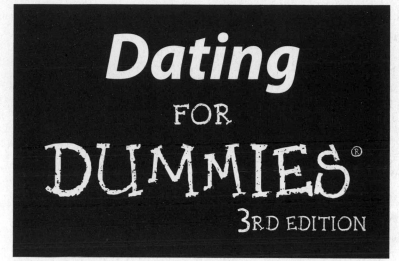

Dating

FOR

DUMMIES®

3RD EDITION

Dating
FOR
DUMMIES®
3RD EDITION

by Dr. Joy Browne, PhD

WILEY

Wiley Publishing, Inc.

Dating For Dummies®, 3rd Edition

Published by
Wiley Publishing, Inc.
111 River St.
Hoboken, NJ 07030-5774
www.wiley.com

3 9082 11748 8331

About the Author

Dr. Joy Browne, PhD is not only a dating guru, but also a licensed clinical psychologist who has hosted her own nationally and internationally syndicated talk show since dirt was invented. She has won numerous awards, including back-to-back female "Talk Show Host of the Year"; was nominated for the Marconi award for best talk show host; was named one of *USA Today*'s 10 most influential broadcasters; and is a member of *Vanity Fair*'s Radio Hall of Fame. The American Psychological Association has awarded her the President's Award, and she is number 10 on the list of the 25 Greatest Radio Talk Show Hosts of all Time. She is the author of 14 books and counting. In her spare time she has appeared on everyone's television show, including her own on CBS and Discovery Health. Dr. Joy enjoys hot air ballooning, yoga, and helping people to improve their lives. She has appeared in two Broadway shows, as well as several well-reviewed documentaries, and has made her singing debut at the Friar Club. Can Hollywood be far behind?

She's gotten her dating experience on the front lines, by watching, listening, and doing, and is always working on a book about relationships.

Dedication

To everyone who's out there giving it the old camper's try — courage!

Author's Acknowledgments

Writing is hard, lonely work, which is why this section is so often over the top in sentiment. People who were there when you were going through the labor, saw you sweaty and cranky, and still stuck by you are much to be valued, and this group certainly qualifies.

Tami Booth was the midwife, if ever there was one. From moment one, she stayed the course, even with elements that seemed part of a cruel joke. Kathy Welton backed the project, even if it meant taking on the gods of conformity and wrestling them to the ground. Tracy Barr kept the work feasible when the effort was literally dissolving before everyone's horrified eyes, and I thank her husband and babies for sharing her with me for weeks of phone calls and faxes and really dedicated work. Mary Hogan slapped life into a project that seemed oxygen-deprived and calmed me with her willingness to help and set limits. Kevin Thornton rode in on his trusty white horse to shepherd the project to the final glory.

For this new edition, Tracy Boggier kept her eye on the project even when it gave her a headache, as is the nature of her commitment. Chrissy Guthrie made online editing fun and a whole lot less scary. Having a team that is smart and also makes you feel smart is a true blessing.

I also want to thank all my callers who've shared their tales of woe or wonder; friends and family members (you know who you are) who've called at 2 a.m. to cry or celebrate; and certainly all the guys who've made me part of the great dating experience.

If you see yourself in this book, think kindly of both of us, because, after all, when it comes to dating, we're all dummies.

Publisher's Acknowledgments

We're proud of this book; please send us your comments at http://dummies.custhelp.com. For other comments, please contact our Customer Care Department within the U.S. at 877-762-2974, outside the U.S. at 317-572-3993, or fax 317-572-4002.

Some of the people who helped bring this book to market include the following:

Acquisitions, Editorial, and Media Development

Project Editor: Christina Guthrie
(*Previous Editions: Tracy Barr, Alissa Schwipps*)

Acquisitions Editor: Tracy Boggier

Assistant Editor: David Lutton

Technical Editor: April Braswell

Editorial Manager: Christine Meloy Beck

Editorial Assistants: Rachelle Amick, Jennette ElNaggar

Cover Photos: © iStockphoto.com / aleksandar velasevic

Cartoons: Rich Tennant (www.the5thwave.com)

Composition Services

Project Coordinator: Sheree Montgomery

Layout and Graphics: Stephanie D, Jumper

Proofreader: Toni Settle

Indexer: Cheryl Duksta

Publishing and Editorial for Consumer Dummies

Diane Graves Steele, Vice President and Publisher, Consumer Dummies

Kristin Ferguson-Wagstaffe, Product Development Director, Consumer Dummies

Ensley Eikenburg, Associate Publisher, Travel

Kelly Regan, Editorial Director, Travel

Publishing for Technology Dummies

Andy Cummings, Vice President and Publisher, Dummies Technology/General User

Composition Services

Debbie Stailey, Director of Composition Services

Contents at a Glance

Table of Contents

Introduction

....

Dating makes everybody feel like a dummy, whether you're 15 or 115, going out on your first date or rejoining the dating scene after your grandkids have started dating. "It's still the same old story" — as sung by Dooley Wilson (or as you probably know him, Sam) in *Casablanca* — "a search for love and glory," and there really *are* some fundamental things that do apply. I lay them all out for you, not so that you can be a stud muffin or the hottest kid on the block, but so that you can understand a bit more about yourself, your date to be, and the whole process. Then maybe the old palms will sweat less, and believe it or not, you may actually have some fun.

After all, dating should be fun. It's not like your whole life or livelihood depends on one date or several dates. The purpose of dating is simple: getting to know someone and letting that person get to know you so that you can decide whether you're interested in spending any more time together. Nothing more, nothing less. Put aside the notion that you're looking for a mate or a one-night stand or someone to please your mom. You're just dating so that you can get to know somebody a bit and let him or her get to know you.

So what are the ironclad follow-these-steps-and-you'll-never-fail, step-on-a-crack-and-you'll-break-your-mother's-back rules of dating? They don't exist. There are some guidelines, suggestions, and observations, but this whole experience is a bit free form since you're unique and so is everyone you'll ever date. So this book is about helping you understand who you are and what you want — some commonly held assumptions, traits, and perils that will allow you to be exactly the person you are. That way, if you're having fun and your date is having fun, you're going to want to do it again.

So why such sweaty palms if this is supposed to be fun? Men and women have been getting together for thousands of years after all. No, it's not because you're the nerd of the universe and everybody else is way cool. It's because the way people date — their expectations and assumptions and goals — have changed with the times.

Adam and Eve were the original blind date (and we know who fixed them up). It's been a lot rockier ever since (ever wonder who Cain and Abel dated?). In the caves, dating was mostly about who had the biggest club (no, not that club) and could carry off the choice woman. I don't think flowers and candy played a very big part. A few eons passed, and we moved from caves and plains to hamlets to villages to towns to cities, and our courting rituals evolved, but still dating really wasn't allowed. Marriages were arranged by families for political and economic reasons. Not only did women have no say, but neither did the men.

Today, not only do we get to pick who we want to marry (at least in this country), but we get to audition them, which brings us to dating. In its purest form, dating is auditioning for mating (and auditioning means we may or may not get the part). Not only has dating gotten complicated (women can ask guys out), but mating has gotten really complicated as well. And then there's romance, truly *the* plague of the 21st century. Romance has made expectations completely unrealistic.

With dating, we're talking individual style — you and your little quirks, which are going to change over time and from person to person, at least a bit. You're going to be a slightly different soul depending on whether you're going out with somebody you met at a bus stop, your best friend's little sister, or your mom's law partner's nephew. So don't go for somebody else's style. If you're determined to mimic your incredibly cool friend, adapt the moves to your style and your partner. The key is to stay light on your feet, be willing to improvise, and believe down to the bottom of your shapely toes that your style is the one that's right for you. (And if it hasn't worked so well in the past, this book can help you figure out why and what you need to do to fine-tune your style so that you're cookin'.)

Before you find yourself hyperventilating over the prospect of dating, remember that there is no single, right way to date or to ask somebody out. And there is no such thing as a perfect experience that will make someone fall madly and passionately in love with you. A date is a unicorn, an imaginary beast that is unique in every situation. But not to worry: This book helps you get it all sorted out so that you can feel like you know what you're doing, have some sense of direction and some idea of what your date is doing and thinking, and even have some fun.

About This Book

Lots of books have been written about how to be the perfect date — how to mold yourself into a package that no one of the opposite sex will be able to resist. *I want you to resist this notion strenuously.* Think about it for a minute: If you pretend to be a stud muffin or a Barbie doll or a pretty woman or a man in black and that's not the real you, and if your date *likes* what you're pretending to be, you have to continue pretending endlessly or, when the real you emerges, the deal is blown. Even if you decide to be your best possible self, are you going to be able to maintain that posture endlessly? If not, when you let yourself unwind you may find your date hurt, angry, and confused about how you presented yourself initially and who you are now. The whole thing about dating is maintainability.

I wrote this book to be about *real-life* dating:

- ✔ In this book, I tell you where to find members of the opposite sex, explain the difference between good and bad pick-up lines, give you pointers on what to wear and what to avoid, describe the perfect place to begin scouting for the perfect date and the perfect date place, and offer a lot of other information, including how much happier you'll be if you don't worry about the "perfect" anything. After all, a little imperfection makes the world go round.

✔ The time frame of this book spans from the time you decide you want to date (or date smarter) until six to nine months after your first date, which is the watershed period: the time when most daters either break up, which means they go back to the beginning, or go on to couplehood. That's a fair amount of leeway, and it depends on lots of factors that I discuss in the chapters that follow.

Dating stops when couplehood begins; relationships deal with commitment and the M word (marriage) and cheating and money and parents and babies and all that sort of stuff.

Remember: The nice thing about a date is that *it's just a date.* It's an opportunity, a time, a place, and a situation for one person to get to know another person. It's not an invitation for sex or marriage or to meet Mom or to find someone to produce a child with or to impress your friends or to get your folks off your back or to prove that you're not a loner. Dating is no big deal. But it can feel really, really scary because it has to do with big-ticket items: the opposite sex and rejection. Yikes! I don't promise to take all the adrenaline out of dating 'cause that would also remove the fun, but at least I can try to smooth out some of the panic and show you why your palms are sweating and the origin of those tummy butterflies so you can enjoy the ride.

Conventions Used in This Book

The following conventions are used throughout the text to make things consistent and easy to understand:

✔ All Web addresses appear in `monofont`.

✔ New terms appear in *italic* and are closely followed by an easy-to-understand definition.

✔ **Bold** is used to highlight the action parts of numbered steps.

What's Not Required Reading

I've written this book so that you can 1) find information easily and 2) easily understand what you find. And although I'd like to believe that you want to pore over every last word between the two yellow and black covers, I actually make it easy for you to identify "skippable" material. This information is the stuff that, although interesting and related to the topic at hand, isn't essential for you to know. (That means no pop quiz, but I did go to a lot of trouble to write it, so I hope you read every word. If you don't, okay — sniff, sniff —whatever makes you happy.)

- **Text in sidebars:** The sidebars are the shaded boxes that appear here and there. They share cool ideas, personal stories, and observations, but aren't critical.

- **Text next to the biology icon:** I went to medical school; I love mind-body connections. Realistically, technically you don't have to read this stuff, but I love it and hope you will too.

- **The stuff on the copyright page:** No kidding. You'll find nothing here of interest unless you're inexplicably enamored by legal language and Library of Congress numbers. Even I have been known to bypass this stuff after being sure my name is spelled correctly.

Assumptions about You

In writing this book, I made some assumptions about you:

- **You are straight, that is, heterosexual:** Statistically, most people are heterosexual, and my goal is to reach the widest audience. Also, many of the issues between opposite-sex dating and same-sex dating are similar, and most are identical. If you find something that I've overlooked, write and tell me what works and what doesn't for you at www.drjoy.com. You can also see current pictures of me there, find out where and when to hear or see me on the radio and television, get my take on current movies and theatre, and see if I've written anything new that might interest you.

- **You are above the age of consent:** This book is a grown-up look at a subject that involves us from childhood, so in reading it, remember that when it comes to the sexual parts, I want you over the age of consent — 18, in most cases. Sex is for adult, responsible folk. If you're a minor, read the stuff about sex as something you're going to do someday, but not now (and when you do, take it seriously and respectfully); the rest of the stuff should be pretty useful to you now.

- **You are dating in the United States:** Because dating customs vary widely in different parts of the world, writing a book on dating worldwide is a whole different project. As an anthropologist (yeah, I have degrees in just about everything), I, too, am fascinated by cross-cultural stuff. This book focuses on what I know best: U.S. dating customs. If you are not from the United States, consider this book as a sort of insider's guide to American dating practices, a kind of roundabout way to see how dating in the United States works.

✓ **You are not a predator:** You genuinely care about yourself as well as others and getting to know another human being in an intimate and meaningful way.

✓ **You wish this book came in a plain brown wrapper:** If anybody sees you with it, you say you're buying it for a friend or you heard my radio program and bought it for a giggle. Even my daughter has been tempted to disown me when a date sees my book in her bookcase.

How This Book Is Organized

I organized this book so that you can find information easily, whether you're using it like a reference or reading it front to back. I've divided it into six parts, each part containing chapters relevant to that specific topic. In addition, I've included an appendix of terms and meanings because I think they're useful but not worth a whole chapter.

Part 1: The Starring Roles: Who Am I and Whom Do I Want?

Any successful dating experience starts with you; that's why the focus in Part I is *you* — getting you ready to begin the glorious adventure of dating. In this part, I give you pointers on being confident, even if confidence is the last thing you feel; getting yourself ready to venture forth into the dating world; and uncovering some of the less than helpful patterns you may have fallen into so that you can be aware and active and can take more control of your behavior. Also in this part, I help you figure out whether now is a good time to begin dating or not.

If you're new to dating, have been away from the dating scene for a while, or aren't happy with the way your dates have been turning out lately, this part is where you want to begin. Even if you read only this part, you'll still find tons of good information about being a happier and emotionally healthier person.

After you figure yourself out, the next item on the agenda is figuring out who you want, where you can find that person, and how you can make your approach so that you two can get together. I give you the lowdown on great places to meet a potential date and pointers on how to approach Mr. or Ms. Intriguing once you do find them.

Making the initial approach is probably one of the toughest parts of meeting someone new — will he like me? Will she turn away? Will I make a fool of myself? I share tips on what works, what doesn't work, and how you can maneuver gracefully through the encounter, no matter how it turns out.

Part II: Setting Up the Date

You've met someone, you think you two click, and now you're at the next step: setting up a date. In Part II, you can find surefire tips on how to ask for a date so that you get the answer you want or, if the answer is no, so that you can bow out gracefully with your dignity intact. I also tell you how to deal with the potentially sticky situation of getting (or giving out) a phone number, and what to look for in the place you pick for the date.

Part III: The Big Day: Preparation and Action

It's date day. You're probably feeling anxious, excited, hopeful, giddy, and a little queasy. This part takes you through getting ready, from the outside to the inside to the last-minute things you do. In this part, I give pointers on everything from what to wear (and what not to wear) to the things you should carry out the door with you to how you can relax and prepare yourself mentally for a great time.

In this part, I also give you the information you need to make it over the first (generally awkward) minutes of a first date: things like what to talk about and what to avoid, how to flirt, how to listen, and how to gauge how things are going by being aware of body language.

Also in this part, you can find information dealing with just about every scenario you may encounter on a first date. I cover how you can turn an ordinary date into something extraordinary and how you can turn that great time into date number two. I also give pointers on how to navigate through potentially embarrassing or awkward moments, how to end the date, how to deal with the kiss questions (do you or don't you and how can you tell whether your date wants to, and even how to), and how to step back after it's over and gain a sense of perspective on the evening.

Since not all dates go wonderfully, I explain how to read the signs of a date going south, and how to handle those not-so-great dates so that you come out looking like the prince or princess you are.

Part IV: The Day After and Beyond

Every date — good, bad, or indifferent — has a day after, and in this part, you can find out how to handle the next day, the next date, and everything that can potentially come after. I also list what things you need to share (and what things you must keep quiet) if your date is turning into a relationship-to-be and when you should share them. I explain the differences between casual, serious, and heavy dating, and how sex can impact the budding relationship. There are also several emphatic words to the wise about silence being golden, especially when it comes to the Internet.

If your date has turned into a relationship and things don't seem to be working out, I explain how to read the warning signs, what you can do to try to save the relationship, and, when all else fails, how to break up without either of you falling to pieces and how to move beyond the breakup. Finally, a real danger when you're feeling vulnerable after a breakup is rebound, so I spend a whole chapter explaining what that is and why you must avoid it.

Part V: Playing It Safe and Keeping It Fresh

This part covers how you can safeguard yourself from potentially dangerous situations, from things as obvious as letting a friend know where you're going to less obvious things like paying attention to your intuition. Also, in this day and age, when people meet online or through dating services or the personals, knowing how to protect yourself when your first date is the first time you meet face to face is especially important. Unfortunately, a book on dating isn't complete without information about how you can protect yourself from the slight but real risks of dating's dark side: date rape and stalkers. And I also cover how to protect yourself from yourself in terms of the blab factor, especially when it comes to Facebook and other social network sites.

And this part isn't just about safety; it's also about how to keep things fresh when your date turns out to be the first step in a long-term, committed relationship. From sending flowers for no good reason to offering to go someplace that isn't high on your must-see list, I explain how to show your ongoing appreciation for this person who has become much more than just your date.

Part VI: The Part of Tens

This part contains lists including "Ten Do's and Don'ts of Internet Dating," "Ten Ways to Know You're in Love," and more. These lists give you good information in quick, snappy bursts.

Appendix

At the end of Part VI, you find an appendix to help you translate common lines like "Can't we just be friends?" or "You're too good for me," so that you can understand what is really being said.

Icons Used in This Book

I include some symbols to make it easier to whiz through the book at the speed of light or to peruse it at your leisure.

You find this icon beside neat things you may want to try.

This icon appears beside information that explains the biological reasons for why things happen. Although you don't technically need to know this stuff, reading it can give you a lot of insight into why humans do what they do. In the nature versus nurture debate, consider this icon the nature side.

Whenever the information relates primarily to women, I indicate it with this icon. This doesn't mean, however, that only women should read this material. In fact, you guys can get quite a bit of insight into female behavior by paying attention to this stuff.

If the information relates primarily to men, I use this icon. (Girls, if you want to understand men a little better, take a peek at this stuff.)

Some things just aren't good ideas: They're dangerous, hurtful, harmful, and to be avoided. I use this icon to flag any behavior or situation you need to steer clear of.

Of course, you could consider this whole book one giant Dr. Joy Says icon; after all, I wrote everything in here. But periodically, I make points that I think you need to pay special attention to, for your own well-being and best interest. Consider this icon roughly equivalent to your momma saying, "I'm talking to you," when she wanted you to pay extra attention.

This icon marks general information that is important enough for you to keep in mind.

Where to Go from Here

You can read this book from front to back or treat it like a reference and hop around, reading only those sections that apply to you. If you don't want to read through the entire book, here is a brief guide on where you can find information specific to your situation (you can also use the Table of Contents or the Index to find specific topics):

If You Are	Read
Young (13 to 17)	Whole book, but ignore Chapter 17 about sex.
Inexperienced (that is, have never dated, have done no serious dating, have dated fewer than three people, or have had fewer than three dates)	Whole book, but go slow. Almost everybody feels like a dummy to start.
Divorced	During the year you are waiting to resume dating (and *no* dating until one full year has passed), read Part I carefully, especially Chapter 4 about figuring out who you are, what you want, what went wrong, and waiting. Also read Chapter 19 on rebound. (It's also not a terrible idea to do some work on self, with or without a therapist.)
Separated	Don't even think about dating. Follow the same advice for divorced (see the preceding), only more so, and *memorize* Chapter 19 on rebound.
Unhappily married or involved	Chapter 17, Chapter 18 on breaking up, and Chapter 19 on rebound. And don't even *think* about thinking about dating yet. Work on your relationship; if it doesn't work out, you still have to wait a year after the divorce or final breakup becomes final.
Widowed	If you're widowed at least a year, follow the advice for divorced (see earlier item). If you're widowed less than a year, put the book aside, hang out with friends in groups, and look at the cover once a month, but no reading until the first-year anniversary.
Senior	If all you are is older and aren't widowed or divorced or separated, start from the beginning and just read faster. When it comes to dating, everyone is in the same boat, regardless of age, so enjoy and be willing to feel inept and young and inexperienced all over again. Is that such a bad thing? Maybe not.

Remember, this is a reference book, not a bible. Write in the margins, underline passages, dog-ear pages, and put that cool contact paper on the front if you want.

No panicking, no whining, and no comparing. Okay. Let's go!

Part I
The Starring Roles:
Who Am I and
Whom Do I Want?

The 5th Wave   By Rich Tennant

"I'm looking for someone who will love me for who I think I am."

In this part . . .

Dating is the emotional apex of who you are at this very moment in time. The way you feel, act, walk, talk, sashay, flirt, or dish the dirt all play a part in attracting or totally turning off the ideal date. So right out of the gate, you've gotta get clear on who you are because if you can't figure out who you are, how are you going to figure out who you want in life?

Listen up: You, and you alone, are the beginning of any dating experience — not your prince or princess charming, not your fantasy or your blind date to be. You, little ole you. In this part, it's time to take a look at your patterns, your tendencies, your needs, your desires, your past boo-boos, and your future hopes. Especially when talking about dating, self-awareness brings action and power and the potential for lots of fun — which is what truly great dates are all about. While how you date may shift, knowing thyself is always the beginning, so no short cuts or skipping through this part.

After you've done the appropriate homework on yourself, you're ready to look for love in all the right places. This part also covers how to dip your toe gracefully into the dating waters without falling flat on your face — and how to use technology to test the waters rather than as a substitute for flesh and blood, sweaty palmed, face-to-face meet and greet.

Chapter 1

Thoroughly Modern Dating

Dating is about two people who are interested in one another and want to get together at a specific time and place. We're not talking rocket science here. Since the original fix-up — you know, the one between Adam and Eve (who had the advantage of the ultimate Matchmaker) — dating has evolved. With the familiar United States version less than 100 years old, the guy is often (but not always) the one who asks and pays, and couples still face the tension of possible sex at the end of the evening.

After some recent reflection about the dating scene, I concluded that the last ten or so years have indeed significantly altered the dating landscape, and anything that alters that landscape is certainly going to alter dating behavior. Technology is a tool, but it is a tool that has profound effects on how and what we communicate, how fast and with whom. The original changes had to do with the ubiquity of online dating: its ease, breadth, and nearly universal acceptance in a very short time. That same technology has now given us social networking, tweeting, texting, and the possibility of seeing and being seen instantaneously and universally, ready or not.

In this chapter, I detail those changes precisely. In addition to key points to remember about modern dating, including dating in the age of social networking, I offer special advice and guidance for folks who are in special dating situations. The chapter concludes with tips for using a dating notebook to keep track of what's going on in your love life. I promise no pop quizzes, but you'll be amazed at how much you can learn about yourself and the process.

Dating is the Wimbledon of social intercourse. So you'll be happiest and most successful if you practice, correct mistakes as you go along, and don't expect to make the finals the first time out. Dating should be fun and interesting. If it feels grueling, unpleasant, or exhausting, take a breath and a break and kick back for a while. You're fine by yourself!

Scoping Out the Changing Dating World

Believe it or not, the changes that society, sexuality, entertainment, and technology have engendered in the dating scene can be distilled into a single concept: the need for speed! The entire process has been sped up so that courting behavior no longer functionally exists. Without some real caution the privacy that allows relationships to unfold can be compromised, and Facebook and other social network sites have allowed dating to become an audience participation sport.

Speed bumps

Admittedly, human beings, when it comes to love, have always been impatient — even though Diana Ross, or at least her momma, said, "You can't hurry love, you just have to wait!" People are under more pressures now to race dating at the speed of light when instead they should be taking very small baby steps, exercising due diligence, and noticing in minute detail what's going on. Talking with a girlfriend about a groovy guy has been replaced by Googling, checking out Facebook, texting friends, chatting at online forums, blogging, tweeting, and texting. I know that the temptation is to close your eyes and just go for it: Tell the world and let the relationship chips fall where they may. Falling makes it seem much more fun, scary, exciting, and fast, but it's not very productive if you're looking for more than just cheap thrills. The exposure factor has never been higher, so the stakes, which have always been high when it comes to matters of the heart (let alone other important organs) are off the charts.

Admittedly, I bear some vague responsibility for this trend: I sort of invented speed dating, accidentally, when I first had a TV show in 2000. Speed dating, as it has evolved, usually gives participants six or seven minutes with each potential date, but I gave them three minutes to convince somebody to go out with them, though I was there to offer encouragement or redirect the Burger King philosophy of life: quick, hot, juicy, and "your way" work in some places, just not in dating! The need for speed is triggered by two equal and opposite tendencies: Ironically, couples are marrying earlier (obvious sexual urgency) and later (increasing fertility concerns), with women feeling that if they wait any longer they won't have the option of raising children of their own.

Changing definitions of marriage: When and why

Dating has changed. Marriage is changing. Gender roles are changing. There are now more single people living by themselves than ever before in the history of the world. This tendency, coupled with the reality that life expectancy has nearly doubled in the last century, means that individuals are concluding that they can hold off on marriage or not marry at all. These options mean that dating doesn't necessarily point in the direction of settling down as it once did. Additionally, settling down could mean spending many decades with one person if they marry early, prompting them to proceed cautiously.

Statistically, more people are marrying and remarrying than ever before. Concerns about fertility are balanced by women deciding that they can have children without the benefit of a partner, another factor that has radically altered the dating landscape. Some people who are raising children are dating but have never married and don't intend to do so.

If all this makes your head spin, you are not alone.

Fantasies and realities

In addition to the census, demographic data, and the changing realities, television shows in the 21st century have significantly changed the dating landscape since popular notions perpetuated by the media, while originally fantasy, have a strange habit of morphing into our shared reality. Dating shows have always been a part of the TV landscape, but the bar has been raised, or lowered, depending on how you look at it. In addition to the traditional plethora of inane reality-style TV dating shows, *Who Wants to Marry a Millionaire?, Who Wants to Marry My Dad?, The Bachelor, The Bachelorette, My Big, Fat, Ugly Fiancé,* and *Millionaire Matchmaker* have not only made dating a blood sport but convinced the viewing public that hot tubs and serial necking in front of a TV camera are normal aspects of dating. Rules about no kissing on the first date and no sex until the third date seem laughably out of fashion if you watch television. Dating as a competitive sport — complete with body contact and backbiting — has cheapened, degraded, and sexualized dating as well as increased hostility in ways we're not even completely aware of.

Okay, so most of us probably look at television dating shows and say, "That's ridiculous!" We know that a lot of editing and prompting goes on. But we are all influenced, subtly and not so subtly, by these shows in how we date, how we view the opposite sex, our own behavior, and what's acceptable and what's not acceptable. Reality TV has made competition, mean spiritedness, and just plain nastiness part of the social landscape between men and women, making the war between the sexes appear as a bombed-out landscape with few survivors and multiple casualties. And the exposure: I'm not necessarily talking hot tub here. No emotion is too raw, no vulnerability too dangerous, no image too intimate. Chapter 10 may make you believe in civilization, manners, and survival as possible goals in dating for yourself and others.

Adding to the general confusion is the fact that so many television shows suggest that being gay is not only acceptable but hip and nearly ubiquitous, which has certainly increased the potential for at least considering yourself bisexual, or even more terrifying, having your partner consider him or herself bisexual. Thus dating has become a question of will or won't your date come out of the closet after you get to know each other. Interestingly enough, the statistics on the percentage of the population reported and reporting as gay are unchanged since Alfred Kinsey's studies 60 years ago. Thirty years ago, TV would have you believe no one was gay; today TV would allow you to assume *everybody* is gay.

Terrorism, war, and recession

The terror attacks of September 11, 2001, have also changed the social landscape forever. In the weeks and months following the destruction of the World Trade Center, the realization that life could be so dramatically fleeting and unpredictable meant folks rethought relationships suddenly: broke up, or committed to one another foregoing — perhaps forever — the sense that we all have all the time in the world. As time goes by, as is always the case, the trauma fades for most, only to be replaced by a devastating recession, double-digit unemployment, a floundering stock market. The point being that as humans are affected by their environment, dating is impacted. In addition, no particular event has consequences that are universal or forever. The human condition is one of change.

Dating in this context has taken on a level of intensity and urgency, with people often looking for instant meaning in an inappropriate way — make my life meaningful, make me happy, make it all worthwhile, pay my bills — a heavy burden indeed for a process that was invented to be light, delicate, and lengthy. Modern dating has always worked best as a carefree, pleasant experience, at least initially, but that evaporated after September 11. Questioning whether coupledom or bringing children into this world was a good idea was offset by the questioning of the willingness to be alone if the world was about to end. The simple question of "Am I willing to spend the rest of my life with you?" has been altered by the fear factor in general and by the threat of terrorism on a daily basis. Intellectually, people may have understood that anybody could perish at anytime, but September 11 drove home that point in a dramatic and tragic way. The years since have provided ample examples of vulnerability — financial, social, and political.

Gadgets, gadgets everywhere!

Modern technology has had an impact on all aspects of our lives, including dating.

Instant coffee, fast food, and instant gratification have been a part of the social landscape for years, but instant messaging, constant access through cell phones, caller ID, the Internet, texting, YouTubing, tweeting, and Facebooking (see the section "Dating in the Age of Facebook" for more) have made it all too easy to act impulsively and regret at leisure. Moving at the speed of light is sexy for sound waves but scary for human relationships, especially when it comes to dating. Exposure works well for photographs, but relationships often flourish with a bit more privacy, especially in the early stages.

Online dating

Even when Internet dating was in its infancy, I understood the advantages and disadvantages of the computer as cupid. Computers dramatically increase the pool of potential dates, as well as offering options, which is never a bad thing. They give people an opportunity to "meet" people from different social circles, creating the delightful sense that somebody wonderful is just around the corner (as long as one is able to resist endless corner peering). But it's important to online date for a minimum amount of time before going in-life. My basic rule of thumb is that you should have no more than a couple of e-mail chats and phone calls over a couple of weeks before you meet somebody face to face.

The last time I checked, literally millions of people are online dating. On a more personal level, I know 12 couples who met online (not all of whom have admitted to having allowed a computer to match-make).

Here's the good news and bad news about online dating (for more info on online dating, see Chapters 5 and 23):

- ✔ The good news about online dating is that it does increase the number of possibilities and can be morale boosting to see how many people are around and available, plus it gives you an opportunity to shop.

- ✔ The bad news is that it can be impersonal, time consuming, and addictive, with a large dollop of fantasy, and there's a tendency to shop.

  Also, people tend not to be 100 percent honest about who they are, what they're looking for, their weight, age, marital history, their past, their sex, or whether they're straight or gay, because dating online is fantasy. Married people have been known to pretend that they were single; gays, straight; older people, young; young people, older. But if nothing else, it'll give you the sense that there are available single people out there.

An inherent Internet temptation: Long-distance relationships

While I cover this topic later in this chapter (see the section "You're in a long-distance relationship"), let me emphasize here that the cute soul who lives half the country away cannot be your soul mate — just your fantasy love. And fantasy isn't what you are seeking in a dating relationship. If you're not careful, you'll end up spending most of your time together in bed, increasing the longing when you're apart and completely blinding you to the underlying personality, quirks, and soul of your partner. Not a great basis for a long-term relationship at all.

Instant messaging

Instant messaging enables you to get in touch with somebody immediately and talk in real time to that person in a completely artificial while seemingly urgent way. Instant messaging discourages self-censoring, voice clues, or reality-based feedback loop. If you're angry with one another (or even if you're not), you may end up typing something that you might not have said if you had a little longer to think it through. Although you do get an instant response, it's not the same as a conversation, so things like tone, sense of humor, body language, and irony really do get lost in typing. No matter how you cut it, communicating through the Internet really is simply typing. If IMing is seductive, how much more is being able to tweet or send a picture from your cell (please tell me you're fully clothed) or posting your latest image online?

Chat rooms

Chat rooms are another part of the fantasy world of the Internet. They've been known to be very disruptive to relationships even when they're not suggestive or pornographic, and when they are, Nelly bar the door! And for those of you who view Internet porn as harmless or private, beware! Because Internet porn is so instantly available (it doesn't even come in a wrapper anymore), it's right there in front of your keyboard. Women tend to be grievously offended by it, and men tend to think, "What's the big deal?" If Internet porn is part of your life and you're dating, you need to think through what you're really doing here, what your intent is, and what happens if you get caught. Remember that very few things are private anymore.

Social networking sites

I talk in depth about these sites in the upcoming section "Dating in the Age of Facebook." Just a few words here: For singles, social networking sites are often a way of checking status ("Are you admitting that we're dating or not?"). But for folks in relationships, whether married or not, these sites are a way to get in touch without any stigma or even having to admit they're looking around. The intent seems harmless; after all, parents are often "Friends" on their kids' Facebook pages, so the whole thing is pretty innocent, right? Sometimes yes, sometimes not so much.

Since you're reading this book, I assume that you're single (even though much of the information is also useful for keeping a marriage strong and healthy if you view yourself as dating your spouse). If you aren't single, social networking sites present a specific challenge. Innocently deciding that you're going to get in touch with an old love and see how that person's doing and catch up can turn into something a great deal more disruptive without some caution and discussion with your spouse. I have always encouraged couples to attend reunions together because the temptation of history and nostalgia can be treacherous to navigate. Social networking sites, including Classmates.com, have become reunions without the need for travel.

Cell phones

To say cell phones have become ubiquitous doesn't begin to explain how common they are. My daughter visited Thailand and was astonished to discover that in a country where the average annual income is $700, everybody had a cell phone! There are actually more cell phones in the world than toilets. No snide comments, please. Smart phones now mean that there is no need for a camera, laptop, phonebook, gaming system, television, newspaper, magazine, ticker tape (does anybody even know what that means anymore?), or concierge. If we could only teach 'em to give backrubs. But I digress.

You need two computers in your life

Dating is a social activity, while work is about competence. Please don't use your office computer at work to instant message, visit chat rooms, view pornography, check to see whether the dating site has gotten much action, check out the latest on YouTube, or see who's friended you. You need to have at least two computers in your life: one at work and one at home. If you don't, you may find that you'll have only the one at home because you're going to get fired from the one at work. Work is about competence; you're not being paid to work on your social life.

With regard to dating, the first thing that you should know about a cell phone is that unless you're late for a date or lost and trying to get in touch with your date by cell phone, turn it off! A date is not the time to show how popular you are by letting your date know how many people call you. That's why voicemail was invented. The worst-case scenario I've ever seen was a couple walking down the street and holding hands, while both of them were talking on their cell phones, so you know they weren't talking to each other. This kind of behavior really makes no sense. Cell phone addiction is evidence of that need for speed and urgency thing, always having to be in touch and feeling like you might be missing something if you're not connected. I actually once did a story about countries where a person having sex is more likely to answer his or her cell phone. If this is you, stop! Get up from the couch, go look in the mirror, and ask yourself, "What are my priorities? When did I become so addicted to being that in touch?"

Another problem with cell phones is that everything on your cell phone bill is going to be listed by phone number. Anybody opening your cell phone bill is going to know exactly who you've been taking to, what time of day, and for how long. Caller ID has also made both stalking and cheating something that you really can't do with much success anymore. If you're dating more than one person and being less than candid with either, chances are you'll be busted by your trusty cell bill.

Use the disposability and portability of cells to your advantage by giving out only your cell number until you've had a number of face-to-face dates, and then only when you feel really secure.

Money matters

The days of men expecting or being expected to pay for everything have come and gone. It makes a women look modern, generous, and interested to at least offer and be willing to pick up the check, especially if she's making a decent living. Even if you're making a mere pittance, offer to do what you can — even if it's a picnic in the park! Guys, offering to split the check makes you look cheap — I know she looks generous, but you'll be labeled chintzy. Times are changing — but not overnight.

Sex

Ah, sex. The fundamental things apply, except that we're not quite so basic anymore when you add in earlier puberty, longer lives, sexually transmitted diseases, birth control, hooking up, women being more sexually aggressive and assertive, drugs, and rock and roll. Relax, go at your own pace, always use protection, and remind yourself to be respectful of your partner and yourself since both of you are susceptible to — but not controlled by — hormones. Discuss exclusivity and commitment before hitting the sheets so you're both on the same page that isn't being blurred by lust. When in doubt, wait! Choice is complicating but eventually empowering!

Safety

Be reasonable and cautious. Dating should be fun — not a walk on the wild side — so make sure you meet a stranger in a public place, make sure someone knows where you are, and use your cell phone initially — don't give your home address or business phone number or address until you know each other really well. Wait to have sex until you feel safe enough to give out a home number. Use protection and floss after meals.

Dating in the Age of Facebook

Facebook is the most successful of the social networking sites and at this moment has over 500 million members and generates more than $2 billion per year in revenues. Love it or hate it, it's a fact of life in this day and age, and if it's a fact of life, it's a fact of dating life. Facebook hasn't changed how people date, but it has changed who knows what and how soon and for how long. It is a voluntary loss of privacy, which can seem very appealing in the first throws of passion. Is Facebook the place to look for dates? The occasional hookup occurs when people check out their friends' hookups, but by and large, the more established dating sites like Match.com and eHarmony have maintained their position of dominance.

Privacy versus publicity: Protection or prudery?

Most young people still date the old fashioned way — through friends, classes, and social events — and the new old fashioned way — through online dating services. Most use social networking for keeping in touch with friends and sharing information about their social lives rather than for finding mates.

However, the uncensored flow of information certainly affects how we date. It changes what we know (or think we know) about one another and how we get our information; we used to acquire knowledge about a person within a relationship, but now we get it online. In the old days, when you broke up with someone you hoped that person would keep his or her big mouth shut and not badmouth you to friends. Now the relationship news is all online: all the hopes, dreams, idiosyncrasies, pet names, favorite places, silly pictures, ad nauseum. Sharing it all seems fun at the time, but it's hard to have it trailing along behind you for the rest of your life.

Facebook: Fame, fantasy, familiarity, and me

In the good old days, classy folks had their names in the newspaper three times: when they were born, when they got married, and when they died. At some point, society recognized that we need heroes and that heroes should be celebrated for good deeds and heroic conquests. Even then, famous people understood that the public was going to want to know more about them than they were willing to share, and the tabloids were invented. Folks who wanted to do good realized that fame was sometimes the cost and sometimes the reward of their work.

At some point, somebody decided that fame could be translated into value — sometimes societal, occasionally political, and often financial. The upset came when those same people realized that notoriety for doing bad actually lasted longer than for doing good, and then all bets were off. Daytime television of the '80s and '90s expanded the concept of evil so that no matter how disreputable one's own behavior, a worse example could be found on television getting nationwide publicity and a free trip to New York and a fancy hotel room to boot. Reality shows became daytime TV on steroids. Some young people today actually aspire to be reality television stars. They have no sense of direction or accomplishment; they just want fame.

Which brings us to social networking sites and the idea of lives lived publicly — again, without restraint, direction, or meaning. The idea obviously appeals not only to the young and inexperienced but also to folks who should probably know better (although the grownups would argue they are only trying to reconnect with old friends, especially those from high school or college). I don't think it's coincidental that this wish to re-experience youth is a ubiquitous (if often unacknowledged) motivating factor.

The perfect storm of Facebook notoriety and celebrity might have been NFL player Jeremy Shockey's 2010 Facebook page contest. Here's what he wrote: "Ok LADIES heres the contest. Post a video on the 'just fans' sectin of my fbk page explaining why u deserve to have me take u on a date 1 nite this offseason…Contest ends sun night 4/18 at 8 pm est…Lets have fun w this so be creative but just be careful its not too inappropriate where fbk deletes it!! Good luck!!" Shockey claims that he wasn't looking to pick up a girl; he was just doing it for the fans. But did some young woman post a video that contained her heart and soul just to be rejected, publicly humiliated, or (even if chosen) treated like a fan? Nothing posted in response to such a "contest" would be private. Obviously, this is an extreme example of "dating" on Facebook, or is it? The assumption that Shockey was looking to meet someone to date isn't so far-fetched, yet in reality has nothing to do with his motives whatsoever. You might argue that this was merely a publicity stunt, and I wouldn't disagree, but you begin to see the issues.

Social networking sites are about connecting in a public way. Most dating is about connecting in a private way.

Avoiding the nostalgia trip trap

Facebook has had the largest effect on dating behavior among those who ought not to be dating at all: the married and nominally committed. The idea of keeping up with classmates has morphed from the innocent every-five-year reunion option with (hopefully) a bored spouse in tow, to a private, intimate opportunity to catch up, complain, fantasize, and generally disrupt ongoing relationships without having to confront the consequences 'til disaster has struck.

Tracking old loves on Facebook shouldn't be a back door to infidelity, and that's the problem: There is a veneer of high school innocence that allows for predators, unexplored motives, and impulses that are facilitated by the extreme anonymity on one end (sitting alone in front of a blank screen) and the extreme intimacy and familiarity of a posting on something as universally available as the Internet. Yeah, I know about private chats, but they require opting out of the default setting and aren't the norm for social networking sites.

Computer common sense

Let's face it: These days people are getting used to exposing everything online, including their physical locations, which can be shared using a GPS-like monitoring service that can be downloaded to a smart phone. Given the fact that nearly one-third of Facebook users access the site via their cell phones, *Katie, bar the door!* because everyone can now find Katie's door easily and directly. (If you haven't heard that expression before, it means "be cautious"!) Users admit there are privacy issues with this smart phone app but continue to use it anyway. Which is exactly my point. Folks, use a little common sense here. Realize that if you wouldn't want your parents to know or have the info on the front page of your local paper, you don't put it on a social networking site. Period.

I am not a Facebook hater: I'm just saying that it's important to see Facebook in the way businesses see Facebook — as an opportunity to advertise a product to a huge, undifferentiated audience and then be able to focus on a particular demographic. It's a lovely sales tool if you're selling toothpaste but a bit more problematic if what you're advertising (selling) is yourself to a large, undifferentiated audience. As a seller of toothpaste, I don't really care if you've lied about your age, your sex, or your motives since there is no harm to befall me either way. If I'm looking for love, companionship, or involvement, trust becomes a huge issue and there is no way of sorting that out.

A documentary made in 2010 called *Catfish* deals with just such a situation, in which a lonely married woman constructs not only an imaginary profile but a whole family including an 8-year–old daughter, a 19-year–old sister, cousins, and friends. The profile entices a smart, educated 28-year-old photographer to travel cross country to meet a woman he has fallen in "love" with on Facebook — only to find she doesn't exist. His brother just happens to be a videographer who documents the pain involved with both his brother and the sad, lonely woman and her husband, who has been completely unaware of the deception.

Personal information is the coin of the Facebook realm, whether for advertising toothpaste or your new hairdo, and the fact that a blank computer screen encourages intimacy has been repeatedly and well documented. "Check out my Facebook page" has become the new calling card. (The latest numbers suggest that people spend three times longer checking out their Facebook account and contacts than they spend on all of Google services *combined,* including YouTube, Gmail, and Google news.) The fact that there is a community on the page gives you a sense of safety, but it's illusory. In the old days you could check out a relative or a classmate and in theory you can do that here, but what are you asking and whom are you asking and do you really want to be the topic of discussion among strangers? If the answer is yes, can we talk?

Being aware of the pitfalls of "friending" a date

For those of you who think that "friending" a potential date on Facebook is a way of getting to know one another, realize that doing so actually increases jealousy and a sense of over-familiarity that can doom a relationship and take away some of the mystery in the early days of dating, according to a study in the journal *Cyberpsychology, Behavior, and Social Networking.*

Checking out Facebook encourages over-analyzing without the option of time and space to reflect. After a date, you may think about each other, but you shouldn't be sorting through pictures, trying to decipher old photos, or checking out what your date is doing online. You shouldn't be trying to second-guess who blabs first about the relationship by changing their status or figuring out whether this date is following a pattern (doing what's been done in previous relationships); those kinds of comparisons are odious and painful. And who needs to be confronted with the thumbs up or down of other FF (Facebook Friends)?

Dealing with Specialized Dating Situations

The purpose of *Dating For Dummies* is to give you the basics on dating, but there are a lot of situations that make the dating experience a bit different for certain folks. The point of this section is to explain the things that can impact specialized dating situations. Find your special definition and then integrate those rules with the basic rules for a custom fit.

One of you is a lot older or younger

In theory, an age difference is the thing over which you have the least control in a relationship. It's the given from day one and shouldn't matter all that much. The younger one of the partners, the more any age difference matters. High school freshmen dating seniors makes parents nervous, and that's only three years. The difference between a 15-year-old and an 18-year-old may mean a jail sentence, whereas the difference between a 70-year-old and a 73-year-old is irrelevant, so part of the issue with age is the starting point.

The issues between age-challenged partners fall into six distinct categories.

Tradition and actuarial tables

Traditionally, in our society and many others, older men marry younger women, which perpetuates the "daddy" school of relationships — that a man should be older, wiser, smarter, better educated, stronger, more powerful, richer, and, in general, higher on the food chain.

As women act more responsible and mature, these distinctions become less relevant and politically viable, but the tradition remains. There is a wonderful movie called *Harold and Maude* in which an 80-year-old Ruth Gordon is pursued by an amorous 18-year-old Bud Cort. No, that wasn't a typo. The woman is 80; her suitor, 18. The movie was made as satire to demonstrate how rigid our rules are for dating, and it's as relevant today as when it was made 40 years ago. (Watch it on Netflix; you'll love it.)

Tradition, tradition: "I do" (and "I don't")

The divorce rate has remained steady at around 40 percent. (The 50 percent statistic often bandied about was a computational error that was admitted in 2005 because it divided the number of marriages by the number of divorces without taking population fluctuations into account.)

But folks are still marrying like crazy — at a rate of 2.5 million per year in the United States.

However, people are marrying later: The average age for a man's first marriage is 27; for women it is 24. The average age of remarriage after divorce is 42 for men and 39 for women.

Movies and tradition aside, age can and does make a difference. If we all mated on a logical basis, women would marry men at least seven to ten years younger so that everybody would end up living their lives out together since men's life expectancy is still that much less than women's.

Sexual viability

One of the major drawbacks of large age differences deals with the age-old problem of childbearing years. An older woman who is through childbearing with a younger man who decides he wants children is going to create chaos, as is a younger woman who wants children with an older man who doesn't. (I recently read a news story about a woman who gave birth at 79. That's not a typo: 79 years of age. Truly terrifying. Science and technology are offering all sorts of possibilities heretofore unknown. Can you say Viagra?)

Since we know that men can procreate until their last rattly little breath, and women (usually) only for the years between about 13 and 50, men who are interested in procreating should choose women in this age bracket. Of course, most states appropriately frown on dating between adults and children, so if we wipe out the lower end of the spectrum up to 18 or so, we're talking viable dating partners between the ages of 18 and 50. Biologically, we know that birth defects are more common at both ends of the spectrum, with both the very young and the very old eggs (not women, just eggs), so we're actually talking ages 20 to 40 here, more or less.

Many men on second marriages decide that they can trade a 40-year-old in for the proverbial two 20-year-olds, which makes some biological sense. But a 40-year-old man with a 20-year-old woman will become a 60-year-old man with a 40-year-old wife, and if you go on to the next section, you will see the potential problem with that formula.

Sexual compatibility

Sexually, men are at their peak at 18, women at around 40 or so. So if sexual compatibility were the issue, women should marry significantly younger men. A woman named Anne Cummings, known as the Randy Granny (a Brit no less), was one of the early "cougar" dating proponents. She actually advocates this kind of pairing — although not necessarily marriage — so that young men can learn about sex from an experienced partner who is less likely to get pregnant and more likely to be sensible rather than lust driven.

If sex were all there was to it, maybe. (In case you're gasping for breath here, remember that a 40-year-old man with an 18-year-old woman would be considered a stud.) Beyond sex is a wider look at biology.

Health

These days, when people are taking better care of themselves and living longer and more productive lives, the idea of an age difference resulting in obligatory nursing duties at the end of one partner's life has diminished. I refuse to deal with the idea of serial marriages here: the idea that you marry one person for one stage of your life and another for another. Since none of us is able to see the future, in theory, it is possible that the older person in a relationship may outlive the younger, but it is wise to at least consider issues of health, energy, and life stages when dating.

Common interests

One of the often overlooked issues of major age differences is what the two of you have in common, not only in terms of life experiences, but friends, perspectives, and whether one of you thinks that the Beatles are bugs or that Nine Inch Nails refers to a Chinese emperor's hands.

These differences at the outset of a relationship can seem charming and fun and don't have to be divisive if the two of you can find some areas of communality to share that are likely to last the length of the relationship. But be aware of pitfalls that can be predicted but that aren't always initially obvious. I know one couple with major age differences who ran into trouble when he retired and wanted to play and she was just hitting her career peak and wanted to spend a lot of time at work.

Personal preference

Issues of control and crushes on mommy figures or daddy figures are going to enter into the age equation. Obviously, all other things being equal, similarity of ages probably makes the most sense, but all other things are never equal. People are as individual as snowflakes and likely to be just as flaky when it comes to matters of the heart. Be aware of the advantages and disadvantages, the potential fun stuff and pitfalls of major differences in birth years. If one of you is ten or more years older, you're talking half a generation here. At 80, who cares? But at 18, everyone will.

Fortunately — or maybe unfortunately — we don't fall in love with birth certificates but with flesh and blood individuals. If you're looking to date someone who is significantly older or younger than you are, ask yourself why and whether it makes any long-term sense. Are you looking to shock or advertise, brag or control? As long as you know what you're doing, you'll get no argument from me, but make sure you've taken your own emotional pulse here; I don't care how old you are.

You're different

In theory, the more similar you are, the more you have in common and the easier the relationship, assuming you can avoid competition. I view relationships as Velcro: The more points of contact that the two of you have with one another, the more likely the relationship is to survive the storm-tossed seas of the tempest of life together. The more points of contact — religion, ethnicity, education, social class, and community of interests — the more likely the relationship will survive. Does this mean that you have to date only people who have the same religion, ethnicity, social status, education, or income you do? Of course not. But it means that you need to be aware of the differences, their importance, and the ramifications of the differences if the two of you are going to survive together.

Some foolish souls believe that dating is all about soul mates. You've undoubtedly figured out that I am certainly not one of them. Working on the assumption that opposites attract and they aggravate the daylights out of one another, I explore some of the more common differences. This is one area that may be obvious or subtle, clear or obscure, depending on your own convictions.

Religion

In theory, in the early stages of dating, religion can be finessed and therefore can be benign, especially if you both assume the relationship is pretty casual. But as the two of you get to know each other better and begin thinking on a long-term basis, religious differences may begin to be disruptive.

First, let's be painfully honest. If you feel strongly that you will absolutely *not* marry outside of your religion, *do not date outside of your religion!* The heart often has its own rhythms and paths and doesn't really understand casual dating. (This is one of the areas where niche online dating sites serving singles in particular religions can be beneficial.)

On the other hand, if you have a preference but no strong commitment and are willing to entertain long-term involvement with someone practicing another faith, try taking turns going to each other's synagogue or mosque or church, take turns sleeping in while the other trots off to services, or schedule golf dates or brunch while your friend is in synagogue. If the two of you can tolerate compromise while dating, you may be able to do so in the future, at least until the wedding or children require more clarity.

You can and should discuss religious differences instead of making the assumption that the differences will go away. Depending on how important religion is to you or your date, there are multiple possibilities. If your two religions are not far apart, you may want to experience each other's religious customs and festivals as a pleasant part of getting to know one another. Or maybe you'll find a third mutually accepted religion. On the other hand, you may find absolutely no room for compromise — meaning that neither one of you will convert (actually or informally) or attend the other's place of worship. Even if the two of you are relaxed about your religious differences, remember that your parents may or may not be as open minded, so be prepared to explain the situation to them.

Ethnicity

Living in a country that prides itself on being a melting pot means that different ethnicities are common almost everywhere you go — reflected in jokes, sitcoms, and songs: the Irish man and the Italian woman, the French man and the German woman, all the way back to Pocahontas and John Smith. The Internet, colleges, big cities, and bars are all venues in which different ethnicities can meet, greet, and hook up. Again, if you're certain that you're unwilling to marry outside your tribe, do yourself and everyone else a favor and don't convince yourself that it's okay to date but not marry outside of your own ethnic group. This is a prescription for heartache for all concerned, including a whole lot of problems with your parents.

The lure of the exotic may be initially attractive, but don't overlook the potential fallouts, including traditions and inborn racial conflict, because even though the two of you may feel very much in love, the people who are in your sphere of influence (your family, friends, neighborhood, grandparents, and country of origin) are going to influence you. To what extent is not entirely obvious, but it is something to be aware of.

We've been talking about differences that you were born with that you may take for granted; the next three issues that I'm going to talk about are ones that you achieve.

Social status

I know that the United States pretends that it has no class system. If you believe that, I have a bridge to sell you. The good news about class in this society is that it doesn't go back very far, probably only a couple hundred years, as opposed to other countries where it goes back thousands of years. The idea that somebody comes from a completely different background socioeconomically than you do and has been in that situation for generation after generation very well may influence how you view friendships, vacations, money, child rearing, naming your children, and traditions. The notion that money is the great leveler — even more so than love — is the stuff of media pipe dreams, but the notion doesn't work very well once the cameras stop rolling.

Be aware that people have all sorts of different expectations depending on their socioeconomic background. I am not suggesting that people from different socioeconomic backgrounds not marry, but you need to understand that there are going to be repercussions, perhaps within the relationship eventually, and certainly within the general society. I have no particular reason to uphold the social order by making sure that people of a certain socioeconomic class marry only one another. But be aware that there are different expectations, including whether it's true love or greed, the ability to fit in, community acceptance, and being snubbed at Thanksgiving.

Education

As a radio psychologist, I often remind callers that, traditionally, American women marry men who are father figures: older, wiser, taller, richer, and better educated than they are. While that is changing, historically it certainly has created some problems, with men feeling that they outgrew their wives, even those wives who may have put them through school.

Although more subtle than race, religion, or age, differences in education in the long run may be divisive because one of you is going to feel inferior to the other, and that inferiority may make you defensive or angry or argumentative. The nice thing about living in this country is that education is available, but it may not solve everything. Don't misunderstand me: As a seriously educated woman, I am a great fan of education. But face it: Some really smart people aren't well-educated. So having matching degrees isn't necessarily a requirement for compatibility.

What is crucial is the respect you have for one another's intelligence. However, your friends and associates can complicate things. I have a friend who is a lawyer, and her boyfriend is a high school dropout. They're having massive problems — not within the relationship itself but because he refuses to accompany her anywhere and keeps referring to her friends as "those lawyer jerks." He feels intimidated and defensive, which translates into rudeness and unpleasantness toward them, and in return she is defensive. This difference can definitely undermine a relationship.

Income

Our society has been set up to accept the fact that as men got wealthier, they could get more beautiful — not necessarily brighter, but more beautiful — younger women. As women have entered the work force and become more successful, the fact that a woman earns more than her partner is no longer remarkable. We know that while these well-heeled women may be thought of as desirable and sexy while dating, once married, the relationship can be threatened by the very financial discrepancy that was enchanting during courtship. This situation is much more disruptive than the converse, which is much more in line with the expectation that the man provides for the woman. When the woman makes more money, the man may initially feel unmanly, which will result in problems in the bedroom as well as the kitchen, living room, and garden and may lead to arguments due to his need to "prove" himself.

I'm not suggesting that women hide their income or their power, especially in second marriages in which women have accumulated (through hard work, inheritance, or a divorce settlement) vast sums of money. That's why prenups were invented. If the two of you have a lot of positive things going for you, a difference in income doesn't have to be destructive, but it will always be disruptive. Does this mean women are limited to guys who currently or will eventually out-earn them? Absolutely not, but it means the two of you need to be aware of the long-term turbulence and even the short-term upset that this inadvertent challenging of the social norm offers.

You're gay

I am one of those people who thinks that we can and should be defined on the totality of our being rather than our race or hair color or height or sex or religion. I believe that all of us would have much easier lives if we could choose who would turn us on (the person who is nice and is crazy about us, our next-door neighbor, our mom's best friend's offspring, the boss's son or daughter, our best friend). Unfortunately, that's not how sex works. We can choose our behavior, not our feelings. It has always seemed unnecessarily limiting to define a person's entire life on the basis of who turns them on. I still opt for sex as being a private behavior, and in the long run, I care more about a person's manners or breath than I do about their sexual preference unless they happen to turn me on.

One of the assumptions of this book is that you are straight, meaning heterosexual. However, gays and straights face many of the same issues with respect to dating.

In my years as a psychologist both on and off the air, I have dealt with lots of folks who were in or out of the closet, gay or straight, and I am struck by the similarities in their dating problems, not the differences. If you are a gay person reading this book and feel that something I have said as a universal statement doesn't apply to you because you're gay, please write and let me know. I may include it in a future edition or write a new book or explain to you why I disagree.

My only real warning here is know thyself. If you're gay, don't date straight people, and if you're straight, don't date someone who's gay. You're both just asking for heartache, and there are enough disappointments in life without a need to go out of your way to ask for that kind of trouble.

If you're muttering, "What about bi's?" I would say get a therapist or a piece of paper or a mirror and get your act together and decide who you are and what you want. Wanting it all is okay; trying to have it all is often both greedy and futile. Sometimes you have to decide the real you: chocolate or vanilla, Christian or Jew, New York or California (all of which you can change); male or female (which can be changed with great difficulty); or straight or gay (a preordained biological orientation like curly hair or left-handedness that you can't change).

You're in a long-distance relationship

You meet someone on vacation or at a friend's wedding, and it's instant fireworks. Will it work? Maybe, maybe not. But if you're more than an hour away and see each other less than a couple times a month, you're talking fantasy. Long-distance relationships can certainly be fun but shouldn't be confused with a reality-based relationship, which is the only way to have sanity in your love life.

Sometimes a couple who has been together for a long time has to be apart for a specified length of time: One has to finish school, a military commitment has to be fulfilled, a job transfer looms. If the two of you have been together for a year or more, you may be able to sustain the relationship over a period of certainly not more than a year (otherwise, you will have been apart longer than together, and people change over a period of a year). Work out the ground rules (basically, don't ask and don't tell about other social engagements, and *don't* commit to one another until the end of the separation).

If you've been together six months to a year, you're best served to believe in fate. Plan to get together at the end of the separation and see what's what. But a lot of visits, if they're less than weekly, are likely to prolong the agony without offering much in return.

If you're sexual, you're both likely to feel used and spend most of the time in bed — without acknowledging how both of you are growing and changing. Relationships that get stuck like a bug in amber are quite brittle. If you're not having sex, it will be easier to maintain the distance, but what about the intimacy?

In general, lots of time apart is hard on a relationship. It doesn't mean you're doomed, but it means things will be and feel different when you reunite. Why not start over then, without ghosts and baggage, secrets or lies, and see where both of you are rather than having to finesse or pretend?

You're involved in an office romance

Americans believe in the *M.A.S.H.* philosophy of life, which suggests that we can have all our goodies in one place: love, family, friends, work, rivalries, food, housing, recreation, flirtations. Nonsense. *M.A.S.H.* is a TV show that hasn't even had original episodes since 1983 (though it thrives in reruns). *The Office* is a more modern cautionary tale. While there is a certain efficiency to the idea of finding someone to love at work (think of how much you'll have in common), what is most likely is that one or both of you will lose your jobs.

Work is about competence, and dating is about compatibility. They have very little to do with one another, and if you think no one will know, think of how obvious it was when that secretary over in Accounting was having an affair with his boss. *Everybody knows.* If for no other reason, keeping your work and love life separate is a good idea so that, if one goes sour, you can throw yourself into the other. If you've got the hots for someone at work, wait until one of you leaves or transfers, and trade phone numbers at the going-away party, unless it would be a long-distance relationship. (And if that's the case, just confess your crush, wax nostalgic, and chalk the whole thing up to what might have been until one of you moves back into the area.)

You're a single parent

Nowadays, nearly two-thirds of all children are being raised in single-parent households, which means there are a lot of parents dating. The number of single mothers (9.8 million) has remained constant (84 percent of children living with one parent are living with mom), while the number of single fathers is growing: Men now comprise one-sixth of the nation's single parents.

As if dating weren't complicated enough, having your child ask *you* what time you're going to be home adds agony to embarrassment. By the way, what time *do* you plan to be home?

Let me make one thing absolutely clear: Young kids don't get dating, and neither do older ones when it comes to a parent. Trying to combine parenting with early stage dating is like walking a tightrope while wrestling a dolphin: highly slippery, inadvisable, and just plain dangerous. Take a look at the possibilities:

- You like your date, your date likes you, the kids hate your date: Problem.
- You like your date, your date likes you, the kids love your date: Problem (believe it or not).
- You like your date, your date hates you, the kids hate your date: No problem.
- You like your date, your date hates you, the kids love your date: Problem.
- You like your date, your date likes you, your date hates your kids: Problem.
- You like your date, your date hates you, your date loves the kids: Big problem.
- You hate your date, your dates likes you, the kids hate your date: No problem.
- You hate your date, your date hates you, the kids hate your date: No problem.
- You hate your date, your date hates you, the kids love your date: Medium-sized problem.

I think those are all the possibilities, but the point is that the only times kids and dating aren't a problem is when everybody hates everybody. And best-case scenario — when there is a genuine love-fest going on — can still be trouble, since this book only covers the first six to nine months of dating and lots of things change. I haven't even mentioned trouble with exes and the confused roles between dating and parenting for you.

It's a common problem that's not going to go away, but you are well advised to keep your kids and your dates separate until you're sure of your date, which takes a while because:

- Introducing a date too soon can make kids either clingy or anxious or both, and unhappy kids do a lot of *acting out,* which is psycho-babble for acting like creeps: hanging up when your date calls, telling your ex, hitting, crying, clinging, telling the teacher your date hit you or the child or kicked the dog . . . you get the point.

- Kids get attached and don't really get hanging out for a while to see how things work.

- The adults need time to see if they're strong enough to be together before they test the do-the-kids-like-me waters.

- Adult sexuality can be really confusing for kids of any age. (Do you like the idea of your parents "doing it"? — and look at how old you are!)

This doesn't mean you have to be celibate or put yourself on house arrest until the kids are married, but you *do* have to be discreet and really good at juggling time and responsibilities, and have reliable babysitters at the ready.

You're dating your best friend's ex

You and your best friend share lots of secrets and have lots in common, but an ex shouldn't be one of them. I don't advise dating your best friend's ex unless it's been a long, long time, and even then, I guarantee your friend is going to feel you're being disloyal.

The Everly Brothers had a song about *bird dogging* (which is dating your friend's date), and the song, not the concept, was a big hit. I know it makes some kind of logical sense. After all, you and your friend do share a similar sense of humor, a fondness for James Bond flicks, and a willingness to cover for each other when necessary, but sharing a love interest, even serially, only works in Hollywood movies, and even Hollywood admits it can get pretty sticky.

You don't have to believe me. Just think about how you'd feel if your best friend started dating one of your exes. Are they talking about you? Comparing notes? What if you come in second? If nothing else, if your friend starts dating your ex, you'll either end up saying, "See, I told you so" or feeling that your friend has something you don't . . . like your ex.

If you're bound and determined to date your friend's ex:

- ✔ **Wait at least a year or so after the break-up.** Any earlier, you're talking rebound: You'll lose a date, a friend, and your mind.

- ✔ **Don't ask permission.** The first date can be kept quiet (after all, who knows how things will go?), but if it seems to have some potential, tell, don't ask. Just explain that you bumped into one another and plan to go out for coffee (you can finesse that first date), but keep the details to yourself, whether it's going very well or very badly.

- ✔ **Ask yourself, "Is it worth the friendship?"** That will very likely be the cost.

You're dating your relative's ex

This is just a specialized and potentially even more toxic case of dating a best friend's ex. I actually know a man who married the sister of his girlfriend of seven years. You can imagine family Thanksgivings are more than a little strained.

Again, if the two of you feel star-crossed, at least wait a while, and then don't share the details but do tell the relative before that person finds out via the family grapevine. If at all possible, avoid this plight. If you can't avoid it, make sure that your motives are pure, and you're not acting out of some ancient feud or competition.

You're a senior

As we get older and wiser, dating should get easier, but I'm not sure it ever really does. If you're a senior (65 or older), this book may be particularly useful to figure out what's changed and what's the same old story.

If you're divorced, it's a good idea to keep your kids in the dark for as long as possible. Don't wait until the wedding or the funeral, but reading the section on single parent dating applies regardless of the age of the "child."

If you're widowed, don't be surprised to find your offspring fairly resistant to a new date. When it comes to our parents, we're kinda frozen in amber. If Mom and Dad can't be together, then the survivor can be a living monument to how things used to be. Besides, if Mom or Dad is dating, she or he may be having sex . . . yech. . . .

If you've never been married, ask yourself why not and what you're looking for now (see the following Part I chapters for information on how to find out about yourself and what you want).

Having said all that, there are several huge advantages to senior dating:

✔ Women don't have to worry about getting pregnant. The woman cited earlier in this chapter was and is incredibly unusual. You do, however, still need to use protection to avoid STDs, which are a problem at any age.

✔ Men don't have to worry about borrowing the family car.

✔ You don't have to ask your parents what time you have to be home (although you may end up answering to your kids).

✔ You don't have to worry about your braces locking when you kiss (although you may have to worry about your canes knocking).

✔ Long-term commitment has a whole different meaning.

✔ You can shop together for eternal housing — a really long-term commitment.

✔ You don't have to worry what religion to raise the kids in.

✔ One word: Viagra.

You're married

I put this specialized situation last because if you're married, you cannot, must not, dare not date — or I'll haunt you. Got it? Good. If you don't want to be married, get a lawyer and a divorce, but under no circumstances are you allowed to date.

You are married unless you are divorced or widowed. Period. Separated? Still married. Staying together for the sake of the kids? Still married. Getting through the holidays? Still married. Waiting for the kids to go off to college (your collie to die, your parents to move to Florida, your stock option to be exercised)? *Still married.* If you're married, you don't date, and if your date is married, don't date your date.

Not only can you not date one another if either of you is married, but you have to wait one year until the divorce — let me repeat, the *divorce* — is final, *one full year.* Not the separation, not when sex stopped, not when one got sick. (If separation was the same as divorce, they would both be the same word, "sivorce" or "deparation" or something. Two different words mean two different things.)

If there is any question in your mind as to why waiting a full year is terribly necessary and important, read Chapter 19, and it will become painfully clear. I know the temptation is common and strong, but resist. Your relationship and your soul and your conscience will be the better for it.

If you feel your relationship is beyond redemption, so be it. If you're not sure, you may want to try dating your spouse. For real. Remind yourself that at some point, you couldn't keep your hands off each other, and it may be that by following along in the footsteps described here you can rekindle and rediscover not only what made your spouse terrific, but yourself as well. What do you have to lose?

Not only is dating your spouse allowed, but it's encouraged. If you spend the time and effort to woo one another, to pretend that it's a first date, to spend the time and energy that is implied and detailed in the early chapters of this book, I guarantee your marriage will benefit. If we took a job and then never worked hard at it or changed any of our work habits and did the same thing day after day, year after year, we would get bored and fired. So don't treat your marriage that way. Date each other if you are married.

Keeping a Dating Notebook

Throughout this book, I include exercises you can do to find out more about yourself and what you want, as well as suggestions for noting your feelings and impressions. Treat this as both an opportunity and a project to find out more about yourself.

Buy yourself a spiral notebook and a pen and write down specifics. (Be sure to write in ink because it's useful to go back and see what you were saying as opposed to erasing it, if you didn't like it, because your musings can be a work in progress, a reflection of who you were and who you're becoming.) Instead of writing in this text (I still haven't recovered from the fact that my second grade teacher would never let me so much as underline in my book), I want you to provide your own notebook. Keep it with *Dating For Dummies*, but make sure no one else can casually pick it up and be privy to thoughts you might want to keep a bit more private. (Actually, as long as you bought this book, you're welcome to underline in it as you see fit. But a separate notebook is necessary as well.)

The undivorced

This is an increasingly growing category of people who are not living together but not yet divorced. I don't care if your prospective date has been separated for decades; the person is still not divorced, and believe me, there's a reason. Do you really need the aggravation of finding out why?

A lot of folks who are really commitment-shy find the limbo of separated but not divorced quite comfortable because it means they are unable to commit to someone new — "I'm not able to marry you because technically, I'm still married." Do you really want to take up with someone who is unable to fish or cut bait, either be married or be divorced? Not a great idea and often a great recipe for heartache down the road.

When you write something down, include information that will help you remember who you were at the time of notation, your feelings, your job, your wishes and dreams, as well as the date, the time of day, who you were dating at the time, how old you were, and where you were living. This info can really be an ongoing log (sort of like Captain Kirk StarDate log as if your dating is entering a strange, new world, encountering exotic new species!).

I know you're thinking, why not blog or keep the record online? But there truly is value in using the old fashioned route: You get privacy, as well as reflection, and no need to reboot.

Chapter 2

Being Confident

- -

- -

*Y*ou have to start with confidence. Not bravado, not bluster, but confidence. This book is as much about losing your fear as anything else. If you want to be scared silly of being rejected and feeling vulnerable, of being too fat or too tall or too noisy or too quiet, you're going to be alone, because I'll tell you everybody's dirty little secret: If we let ourselves, we'd all be frightened all the time. It's not that there are brave people and cowards; it's that there are people who decide their fear is too heavy and can and should be left behind. These people get on with their lives: They focus on other people, have fun, have sex, have picnics, have colds, and even have doubts. But the emphasis is on doing, not on worrying. Checking out the latest movie star's pecs or bosoms is not a way to start dating. They're airbrushed, and you're air-breathing, so let's get on with it.

Handling Fear

The T-shirt that says *No Fear* is probably the only profound T-shirt in the history of the world.

Fear can paralyze you; it can stop you from looking for a job, looking for love, looking in the mirror. It can keep you from asking for what you want, saying what's on your mind, saying "ouch" or "hurrah." Fear eats away at your time, your energy, your very self, and it has no place in your life. Caution? Perhaps. Knowledge about why something isn't good for you? Certainly. But fear is a waste of time; most often, it is the boogeyman of your imagination, the monster that says, "Boo!"

Fear is an awesome and formidable power that scary things don't deserve, so turn on the lights and look at what you fear. Figure out what you can do to be strong, and bypass or tame what frightens you. Don't let fear have the power to control you. Take control of your fear.

What you already know is fine and comfortable and perhaps even useful, but if you spend your whole life with the familiar, you miss out on a lot of potential pleasure. The only way to truly appreciate what you have is to measure it against what else is available. You're shopping in a one-room shack when a whole mall awaits you. To paraphrase Auntie Mame, "Life is a banquet, and most poor dummies are feeding on crumbs."

I'm talking about blasting off and going bravely where you haven't been before: a land where you rule by laughing, singing, having fun, meeting new people, encountering new situations, finding new muscles and a sense of perspective. Okay, okay, I can hear you now: "Blastoff is scary. What if I get blown up on the launch pad or end up where there's no oxygen?"

Go for it. Lose your fear, and focus on your curiosity and strength. Think of other new experiences you've had: your first day of school, the time you tried a mango, your first airplane trip, the time you let your friend talk you into riding the giant roller coaster, and so on. Admittedly, not all new experiences are fun, but think of what you miss when you let your fear of the unknown keep you from trying. You may miss things like lobster or chocolate or a Jacuzzi — and a lot of exhilaration.

Even Captain Kirk, Spock, every astronaut, *and* every gorgeous creature and manly stud has been fearful. The difference between being paralyzed and going for it is a basic faith in yourself. This faith is really what confidence is all about. Even when you're not quite sure, the *appearance* of confidence can get you a long way. In the long run, looking like you know what you're doing is almost as important as knowing what you're doing. Almost.

Whining

You know about whining — the obnoxious, nasal complaining that serves no purpose other than to say, "Pay attention to me because I'm helpless and weak and irritating, and I can't get your attention based on strength or knowledge or reason so I'll drive you crazy by pitching my voice and my grievance in such a way that you'll do anything to have me stop, but you'll hate both yourself and me in the morning." The word actually comes from the Anglo-Saxon word for "whizzing" — which *must* have meant something different to them than to us — so obviously the concept of whining has been around for a very long time.

If you've got a legitimate complaint, say it clearly and cogently and respectfully and see what you can do to solve the problem. Leave whining to 3-year-olds who don't want to take a bath.

Remember the musical *The King and I* (which is based, by the way, on a true story)? Anna and her young son arrive in Siam, a strange foreign country in which they know no one. While they're awaiting the summons of the king, who has a nasty reputation, Anna tells her son to whistle a happy tune to fool everybody into thinking that they're not afraid. This isn't just a movie moment. The truth is, if you pretend you're not afraid, before you know it, you're really not afraid.

Be afraid of not taking chances, not of making mistakes. Look both ways before you cross the street, but don't stand in the middle of the crosswalk and tremble; you'll get run over.

Winning the Confidence Game

So let's talk about this confidence thing. Are some people — the gorgeous, smooth, and successful among us — born with it? Nope! These people got to be successful and smooth by *appearing* to be confident. And what about those who were smart enough to choose the right parents or get dipped in the gorgeous-gene pool? Well, I know some of the most stunning people on this earth, and most of them are surprisingly *insecure* and *frightened* — of losing their looks, of appearing stupid and superficial, of growing old, of putting on weight, of having no one love them for any reason other than their cheekbones, of having no one love them at all.

In spite of what we've been led to believe, you don't have to compete against the whole world (including the gorgeous, smooth, and successful). Compete only with yourself, being the best you can be, and you will find comfort and serenity that others will see as confidence and that will keep you calm and focused — all of which are incredibly attractive characteristics.

I'm not suggesting that you petition to be hit upside the head with the ugly stick, just that you get on with your life, whatever you look like. Accept the ride home with the too-cute guy from your building who you never thought would ask you out — rather than worry why he'd ask *you* out. Introduce yourself to the fascinating woman you'd really like to know better. Or at least say "hi" to the person you see daily at the bus stop. Smart people do the best they can with what they've got, and they don't whine too much in the process.

Take two lefts . . .

I'm one of those people who give instructions like a girl. Where a guy would say take two lefts, go a half mile, and take a hard right, I include lots and lots of checkpoints: Go until you see the red barn on the left, turn at the Dairy Queen sign just before the house with the magnolia bush — you get the picture. (Undoubtedly, this habit's a leftover from being the navigator when I was a kid and not wanting to hurt my mom's feelings because she was hopeless with a map. If I sounded like I wasn't quite sure, then my being right wouldn't make my mom feel so incompetent. Of course, I now realize that she was delighted to be relieved of the task.)

I almost always know what I'm talking about, but I never sound like it when I'm telling people how to get somewhere. And they always seem surprised when I'm right because my tone and demeanor give exactly the wrong message. Even though I know what I'm talking about, I don't *sound* like it.

Fortunately, this equation works both ways. Just as sounding tentative convinces people not to take you seriously, sounding like you know what you're talking about convinces them that you're right. In other words, to a surprisingly large extent, how people view us is up to us. Got it? Good. I cheerfully refer to this as the Anna and the King of Siam school of life. Whistle a happy tune and you fool not only yourself but everybody else as well.

Appearing confident

Confidence is the ability to trust yourself and convey that sense to others, and appearance is half the battle. If you want to appear confident, whether you feel confident or not, try the following (and for more information about confidence and confidence building, see Chapter 3):

- ✔ **Stand up straight.** Posture counts. A straight spine denotes purpose and strength (*spineless* means cowardly, after all). Face forward. Think military bearing rather than bent-over hag from *Snow White,* and you'll get the picture.

- ✔ **Smile.** Not only is a smile a good umbrella to the slings and arrows of outrageous fortune, but it also convinces others that you're happy and healthy and *wise.* A frown makes you look like you're worried or frightened.

- ✔ **Make eye contact.** It's all in the eyes. Showing that you're not afraid to look people in the eye means that you're strong and truthful and willing to meet their scrutiny.

  One of the most blatant tip-offs to a lie is the liar's inability to make eye contact — unless we're talking pathological liar here, and then you're sunk anyway. Your momma knew that when she said, "Look me in the eye and tell me you were studying."

✔ **Lean slightly forward.** Whether you're standing or sitting, leaning forward rather than pulling back denotes energy and forthrightness — and *that* signals strength and willingness. It also lets your energy move forward. Leaning forward is a bit aggressive or at least assertive rather than defensive or passive.

✔ **Shake hands firmly (yeah, women too).** Upon entering a new situation, walking confidently into someone else's space and putting out your hand and firmly — not crushingly nor limply — offering a part of yourself in a friendly but assertive way says gobs and gobs of good things about you: You're unafraid, you're an equal, you're friendly, you're engaging. A firm handshake while you look someone in the eye works wonders in business and personal situations.

It's okay to feel nervous or excited, especially in new situations. An actor will tell you that unless she feels that adrenaline rush, she's not going to give a really top-notch performance. Make those nerves work for you. Remind yourself: *I've felt this way before, and I survived; what's the worst thing that could happen, and how likely is that? It's okay to feel a bit edgy. I can do this.* Confidence is both that quiet inner voice and that more obvious outer show.

As I'm sure you've figured out, the woman who wears the flashy, low-cut dress and the man who brags about his conquests may be insecure and trying to convince other folks of their appeal rather than trusting themselves. Anything you use to build confidence needs to go deeper and work for you, not against you. You don't want to send an easily misread or misinterpreted signal. Doing something harmful to your basic sense of self doesn't make any sense. On the other hand, positive activities build real self-assurance. When you whistle, for example, you hear yourself sounding happy, control your breathing, and entertain others. Pretending to be interested may teach you something; after all, you are listening. Pretending to be interesting makes you more informed; how else would you be more fascinating? Get it?

COOL IDEA

Handshakes and other coded messages

I learned the importance of a firm handshake when I was 16 years old and the only woman working on an archeology dig in southern France. I noticed that all the men strode up to one another and firmly shook hands by a grasp and a single downward movement and then went off to talk. They would politely — but dismissively — acknowledge me first, and then they would shake hands with one another and be off.

The first time I used this handshake, I was being a smart aleck. I just wanted to see what would happen. What did happen was that their eyes widened and then they included me in the conversation. I've practiced a firm handshake ever since.

> ## Lights, camera, *action*
>
> When I have a moment to prepare folks who are doing TV with me for the first time, I always tell them to sit forward in their chairs. Doing so puts them right in the middle of things, ready to go and participate. If they sit back, just moving far enough forward to be heard takes energy, and then their moment in the spotlight may be gone.

Confidence on the inside

When you begin building confidence on the inside, you inventory all the things you do well, from tying your shoelace to helping your mom cross the street to making a great cherry pie to sneezing really well.

Everybody does *something* well, and the place to begin building confidence is on that sturdy foundation of being able to do something — *anything* — with a degree of proficiency.

If you can't think of one thing you do well, then you're probably having a pity party, which is toxic for confidence. You're also not looking at yourself objectively, so have a friend help you recognize your talents. If a friend's not available, ask your mother, who probably loves *everything* you do. If that doesn't work, immediately turn to Chapter 3 to understand why pity parties are toxic. If that doesn't work, see a therapist.

Confidence on the outside

To begin on the outside, you can develop a sense of personal style — knowing what looks good on you, your own personal statement, the attention to detail that sets you apart. Regardless of your age or economic circumstances or bone structure, you can make a statement that makes you feel good about yourself, and *that* is the best accessory you can have whether you're looking for a job or a loan or a date. A fun and easy way to develop a sense of personal style is to liven up your wardrobe with clothing and accessories that accentuate the traits you like best.

If you're not sure what becomes you, take a trusted friend to a dressing room or have someone whose style you admire go with you. (Of course, don't try to copy someone else's style, but if your friend has an eye for what looks good, he or she can probably help you.) Public dressing rooms are also great places to ask strangers whether they think a style looks good on you. Strangers are often brutally frank and even make suggestions. You can also ask a salesperson, but be a little careful about trusting someone who's working on commission. The good ones are honest, but knowing which clerks to trust is hard if you haven't shopped much at a particular store.

I know a couple who actually e-mail pictures of potential outfits to wear or buy when they're apart. Please do *not* view this suggestion as an invitation to use the camera on your cell to send naughty pix, just potential outfits — are we agreed here? If you're looking for a bit more self reliance, take your own picture in the dressing room, put the outfit on hold for 24 hours, send the picture to your e-mail, enlarge it when you get home, and decide whether the outfit makes you look, well, you-ish. Also, do you like it better than what you already own?

If you're feeling a bit scared about trying something new, shop at a resale or discount store. These places often allow you to get more bang for your buck. Don't spend a fortune, but be willing to experiment a bit. You don't have to do anything drastic to find a new look. If your wardrobe consists of dark, sober colors, try livening things up with a bright blouse or scarf or striped shirt or tie. If your idea of casual wear is limited to jeans and concert T-shirts, consider getting a pair of khakis and a shirt that can be worn with or without a tie. Look through a magazine and see what look may work for you. Trust your mirror: Which clothes do you already own that are most you-ish and most flattering?

In general, wear something you like and know you look good in for a first date instead of something very different from the real you or something brand new that might pinch or fall apart or chafe. Your lucky dress or tie or color is a better choice for a first date than that brand spanking new bolero jacket you bought because you thought it looked good on Zorro or the Jacksons (either Janet or Andrew). Also, beware especially of new shoes. They can literally cramp your style faster than anything I know. It's hard to stride confidently into a room if you have a gigantic blister on your heel or your toes are folded back onto each other like an accordion. Clothes should be comfortable. Wearing something that looks good but feels lousy (a too-tight waistband or collar) is distracting and worrisome and unproductive.

Boogie-woogie, baby: Letting your confidence flow

When I first moved to a new city, I didn't know a soul. I was working out a lot to stay sane, and unfortunately I stumbled into the gym where Mikhail Baryshnikov and other folks from the American Ballet Company worked out. There I was among world-class dancers, so I took my own advice, stayed in the back row, and comforted myself with the thought, "Maybe these folks can twirl their left legs around their right ears, but *I* have a Ph.D." And I kept going. The point is that confidence in one area allows us to take chances in areas where we feel like a jerk.

How you conduct yourself has a big impact on how other people act around you. Think about someone who's really fun to be around. Usually that person makes you comfortable because he or she is comfortable in his or her own skin. Conversely, somebody who's nervous and fidgety and needy makes you break out in hives. Remember, people accept your version of yourself until they know you better or have some reason not to. So put on that smile, shine those shoes, remind yourself why your momma loves you, and keep in mind that everybody's nervous on a first date. If you can allow that nervousness to be only a tiny layer of a nice, deep coat of confidence, both you and your date can calm down and begin the hopefully enjoyable task of getting to know each other.

Please don't be tempted to use your cell as a tool to show how popular or how important you are. Voicemail was invented to allow you to get through a date uninterrupted. If you're afraid that you will be valued only if you seem unobtainable, you're with the wrong date or you need to chat with a therapist.

Confidence builders

This section gives you some ideas about how you can go about building your confidence. For more in-depth suggestions about building confidence and getting ready to venture into the dating world, see Chapter 3:

✔ **Catalog traits you like about yourself.** Start with a pencil and paper and write down the things you like best about yourself. Be specific: No sentences like "I'm really a nice person" — what does *that* mean? It may mean that you're really good to animals, handle a calculator like you were born with it in your hand, make a mean burrito for your friends, have a great singing voice, or always clean your plate. So if you mean that you don't fly off the handle every time something goes wrong, write that. The more specific the items, the better for confidence building.

✔ **Help someone else.** The ability to do something for someone else builds confidence because not only does the person you help say thank you and appreciate what you did for him, but he appreciates *you* in the process. So if you feel your confidence is a bit too soggy for serious interaction with the opposite sex, do someone a favor, find a volunteer activity, or deal with kids (so you can feel more powerful). The other terrific advantage of volunteer work is that you're not locked in: You can feel good quickly and not feel like you have to stay doing something forever.

Keeping some do-good stuff in your life is a way to be connected and keep a balance in your life, as well as maintain good feelings about yourself and the world at large.

✔ **Try a challenging activity.** Try doing something you didn't think you could do. Even if you don't do a great job, you'll feel much better about yourself when you try something really difficult. Even succeeding at something easy often doesn't feel as good as attempting something hard. And if you succeed at the hard stuff? Well, gangbusters!

It is actually okay to feel a sense of accomplishment by doing something you know you can do. It's a good start for confidence. Just as feelings of incompetence seem to spread, so, too, can the more positive feelings. So get out there and get started.

When you're confident enough to date

Nobody feels sure about every part of his life, and all of us feel most insecure about dealing with the opposite sex because we feel vulnerable and really want things to go well. So don't put off dating until you feel really, really sure of yourself, because you'll find that, by then, you're 90 years old. Just try to bolster your confidence enough so that you're not whiny or so incredibly needy that you're falling apart (see Chapter 3 for tips on building confidence and Chapter 5 to find out when is the right time to begin a dating relationship). Sweaty palms and dry mouth and a bit of anxiety are okay.

You want to know how much anxiety is okay and how much is too much, right? Not an unreasonable request since dating really can drain the confidence banks. If you're feeling really rocky on your feet, stabilize before you venture forth. Don't wait till everything is ducky, although ducky times are the very best times to get yourself out there. Clinging to someone for dear life isn't sexy or stable enough to work for any length of time, and the only people you'll attract in times of trouble are control freaks who really want and need to call all the shots. Also, don't look for a parent figure or someone as a crutch to lean on when you're starting the dating game, or you will find that dating is not at all fun and not a game but a desperate bid for survival.

The secret to sex appeal

Think of the sexiest person you know. My guess is that if you take the person apart feature by feature, she or he may not be as good-looking as others you know with more perfect features but less *élan* (a cool French word for confidence, style, and poise). In any country but ours, people think of older women as incredibly sexy because they've come into their own and accepted themselves.

Sex appeal is confidence, the ability not to ask anything of another but a willingness to offer yourself. What can be sexier?

You're ready to date if:

- ✔ You've got a stable place to live and a way to make a living.

- ✔ You have a reasonably good working relationship with your parents (okay, so long as you're not at war; a cease fire is good enough).

- ✔ You have a friend or two hanging about.

- ✔ You know how to make yourself reasonably happy.

- ✔ You'd really like some tension and aggravation and excitement and fun and worry and uncertainty in your life.

If you can answer yes to the preceding conditions, well, bunkie, sounds like you're ready. If you haven't passed muster in any of the preceding, it's time to work on your life and put off dating temporarily. If nothing else, having accomplished these things will give you a nearly giddy sense of confidence, and that's not only the name of this chapter, but the name of the game.

False Confidence

Just a word here about false confidence, the kind you purchase with alcohol or some other chemical. Don't do it. You can't gain confidence through some substance. It wears off, you get hung over, and it's absolutely obvious in the worst kind of way. You may think you appear confident, but everyone else just thinks you're drunk, high, a jerk, or all of the above. Think about how uncool you notice some people to be when you're the designated driver — stone cold sober — and *they're* three sheets to the wind. 'Nuff said.

When I'm talking confidence, I'm talking the real McCoy that comes from knowing and trusting yourself, knowing that you're not perfect but trusting that you'll do the best you can with what you've got.

Chapter 3

Polishing Your Social Self

Dating is anxiety-provoking, exciting, common, and individualistic, as well as potentially straightforward and simple. The best way to have a good time dating — not just on a date, but throughout the whole process — is to be relatively sane and happy before you begin. Notice, I did not focus on any particular date because you have surprisingly little control over that. After all, there is another person involved and lots of imponderables. I don't say this to scare you, only to prepare you for what you already know in other situations: Life is full of surprises, and even with great preparation, things can go wrong, and sometimes, with absolutely no preparation at all, things can go astonishingly well.

The point is not to throw up your hands in frustration, but to realize you do the best you can with what you've got and be prepared to go with the flow a bit.

In this chapter, it's crucial to take a hard look in the mirror to determine whether your social skills are up to par in order to make and keep friends and date successfully. If you're good to go, you can skip right to the dating advice later in the book. But if you have some work to do, I've provided you with some tips on what to do (as well as warnings about what not to do) to prepare yourself mentally and physically for dating.

Self-Assessment 101

The happier you are, the more ready you are to date. A contradiction you say? Nay, nay. To figure out the right and wrong times for dating, see Chapter 4. This list gets you started by showing you some signs that you're *not* ready to date:

- ✔ You've lost your job.

- ✔ You've lost your housing.

- ✔ You've lost a friend.

- ✔ You've lost a parent.

- ✔ You've lost your dog.

- ✔ You're lost.

- ✔ You're married.

- ✔ You're still involved.

- ✔ You're separated.

- ✔ You've been divorced less than a year.

You have undoubtedly noticed that the operant word here is *loss.* Trying to fill one portion of your life by dating is not only bad karma but also futile and doomed. I know Hollywood would have us believe that if you're "on a break," staying together because of the kids, not in love anymore, yada, yada, dating is great. It's not. We are not robots, and it takes time (and we deserve the time) to focus exclusively on self after a marriage or a relationship goes south. Give yourself that gift of time, and you'll find yourself much less prone to serial dating and breakups. Admittedly, the beginnings are fun. The endings: not so much.

If your life feels terrific, but you'd just love to have a special someone with whom to share it — in other words, if your motivation is more focused whimsy than desperate need — you're prime dating material. Jump right to Parts II and III, where you'll find all sorts of tips and advice on making dates.

If you're unutterably lonesome, desperate, miserable, or need cheering up, this chapter is definitely for you. I'm gonna get you in shape to date. Just as an athlete prepares for an important event or the opening of the season, I'm going to coach you about how to prepare yourself to begin. Yep, that's right, this chapter deals with preparing to date, not actually dating. But don't get impatient. The mission of this chapter? Creating a person who is healthy and happy and okay, maybe a little excited, but under control and ready to put in the time to do the job right. I can hear you thinking: "Yeah, yeah, but I think I'll just go online and see who's out there or check out a chat room or troll through Facebook or flirt with someone on Match.com." Please, hang in there and be patient for a moment. This first impression thing is real. You don't want to bump into the right person at the wrong time, before you're ready, willing, and especially *able.* So chill and learn and trust yourself to become the best and sanest and most datable you can be.

I've divided the rest of this chapter into terrific ideas and horrific ideas. These ideas are each given a rating, that is, a heart (what else would you expect in a book on dating?): the higher the heart count, the more important the idea and the more critical to your dating health and preparedness. A broken heart is self-explanatory: Don't go there, even if you're tempted, even if it seems logical; the disaster is predictable.

The ideas are presented in sequential order. To get the most benefit from this chapter, perform the suggestions in each section, in order. Begin with the three-heart ideas, move to the two-heart ideas, and finish up with the one-heart ideas. (Of course, avoid the broken heart ideas.) But even if you don't want to read this chapter from first page to last, you can still get a lot of good information by jumping around.

♥♥♥ *Three-Heart Ideas*

These tasks are the most critical to your personal understanding and dating well-being. They may seem like the hardest because they require that you get out into the world and make connections with other people. That can be a scary idea, especially if you're unsure of yourself or shy or have been hurt or just don't know where to begin. But the benefits derived by getting yourself out of the house and meeting new people are definitely worth it. No guts, no glory — and, hey, this is dating, not dental extraction.

Taking yourself off house arrest

A wounded animal seeks shelter, but animals don't have to date, just mate. As far as we know, animals don't have to worry about job descriptions, well-meaning parents who nag, and a few extra pounds that don't look terrific in a bathing suit. Animals don't get hurt by misunderstandings or insecurities, animals don't feel self pity, and they don't have TV as an anesthetic (or the Internet or video games or Facebook or even chat rooms). In other words, animals don't become couch potatoes because their true loves didn't come along. Although seeking shelter is fine if you're a four-legged forest creature, if you're a human, you need to get out and about. After all, we humans are usually not very well-served by hibernating. We sulk and obsess and analyze and feel more and more cut off.

Therefore, bunkie, if you're spending most of your time in front of the tube, hoping the good fairy of dating will come and hit you upside the head with an inspiration stick, you're wasting time. Get off your butt, turn off the tube, and *get out of the house, off line, and into life with a capital L.*

Sulking is not sexy, and it's not productive. Your vocal cords will seize up if you don't use 'em, and your social skills will shrivel. When you're feeling sorriest for yourself is when you most need to use your gumption rather than wishing you'd inherited straight teeth, a crooked smile, and a charm gene — and when you most need to *get out of the house.* Take a walk, take a course, take a hike (literally). The more sedentary you are, the less you feel like moving, and the less you move, the less you *feel* like moving. Emotionally, you can experience extreme sludgy-ness, and the computer only *seems* to connect you with others.

If you're not working, get a job or do some volunteer activity. If you're still in school, join a club. The point is to get out of your cave and visit the rest of the tribe. Doing so will change your perspective, clear up your skin, and keep you from brooding and thinking only about yourself.

This isn't just a way to get a date; it's a way to get a life. Even if you've broken your leg, unless you want to be in a wheelchair the rest of your life, you've got to move that leg and re-energize the muscles. True, it won't be much fun to begin with, but it's the only way. Don't put yourself in the prison of your loneliness. Nobody but you has the key. Following are a few ideas you can use to get yourself out of the house and meet new people:

- ✔ Make a plan to be out at least three days or nights a week — that's less than half the time — and to talk to at least three new people on each outing. I'm not talking about picking somebody up; a simple "hi" or a conversation about garbanzo beans or the weather will do.

- ✔ Try going to new places, taking a different route, or checking out a new store. Shake up your world a bit. What do you have to lose? Only your sadness.

- ✔ One of the best ways to make the transition from lonely to lovely is volunteer activities. Because you're not getting paid, you feel more in control, and because what you're offering (basically yourself) is valuable to someone, volunteer work is a great way to build self-confidence.

A note here about online "relationships." These relationships still count as house arrest. Face-to-face is the way human beings relate best, and if you're using your PC or your cell for your social life, you're literally keeping others at arm's (or at least keyboard's) length even if you're sharing video and making online "friends." It's not healthy or productive. If you've got flesh-and-blood contacts and want to fill in some of the spaces between seeing each other with online friendships, fine, but don't substitute e-mail for emotion or mistake online for alive. We know that a blank computer screen is really seductive, lowering your inhibitions, but don't even think about typing or texting when you've been drinking because once it's online, it's immortal. Who among us needs to be reminded of our pathetic selves just following a breakup? We've all been there, whined that, but we don't need for it to be a permanent part of our Internet résumé.

When you get out of the house, you discover that you're in charge and valuable. You're wanted and needed, and you'll feel a lot more loving toward yourself, which is the beginning of allowing other people to love you.

BIOLOGY

Dealing with depression

If you feel incapable of moving off the couch; if you're not sleeping well or your eating habits have changed; if you feel sad most of the time, it's hard to concentrate, and you're noticing your body doesn't feel well, you may be depressed. First get a physical to rule out any treatable underlying condition.

If you get a clean bill of health and still feel really lethargic, it's time to make an appointment with a psychiatrist. Depression is the most common and untreated illness in our world, and that's literally a crying shame because it is a very treatable condition. Medication and talk therapy can change your life and give you back the person you used to be.

Making friends

Before love comes like, and liking is what friends do for one another.

Let me say at the outset, I'm talking about flesh and blood, face-to-face, real life, eyeball-to-eyeball relationships, not computer-generated or accessed "friendships." Making friends is one of the most difficult and worthwhile experiences of human life because it requires time and effort and patience and understanding and acceptance and honesty. Many people confuse friendship with acquaintances, and they're not the same at all. Acquaintances are people you hang out with; they're convenient but interchangeable. Friends are people you actively seek out, people with whom you have something in common, and the link is deeper and stronger. It is very possible for one to become the other: Everyone who becomes a friend had to be an acquaintance first; and friendships can be downgraded, for example, when two people move apart geographically or emotionally or situationally — changing jobs, marital status, and so on. (Of course, this section focuses on *getting* friends, not losing them.)

If you've taken yourself off house arrest (see the preceding section for pointers), you've begun making acquaintances. The question then is how to turn an acquaintance into a friend.

A friend indeed

The place to start is with an acquaintance you really like, who seems to have some time available, and with whom you have something in common. Adult friendships are based on characteristics that you share or with which you're compatible, not overall similarities, so your friend-to-be may be older or younger than you, taller or shorter, smarter or slower, richer or poorer, or more or less energetic.

Did you hear the one about . . .?

This is a really silly joke, but I hope it will convince you to take yourself off house arrest. A guy was in a terrible accident, and he lost his eye. Fortunately, he was a really talented wood carver, so he undertook the task of making himself a new eye from wood. Although his new eye looked real, he was understandably self-conscious, so he put himself on house arrest. Eventually, he realized that this was not making him very happy, so he worked out a plan where every day he would take a few more steps outside. The first day, he took one step, the second day, two, and so on until after several months, he was at the end of the street, where he saw a huge banner proclaiming "Come one! Come all! Free admission! Dance tonite!"

Now he was still understandably self-conscious about his eye, but he decided "no guts, no glory," and went. He stood in the doorway and was just about to lose his nerve when he saw a woman across the room, sitting by herself. She was quite attractive except that she had the biggest ears he had ever seen (I mean she made Dumbo's ears look small). He decided then and there to ask her to dance, deciding that she wasn't perfect so he felt a bit safer.

With his heart in his throat, he threaded his way among the dancers and said, "Care to dance?" She smiled delightedly and said, "Would I!" Stunned, he hollered back, "Big ears, big ears, big ears!"

Well, I thought it was funny. I feel sure they will get the whole thing worked out and enjoy the dance and go on and live happily ever after. This joke is also a cautionary tale: You might be a bit self-conscious and overly sensitive at first, but you should persevere.

Beware of using the same criteria for adult friends that you used when you were 12. Twelve-year-old girls' minds meld: They essentially become one person because they have everything in common — boys, parents, braces, new breasts, bratty sibs, geometry, and zits. Also, 12-year-olds don't have a fully developed personality structure intact yet; they are still a less solidified version of the person they will become: less rigid, less defined, less sure. You will never again feel as close to another living soul as you did when you were 12 (unless you happen to be an identical twin). If you look for that same degree of intimacy, you're going to spend your whole life being disappointed for no good reason.

Are you friend material?

A friendship can be an important part of your life, but not the totality of your life as it was when you were a kid, so don't try to take over your friend's life or let your friend take over yours. (Just because your best pal hates your hairdo, thinks your career is in the dumps, or isn't as fiscally adventurous doesn't mean you need to change hairdressers, go looking for another line of work, or choose a different investment counselor.) If you're old enough to date, you're old enough to be self-reliant, and the same characteristics that make a good friend make a good potential date. Not to mention, our friends sustain us while dates often come and go. Don't be discouraged; just understand that making friends is important whether or not your dating works immediately. Who couldn't use the practice in building and maintaining relationships?

Friends grab our heads as well as our hearts, and most of us have heads that are a lot harder to fool than our hearts. Friendships employ less chemistry and much more sense. Good friendships are also based on give and take, without preordained roles of what one *should* do. You might expect your date to pay for your meal, but you certainly wouldn't expect a friend to; similarly, you would never expect a friend to read your mind, even though you may expect your date to ("If you loved me, you'd know"). A good friendship is based on reality, not fantasy; equality, not dominance; and rationality, not romance. The healthier both participants are, the better — and healthier — the friendship will be.

Adult friendship is based on caring about someone because of, rather than in spite of, their warts, and the best way to have a friend is to be a friend. You don't have to be perfect to have a friend or be a friend. Just be flexible and loving and honest. If you're getting the idea that friendship is a great potential basis for romance — bravo! — you're right. The only tricky part is chemistry.

Take out your dating notebook (see Chapter 1) and answer yes or no to the following questions to find out whether you're ready to be a friend and have a friendship with another adult. Keeping a notebook lets you see what you're doing, where you've been, and where you're going. Haven't started one yet? Not to worry. You can buy a spiral notebook or a three-ring binder and start one now. Make this exercise one of your entries:

Tell it like it is, sister

I had just moved to a new city and didn't know anyone. One of the news anchor women shared a cab with me on the way home, and she said, "I don't have any really good women friends, and you just moved here, and I'd really like to be your friend." I was touched by her honesty and her urgency, and while we didn't have a whole lot in common, we did become friends because her urgency really started the ball rolling.

Although it doesn't always work, starting off with an honest statement doesn't hurt because friendships have to be honest — not brutal, but honest — to qualify and to survive.

✔ Expectations:

- Am I able to separate who I am and what I want from who my friend is?

- Do I accept that my friend is not just like me?

✔ Tolerance:

- Am I as tolerant of my friend as I would like him/her to be tolerant of me?

- Do I apply the same standards to myself that I expect of my friend? (In other words, do I have the same set of rules for myself and my friend?)

✔ Availability:

- Am I willing to put myself out for my friend (that is, the relationship *isn't* all about convenience)?

- Do I have the time and energy to invest in being and having a friend?

✔ Honesty:

- Am I willing to be my true self?

- Am I willing to say what I feel?

✔ Openness:

- Am I willing to be vulnerable and intimate and share my feelings?

✔ Dependency:

- Am I able to stand on my own?

✔ Empathy:

- Am I able to look at a conflict from someone else's point of view?

✔ Perspective:

- Do I like something about my friend other than the fact that he/she likes me?

- Can I be a bit unselfish and less self-centered?

You can see from this list why friendship is such a good basis for dating and just about any other kind of relationship. If you answered yes to most or all of the questions, you're great friend material. If you aren't capable of friendship, you might think about working on that before you take up dating. Friendship isn't easy. It is important, and it doesn't even have sex to heat things up.

Friendship is truly a uniquely human and undeniably valuable exercise in being our most basic and terrific and honest and self-reliant selves. Time spent making friends is always time well spent. When you do launch your dating self, you'll have your friend to commiserate or share the joy.

Same- versus opposite-sex friends

Can a man and a woman be *just* friends? Well, yes and no. Most women say yes; most men say no. It is certainly possible for friendship to blossom into a sexual and romantic thing. (Why do you think *When Harry Met Sally* is still such a popular video rental, and *Friends* and *Dawson's Creek* still rule in cable reruns five days a week?)

Often exes can be friends after the sexual passion has gone and some time has passed so that neither is confused by kindness or emotional intimacy. I say this with a slight amount of trepidation because I have seen the demise of some fairly good marriages when an ex gets curious about an old flame and gets in touch via someone's Facebook page: Can 500 million people be wrong? These same people would likely never pick up a phone and call to satisfy the curiosity or longing; it takes so much less

courage or questioning of motive to Google an ex and share confidences and pictures. I continually remind you of the seduction of an empty screen. Fantasies are easy, especially when tinged with nostalgia and abetted by the realities of a long-term marriage or committed relationship. The world's easiest job description is that of lover rather than partner or spouse, and the Internet can fuel that fantasy without any initial acknowledgement of intent or guilt. Careful, careful, careful. Remembering what was or what might have been is harder than starting from ground zero, with no history.

The advantage of opposite-sex friendships is that you can share dating tips and insights. This is probably why so many women have gay male friends: They can get the insight without the hassle of wondering about sex with one another.

 **Two-Heart Ideas**

You've now performed the most fundamental things: gotten yourself out of the house and begun the process of social interaction that isn't sexually based. Good on ya. But how, I can hear you asking, do you go from friends and volunteer activities to dating? Well, stay tuned, I'm gonna tell you.

Charm practice

Charm is simply the practice of making someone know that you feel good about them without embarrassing them or asking anything of them in return, and it's really, really seductive. It's being a fancy maitre d' at a French restaurant without the tip — making someone feel that he or she is the most important person in the world to you at that moment. Keep in mind:

- ✔ Charm has to be sincere. Charm is its most potent when *you* believe what you're saying.

- ✔ Charm *must* include eye contact. If you're good at eye contact and vocal warmth, it's almost impossible to lay it on too thick.

- ✔ Charm may include compliments. What to say is relatively easy: Figure out what would feel the best to you if someone were making you feel good. This technique doesn't work 100 percent of the time, but it works more often than not, and because you're tuned in to the other person (a large part of the charm experience), you'll be able to adjust accordingly.

- ✔ Charm is done lightly and pleasantly.

- ✔ Charm isn't sexual; it's just warmth.

- ✔ The trick to charm is to be selfless: You're not asking for anything here, not even feedback. Charm is independent of response (well, almost independent; all of us like to feel appreciated, but with charm, being appreciated isn't the point).

  The difference between charm and flattery is that flattery has an agenda — I'll give you compliments so that you'll give me what I want. Charm is a way of being, rather than a tool to achieve something.

- ✔ Charm at its simplest just says, "You're terrific; thank you for letting me bask in your glow." Who among us isn't going to respond to that pitch?

Like most things, charm benefits from practice. So where do you start? Any place. Practice on your mom, your cat, your neighbor, your dad, your boss, your teacher, the cop on the corner, the 2-year-old next door. You will also be amazed at how charming people will be in return, the smiles you will glean, the fun you will have.

In short, charm is a butterfly's touch on a flower petal, the breeze of a hummingbird's wing: The key is easy does it. Charm is fun and potentially a very profitable tool in interpersonal relationships, and it's crucial to dating. So practice and enjoy.

Reading the personals

In the age of disco, the Cold War, and Johnny Carson, (a mere 30 years ago), personal ads were considered sleazy, sexual, and sometimes perverted — a backstairs way for people to manage what they were ashamed to admit to. These days, personals — both online and offline — are one of the most common and accepted ways for people to meet one another. By spending a couple of hours reading through the dating ads in whatever newspaper or magazine you normally read anyway or at popular dating Web sites such as Match.com, eHarmony.com, or any of the specialized dating sites, you can get a really good idea of who's looking for what. While not exactly an unimpeachable source, Match.com reports that these days, a full 25 percent of relationships are starting online. My own experience with friends is that while not all admit to meeting online, at least half of my friends are with someone they met online, so there.

Are personal ads completely accurate? Can they be useful? Good questions. If you believed everything that was written, you'd believe that all women are raven-haired, svelte, emerald-eyed owners of their own antiques-importing businesses, and all men are handsome, chisel-chinned CEOs looking to settle down with a wife and kids after taking long romantic walks on the beach on their private islands.

If you're already feeling outclassed, if you're not skinny, or if you don't own your own business, not to worry. Having done some research on the personals, I can assure you that people are not necessarily very accurate in their self-descriptions. (If you don't believe me, just spend a little time in the cookie aisle of your favorite grocery store, or — even better — think about how you described yourself in your yearbook.) But that's not the point of this exercise.

What this exercise does is help you figure out how many people are looking to connect, how they describe themselves, and what they're looking for. If nothing else, this exercise helps you realize that you're not alone, that lots of seemingly normal, happy, fun people are out there looking. Once you're ready, you can hop right on out there and answer — or even write — an ad if you wish. The following section tells you how.

Writing a personal ad for practice or real

When writing a personal ad, you need to consider where you're going to place your ad. If writing it for a newspaper, keep in mind that you have to pay per word, so being succinct is an advantage. If you are placing your ad online, you don't have to worry about a per-word charge. But no matter where you're advertising, writing a personal ad requires the same kind of discipline that you would use so as not to break the bank — pithy and succinct beats wordy and rambling every time. For more information on writing a personal ad, see Chapters 5 and 23.

Stop sweating. This is an exercise to limber you up, not a performance piece. You don't have to send the ad anywhere, but writing a personal ad does a bunch of cool things for you:

- Makes you admit that you're really ready to start looking to date
- Allows you to be specific about the kind of person you're looking for
- Forces you to look at who you are (and that's really, really, important)

The birth of an exercise

I discovered this technique of writing personal ads quite by accident in therapy with a young woman who tearfully told me she kept picking the wrong guys. I had her write an ad. She initially focused on what she wanted in a guy, and we looked at that together. It turned out she was looking for a daddy to take care of her, but then she would get aggravated when he treated her like a child. Bingo. This discovery short-circuited months or maybe even years of therapy.

Then we turned to a description of herself, which she hadn't even included originally beyond the physical description (you know, single white female, 28, and so on). It was a very efficient insight into what she felt her strengths and weaknesses were. She focused on her generous hips while completely overlooking her gorgeous skin — although she did realize her eyes were her best feature.

When you write your personal ad or profile in your dating notebook (see Chapter 1), think about the following:

- ✔ Who you are
- ✔ Your assets and your liabilities
- ✔ What your mom loves about you
- ✔ What your friends criticize
- ✔ Your favorite thing to do (no, don't put *that* in the ad just yet, thank you very much; I mean your favorite thing to do vertically, with your clothes on . . . in public)

When you describe your perfect companion, try to get beyond the physical description and age to the person's soul and consider these qualities:

- ✔ What is the person like?
- ✔ What do the two of you enjoy together?
- ✔ What do you talk about when you're alone?

Other things that you might think about are:

- ✔ Sex (come on now, no giggling) — your sex and the preferred option for your date to be. In other words, are you straight or gay?
- ✔ Age range.
- ✔ Race, if it's an issue.

✔ Educational background.

✔ Work.

✔ Geographic proximity. Don't start with long distance unless it's preferred, and then you need to think about why you opted for distance rather than closeness. I'm of the belief that more than a 25-mile radius is self defeating.

✔ Height and weight.

✔ Religion.

✔ Smoking preference.

You should also think about whether you're looking for:

✔ Friendship and whatever else

✔ A mate

✔ A date

✔ A discreet nooner

✔ Commitment

✔ Kids

✔ Marriage

✔ A prom escort

✔ Permanence

If you're going the online route, think about what picture you'd choose: sexy, serious, sleazy, suntanned . . . I think I've run out of *s* words. Your picture should be recent and flattering but seriously resemble who you actually look like. While a fabulous picture may seem like good bait, remember two things: You may actually want to meet the respondent (no nasty surprises, please), and overly beautiful people actually have a lower success rate in terms of responses than the more ordinary looking. Leave off the props: dogs, cars, boats, kids, the ocean, flowers. Just post a recent, clear picture of you wearing something flattering, not suggestive. Don't even think of photo-shopping that picture with you in formal wear with your arm around your date. And please, no nudity. Have a friend do the honors rather than posing in front of a mirror with your cell phone camera, okay?

The lists in this section are only the beginning of sorting through who you are and what you want, and writing a personal ad or profile is a cool shortcut. In writing your practice ad, allow yourself to be honest, creative (not with the facts, with your thoughts), and specific, as well as flexible. This exercise should be fun and really helpful. You don't need a book to tell you how to write the ad, just the ability to write about who you are and what you want.

♥ One-Heart Ideas

Now that you've gained some confidence, some outside activities, some sense of who you are and what you want, it's time to do it: Take a closer look at you and who you are. The exercise of writing a personal ad or profile should have gotten you a lot closer to the basics than you were before. We're almost ready to begin looking beneath the surface, but first, the surface.

Making a good first impression

First impressions count. What do you see when you take a good look? I don't mean Mom's eyes and Dad's hairline. I mean, if you just walked into a room, what would you see if you were looking at yourself? What do you say about yourself?

- **Look at your clothes.** Do you dress age-appropriately, like your grandparents, or like a 12-year-old? Does your wardrobe scream rich or sexy or uptight or casual or poor or insecure or "I hope nobody will notice me"?

- **Look at your shoes.** Are they shiny or worn, fashionable or comfortable? Do they match? Are the laces tied or broken or mismatched?

- **Look at your hair.** Is it neat and becoming, stylish or simple? Are your roots showing? Does your part start below your ear, or are you wearing an obvious rug?

- **Look at your face.** Is your makeup subtle or heavy? What's your best feature? What about facial hair: Are you shaved?

- **Look at your hands.** Are your nails clean, polish unchipped?

- **What's your look?** Is it preppy or sexy? Conservative or out there? Business-like or fun?

REMEMBER

Your look should be consistent with your online picture and vice versa.

Considering a mini-makeover

To change your look, you don't have to spend a lot of money or win a makeover on a talk show. You just have to be willing to see what you want to change without a lot of self-loathing. You can change your

- Wardrobe
- Look
- Waistline

   ✔ Hairdo and/or hair color

   ✔ Attitude

This makeover isn't about changing your nose, height, bone structure, or parents. It's changing the seat covers, not replacing the couch, or touching up the paint job, not selling the car.

The wardrobe department

Presumably you're smart enough not to wear the same thing to the office that you'd wear to the beach, but if you look through your closet, you'll see a lot of consistency: your comfort clothes (you may need to jump-start this part of your wardrobe a bit) and stuff that is more costume that you wear to make a statement. It doesn't matter what the statement is as long as you're aware of the statement and it squares with how and what and why you want to present yourself.

You can start with your closet if you like, and get rid of all the stuff that doesn't make you look and feel terrific. All of us have more clothing than we need, so if something doesn't look and feel wonderful, give it to a friend or Goodwill, but get it out of your closet. If your shoes hurt your feet, get rid of 'em. Nothing makes people look worse than when their feet hurt. That's the easy part.

You want to focus on flattering colors, but you don't have to spend gobs of money getting your colors done. Go to a large department store with good lighting (not fluorescent), pick up the same shirt in a bunch of different colors, and see which color looks best with your skin and eyes. Then decide which color looks worst. Avoid the latter and focus on the former.

Where, oh where, has all my hair gone?

I know guys worry a lot about hair and losing it, but most women would prefer a cool bald guy with nice manners who's interested in them to a dope with a gorgeous head of hair — which gets us to the rug question. Should you or shouldn't you?

Toupees aren't usually all that convincing, but if you want to, go ahead. What you might want to try is just being yourself and letting your hair, or lack of it, be. Go au naturel on vacation, and see if you don't feel more relaxed and happy. A shaved head is very hip right now and bespeaks *loads* of confidence, which is what true sexiness is all about.

What you *shouldn't* do is take that one wisp of hair and wrap it 12 times around your head. If a wind comes up, you're sunk, and even if it's dead calm, you're going to be fiddling with it and patting it, and you'll look distracted and unhappy.

And remember, women don't care nearly as much about hair as you think.

Snow White and Rose Orange, a story of two sisters

Two-thirds of all women and one-third of all men color their hair. I learned a lesson very early on with two sisters, one of whom had gorgeous white hair and the other of whom had bright orange hair, which was obviously not any color momma nature had invented. I thought they were 20 years different in age. They were three years apart. (Oh, *please* . . . of course Ms. Prematurely Orange looked much younger!) Lesson learned as far as I'm concerned.

Mirror, mirror

Take a close-up look in the mirror. We're not talking plastic surgery here, just a look at hairstyle and color (yeah, guys, you too), facial hair (yeah, gals, you too), and makeup.

✔ **Hair:** If you hate your hair, it's probably because you haven't come to grips with what looks good on you with your particular style and texture. Look through a magazine and pick out a couple of styles you like, and then make sure that the people wearing the hair have your coloring or kind of hair or features. In fact, rather than focus on hairstyle first, look for magazine models who look like you (more or less, remembering that even those models don't look like that in real life), and then see what style they're wearing.

Don't assume that a cool hairstyle is going to cost a fortune. Find somebody who knows and likes your kind of hair, and make sure that everybody that person works with doesn't look exactly the same. Also be willing to experiment a bit: Remember, it's only hair, and it grows back.

All of us grow up with notions of what we hate about our bodies, and we unconsciously try to cover up even when the problem is gone or the cover-up only emphasizes the problem. So it may help to have an astute salesperson or a friend with a good eye stand you in front of a mirror and show you what looks good and why, and show you what you should avoid like the plague.

As long as you're preparing to launch yourself, you might as well look and feel your best.

✔ **Makeup:** Makeup is a strange and wonderful thing. Men all say they hate it 'til they see us without it. What they hate (and what we hate, too) is someone who looks like she has just walked off stage or out of the circus. Makeup can enhance what you've got and hide a bit of what you wish you didn't have, but in the same way that men who try and hide a bald spot can end up showing it off, too much makeup can actually emphasize the very things you were trying to hide.

Remember, your face is you. A good makeup person can show you how to look your best rather than someone else's not so good. Often department stores will do your makeup for free (although they try to sell you the products afterward). Pick someone whose makeup looks good — especially if she's got your skin, hair, and eye coloring as well. But don't try to look like her. You just want to look like you, only better.

✔ **Physical fitness:** All this stuff — the hair, the makeup — is the stuff someone else can do for you. A bit harder is the stuff you have to do for yourself. You can't change your bone structure or your eye shape, but you can lose ten pounds if you'd feel better (joining a health club or jogging also gets you out of the house, and physical exercise is its own happy pill) or put on ten pounds.

If you can figure out something to do that makes you happier with yourself physically — whether it's gaining or losing weight, changing your hairstyle, or buying high heels or cowboy boots or a Wonder Bra or Spandex swim trunks — then do it.

After you deal with the easy, outside stuff, it's time to dig a bit deeper.

Learning from past experiences

None of us sprang from the head of Zeus fully armored. We all have a past: things that made us happy or unhappy as a child or a youngster, and previous experiences with people of the opposite sex, parents, teachers, employers, next-door neighbors, crushes, loves, lovers, maybe even spouses. If you can pinpoint something making you unhappy, you can begin working on it. If you feel you are the problem — and have felt that way for more than a couple of weeks — it's time to think about getting some professional help. Therapy is a very good investment in you, especially if you're really, really unhappy (then I definitely am not only suggesting it, but ordering it). For most of us, getting out a pencil and paper is the first step to better mental health. Just as you wouldn't go out on a date with a raging virus, a runny nose, and a temperature, starting to date with an unhappy head doesn't make much sense either.

Because the focus here is dating, start with your earliest boy-girl stuff. Don't edit or prettify — just write 'em down as they occur to you.

✔ When you were younger, even in kindergarten, what characteristics were you drawn to? Has your taste changed? (Okay, I know you're not interested in preschoolers; let's get focused here.) Do you like high energy or quiet types? People like you or your opposite? Athletes or scholars?

✔ What personality types draw you? What constellation of characteristics attracts you? Warriors or scholars? Introverts or extroverts?

- Are you passive with the opposite sex or more aggressive? Do you like to be in charge or told what to do?

- Do you make decisions easily or do you prefer that someone else take the responsibility?

- Are you drawn to high or low energy, quiet or bubbly, shy or outgoing?

- If you had to make a list outlining a perfect date, what would head up your list? Is having a sense of humor important? Being well-read? Talking or listening?

- What have been the best parts of your interactions with the opposite sex?

- What goes right the most often, and yeah, what goes sour? The point here isn't to fix blame but to understand what your patterns have been since your first crush. You can't control chemistry, but you can understand it and try to compensate for it because you *can* control behavior, at least your own.

- Are there situations in which you shine or fold?

- What makes you happy, anxious, ambitious?

- What challenges you?

Yeah, I know these are personal questions, but dating is pretty personal stuff, and the more you know about yourself, the more confident you can be, the better the presentation you can make of yourself, and the more successful the experience will be for the both of you. So dig away.

If you're reading this book because you've never had a date, don't worry. You have patterns to discover with your friends, your crushes, your fantasies. If you're a veteran of the dating wars, the more reconnaissance the better. Knowing yourself is the best possible preparation for getting to know someone else.

Turning your fantasy self to reality

Fantasy is a terrific indicator of the difference between what we have and what we want. In our fantasies, we can do and be anything, and understanding what we *really* want allows a perspective on who we are and how we should proceed.

Don't misunderstand me: Fantasies aren't exclusively or even primarily about sex. They're just about what you want without hearing your mom or your Sunday school teacher or your big brother saying no. Fantasies are just feelings given form, and they are safe if understood.

In this exercise, you write down the words that best describe your fantasy self and see how those words compare to who you are and what you're feeling at this moment. Figure out what matches up and what doesn't, and then think about what you can do to bring your fantasy self more in line with the real you.

Answering the following questions in your dating notebook (see Chapter 1) is the place to start. Then you have to decide whether you want to do the work, practice different behaviors, learn new skills, be more honest. Change isn't easy, but it can be very worthwhile to lighten up, become more informed, become more assertive, tune more into others, be more (or less) aware of yourself, and so on.

- ✔ Who you are:
    - Who are you?
    - Who would you like to be?
    - How can you bring the two together?
- ✔ What you want:
    - What do you want?
    - What do you have?
    - How would you go about making one into the other?
- ✔ How others respond to you:
    - How do people respond to you?
    - How do you wish they'd respond?
    - What can you do to get the preferred response?

Are the fantasies just frustration, and what can you learn from frustration? (Frustration is probably the only true trigger to learning because it's bumping up against something that doesn't feel good, which makes you look for new pathways.)

Looks good to me. . . .

Presumably one of the reasons we are so influenced by what we see is that animals, when mating, have to determine healthy characteristics so that the line will survive. While survival is still pretty basic, a cute nose or a full head of hair is a lot less crucial to good breeding genes and survival than it used to be (if you're a wolf or a sheep or a saber-toothed tiger). Just one more of those charming contradictions of being human these days.

After you've taken a good look at your fantasies about yourself, imagine what your fantasy partner is all about. Okay, okay, indulge yourself for a minute (I mean with clothes on):

- How does this person act, talk, think, respond to you?
- Would you be happy with this person for any length of time?
- What could you offer in return?
- How would you attract this kind of person?
- What would this person likely want from you?

Don't allow yourself to spend too long thinking about the purely physical. All things being equal, we would all probably prefer attractive to unattractive, but you'd be surprised how many people, both men and women, aren't all that turned on by in-your-face gorgeous. When it comes to physical beauty, seldom are all things equal. Pretend for a moment that you are blind, and describe your perfect date. Interesting, yes. It's quite possible that you didn't mention even one physical characteristic. Why do you think they say love is blind? It's because sight is probably the least important sense we bring to the table when our hearts get involved. (To find out how important first impressions are, see Chapter 10.)

When you think about fantasies, think about both long- and short-term time frames: your perfect lunch vs. your perfect vacation vs. your perfect home vs. the school you'd like your unborn children to attend. What would you and your fantasy date do on your first date, your second anniversary, your second decade, your second grandchild?

Fantasy and frustration

Fantasies offer us insights into the discrepancy between what we are and what we have and what we want. I used to do a program where I would ask people if they had only a year or a week or a day to live, what would they do. Since none of us know whether we have any more or less than that amount of time, thinking about these things is a good way to get a clearer take on what we want. If you won the lottery, what would you do? If you could do anything in your life, what would you do?

I often loan people my magic wand for a couple of days (no more than a week or the magic goes away). Now I'm offering it to you to borrow. Instead of whining about what you don't have, set yourself free to figure out what you want. Then you can settle down and do the work of figuring out how to get it.

When things are going well, we're foolish if we don't just enjoy; it's when we hit a bump that it's time to figure out what to do differently. In that way, frustration is really the doorway to fantasy and a better way of doing things. Start with the dream and then figure out how to make it happen.

❤Broken Heart Ideas

Sometimes the best way to understand conclusively how to do something is to understand very specifically what *not* to do. All of us have committed at least several of the no-nos listed here, but if you can minimize them, you'll save a lot of wear and tear on yourself and everybody else.

Comparing yourself to others

This is not about entering the Miss USA or Mr. World contest or surfing the Web to be truly masochistic. This is not about comparing yourself to Brad Pitt or Angelina Jolie or anybody you see on a billboard or in a magazine. Those photos have been retouched to a fare-thee-well (trust me, I've met and interviewed bunches of these people). They've been powdered, primped, airbrushed, oiled, and lit so their own moms wouldn't recognize 'em. If you don't believe me, Google the famous Jamie Lee Curtis article where she allowed herself to be photographed before and after a magazine shoot. She is a smart, lovely, brave, beautiful woman who wanted to show the difference between real life and the fantasy that Madison Avenue sells us. The Dove ads also point out the real beauty in real bodies and real women. Besides, if you read any of the fan magazines, you know that beautiful people don't have all that easy a time dating either. So cut it out.

While you're at it, don't compare yourself to the homecoming court either, male or female, or to your next-door neighbor or your older or younger sibs or your parents' wedding picture. You are who you are, and if you want to do a little fine-tuning there, fine. (That's not to say, of course, that you can't change and grow, and I'm not even against plastic surgery, but not before your first date, please. Know yourself, like yourself, and work on yourself.)

You'll only make yourself miserable for no reason if you continue to compare your own light to someone else's bulb. You can choose to be either a pale imitation of how someone else looks or a vibrant, one-of-a-kind you. Guess which I suggest.

Throwing pity parties

You can see how viewing your life as a beauty contest is hopeless and self-defeating and just a short step away from a pity party — you know, woe is me, no one likes me or loves me, I can't get a date, I'm doomed to spending the rest of my life alone diapering cats, I think I'll go eat worms. The self-loathing can move from face and body (I've got a zit farm and a spare tire that any sports utility vehicle would envy) to heart and soul (I'm not a worth-while person) with incredible speed. If you really feel you absolutely must throw a pity party, stay in bed for a day, play sad music, feel incredibly sorry for yourself, and then *cut it out*. It's boring and no fun to be around and *very* counter-productive to dating.

Why would anyone want to spend time with you if you are so self-centered and sad? And if you've been saying the same thing to yourself — quick! — think of three cool things about yourself. If you can't, call a therapist now. I'm not kidding. Pity parties you can decline; depression is another thing completely. See the earlier sidebar "Dealing with depression" if you're not sure whether you're just momentarily down on yourself or truly depressed.

Vowing never again

I have nothing against your taking a vow of chastity if you plan to enter a life of service and quiet contemplation, but why then did you buy a book about dating? This book is *Dating For Dummies,* not *Dating For Those Headed For the Priesthood or a Convent,* so cut it out. Don't disguise a pity party in clerical robes. It's okay to take a break from dating if you wish, but don't kid yourself as to the reasons. Deciding that you'll never date again may be a thinly veiled hatred of the opposite sex: Poor little you is just too fragile to get mauled by "them."

Hey, if you've got a leaky pipe and you call a plumber and she doesn't fix it, does that mean you just let your basement fill up? I think not. You call another plumber. (All right, smart aleck, I can hear you saying, "Okay, I'll fix it myself." Yeah, yeah, that's the problem about analogies, not to say plumbing. What if I made it an electrical problem?) The point is, no need to blame, just figure out what's going on.

Swearing off the opposite sex so that you can catch your breath or if you've just come out of a tough situation is not only fine, but wise. But don't confuse this break with fear or hatred. You need to be aware of your feelings so that you can use that big fancy cortex on top of all your other organs — including your heart — to figure out what's going on.

Beating yourself up

Beating yourself up is a waste of time and painful, and because you're the only person you are guaranteed to be with your whole life, why hurt yourself? I'm not saying that you shouldn't take stock when something has gone really wrong (see Chapter 19). Who needs to walk into a propeller blade more than once?

Instead of beating yourself up, why not ask yourself what you could do differently next time? Make sure your answer is very, very specific.

Beating up Mom

I've already told you not to blame yourself and not to blame the entire opposite sex. Unfortunately, these days, I may need to remind you not to blame anybody else either: not your parents or your first-grade teacher or your babysitter. If you think you've got a problem because of something that someone did or didn't do at an earlier time in your life, ask yourself whether there is anything you could ask of that person now — other than an apology — that would help you. (Styles of parenting change every ten years or so, which means everybody gets caught. Most of our parents did the best they could with what they had, and the rules keep changing.)

If you think your mental health and dating abilities would be helped if you had a better relationship with your dad, get baseball tickets and invite him, but don't expect him to apologize for the person he is. He may not have been the perfect dad, but you may not have been the perfect kid, either, so let it go. Or find a therapist.

If talking to your mom about the things she told you about sex would help — and if you can manage such a discussion without making her feel defensive or guilty — go for it. If you can't manage it without making her feel bad, you'll end up feeling awful, too. Then what have you accomplished?

Blame locks you in the past and makes someone right and someone wrong, which means it's likely that someone's going to fight you if you're blaming him or her. Or, if you're doing the "it's all my fault" routine, you're making yourself unhappy. Who needs it? So go to a therapist or go to a ball game, but whatever you do, get on with it. Figure out what to do differently and let's go.

Putting yourself under house arrest

If the first way to get on with this dating stuff is to get out there, don't put yourself in prison, even if it's homey and comfortable to begin with. It is very unlikely that someone is going to come up to your door and ask you for a date (and even if someone does, think about what you'd be wearing . . .). Don't allow yourself to fall into the La Brea Tar Pits in front of your TV. Get out and be active — and that doesn't mean finding a neighborhood bar as a substitute home away from home either. Bars aren't the best place to find anybody other than lonely people drinking in the dark. Let's make a deal: Avoid any place with bars — they're all a kind of lock-up and confining. Let yourself be free.

Whining

Whining is the vocal manifestation of house arrest, pity parties, blaming, and comparing. It's hard to listen to, will give you wrinkles, and is social suicide. Nobody likes a whiner, which makes it so remarkable that all of us do it from time to time. The worst of it is, the more we whine, the whinier we feel, so make a big sign with a goblet inside a circle and put a slash through it. Get it? No whine (or wine, as the case may be).

Occasionally whining is okay — that's what friends and family are for — but the amount of time you spend whining should certainly be no more than the amount of time you're willing to spend listening to someone else whine. Let me also remind you that you may run out of friends much more quickly when whining is always on the menu. And if, heaven forfend, you've made whining a habit that you continue once you start dating, your friends will learn to despise the subject of your whines. Anyway you cut it, it's a valuable habit to lose.

Chapter 4

Finding Out What Makes You Tick

· ·

In This Chapter

▶ Understanding how Mom and Dad affect your dating decisions

▶ Figuring out your dating patterns

▶ Taking a close look at who you are and what you want

▶ Finding the right person at the right time

· ·

*W*hether you're going to build a house, a patio, a hot fudge sundae, or a garden, you would never start a project without figuring out what you hope to accomplish, what tools you have on hand and what tools you need, how you're going to proceed, and when you're going to start. The same goes for a date.

One of the reasons dating seems so scary and so magical is that you focus on the endpoint instead of breaking the process down to manageable (even baby) steps. Not to worry. That's exactly the point of this book, and believe it or not, this chapter starts with the most important part of the equation: *you*.

You may think that you know how to date, but unless you're viewing dating as a process rather than a make-it-or-break-it one-time event, you're missing the point. Sure, the date itself is fun and exciting to think about, but important things come before the date and important things come after. To date successfully, you have to think about the whole shebang. Thinking about only the date itself is like thinking about a dinner party without working at the menu, the ingredients, the preparation time, and the cost and then trying to put the whole thing together so that the food looks terrific, tastes yummy, is all ready at the same time, and is enough to feed everyone.

The crucial factor isn't getting someone else to like you or to go out with you; it's making sure that you sorta like yourself. This isn't a book about saying, "I'm a great person, and everybody should love me," because I have no idea who you are. By the time you work through this part of the book, you'll have a much better notion of your strengths and weaknesses. Although examining your weaknesses may not sound like much fun, some things are better to know than ignore. It's that ignored stuff that makes you really anxious, because only part of you can really ignore it anyway; the other part — abetted by the slight feeling of unease, the quick flashes of anxiety, the scary dreams — is whispering or shouting in your ear, "Listen up!"

Not to worry; we're all products under construction anyway.

Starting with Mom and Dad

Okay, where to start? How about at the very beginning: parents? Who you are, especially in relationships, is determined by watching your own personal Adam and Eve, alias Mom and Dad. Even if you didn't grow up with both, how each parent acted and talked about the other — and how each related to you — influences you.

How Mom and Dad can still ground you

The purpose of this exercise is neither to prove that there is a terrific set of parents who would have sent you forth with all you needed nor to prove that the parents you got have emotionally maimed you. The purpose is to show that anything your parents did has some positive and some negative possibilities. Once you understand the consequences of parental influence and behavior, you can emphasize or compensate for them. Consider the following examples:

- If you felt your parents never had time for you, you're probably self-reliant but find it difficult to trust and are a bit brittle on the outside. What you most want is someone to hug you and tell you that you're great.

- If your parents were really lovey-dovey with each other, you may have felt envious and excluded. As a result, you may look for a date who ignores everybody and everything but you.

- If one or other of your parents doted on you — and I mean *really* doted — you may feel an overwhelming need to perform or be perfect. A date who asks what you were doing last night may make you feel claustrophobic, as if you're being monitored or graded again.

Once you know that, you can look for someone who *isn't* like the parent, who is self-sufficient, and who is not overly sentimental. Unfortunately, most of us choose someone who's like the parent who didn't do whatever we wanted him or her to do when we were kids, and — voilá! — because we pick the same kind of person, he or she acts in the same kind of way.

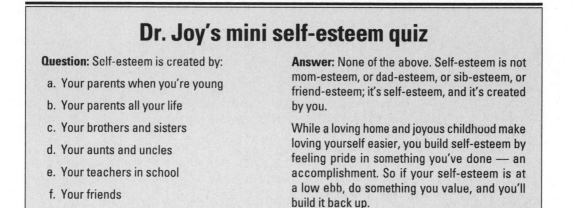

Dr. Joy's mini self-esteem quiz

Question: Self-esteem is created by:

a. Your parents when you're young

b. Your parents all your life

c. Your brothers and sisters

d. Your aunts and uncles

e. Your teachers in school

f. Your friends

Answer: None of the above. Self-esteem is not mom-esteem, or dad-esteem, or sib-esteem, or friend-esteem; it's self-esteem, and it's created by you.

While a loving home and joyous childhood make loving yourself easier, you build self-esteem by feeling pride in something you've done — an accomplishment. So if your self-esteem is at a low ebb, do something you value, and you'll build it back up.

Escaping parental haunting

The solution to parental haunting is to figure out how your parents acted, figure out what you wanted them to do differently, and determine how, logically, you can fix it so that this pattern of behavior doesn't control your dating behavior.

Because you're doing an inventory here, keeping a notebook in which you can jot down thoughts and impressions is a great idea (see Chapter 1). Make sure your notebook isn't left around for other folks to read; it's personal and just for you and your work.

1. **Start with a heading called "Mom and Dad," leaving a page for each, and write down any thoughts that occur.**

   On Mom's page, you might write, "Neat-freak, warm laugh, takes care of the finances, whines," and so on. On Dad's page, you might write, "Rarely home, drinks too much, loves fishing, gives good hugs."

   It's a good idea to leave lots of space so you can let your mind roam.

2. **Now go to a new set of pages, again one each for Mom and Dad, and try to organize your thoughts into positive and negative.**

   For example, on Mom's page, you might put her warm laugh and the fact that she's in charge of the finances on the positive side and "neat freak" on the negative side. Of course, if you're being honest, warm laugh might be positive, but "doesn't take me seriously" might be the downside of her sense of humor. See if you can use your grown-up self to look at things fairly.

3. **Once you've got a good list going, begin to relate the items on your list to dating behavior.**

    For example, a sense of humor may be important, but so, too, may be someone who won't laugh at you. Which is more important: having someone who listens a lot or someone who talks a lot? Make sure that the characteristics you want aren't mutually exclusive. For instance, on one hand you want a man who is really successful; on the other, you want someone for whom you come first. Nope! Doesn't happen that way.

When you understand which of your feelings about the opposite sex are directly related to Mom and Dad, you may be able, with your grown-up mind and paper and pencil, to free yourself of some of the knee-jerk responses that all of us have. Consider these examples:

- ✔ If your Dad always beat you at checkers, you may go for the kill in games, taking all the fun out for both of you, or you may be unwilling to play at all. Finding a game at which you can best your Dad might free you, but at least understanding the cause and effect helps.

- ✔ If your Mom was a worrywart, you may feel great anxiety before you leave the house. Your adult self can understand Mom's fears and separate them from your own.

Looking for Patterns

Since you're old enough to read and think about dating, you have some patterns to go on. Even if this is your very first dating experience, you've talked to the opposite sex, fantasized, and interacted. In this section, you look at those patterns (this is also good information to put in your dating notebook):

- ✔ **Who you choose:** Are you drawn to blondes, bullies, actors, athletes, people who hold you too tight, or people who seem to disappear? Are you talking down-to-earth or mysterious, bubbly or reserved, serious or silly?

- ✔ **How you act:** All of us act in characteristic ways, and once we understand those ways, we can see our behavior and the effect it has. Understanding this, we can then begin to see alternative ways of behaving — what to do more of and what to change — before our emotional bruises become permanent.

    In your notebook, put down what works really well for you and what bombs. Are you really a good listener, or are your jokes terrific? Do you dance well or help everybody with homework? Can you remember your first grade teacher's name? Do you do well at Trivial Pursuit? Do animals love you? Are you great at crossword puzzles?

> ✔ **How you react:** Where are your buttons? What makes you blow up — what words or phrases or situations? We all have them, and they're often connected by a long, sturdy thread to our past. I hate being told to shut up. "Keep quiet" is okay; "stop talking" is okay; but someone's saying "shut up" makes me see red and purple and black and blue.

Don't get hung up on the belief that some people are just naturally good at dating and some are awful; it's basically not true, and even if it were, it has nothing to do with you. The goal of this book is to help you figure out how to build relationships in a way that makes some sense to you and is effective and honest and sincere and fun.

Don't assume that everything you can do, everybody else can do. It's just not true, and the beginning of any good relationship is the relationship you have with yourself. Don't be shy and don't be overly critical or overly kind. Paper and pencil can help you to focus on your strengths.

When you're done, you'll probably have a pretty detailed list of the most super New Year's resolutions of all time: how you're going to polish, trim, highlight, and embrace who you are and who you are cheerfully and enthusiastically becoming. The more specific the list, the more obvious the path and the more straightforward the task.

Who Am I?

All of us are the products of our gene pools (that's why this chapter begins with parents); our experiences (that's why the preceding section looks at patterns and fantasies); and our choices, intellect, and emotions, which is what this section looks at. By now, you're beginning to understand that there are no perfect people and no perfect characteristics. Almost anything can have a plus and a minus. You can't begin to work on emphasizing the good stuff and downplaying the icky until you know exactly what and where each is. So to work:

1. **List the things you really love about yourself in your dating notebook, and be *very* specific.**

   What you love about yourself is the basis of everything else, but for heaven's sake, don't write, "I'm a really nice person." What does *nice* mean? Instead, write that you are patient with your little brother, impatient with a check-out clerk, likely to snitch a candy bar if no one's watching — well, actually, that part goes in the next step; so carry on with the good stuff, or if you can't separate 'em, begin the "what I'm not crazy about" list and come back to this one after you've purged yourself.

   Make sure that this list is long enough to withstand the next task, which is to list what you don't like about yourself. If you can't come up with at least ten specific good things, you're having a pity party or you need a therapist, seriously. We are each responsible for fashioning ourselves as likable by our own standards, at the very least. If you can get other folks to agree, terrific; if not . . . well, we're not talking crazy here.

2. **Now complete the *I'm-not-crazy-about-these-things-in-myself* list.**

Just bedrock — who you are and what you can change and what you're going to have to learn to live with — goes here.

Some of the things you're proudest of often have a downside. For example, if you're independent, you may not be as attuned to others' feelings as you would like. If you're sensitive, you may be too dependent on others' opinions.

The point of this exercise is to emphasize the positive and either downplay or obliterate the negative. The very act of thinking about yourself in this way, being specific, and taking inventory is the first step toward taking responsibility and changing what you can and want to change about yourself. Then you can begin to repattern your behavior: Snap that rubber band against your wrist when you lose your temper or fine yourself when you gossip; focus on your great posture and ability to put others at ease.

Describing an Ideal Match

Now that you know who you are, what would you like in a partner? I'm not necessarily talking about the rest of your life — after all, you may very well want different things in someone at one stage or another of your life — but it makes no sense to date someone who loves kids and animals if you want a lifestyle of travel and high adventure and risk with a partner. Similarly, if sex is crucial in your life, dating someone who thinks sex is dirty is somewhat counterproductive.

Love, hate, ads, and dating

It's amazing how most of us are much more able to list the things we loathe about ourselves than our assets. I'm convinced it's because we live in a capitalist society that creates a desire for things we don't really need by convincing us that the way we look and smell and taste and live isn't really all that cool. If you can't value yourself, how and why should anyone else? Confidence isn't conceit. In fact, it's the opposite. Conceit says, "I'm better than you." Confidence says, "I'm good." It isn't competitive or comparative.

Think about what most ads promise: that if we use this mouthwash or drink this beer or drive this car, then some hunky guy or gorgeous babe will love us — which is why we all break out in a sweat when it comes to the idea of dating. We've all been convinced that whatever we are isn't okay and that somebody else is going to beat us out. (That old capitalistic urge to win so somebody loses crops up.) With that in mind, your dating profile should be upbeat (not whiney), imaginative, and honest whether online or in a newspaper.

Friendly and not-so-friendly ghosts

When you begin thinking about who you want in your life, the kind of person who makes sense, you may be influenced by a ghost — not Casper and not necessarily friendly, but someone who haunts you without your even being aware of it. This ghost is someone who rearranged the emotional furniture in your room and is likely to be someone who you cared about but who didn't turn out as you wished. It may be a first-grade teacher who seemed to like your best friend best, a best friend who moved away, or someone who didn't give you a Valentine. It could also be a traumatic experience, like over-hearing a remark from a supposed friend that hurt your feelings. And just like ghosts, who are assumed to be souls who haven't found peace, your emotional ghosts are fueled by lack of resolution in your head or heart.

Because this chapter is about laying the groundwork to go and do something that's scary and fun and exciting (that is, date), it's a great idea to have as much of your energy at your disposal as possible. Therefore, an exorcism is in order. You don't need holy water, incense, or a priest, just a bit of courage and a paper and pencil. If you're haunted by an emotional ghost (what an image!), write down the specific characteristics of the ghost — turn on the light of your intellect and understanding. Ghosts need darkness, fear, and tension to survive. You may not be able to get rid of all the thoughts, but you can probably keep yourself from being haunted by just getting all those thoughts out into the open and into your notebook. Ghosts can only haunt you in the dark, so turn the light on.

Look at a specific list of the characteristics that would balance your good and bad points. For example, if you're shy, would you be happier with someone who is more outgoing or shy like yourself? There is no right or wrong answer here, just good questions.

Start with the fantasy list describing your ideal partner, and compare that list to the list describing your characteristics. See if there is a fit, a match. Are you looking for security or excitement, domesticity or adventure, stability or thrills? Are you looking to balance who you are or find someone just like you?

Being the real you

Once you're aware of *who* you are, you can begin working on *how* you're you. You can look at your body language, your wardrobe, your vocabulary, your tone of voice, your fears, and your desires and make sure that there is some consistency between what you truly want and what your behavior indicates you want. It's amazing how often we all give out the wrong clues in an attempt to pretend to be someone we're not. When you're more knowledgeable about yourself, you can hold a mirror up to your behavior and see what others see — and respond to. Think about how you present yourself and determine whether you send out signals that are consistent with what you want.

Are you timid and looking at the floor or confident and covering up sweaty palms with a bit of swagger? Are you noisy because you're fearful no one will listen to you, or do you whisper so that people have to stand close because you're afraid of your own power? Do you stoop to appear short or fluff your hair to appear bigger?

A personal ad with no purse strings attached

In Chapter 3, I talk about writing a real personal ad or a profile. Here I want you to use the gimmick simply to get in touch with *you*. The major distinction between a real personal ad or profile and this exercise is that real ads are limited in number of words and just focus on the tip of the iceberg. Your musings here will likely not see the light of day without some serious editing, but allow yourself the luxury of verbosity at this moment: no charge by the word. Without these restrictions, you can look well below the H_2O level.

A personal ad or profile can tell you very quickly whether what you want and how you're advertising are out of whack. If you're looking for someone with whom to settle down, for example, then looks should be less important to you than stability, sincerity, and fertility. If you love to travel, you shouldn't be trolling for a homebody.

To use your personal ad for this exercise, look at what you said you wanted in your mate (your fantasy) and what you said about yourself (your reality). Look for compatible or complementary traits. For example, if you listed that you want stability and commitment in your About Me section but listed adventurous risk-taker in the About Him/Her section of the ad, you've got some work to do in order to achieve some semblance of compatibility.

In determining whether the lists are compatible, look for overlap in words or ideas. If you see "fun-loving" in your list, you probably want to see "fun-loving" — or a concept like it — in the fantasy date's list, too; be careful if your fantasy date's list includes qualities that conflict with yours, like "down-to-earth and serious." You'll think of them as a stick-in-the-mud, and they'll see you as frivolous, flirtatious, and untrustworthy.

You may be saying to yourself, "Hey look, I'm only talking about a date." But don't go off in a direction that makes no sense (why date someone of another faith if you would never allow yourself to fall in love with that person or marry out of the faith? Why date someone who smokes if you hate smoking?) *unless* you simply want a diversion, which is expensive in terms of time and energy and emotion. Of course, if you want to do that, it's fine with me. Just make sure that you make your intentions clear upfront to all parties concerned, including yourself.

Mixed messages and other near disasters

A close friend of mine wants nothing more than to be married and have a vine-covered cottage and a collie and a station wagon and a bunch of kids. Even these days, she's a throwback to the 1950s. Unfortunately, she presents herself by going to bars in tight, low-cut dresses, and she attracts guys who respond to her overt sexuality. She scares off the very kind of guy that she would really like, who probably wouldn't be in a bar in the first place, would be terrified by her sexual aggressiveness, and would be unwilling to fight through the guys drooling over her cleavage. She is convinced that men are no damn good and just users, which certainly isn't true of all men. It's just that how she is presenting herself and who she really is don't have much of an overlap. This is a woman who hasn't done her inventory of what she likes about herself (not what others notice) and what *she* is looking for. This is an extreme example, but it's extraordinary how often all the rest of us do a variation on the same theme.

I also knew a guy who used to date gorgeous, tall, blonde women, saying he was looking for great breeding material. Understandably, many of these gorgeous women were not all that thrilled about settling down and having gobs of kids anytime soon. They tended to treat him badly and leave him after getting what they wanted from him. He decided all women were leeches. Again, not really the case. It's just that what he wanted deep down and the women he was choosing had nothing in common. When he finally showed up with a short, less-than-gorgeous woman who adored him, I knew he was in love.

If you're not sure what you want, it's okay to experiment, but make sure that your uncertainty isn't based on an unwillingness to face up to who you are and what you want. That's an expense none of us can afford.

Because this ad isn't going anyplace, don't worry about how many words you use, but do make sure that you're not avoiding reality by tap-dancing with a lot of words. Are you looking for romance *or* companionship *or* commitment? Don't tell me all of the above, because they're really not the same thing.

If your ad sounds like every ad that you've ever read, start again. This is you. The *real you*, the honest you, the specific you. No one ever has to see what you really want, but doing this exercise can focus you in a very helpful way.

What you're looking for in your personal ad is something that really says *you*. The fact that you love grape jelly and Bob Dylan and are allergic to cats says a lot more than that you like moonlight and long romantic walks on a beach. Puh-leeeeze. If there was ever a time not to be trite, it's when you're talking about yourself and who you are and what you want.

Don't worry that you're being too specific. If your ad seems too picky, you can always modify it and try that approach for a while or rely on the Fates and chemistry to steer you. Keep in mind, though, that a little bit of that unwillingness to take responsibility goes a long way. So do be careful.

The hairdresser, the psychic, and the cue ball

When I had just moved to San Francisco, I noticed that my first hairdresser was wearing a hunk of an engagement ring. I was suitably wowed and said so, to which she said she was getting married the following week. She was no spring chicken and explained that she'd been about to give up on men; then she'd gone to a psychic who told her to write down everything she wanted in a man. She'd written that she wanted someone who was intelligent and kind, who had a sense of humor, and who already had kids and was ready to settle down. Three days later, she'd met the guy she was about to marry (don't panic, they'd known each other for almost two years). She laughingly noted that next time she was going to put "full head of hair" on her list because he was as bald as a billiard ball.

It wasn't the psychic who did it, but the specificity of the hairdresser's list — or more likely, her being aware of what was important to her and what wasn't. She no longer allowed herself to be diverted by the irrelevant, like a full head of hair.

Do not be tempted to send this ad *anywhere*. Personal ads can certainly jazz up your social life, but don't waste the time or the money on a personal ad until you have a bit of conventional dating under your belt. You want to make sure that you have most of the details worked out before you take the act on the road.

Tuck the ad away in your notebook for a while and go on to the next chapter. If, after dating for a year or so, you feel like you know what you're doing but would like to widen the dating pool, you'll be prepared. Do read the ad again to make sure that everything is accurate in terms of how you see yourself and your prospective date. (Of course, it certainly should have changed a bit once you've been out there — nothing's quite as valuable as a bit of experience.) You're now most of the way through armchair dating. Just a bit more and you can get out there and strut your stuff.

Figuring Out If the Time Is Right for You

Before you get out there (and I know you're raring to go — you've definitely laid the groundwork), you need to know when NOT to date. Timing is crucial in many things in life, and dating is certainly no exception. Finding the right person at the right time increases the probability of a cool experience. Finding the right person at the wrong time is going to be a problem. And finding the wrong person at the wrong time? Well, heaven help us all.

For the wrong person, there is no right time. Trust me on this.

So how do you know when it's the right time for you, the right time to launch yourself into someone else's orbit and try to convince that person to ride your trajectory (and no, I'm not talking dirty)? As is true of much in life, not only can understanding the wrong time give you insight into what to avoid and the warning signs, but it can also help you tell when the right time is just about to arrive so that you can be ready.

The wrong time

The wrong time is any time when you're feeling blue and lonely, sad and sorry for yourself — which is, of course, the time when all of us decide, "Okay, I *need* to find someone." You may be particularly susceptible to this type of thinking when your boyfriend just dumped you, your girlfriend told you she just wants to be friends, you've just moved to a new city and are lonely, or any other time when attaching yourself to someone else sounds easier than being alone.

I know the songs all talk about "I want you, I need you, I love you," but need means dependency, and if that's how you set things up, you'll distort any potential future you could have with someone. Either you will be nurtured (and thus less needy) and the whole reason for being together evaporates, or you'll continue to be needy. What a drag — literally! Need is a lousy basis for anything other than employing a nurse; need won't hold up for any length of time, and breaking up is always the pits. So pull yourself together and get yourself better before you even think about hooking up with someone else.

When you're needy:

- ✔ Your feelings are so clouded by your pain that you can't make sound choices regarding what you want.
- ✔ You ask another person to make you okay.
- ✔ You can't see objectively what the other person is able or willing to give.
- ✔ Dating leaves you in a worse situation than you were in before.
- ✔ You can camouflage or ignore growth areas (for a while) that need and require your concentration.

When this relationship ends (which it's bound to do), not only will you not be better off, but you'll actually be worse off because you'll have all your original issues to deal with in addition to anything that came up in this last relationship.

If depression and anxiety were attractive and neediness were sexy, it would be okay to whine on a date, and everybody would fall madly in love. But you know that's not the way the world works. The *need* to find another is the world's worst reason to try to find another.

Following are some especially bad times:

- **You're coping with the death of a parent, a dog, your best friend, or anybody you feel close to.** The human psyche needs to reaffirm its mastery over death, so the impulse not to be alone and sometimes even to mate can be really strong when you're feeling bereft. Unfortunately, another person can't act as a human bandage. You need to be able to embrace the sorrow of loss and let it go before you can resume your normal life. Not only can beginning a dating experience with someone before you've healed mess up a potentially good situation, but it can slow the healing process as well.

- **You've just lost your job.** First things first. You need to find another job, not a date. Because both a new date and a new job take time to find and time to get used to, stabilize before you add a complication. Because you won't starve without a date and you may starve without a job, get the job first. Additionally, getting fired feels lousy, and finding a job feels good. You want to feel stable and healthy, not like somebody's charity case, before you begin dating.

- **You've just lost a place to live.** This may seem like a really good excuse to latch onto somebody who has a place to live and a bed and a stable existence, but that *n* word (*need,* for those of you not paying attention) has to be a tip-off. Need is not good to put on another soul. I want you. Yes! I love you. Yes! I need you. No, no, no! If you don't have a place to live, you don't have a place to take a date, a place to sleep, a place to get phone calls at night — all that's pretty basic. So take care of the basics and then go for it.

- **You're depressed.** There are times when all of us feel lost and alone and out of tune with the universe. The priority at that moment is to get back in tune, not to find a human teddy bear to keep the monsters at bay. Being depressed doesn't mean you're hopeless; it just means that dating is going to tax resources that are stretched pretty thin already.

If you've been feeling really sad and bummed for more than a week or two; if you can't eat, sleep, or concentrate; if you cry easily and feel hopeless and tired all the time; and if things that used to make you happy really don't anymore, the cure isn't a date — it's a therapist and medication. No kidding. Those are signs of a serious, but very treatable, illness. However, the prescription isn't a hug; it's some important work so you won't feel like that again.

- **You've just broken up with someone.** There is a piece of folk wisdom that says if you've just been thrown from a horse, the best cure is to get right back on. That may work really well with horses, but don't even think about applying it to dating situations. If you've just broken up with someone, don't use another person as proof that you're still lovable. It's not fair to you, and it's not fair to the human aspirin you're using to make your headache go away, at least temporarily.

Think of going to your bank and trying to borrow money. If you go in looking all raggedy and dirty and seedy, do you think the bank is going to loan you money? No way. If there isn't some indication that you'll be able to pay back the loan, the loan officer may feel sorry for you but won't loan you money. Relationships are based on surprisingly similar theories. Somebody looking to get involved with you expects to give but also to get something back, and expects you to show a little interest (pardon the rather obvious pun). If you're getting the idea that misery is not a very good motivation to date, you're exactly right.

The right time

The best time to begin dating is when your life is really in gear, your friends think you're swell, you're relatively content with the way you look, work is going well, you're even on speaking terms with your parents, and you can think of exes without raising your blood pressure. Hey, you're ready. If you're so all-fired happy, why go through the hassle of dating, you ask. Good question, I respond. Because, let's face it: The right person can make a good day great and a great day simply fabulous, and there *is* something about that chemistry thing.

Following are some scenarios that may motivate you — happy, well-adjusted person that you are — to jump into the dating arena:

- ✔ **Your friends are involved.** Often the trigger to get you going is that all your friends are involved, and they seem really happy. Equally important, they also don't have a whole lot of time for you these days, or at least not as much free time as you find yourself with — good motivating factor.

- ✔ **You're feeling great.** Feeling much better about your life than you have for a long, long time — cheerfully assuming you're stone cold sober and not high when you notice the feeling — is also a great sign that it's time to begin. Remember, it's always easiest to borrow money when you seem not to really need it, and the same is true with relationships. You're your coolest self when you're happy and relaxed. If you could bottle it, you'd be rich. You don't have to bottle it, but you may want to spread it around.

- ✔ **You're in a new city.** You've made new friends, you're not on house arrest, there are new restaurants to experience, new parks in which to picnic, new museums to explore. Don't substitute a search for dates before friends, but once the friends are in place, it's quite kosher to mention that you're new in town and looking — talk about your clean slate. Moving to a new city is a really good time to get in the swing. You'll learn the city faster and have someone to share it with, someone who knows the sites taking you around. Be sure to leave some time for you to be by yourself. Although having someone along is great, time alone to explore your new surroundings is important, too. When you're alone, you get to concentrate on the parts of the city that really interest you.

✔ **It's New Year's Day.** Although a New Year's Eve party is a really treacherous first date experience, New Year's Day itself can be a good reminder that time is marching on, and if you want someone marching with you in your parade, it's a good time to push yourself a bit. (A New Year's Day introduction also can make a great opening line: "I decided meeting you was going to be the first terrific thing I did for myself this year.")

✔ **A big event is coming up.** A big deal event coming up in your life — a wedding, a party, an anniversary — can be a useful motivation to offset your lethargy or fear and inertia when it comes to dating. It can be a good opening gambit. If you feel compelled to take a date to the big event, do be a bit careful about making the big event the very first date. It's preferable to have a couple of date-ettes to break the ice before the big event. If possible, give yourself enough time to have a couple of dates or even a couple of months before the event.

If you're getting the idea that the best time to begin dating is when you're feeling terrific and cheerful and confident and busy and happy, whether for the first time or after a hiatus or break from the action, you're right on target. The happier and more stable you are, the more attractive, the more confident, and the more able you are to assess want you want *while* presenting an accurate picture of who you are. If you're going through a rough time, don't despair; it happens to all of us. Keep in mind that dating isn't the cure; it's a complication. If you're feeling great and stable and happy — and most of all ready for an adventure — it's your time.

Chapter 5

The Perfect Date: Person and Place

*O*kay, if you started in Part I, you've done the hard work: You've looked at who you are and what you want. You've examined those cute little quirks that your Auntie Gertrude loves but that seem to drive your roommate to distraction. You've been realistic about the kind of person you're looking for, and you've thought about how this hypothetical person would merge with you to make a divine duo or at least a viable date. So what now?

In this chapter, you go hunting for Mr. or Ms. Right. (And if that's too much pressure, you can scout out Mr. or Ms. Maybe or Mr. or Ms. Right Now.) There are terrific places to look, places to look with caution, and places where you absolutely, positively don't want to look. (I'll bet your first three choices fall into the don't-even-go-there category.) So if you're looking for information on where, and where not, to go to meet people, you're in the right place.

Overcoming shyness

Most people are a little shy around new people, especially people to whom they're attracted. A little shy is okay. A lot shy can keep you from the three fundamentals of dating: 1) getting out there, 2) taking chances, and 3) enjoying life. It's important to shake that shyness if it's getting in the way. To do that, here's some stuff you can try:

- Meander around a busy public place for an hour or two so you get used to being around people.

- Practice smiling and making eye contact. Lift your chin off your chest and nonverbally connect with people who seem nice and interesting to you. (No touching; just look and smile.)

- Decide to chat with one new person a week. You can do this in the grocery store, the school cafeteria, or the line at the bank. Nothing breeds success like success.

- Act "as if." If all people waited until they were totally comfortable before trying anything new, no one would do anything new! Pretend you're not shy and act "as if" you're full of confidence.

- Calm yourself by telling yourself over and over again that you're safe and everything's going to be okay. Say it aloud in private and in your head in public as often as necessary.

- Identify the worst-case scenario. What's the most hideous thing that could happen if you walked up to someone you liked and said, "Hi"? Putting a face on your fear helps reduce it to a manageable size. For example, the worst thing that might happen is the person turns around and walks away. Yeah, rejection hurts, but you're not going to die from it. Acceptance feels great, and you'll never experience it if you don't take a chance.

- Have fun! Shift the focus away from your own fears and zero in on what makes someone else tick. Before you know it, you'll forget all about being shy.

At first blush, the Internet seems like the answer to a shy person's prayers, but do not be misled. Don't be tempted to use a crutch to keep you in a negative place. Shyness is a particular form of self indulgence. Thinking about someone else — not what that person thinks about you, but truly being focused on him or her — is the cure. If it's any comfort, 83 percent of people surveyed said they're shy in certain situations, so suck it up and get out there, bunkie.

A Word about Attitude — Yours

Before I begin listing some of the good places to find somebody fun, let me encourage you to be open — not only open-minded about what I'm going to suggest, but also open to spontaneity. If you're in Macy's and a great-looking person asks whether a particular color looks good with his or her hair, you should hear bells and whistles: potential date, potential date, potential date. Potential dates are *everywhere,* once you start looking. Just keep a few things in mind:

✔ **Be aware.** Both men and women are understandably cautious about being picked up by strangers, so if you're the one doing the approaching, the hallmarks of your approach have to be gentility, civility, humor, and gentleness. Otherwise, somebody's likely to call the cops on you. I know — so what's the problem? Cops are cute. Pay attention here; I'm being serious.

✔ **Be considerate.** If someone has found the courage to approach you and you're not interested, unless that person is really, really scary, say no civilly. You don't have to be nasty.

✔ **Don't panic.** If I were to promise you that you would meet the person of your dreams in ten years, and the two of you would be wildly happy for the rest of your lives, would you be willing to wait that ten years? Of course you would (unless you're already 110 years old). So assume that meeting your dreamboat is just a matter of time and, in the meantime, *have fun,* which definitely increases your chances of being appealing when you run into that date-to-be ten minutes, months, years, or decades from now.

✔ **Be geographically conservative.** Honestly, long-distance relationships suck. If you're going to all the trouble to write a personal ad or profile, stick close to home, but not too close. The same job, building, or block is probably going to be a bit close for comfort. On the other hand, more than 25 miles away is going to create its own set of problems.

✔ **Be honest.** Getting in touch with old loves via their Facebook pages is tricky and treacherous if you're looking for a date. You're better off admitting your motives and going to a dating Web site. No back doors allowed.

Searching for the Best Places to Meet Someone

The best places to meet people are ones in which

✔ You can see clearly, hear clearly, and respond honestly.

✔ You have an interest in what's going on, increasing the likelihood that you'll have something in common with anyone you meet there.

✔ The atmosphere feels safe and familiar.

It makes no sense to hang out in places where you hate the activity. Doing so is kind of like people who feed their babies Gerber's veal and then are surprised when their kids like only veal, which the parents never eat. Hang out in places where you would be happy even if you weren't searching, and — bingo! — you're happy.

A place you enjoy, where you feel comfortable and safe, solves the problem of what to talk about. The key is to be lighthearted about approaching a stranger. The situation is similar to baking a soufflé. You need to tread gently and avoid loud noises, early peeks, or banging doors. Otherwise, you'll end up with a dessert that nobody wants — flat, ugly, and unappetizing — despite the effort and right ingredients you put into it. But be a bit careful about hanging out in only the places where you and your friends hang out. You don't necessarily want early dates to involve audience participation.

The halls of academia

High schools, colleges, and adult education classes are all dating mills. You can sit next to somebody in class for weeks, smile shyly, and eventually get up the nerve to say, "Hi" or "Can I borrow your notes?" or "A bunch of us are going for coffee." So number one on the list of places to meet somebody is a classroom: high school, college, traffic school, cooking school, power squadron course, art history course, computer course — you get the point.

Find something you've always wanted to learn about and take a course. Even if you don't see any datables in your classroom, you're out of the house, learning and relating, and your chem partner may have a cute sibling who's single.

The people in your neighborhood

You may find some very datable people in your own neighborhood. Familiarity breeds comfort, and feeling safe and making the other person equally comfortable are important. So somebody you frequently run into or who knows the people you know works for both of you.

Dating a neighbor has some advantages:

- ✔ You may already be acquainted with each other, and therefore, the situation isn't as scary as approaching or being approached by a stranger — and making somebody feel safe is a priority in this exercise.

- ✔ You probably run into the person often, giving you plenty of opportunities to take the bull by the horns (so to speak).

- ✔ You probably know many of the same people.

The only reservation about dating someone in your neighborhood is that you should be careful about next-door neighbors. If the thing doesn't work out, the possibilities of being spied on increase greatly. Even if this person doesn't own binoculars, the "bump intos" could feel uncomfortable, awkward, painful, or embarrassing.

Parties, vacations, and other fun stuff

Fun places are some of the best places to scout out datables. Everybody's relaxed, open, less uptight, and prepared to be happy and smile. (It's the reason for so many vacation romances.)

Smart phones and apps have made being single easier than ever in terms of finding out what's happening and where it's happening. Just beware the crowd mentality; you want to be able to hear and see without hollering or competing.

Here are a few of the best places to look:

✔ **Parties:** In terms of comfort, meeting someone at a party offers one of the same advantages that meeting someone in your neighborhood offers: You both know somebody in common.

✔ **Cruises:** Cruises can be the perfect vacation if you're single, especially if you don't emphasize the need to meet someone. Cruises meet the criteria for comfort and safety and, after a day or so, familiarity. Be aware that vacation atmospheres are more fantasy than reality, but don't overlook the potential here.

Also beware the long-distance relationship problem. Returning to a shared home port where the two of you aren't more than a cab or car ride away makes a lot more sense than trying to book cruises once a year to keep in touch.

✔ **Movies:** Not everybody in line is coupled up; lots of singles go to movies, so the line into the movie, especially if it's a long line, is not a bad place to get to know somebody. If you have the time to get to know each other before the movie begins, offering to share popcorn can work, too. (Yeah, I know the old joke about the chicken in the popcorn box. Puh-leeeeze.) But if you talk in the movie, I'll give you a piece of my mind.

✔ **Dances:** Folk dancing is great, as is square dancing, because the caller tells you what to do, and you're always changing partners. Ballroom dancing is a bit iffier in that there is a huge premium put on doing it well, and you're pretty up-close and personal with someone. But if you love to dance and you're good at it and you don't mind your feet getting stomped occasionally, dancing does meet the something-in-common, sorta nonthreatening thing.

Since *Dancing with the Stars* and *So You Think You Can Dance* have become so popular, lots of places offer inexpensive classes that are then followed by a group party. They're a great way to get some exercise, change partners, and shake your booty.

If the music is loud, it's often hard to talk when you're dancing. If it's disco, forget about it — you'll never hear a word each other speaks, but then again, at least you don't actually have to follow your partner.

✔ **Singles dances:** The air of desperation may be palpable, but if you can go and have fun, you'll probably do okay because you'll stand out as the only person really having a good time. If you've taken a few dance lessons, you'll likely be more accomplished and less sweaty and much more in demand, but it's not necessary to be a great dancer. Just be willing to get out there and shake your booty.

Grocery stores, bus stops, and other public places

Ordinary places can be extraordinarily effective as meeting and greeting grounds:

✔ **Grocery stores:** Buying food in the local market has that comfort/familiarity/nurturing thing going. It's a (usually) nonthreatening environment, you've probably been there before, and if no one datable happens to meander in front of your grocery cart or pause invitingly in the produce section, you can still pick up your milk and Ding-Dongs.

✔ **Bus stops:** Waiting at the same place and at the same time every day creates a sense of community. You see each other — and every other regular passenger — here all the time, and you can sit together. The trick here is to go slowly (pun intended). Don't worry unless the person you're interested in moves or switches jobs; you have plenty of time.

✔ **Laundromats:** What's more domestic than airing your once dirty, now clean, laundry in public? Always carry extra fabric softener and change (you never know who may need to borrow something) and *under no circumstances* mention underwear.

✔ **Bookstores:** In some bookstore chains, you can curl up in a big comfy chair and listen to jazz quartets — and even be tempted to chat each other up. And if you happen to spy some cutie perusing your favorite author's latest, discussing the finer points over a soy latte in the bookstore café seems fun, savvy, and safe. Somehow being picked up in a bookstore seems really smart, dontcha think?

Heading to the "meet" market

When I lived in San Francisco, the Marina Safeway was a famous place because you could wander the aisles and talk broccoli, and those really clever people would hang out at the meat counter and offer to split the special large orders that were "much too much for someone living alone." Cool, huh? You see the grocery store theme at work here.

- ✔ **Restaurants:** Asking to join someone sitting alone is a bit iffy. If the person says yes, you don't have to eat alone, but if the person says no, you may lose your appetite. I once got up the nerve, after I'd finished my meal, to ask someone if he would like company, and he said no; he really liked eating alone. I was so rattled that I left the restaurant without signing my bill, and the waiter came running after me. But if you have nerves of steel, go for it. My experience is mercifully unusual. Most folks would be both charmed and charming!

- ✔ **Airplanes:** You're both together, going to the same place, side by side, with a flight attendant to take care of everything you need — in addition to the hint of being united against a common danger in the clouds. Hey, don't miss the opportunity. Buses and trains have much of the same criteria, but a little less of the cool factor. (Still, some pretty cool movies have focused on train trips; think about the possibility of meeting a Cary Grant, Mimi Rodgers, Gene Hackman, or Ingrid Bergman in the dining car.)

Spirituality and altruism — a dating duo

The tips in this section can be good for a twofer: good works and good vibes — a cool dating possibility:

- ✔ **Places of worship:** Many churches, mosques, temples, synagogues, and other places of worship or spiritual activities have special singles services and events, figuring that they're safe and familiar and spiritual and, with any luck at all, have the potential to increase the wedding business. The only problem here is that you can't date lots and lots of folks at the same place of worship, or you'll get a bad rep. So either be selective or plan to change congregations should the need arise.

  Converting just to find a date seems extreme, which is probably why some of the most popular online dating services focus on the religious connection (for example, JDate.com, which connects Jewish singles, Muslima.com, ChristianCafe, and CatholicMatch). You get all the advantages of the spiritual without a sermon or the chance of getting a rep with the congregation.

✔ **Volunteer activities:** Being your most altruistic self is hard to resist, and having something in common with another altruistic soul gives you lots to talk about. Just make sure that you like the activity itself. After all, you don't want to end up licking hundreds of envelopes to save sperm whales because you heard fishermen have great poles.

✔ **Political campaigns:** Political campaigns offer a nearly perfect environment because volunteers share a common goal, campaigns don't go on forever, and the atmosphere is exciting and intense.

Good sports win big

You've probably always known that physical activity is good exercise and great for your heart. You just didn't know *how* great until now. Attention couch potatoes: There are dating benefits to being even a spectator at a sporting event, but active is best!

✔ **Sport teams:** Even if you're a klutz, find a sport to play. It's generally safe, it's fun, it's physical, and team members almost always get together afterwards — especially if they win. Even if you view yourself as the ultimate klutz or hated gym, more and more leagues are demanding co-ed-ness. (Please don't tell my English teacher I used that word.)

✔ **Health clubs:** Health clubs have a lot going for them: You're among other people doing essentially the same thing. You see the same familiar group of people all the time. Keep in mind though that most people are in spandex and therefore often a bit shy, so be willing to go slowly. On the other hand, there are going to be a lot fewer anatomical surprises down the road, and you can definitely find out who's into sweat.

✔ **Individual sports:** Even if you embrace the loneliness of the long-distance runner, skier, mountain climber, shot putter, or cycler, there are clubs that support your individuality while having great parties, like-minded souls, and useful Web sites — even dating sites. If you run into the same person daily as you scoot around the reservoir, walk your dog, or peddle uphill, smile as you gasp.

✔ **Sporting events:** Most people are really relaxed when they watch sports — unless it's the playoffs — and they are quite willing to explain what's going on or to argue about who's best. So asking the cute person next to you, "Why did the ref call that penalty?" will likely result in a smile and an explanation.

Picking the perfect date by birth order

If you want to know more about a guy or girl you're dating, the family tree is a good place to look. Certain personality traits, unique to birth position, tend to show up again and again in family after family. For instance:

✔ The oldest child: He or she will tend to be bossy, super-responsible, competitive, and assertive.

✔ The middle child: A people pleaser, he or she will often "make nice" in an effort to keep things calm. Middle kids tend to be the diplomats in the family and in life. It's hard to get them to take a stand or figure out what they really want, and they can be a bit manipulative.

✔ The youngest child: Adventurous, creative, and confident, youngest children also tend to be hyperemotional and needy at times. They like being babied.

✔ The only child: After a childhood of being in the spotlight of their families, only children tend to crave attention and will aggressively and charmingly seek it from you. They tend to be disproportionately successful.

Friends, relatives, and — believe it or not — exes

The less strange the stranger you're finding to date, the easier and more comfortable the early stages. People you both know and trust are a great bridge. Whom can you trust more than your friends, your Mom, or your ex (assuming that you two are still friendly and that alimony is not the primary motivation to get you paired up with somebody new)?

✔ **Friends:** Fix-ups are good news/bad news. On the good side, your friends presumably wouldn't fix you up with Jack (or Jackie) the Ripper, and they probably know you well enough to know what you like. On the bad side, often they want to know specifics, may choose sides, and will likely be miffed if you don't treat their friend right, don't come up with the details, or don't spend as much time with them as you used to because you're seeing the friend. All things considered, fix-ups are often worth the risk of somebody knowing your business, especially if your friends are perceptive and know cool people.

A special note needs to be taken here about the newest, hippest use of the friend word: Facebook pages. Surfing Facebook for dates is tricky; *friend* can mean different things to different people, and if you're married and trying to hook up under the guise of being a friend . . . fuhgetaboutit. Don't do it.

✔ **Relatives:** Isn't it fascinating what people who love us think we'll love? This outlet has all the problems of a friend fix-up with the added problems of gossip and the inability to ever go home for Thanksgiving if it doesn't work out. On the other hand, presumably they do love you and will have to answer to your Mom if they come up with a real loser.

✔ **Exes:** Allowing your ex to fix you up with someone can be a bit dicey. (After all, an ex with an ax to grind can come up with a doozy of a loser.) On the other hand, who knows ya, baby? Whether you agree to such a fix-up or not probably depends on the comfort of the break-up. If it was super icky, you're probably not speaking anyhow. But if your ex is still a friend and other signs seem right, go for it. If your split-up was marked by scream fests and flying fur, and you still refer to each other by unprintable expletives, my advice is to politely decline.

The personals: Online and off

If you're going to write a personal ad, find a journal, newspaper, or magazine that reflects your interests and is available in your geographical area. For example, if you enjoy sailing, then a sailing magazine may be a great place to place an ad. ("Hi sailor, new in town?") Or if you have a publication that you read regularly — whether it's the *Times,* the *Mirror,* a daily or weekly paper, or a special interest magazine based on skills, industry, geography, sports, interests, or income — a personal ad allows you to connect with readers with whom you have something in common. As long as you're going to the trouble and expense of placing a personal ad, be specific and pick a publication that reflects who you are, not who you'd like to be.

To a large extent, printed personal ads have been supplanted by the Internet: The scope is wider, the costs are lower, and the possibilities are nearly endless. The technology hasn't changed the basics, but some additional caution, as well as optimism, is warranted.

If you write well and can be very specific about who you are and what you want, personal ads and profiles can work well. The main thing is to play it safe:

✔ Don't provide any identifying information (such as an address or phone number) in the ad.

✔ Meet in a public place.

✔ Tell someone where you're going and when you plan to be home.

✔ Don't let anyone bring you home.

If you exercise reasonable caution in using a personal ad or a profile, there's potential here. For information on how to write a personal ad, see Chapter 2 and 20.

A personal ad or a profile is a good way to jazz up your social life and be clear about who you are and what you want, but remember that the person responding to it is a stranger. Use the same caution you would with anyone you don't know, and see Chapter 20 for information about dating someone you haven't "officially" met.

The same general rules that apply to print personal ads apply to online dating. It's in the same way that 20 years ago, the personals were considered fringe and then moved into the mainstream. Although ten years ago the Internet was considered marginal and overtly sexual, primarily for kinky liaisons or questionable activities or participants, these days Internet dating is pretty darn mainstream and popular, encompassing literally millions of people. Although some people may still be a bit shy about admitting to online dating (how come I can't find a date the "usual" way?), millions of folks view the Internet as a great way of increasing the pool of eligible possibilities. (To maximize its potential and minimize heartbreak, let alone catastrophe, see Chapter 23 for the list of ten do's and don'ts of online dating.)

Your online profile should look very much like the one that you would put in a magazine or newspaper: Pretend that you're paying by the word (even though you're not) so that you are succinct and specific. Studies have suggested that the longer the personal ad (when wordage is charged), the greater the response. (Presumably the reader is implying that the author has a vast and unlimited bank account.) But because there is no per-word charge for online ads, the green effect is less likely, and going on and on may make you look desperate, lonely, and disorganized. Be succinct by giving an idea of who you are and what makes you unique, as well as specifically who you're looking for. For more info, check out *Online Dating For Dummies,* by Judith Silverstein, MD, and Michael Laskey, JD (published by Wiley).

By using some sense, sensitivity, and specificity, online or offline, personals can energize your dating possibilities.

Avoiding Certain Places like the Plague

You may be sorely tempted to go scouting for a date at the office, at a bar, or online at work, *but don't.* Trust me.

- ✔ **The office:** I know, you think, "Well, it's nonthreatening and familiar." Yeah, and *everybody* will know about it, and one of you will very likely get fired. Work is about competence, and anything that interferes with that is poison. Most of us succumb to the *M*A*S*H* philosophy of life, based on the popular TV series, but think about it this way: Want to lose your job and your love at the same time? Dating someone from the office confuses your work life with your love life and makes you a likely target of office gossip.

You may be tempted to date friends, sibs, or exes of people you work with, but doing so is still not a good idea, so don't, at least unless you plan to change jobs — voluntarily.

✔ **Bars:** "What can she possibly be thinking here?" you may wonder. How about it's dark, almost everybody has been ingesting substances that alter perception, and who needs a relationship based on blurred sensibilities? Plus, bars are too noisy to talk in, and you can't see what the person looks like. If nothing else, how do you answer, "Come here often?" It is probably worth mentioning that alcohol is the major drug of abuse in this country, and if you're spending most of your time in bars, you're going to compromise not only your dating possibilities but also your liver and well-being.

✔ **Online:** Even though I'm a fan of online dating, there are four caveats here: 1) Never use the office computer — it's not private, it's not smart, and you could get both busted and fired. 2) Don't spend too long online before you actually meet in a safe, controlled environment. 3) Because it's so easy and private, the resultant false sense of intimacy can allow you to divulge too much too soon. 4) The accessibility gives rise to a "shopping" mentality — "I'll just keep looking; I wonder who else might be out there. . . ."

Online dating is primarily about fantasy. It's the illusion of intimacy while still being at arm's length. When you do meet face to face, there is all that expectation. Even with a blind date, you *know* that you don't know. It's okay to chat, but online is the ultimate long-distance relationship. You'll think you know much more than you really know, and that's really tricky. So get off-line quickly.

✔ **Singles weekends:** These weekends mean too much stress and expectations that are too high. You're better off spending the same money and taking a cruise; at least that way you can feel your money is well spent even if you don't fall in love.

The breakfast of ex-companions

A guy I dated, but with whom I felt no chemistry, and I hosted a series of brunches with all of our "rejects." Not only were they fun and low-key, but both he and six other couples found each other and actually ended up married. Exes have a history in common with you; there's a common link, so it's not strangers meeting (you can both talk about old Joey); and brunch is a pretty nonthreatening meal.

Of course, you don't have to have a brunch. You can organize singles parties at a Chinese restaurant, a progressive supper (one that travels from house to house), or a picnic in the park. The ticket of admission is a covered dish and a friend who you think is quality material but who doesn't make your heart beat fast. Just make sure you have the same number of men and women.

Singles activities are designed to pair you off, but you may have nothing in common but desperation or loneliness, which won't work and doesn't make you look anything but pathetic. If you're going to adopt this approach, at least build up some experience and confidence by doing some of the preferred activities included in the earlier sections.

Planning a Cool Approach

Okay, person who's ready to begin dating for real, we've discussed *who* (both you and other, in Chapter 4) and we've talked *where* (both places to look and places to avoid, earlier in this chapter). Now, you with sweaty palms, let's talk *how:* how to turn possibility into opportunity, how to go for the gold, how to make the sale — in short, how to get a date.

The eyes have it

First rule: Eye contact is crucial. If you can't connect with eye contact, you can't connect. Eyes are not only the window to the soul, but being connected directly to the brain, they're the primary information gateway for human beings (and we know that everything comes from the brain, in spite of your humming hormones). Make eye contact. No looking down at your shoes. No checking out buns or breasts or legs.

Focus *your* baby blues on the potential date's baby blues. But for heaven's sake, don't stare (and remember to blink). You want to be perceived as soulful, not psychotic. The goal here is to show that you're interested *and* sane.

From your mouth . . .

After you make the contact with eyeballs, you need to verbalize what your eyes are telegraphing.

Using what works

When you approach someone, take this advice:

- ✔ **Be sincere.** The key to being sincere is to mean what you say. Pleeeeze don't practice sincerity in front of the mirror. For sincerity to work, you have to focus on the object (person, please) of your desire and believe what you're saying. In the most basic sense, you are selling yourself, but the soft sell works the very best.

✔ **Be honest.** If you're a rotten dancer, say in a self-effacing, engaging way that you have two left feet. Don't try to make yourself someone you're not to impress someone you may or may not like. Don't pretend to love jazz, collect Porsches, or own a yacht. On the other hand, telling the truth isn't the same as baring your soul. To find out what you should and shouldn't divulge, see Chapter 15. Also, when it comes to discussing the other person, remember what your momma said: If you can't say something nice, don't say anything at all.

✔ **Be friendly.** Who doesn't like friendly people? When you're friendly, you smile, you're open, and you're fun to be around.

✔ **Be positive.** I'm not talking goody-two-shoes here, just pleasant and upbeat.

Avoiding what doesn't work

When you're approaching someone, don't be any of the following:

✔ **Cute:** Unless you're 6 years old, the Little Bo Peep routine gets pretty annoying pretty fast.

✔ **Slick:** When you think of slick, think of snake oil salesmen. People don't trust slick.

✔ **Obscene:** Nothing is a bigger turn-off than lewd or disgusting gestures, jokes, and personal observations. Remember you're in civilized society; if that doesn't work, pretend your mother can hear every word you say.

✔ **Silly:** Straws up your nose and lampshades on your head have never been attractive, so give it up and act like an adult.

✔ **Stupid:** Acting stupid puts you in a catch-22: I mean, *really,* you act stupid to attract someone's attention, but do you really want the attention of someone who finds stupid attractive?

✔ **Negative:** Gossiping about someone brings up the very real possibility that you would gossip about present company.

✔ **Whiny:** Please . . . I really don't have to explain this to you, do I?

A word on compliments

It's okay to be complimentary as long as the compliment is sincere and at least fairly reasonable and stays away from body parts below the neck and above the ankles. Saying to a fat person, for example, that he doesn't sweat much isn't even in the compliment ballpark. Saying "You remind me of my grandmother" (for either sex) isn't too hot, either.

COOL IDEA

How to flirt

I know many of the online dating sites encourage you to "flirt." Here we're talking about the old-fashioned flirt: what your granny and poppa did, as does your roomie. Flirting online is a whole different ballgame that seems to me more teasing than anything else, but here, you've got to be within eyeballing proximity. Telephone flirting is also another science, which we can discuss later. Focus your eyeballs here and pay attention.

Successful flirting is all about fun and confidence and playfulness and sexiness. Unsuccessful flirting is about being too out-there, too sexual, too self-absorbed, and too eager to flirt with anyone. Basic rule: Flirt with your date, not the waiter, hostess, your date's best friend, or her mom. That said, you can find more about flirting in Chapter 10, but here's some info on how to flirt with style:

✔ **Be interested.** Few things are sexier than someone who's totally into you. Paying genuine attention is a great place to start.

✔ **Lock eyes.** Don't stare, but connect with your eyes and you have a better chance of connecting with your hearts.

✔ **Play.** Good flirting is fun. Don't be afraid to giggle and tease.

✔ **Touch.** Brush arms, bump knees beneath the table, tweak noses.

✔ **Flatter.** A sincere appraisal of what you really like about this person is a turn-on. False praise, however, is a total turn-off.

✔ **Take a chance.** Flirting, by its very nature, is active. Sitting back and waiting for someone to flirt with you may mean you put in more couch time than flirt time. Take a stab. Unless you drool all over your date or flirt-mate, you have nothing to lose. Who doesn't like a little flirting?

GIRL STUFF

It's okay to compliment men on their:

✔ **Hair:** Thick, shiny, wavy, healthy locks, a nice cut, an attractive color. Talking hair is pretty safe. But *don't* talk about receding hairlines, bald spots, early graying, or anything else that may be a sensitive topic. Don't make even a casual reference to dandruff; avoid the words *flake* and *flaky* for at least five minutes after talking about hair.

✔ **Eyes:** Blue, green, black, or brown, all God's children love to hear that they've got nice eyes. Some particularly good adjectives? Try *bright, clear, beautiful, expressive, warm, laughing,* and *sensitive.* Avoid *sexy* until the third date.

✔ **Neck:** If he's got a neck like a wrestler, tell him. If it's a chicken neck, let it pass.

✔ **Tie:** Cut, color, style. But don't say you want to use it to tie him to a bedpost — at least not yet. Make sure it's patterned and not grease stained before you comment on the unusual design.

✔ **Socks:** Some men take a lot of care picking their socks. Stun — and impress — him by noticing, but never lift his pant leg without asking.

✔ **Smile:** Men love to hear that they've got a charming, handsome, alluring smile.

✔ **Teeth:** A bit more personal. *Shiny* is good, but *big, dangerous,* or *sharp* should not be noted.

GUY STUFF

Women find praise for essentially the same things really cool:

✔ **Hair:** Women spend a lot of time on their hair, and they like the effort to be noticed. But don't touch without asking, be careful about noting an unusual color (two out of three women in America color their hair), and *never* say "dye."

✔ **Eyes:** The same rules apply for women that apply for men. Like I said before, everyone likes to be complimented on his or her baby blues (or greens or browns or even hazel).

✔ **Neck:** Complimenting a woman on her neck can be a bit iffy — unless it's long and slender. If her neck is as thick as a linebacker's, you can comment on skin — unless she's wearing something really low cut.

✔ **Smile:** Women love to hear that they've got a warm, engaging, sweet smile.

✔ **Teeth:** If you don't know how to give a compliment on teeth without coming off as an oral surgeon, go for the smile instead.

Just when you think a compliment's safe . . .

Believe it or not, even conservative compliments can occasionally get you in trouble. I was working on a TV show and a very well-known actor was in makeup with me.

I said, "Love your hair."

He said, "It's a piece."

"Nice teeth," I responded.

"They're caps," said he.

"Beautiful eyes?"

"Contacts."

At that point, I said, "Nice package," and left it at that — and I wasn't even flirting.

Stay away from body parts — even muscles (in *either* sex). Also, complimenting women's shoes can be a bit tricky, raising the possibility of a foot fetish. It's just not worth the risk this early on. Avoid the killer *b*'s: buns, breasts, briefs, bazooms.

Admitting you're not perfect

Given the reality that making the acquaintance of a stranger is tricky stuff (even if you believe that a stranger is just a friend you haven't met yet), the idea is to be nonthreatening without looking like a complete wimp. That's why being vulnerable really works. Consider the following:

- **Asking for help, directions, or an opinion:** Most people are more than willing to jump in and help out, so take advantage of that tendency. Helping others brings out the best in all of us and also feels safe. At that moment, you're in control. (Supermarkets are a natural.)

- **Admitting that you're nervous:** Admitting that you're nervous because you think someone is so cool is complimentary and sweet and honest. But once is plenty; more than that is whiny and makes you sound like an overstrung bundle of nerves. Panic isn't sexy, and it's sometimes contagious.

- **Admitting that you don't normally do this but you're so inspired that you've ignored your usual shyness, fear, or sense of propriety:** Think about it: Aren't you impressed when someone puts in extra effort and seems to be doing something for the very first time and *you* are the motivation? Heady stuff.

Being persistent is okay as long as your persistence can't possibly be mistaken for stalking behavior (see Chapter 21).

Perking up pick-up lines

Don't even think about using lines like these:

- "Come here often?"

- "What's your sign?"

- "I must have died and gone to heaven, because where else would I see an angel like you?"

- "If I told you that you have a beautiful body, would you hold it against me?"

Do or dare: Making the approach

I was once at a wretched party in the back room of a bar in San Francisco. To make matters worse, the women outnumbered the men 10 to 1. But in the front part of the bar, there were all these cute guys. So I said to the hostess, "Why don't you invite them?" She snottily replied, "Why don't you?" I took it as a challenge and meandered up to a group of five guys and said, "Somebody just bet me a dollar I couldn't convince the five cutest guys here to come to the party, and I could use the money." Not only did they laugh and join the party, but three of 'em asked me out. This is something I never would have considered doing if I hadn't been "dared." Remember what Helen Keller said: "Life is daring risk, or it's nothing at all."

The danger with overused, hackneyed pick-up lines is that they generally end up sounding like the equivalent of "Oh, baby, baby, hmm, hmm, hmm."

So rather than practicing a pick-up line, follow these two guidelines:

- **Focus on the situation and your feelings.** "I couldn't help myself; I just had to come over and tell you your smile was keeping me from concentrating" is ever so much better than "New around here?" "Do you know the hostess?" "Heard any good jokes?" and so on.

- **If the line sounds like a title to a country song, don't use it.**

Of course, an original pick-up line can be memorable. I have never forgotten a guy who said he knew I wasn't from around here (I was in Alaska at the time) because I didn't smell like fish. While I'm sure this line probably worked for him once or twice, I just giggled and remembered the line, not him.

Never say, "My wife doesn't understand me" or "You're the best-looking person in the room" or "Want to spend the night with me?" on the assumption that if you don't ask, you don't get. We're talking about finding a date, not spending the night in jail.

I know the Internet encourages premature revelations, but don't try to match your speech to your Facebook comments, and don't comment about how your date really seemed different online. Dating is about getting to know one another organically, not running your own version of spy school or a lie detection agency. Don't reveal too much initially or make yourself look like a spy. Go gently into this dating game, and you'll have a great deal more fun — not to mention success.

Part II
Setting Up the Date

In this part . . .

Popping the question "Will you go out with me?" is scary and thrilling and sweat-producing and a whole lot like leaping backward off the high-dive if you don't know what you're doing. How do you up your chances of getting a yes while leaving enough room to bow out gracefully if the answer is no? Good question, and one that will be fully examined in this part — along with the dreaded phone number thing (yours, mine, cell or landline?), e-mail, Facebook, texting, sexting (don't even think about it), transportation concerns, and, of course, date location, location, location.

Not to worry. You'll get all the info you need to sail smoothly over each hurdle . . . or at least be able to pick yourself up off the blacktop, brush off your knees, and walk with dignity back to the starting line, to a bandage, or to the locker room to gear up for the next race.

Chapter 6

Asking for a Date

Whether a date's spontaneous or planned, the first or the last date, or you're young or old, sooner or later, going out with someone comes to this: Somebody has to ask for the date. No matter how much or how little you plan, nobody (with the possible exception of Adam) ever made a date without asking for it. (I bet that even with God as the go-between, sooner or later Eve expected Adam to pony up and find the courage to ask if they could take a walk in Paradise, and if he didn't, well, it explains a lot about the snake, don't you think?)

Face it, the only thing scarier than the first date is *asking* for the first date. But if you can remember that you're not looking for a cure for cancer, and that life as you know it will continue no matter what your potential date's response, you may relax enough to actually (gulp) ask for a date.

Gazillions of perfectly normal (and lots of less than normal) people have all gotten nervous about asking for a date. You and I and everybody else are connected to a long line of sweating, nervous, stuttering, tongue-tied souls, and even the slick ones feel anxious on the inside about asking for a date. Do you feel better? No? Well, I was afraid of that. Never fear — in this chapter, I tell you some things that should comfort you in the asking, help you in the consummation, and protect you from any possible devastation beyond a teensy pinch on the ego.

Also, if the two of you are ever going to have a date, you have to be able to connect. Of course, you could agree to meet on a specific street corner or at a party or restaurant or after a class. But sooner or later, it will occur to one of you that being able to get in touch if plans should change would be nice — and that means a more personal way to connect, and *that* means a phone number. Sure, an e-mail is groovy, and Facebook allows for contact, but both are literally at arm's length. Typing is not the same as connecting. To help you, I also cover how to both get and give a phone number — with the minimum wear and tear on both of you. I also cover what to say during the call, and if you're hesitant to hand out your home phone number (as most people are, which is one of the reasons cells were invented, as well as caller ID), you can also find phone number alternatives.

Risking Rejection

The First Rule to asking for a date is this: no guts, no glory. The worst-case scenario is that the prospective date says no. At that point, you're no worse off than you are at this very moment.

Rejection is definitely not fun, but a rejection is only one person's opinion of you. You don't like everyone, and not everyone is going to like you. If someone says no, then he or she misses out on getting to know how truly terrific you are.

Rejection can be the beginning of opportunity. Scads of hugely successful people just wouldn't take no for an answer. Think about Fred Astaire: When he first went to Hollywood, a talent scout wrote, "Big ears, too skinny, big nose, can dance a little." Many famous beauties and stars in many fields had to cope with someone's negative opinion of them — nobody hasn't faced rejection. The question is: Are you going to let it get you down? Of course not! Alexander the Great probably conquered the world by the age of 30 because some short-sighted lass turned him down — maybe because he was too intense or short or something. Maybe that rejection made him want to make more than most Grecians earn. (It's a pun; say it out loud — but definitely don't use it until the fourth or fifth date or after you're married or your last kid leaves for college or your hearing has gone.)

Rejection means that one person says no — not that everyone will. The question facing you is this: One "no" is not universal, but how quickly should you be deterred? When does "no" mean that someone's showing absolutely no interest, and when does it mean he or she just can't be available for the time you have stipulated? If someone consistently says no when you ask for a date, it's okay to say, "Look, I hear that you're not interested, and I don't want to be a pest. If you ever change your mind, here's my number," or "I'll call you in a year," but then for heaven's sake, don't call any sooner than that. With time, the sting really does go away.

A brush-off with style

The coolest rejection I ever got was from a guy who told me that he'd just gotten a call from an old girlfriend. He said, "She's reemerged in my life, and I need to see where it goes. I'll either marry her and invite you to the wedding, or I'd like to finally put it to rest. No matter what happens, I'd like to be able to call you." Cool, huh?

Conversely, if you really don't want to go out with someone, don't say, "Maybe" or "Call me next week." Just say, "Thank you for asking, but it's just not possible." Remember that the world is a very small place. You may change your mind, or that person you turn down may marry your best friend or be in a position to hire you someday. There is no reason to ever hurt someone whose only sin is being interested in you, so be gentle but firm.

Rejection isn't gender specific. It's not any easier for guys to face rejection than it is for women. We've just programmed men for power, and asking someone out is boss, even if the whole experience is tinged with fear. Both men and women can feel more powerful by taking the initiative and asking someone out.

 Biology has nothing to do with the ability to tolerate possible rejection. Women, if you've never asked a guy out, you should do it for your own liberal education. Guys love it. However, they may think you're hotter to trot (sexually) than you really are, so take that into consideration.

If you're afraid of rejection, you may miss out on a lot in this life, which is pretty darned short as it is. See if you can put that angst away, take the chip off your shoulder, and go for it.

Improving Your Odds

When asking for a date, having a plan is crucial, but you've got to stay a little loose. The more structured you are, the more dependent you are on meshing well with a stranger. Therefore, you need to read the signs, stay loose, and keep things light, flexible, and open. You can seriously improve the chances of getting a yes if you keep these tips in mind when you ask for a date.

Never ask for a first date for a Friday or Saturday night

These two main, big, serious date nights are too important a place to start. Asking for a first date on a Friday or Saturday is like playing at Wimbledon without a tennis lesson or having ever played on grass or at all. Even people who don't have dates and haven't had one for ages are often loathe to admit their plight to a stranger (and if you haven't had a first date, you're still strangers).

Start off with a Wednesday or Thursday night, which are nights when people generally don't have much planned. Also avoid Mondays like the plague. Everybody hates Mondays.

Never say, "Would you like to go out sometime?"

If you phrase the invitation like this and the askee says "no," you've left yourself absolutely no out except to be swallowed up by a prayed-for earthquake. If the person says "yes," you still have to ask him or her out. Yikes. All that stomach acid, and still no date either way.

Instead, be specific. It's much better to say, "I'd love to see the new exhibit at the museum. Any interest in going either Wednesday or Thursday?" You offer a specific opportunity (as well as alternative days), and at the same time, you give your potential date a great deal of room in which to negotiate without sounding wishy-washy or desperate. Giving specifics also allows your potential date a couple of seconds to think about it, rather than getting caught completely off guard. You've displayed your ability to have a plan in life while simultaneously eliciting this person's input for a fun date. These combined attributes make for a great date and a great relationship. That combination of flexibility and creativity rocks.

Always offer options about the date

Options can include the day, time, activity, and transportation. Options make you sound organized without being bossy or rigid, as long as you keep them limited. Offering a few choices at the outset makes you sound less panicky than you would if you were to offer them after the potential date says no to your initial suggestion.

If you're specific about the date and your potential date doesn't like the suggested activity but does like you, you can modify your plan.

Also, although a plan with several separate possibilities requires more work on your part, it offers a better chance of success — and a chance to figure out whether your potential date has any interest in you. After all, if you've offered all options regarding place, time, date, activity, and so on and the answer is still no, the problem is as clear as the writing on the wall, and you've hit the wall. Take a deep breath and move on. It's not the end of the world, just this potential date. Scary but efficient.

By offering to meet there, go in separate cars, or pick her up, you instantly show yourself to be considerate, capable, and sensitive to the fact that females have heard horror stories about being abducted by a date and never seen again. Although you're not Jack the Ripper, understanding that she may feel a little uneasy about being in a car with a stranger makes you a liberated and cool guy for thinking like a modern woman. You will score major points.

In the initial stages of dating, people sometimes want so much to be liked that they agree to things at the expense of their integrity. If your potential date has enough sense to say, "I'd love to do something with you, just not mud wrestling," then give that person a gold star. Don't be offended — be pleased. You have just found someone with brains, courage, and honesty.

Remember that timing is everything

Don't ask for tomorrow or next year. A basic rule is to ask for a first date a week to ten days in advance, but you can break this rule with impunity as the need arises. You can ignore these guidelines if the spirit moves you to be spontaneous. For example, "Hey, got time for an ice cream cone?" can get you an immediate yes; you can also expand this invitation to a "maybe next week" if you get a no. I refer to these as *date-ettes:* spontaneous, lightweight, inexpensive, low risk.

Now is always a better time to ask than later because your courage may diminish over time. There are some obvious exceptions to this rule: Don't ask someone who is in a crisis (never ask for a date at a funeral), just getting out of a relationship (never ask for a date at a divorce hearing, even if the person isn't one of the parties involved; it's bad karma), or going through any other experience when you may appear to be exploiting a weakness. You need to take the other person's life situation into account as well.

Always go for it if you're having a good hair (or anything else) day

You're cuter when you're happy, and self-confidence is sexy. Don't get into the "well, today is a write-off, I may as well ask, get rejected, and make it a perfect score" mentality. You can tolerate being turned down more easily when you're feeling strong — not to mention that rejection is a lot less likely.

Asking someone out for a first date isn't the time to trot out your best anything, including your imagination, checkbook, or best friend. This is a time to think KISS: Keep it Simple, Sweetie. All you want to do here is send a clear and gentle but important message: I'd like to spend some time getting to know you better. Are you interested?

The Invitation: Sending the Message

You have several options when actually asking for the date. The choices may be influenced by circumstances (like distance), personality, and personal style. In general, the closer you are when you ask, the better. When you're close to the person, you get more information, you appear more courageous, and you get some practice for the date.

You can adapt any of the following methods for sending the message to your level of comfort. But be careful that you're not hiding behind your comfort level — sooner or later, you're going to have to get out there and actually date.

- ✔ **Asking in person:** When possible, this is the best way to ask by far because seeing the person face-to-face gives you the most information. You can read body language and see whether the potential date looks pleased, terrified, God-forbid-revolted, or delighted. Based on the other person's reaction, you can then modify your behavior accordingly — or run. The disadvantage with asking in person is that it's also the scariest for the exact same reasons. But it's still preferred and also the friendliest technique.

- ✔ **Asking on the phone:** This method gives you less information, but if you get panicky, you can always hang up before the person answers (although caller ID has made hanging up without saying anything a great deal trickier). When you ask over the phone, nobody can see your palms sweating; but then again, you also can't see your potential date's reaction. Just make sure you haven't called every 15 minutes for a period of three days before you finally connect. Stalkers are not date bait (in spite of Sting's anthem "Every Breath You Take").

Never ask an answering machine for a date. It's cowardly, sends the wrong message (you're manipulating this person by making him call back before you ask him out), and occasionally, the machine actually eats the message. You never know if your potential date got the message or if it was intercepted by a protective parent, a jealous ex, a careless roommate, or the Fates.

✔ **Asking in an online dating site message:** You've exchanged a few messages, displayed your mutual ability to converse socially, and are interested in meeting face-to-face. It's time to step up to the plate, take a deep breath, and ask to meet for a date. You do not have to first exchange phone numbers and then ask for a date on the phone. You can even make all the logistical arrangements via your message exchange.

However, before you two actually meet, exchanging phone numbers and having a voice-to-ear conversation at least once not only ups the ante but also establishes a minimal connection while affirming that at least each of you is the sex you claim to be. While you are using the Internet to be efficient in your dating, to date you actually need to connect with each other. Getting a head start before you meet face-to-face reduces a teensy bit of the anxiety.

✔ **Asking through a third party:** In elementary school, you may have asked your best friend to ask her best friend if someone liked you. You may have even eventually gotten an answer, but after Suzy told Peter, and Peter told you, were you really 100 percent sure about the answer? Third parties are a very unreliable method of information flow.

When other people get involved, sometimes they add their two cents to your message. For example, what if your best friend liked me and wanted you to ask me if I'd go out on a date with him? Can you see lots of room for sabotage and miscommunication?

Remember the story of our Pilgrim forefathers, John Alden and Miles Standish? Miles was the governor who asked his best friend John to intercede on his behalf with Priscilla Mullens. Priscilla decided she liked the messenger, and Miles was left out in the cold. Don't ask somebody else to ask for your date. The messenger may end up taking your potential date, and then not only do you still need a date but you also need a new friend.

✔ **Asking with a note:** Ever since junior high school, the idea of slipping somebody a note to ask about the prom has seemed less scary than face-to-face asking. The problem is that most of us aren't in junior high anymore, and notes can be intercepted and misinterpreted. I know a number of folks who have slipped their number to the cute cashier at the grocery store — or even the butcher. Better than nothing, but still more than a little risky. Snail mail (through the post office) means that you know where the person lives, which may not feel comfortable. Or, if you send a snail mail letter to someone's office, it could be intercepted by the boss.

When you ask with a note, you also don't know the mood your potential date may be in. In addition, a note opens the opportunity for interception, misinterpretation, a delay in feedback, and a lack of flexibility. Ask anybody who's asked for an RSVP to a written invitation, and you begin to understand the problem with asking for a date through a note. Admittedly, e-mail has made notes faster and sexier, but notes still don't offer you much information and feedback and can be intercepted, misinterpreted, or even spammed.

Voicemail etiquette

A voicemail message, unlike an off-the-cuff remark or rumor or discussion, can be saved and replayed and misinterpreted and overanalyzed and overreacted to and thrown back in your face. Not only that, but you never know who's going to be listening on the other end. Here are six messages never to leave on a date's machine:

- You're the best I've ever had.
- I never want to see you again.
- It's me. Give me a call.
- Next time, we'll go out.
- Your mother is hot.
- Can I have your friend's phone number?

When you ask for a date — no matter how you do it — don't even think about bearing gifts such as flowers, cigars, wine, a baseball hat, or a ticket. For that matter, don't show up on a first date with the same sort of gift. You don't want to appear to be bribing your date on the first date. Gifts can be a token of respect and admiration and are okay and even valuable as you're getting to know each other, but they can be too much too soon. Besides, you don't want to have to top yourself later and end up buying your date a small country by the fourth date. Start out simply.

Knowing What to Do with the Answer You Receive

Okey dokey — you've made plans, offered options, and asked for a date. Now what? Well, either the answer is yes, you have a date, or no, you don't. If the answer is yes, the obvious thing to do is to go on that date already! If the answer is no, you may need a little advice on what to do next.

Dealing with a no

If the answer is no, you have nothing to lose by asking if another day, place, time, or event would suit the person. Listen to the response carefully. Often people really are tied up working late, taking care of a sick parent, getting out of a relationship, studying, or being distracted and would be willing to consider an invitation in the future, just not now.

If you're feeling brave, you can say, "If not now, how soon?" If you're feeling a bit vulnerable, you can say, "Let me give you my number, and you can give me a call when you're ready." The middle ground is to say, "Why don't I give you a holler in a week or two and see how you're doing?" If your potential date says fine, then do it. If he or she says "I'll call you," don't hold your breath. Who needs to turn blue? (All of this should make it clear why face-to-face contact is preferable to anything that conveys even a teensy bit less crucial info.)

Getting some feedback

If you get a no, you may want to take a minute to try to figure out why. Make sure you haven't gotten into some bad habits. You may need to ask yourself some tough questions. Are you too eager, too desperate, too whiny, too silly, or too tense? Is your breath okay? Do you make eye contact?

No matter how honest you think you are, give yourself some balance by asking a willing friend to critique your approach. (You've seen it in a million movies where the hero or heroine practices in front of a mirror — no, not Travis Bickle's "You lookin' at me?" line.) Balance your friend's feedback with your own opinion so that you're not being too easy or too harsh on yourself. If you mess up your careful scenario, your friend can give you some tips and hints on improving it, and you can make sense of what you meant to say or do. It's even okay to videotape yourself. But be very careful about circulating this learning tool — it's useful but a bit embarrassing if viewed by anybody other than yourself.

Practicing can help you get a grip on your nerves. A little nervousness is flattering to the potential date because it shows that you *really* want to get to know him or her. Too much nervousness can panic both of you. All things considered, it's probably even better to be a little bit nervous than so nonchalant and cool that your potential date has the sense you couldn't care less if he or she accepts your invitation because if he or she isn't interested, no biggie, you'll just move on to someone else. It's not a terrible idea to start a first date on an honest basis. I know — don't tell anybody I told you, and we'll try to keep it our dirty little secret.

Asking for a Phone Number

Whether you were introduced by friends, ran into one another on the street, or met at a party, unless you believe that the two of you share a karma that will cause you to run into one another again and again, you're going to have to get a number. It can be a home phone number or a cell number (a great option because it allows you to give out a number without having to transpose one of the last digits for someone you don't really want to give your home number to). If you really don't want to give a phone number, don't do it.

I certainly don't recommend giving out your street address or even alluding to the general vicinity of your home. Offering your e-mail address or a business card can be a stall, but this shouldn't be a game of "How can I deceive this person into thinking I'm interested when I'm not?" If you're truly nervous about giving out your personal information, you can always take the mutual friend route, but you're not in seventh grade anymore — I hope. Plus, if you contact the other person directly, you get a lot more — and more reliable — information. If your gut is telling you that this person is dangerous, not a bit exciting but dangerous, trust your gut and opt out, permanently, no games, no info. Period.

There are only a limited number of reasons why you might ask for a phone number:

✔ You want to call the person.

✔ You're not sure whether you want to call the person but want the number just in case.

✔ You know you don't want to call, but you don't want to appear rude.

The following sections give you tips for handling each of these scenarios.

You want to get in touch with the person

When you know you want to call someone, obviously you need to ask for the phone number. One of the best ways to approach getting someone else's number is to demonstrate your good faith and to show that you're not Jack or Jacqueline the Ripper:

✔ **Smile, talk softly, and make eye contact.** See Chapter 5 to find out how to approach someone without scaring the daylights out of that person.

✔ **Ask for the number in a friendly, nonthreatening way.** For example, instead of saying, "So, can I have your number?" try something like, "I'd really like to stay in touch. Is there a number where I can reach you?"

Giving out your phone number if you want to is certainly okay, but doing so puts you in the position of waiting for his call. The best way to offset this position of passivity is to ask for his number as well. Or you can take his and not give yours. (Of course, if you have no intention of calling him, don't ask for the number. It's just as nasty for you to ask for his number and not call as it is for him to ask for your number and then not call you.) See the section "Giving Your Phone Number" later in this chapter for advice on how to take an active role in getting together.

✔ **Offer your own number.** Offering your number is a great way to deflect suspicion by putting the proverbial ball in the other person's court. Offering rather than asking also allows you to be vulnerable first.

You can win sensitivity points by saying, "Look, I know these days, a gorgeous woman like you has to be careful, so if you would prefer, I can give you a way to get in touch with me. I'd love to court you the old-fashioned way and call you, but I don't want to make you feel uncomfortable by asking you to give me your number if you're not ready."

You want to keep your options open

In a perfect world, you could actually say, "I'm not sure I want to call you, but what the heck, give me your number just in case." Of course, a line like that isn't exactly flattering. You're probably better served by expressing an interest but giving yourself an out by saying something like this:

"Look, I'd really love to call you, but I'm . . ." (pick one):

✔ Really busy at work

✔ Traveling a lot

✔ Getting out of a relationship

✔ Covered with herpes

✔ Feeling poorly (not *poor*, which means you're in the midst of pecuniary strangulation)

✔ Scheduled for surgery

✔ About to be drafted

Advice from the animal kingdom

Yes, even at our most well-behaved, we're still animals — human animals, but animals nonetheless. As a result, the same rules that apply to the larger animal kingdom sometimes apply to us.

Lionel Tiger, an anthropology professor who has done a lot of work on animal behavior, reports that, to show that their intentions are honorable, animals bare their necks, the most vulnerable part of any animal's body. Where do you think we got the phrase "Go for the jugular (vein)"? And you thought it came from a Dracula movie or *Twilight* or *First Blood*. Nope.

Therefore, the best way to show how honorable your intentions are is to bare your neck metaphorically: In other words, to get a phone number, offer your own.

". . . so if it's okay, I'd like to take your number and call you in a month or so." (Of course, if you use the herpes line, don't expect the person to be too enthusiastic.)

When you take this approach, you're not misleading anyone or setting the other person up to hang by the phone waiting for you to call. You're simply keeping your options open without doing so at someone else's expense.

The same general rules apply to getting an e-mail address, although because it's that famous one step removed, it may seem safer to both of you. But asking for an e-mail address is an ambiguous request: Are you interested or not? Again, remember: no guts, no glory.

If you're feeling really ambivalent about asking for a phone number, you can always offer yours, saying, "Why not take my number?" Then if the other person calls, you can go out on his or her nickel and enthusiasm. After all, all of us like to be courted. Again, e-mail is safer but much murkier in terms of enthusiasm and intent.

When not to "cell"

As long as we're talking here about phones and the advantages of smart phones, cell phones, and hands-free devices, let me diverge for a moment and pound into your receptive little head some cell etiquette.

Somehow cell phones have allowed folks to forget basic manners and common sense. If the following list of times not to use cell phones doesn't seem absurdly obvious and straightforward to you, you need a basic attitude adjustment. If the list seems like silly fun and you suspect that my tongue is parked firmly in my cheek — bingo!

- At a wedding
- At a funeral
- At the altar
- On a date
- During sex
- In the shower
- When comforting someone who is crying
- When celebrating birthdays or anniversaries
- When breaking up
- When making up
- In a movie

And if you shouldn't be calling, don't even think about texting. Not ever.

You're not interested but don't want to be rude

If you're not interested, don't ask for the number or an e-mail or any other information. If you ask for a number or e-mail, the assumption is that you intend to use it. Don't spread misery like peanut butter. If you have absolutely no interest in the other person and have no intention of calling, just don't ask.

Men especially feel that not asking for a phone number is really rude, but if you can just confine yourself to "See you around," or "Nice seeing you again," or even "It was lovely meeting you," you'll spare yourself and the other person some wear and tear.

Giving Your Phone Number

You've been enjoying the conversation (or not), have been flattered by the attention (or not), and now you're in the spotlight: Your phone number has been requested, or his/her phone number has been offered. Now, whether you're wildly euphoric or praying that the floor will open and swallow you whole, you have to respond.

If someone wants to contact you, you may be tempted to give your phone number or e-mail address for these reasons:

- ✔ You want him or her to get in touch.
- ✔ You're not sure that you're interested, but you want to keep your options open.
- ✔ You wouldn't spit on him if he were on fire, but you don't want to appear rude.

The following sections help you maneuver gracefully through these scenarios.

You'd like to see the person again

If you're interested and want to stay in touch, give out your number, but also get the other person's number. If you only give your number and don't get a number in return, you're setting yourself up to hang around the phone, waiting for a call. So make a deal. Say, "I'd love for you to have my number, and I'd love to have yours as well." Exchanging numbers has the following benefits:

- ✔ You can give the other person a jingle if he/she doesn't call on your timetable.

- ✔ You don't have to be passive or nasty, just a co-equal. No more waiting around for a call, and no more fuming because you never heard from Prince or Princess Charming again.

- ✔ If the person turns out to be a bozo, you have something to fantasize about pasting on bathroom walls — "For a good time, call. . . ." (But don't do it! Paybacks can be really harsh, and putting it on Facebook is just as low rent if it's nasty.)

You're not sure whether you're interested

When you're not sure that you want the person to call, you can always say you're about to change your number because you've received too many hang-ups, the number used to belong to an escort service, or you want a cuter number.

If you decide that you want to give out your number and then, upon reflection, decide that it was a mistake, you can screen your calls. Isn't it terrific that all cells have caller ID? Plus, if it's really crucial to you, you can set different ring tones for different folks so you don't even have to glance to see who's calling. I have also heard rumors that you can finally have calls blocked on cell phones in the same way you can on land lines. If it turns out that the person is more persistent than you'd like, you can change your number or talk with your carrier about your options. Electronic stalking is illegal in most states.

Another alternative if you're not sure whether you want to give out your phone number is to get the person's number instead. Of course, doing so means you have to call the person. (See the section "Asking for a Phone Number" earlier in this chapter to find out why.)

Don't ask for a phone number as a defensive measure, as in, "I don't want you to have my number, but if I ask for yours, you'll be less intense about getting mine." Then you're just being creepy.

No way, Jose

If there is no way that you'd ever want to see this person again, don't be tempted to give out any information: graduation year from high school, e-mail address, spelling of your best friend's name, Facebook page, or number and placement of tattoos — let alone your phone number. Doing so may be easy for the short term, but it actually makes the situation more uncomfortable because you'll end up causing yourself and the other person heartache not very far down the line. Even though it's difficult, it's better not to mislead him or her or give false hope. If you're not interested, be (gently) upfront about it and say, "Listen, I'm going to be very busy," or "You're very nice, but I'm going through a tough time right now," or "I'm about to move," or "I'm joining the French foreign legion." The main point is *don't give someone your number or any other information if you'd rather eat glass and die than spend any time with this person on or off the phone.* If you don't want the person to call you, for the sake of karma and your soul, don't give him or her your number or anything else. Be firm, polite, and obscure.

Don't you dare give a wrong number (and yes, deliberately mixing up any two numbers in the sequence counts as a wrong number) or your mom's — or your best friend's or an old boyfriend's — number. Come on, this is dating, not terrorism.

Deciding whether to give out your home phone number

Many women are reluctant to give out home numbers for safety's sake and are much more willing to give out work numbers because they're not alone at work and they (generally) work during the day. Work phone numbers create their own problems, however:

- ✔ At work other people are around, which feels safer, but it's also less private.
- ✔ Many if not all businesses frown on personal calls during the workday. If you've been given or are giving out a work number, understand that the conversations have to be shorter than they would be if you were using a home number.

Of course, not all home phone numbers automatically eliminate these problems. Sharing your home phone number with roommates or family can limit the length of the calls. If the phone has extensions, you may find that you restrict the content as well because you never know who may be listening in.

Decoding girl time versus boy time

Girl time is quite different from boy time. When a guy asks for a girl's number, she assumes that means he's going to call on the way home from the party. She checks her machine twice an hour, has the phone company check to make sure the line is okay, and won't take a bath for fear she'll miss the call. If Mom calls to talk about Dad's surgery, she'll politely mention that she's expecting an important call and will call back. And she is convinced that her cell needs recharging, her server is down, or her voicemail has been compromised.

Guys, on the other hand, will almost *never* call on the way home from the party or even the next day. They think it makes them look too needy. Because nobody ever calls near a weekend for a first date, the better part of a week may pass

before a guy even thinks about calling. If he left the number at home or gets busy or gets a cold, well, it may be two weeks before he calls. By this time, the woman is just plain furious.

It doesn't have to be this way.

Guys, if you really like a woman, it's okay to call the next day. It's also okay to make a date. Just don't stay on the phone too long, and keep the patter light.

Ladies, cool your jets a bit. You've been smart enough to get his phone number, so you can wait this one out a while. If he hasn't called in a week or so and you want to give him a ring, fine. Just keep the conversation light and short and don't ask why he hasn't called.

Life-saving cells

When it comes to dating, cell phones are really lifesavers, allowing you to remain coy about home and work numbers. Giving out a home number is giving an awful lot of information to a stranger. Giving a work number may compromise you at work because when the person calls, the timing may be unfortunate due to lack of privacy, running afoul of company policy, or any one of a number of constraints. An operator or a voicemail may identify the name and/or address of your workplace, which may be more information than you want a stranger to have about you initially. Ta-da — cell phones to the rescue! Among other things, cell phones have caller ID and are mobile, thus not identifying any geographical location where you can be found. The disadvantage of a cell over a land line is you ordinarily can't block a cell number, but you know who it is before you have to answer. Also, if someone is sneaky enough to use "restricted," you can just let it ring through to voice-mail. In a worst-case stalker scenario, it may be a lot easier to change your cell phone number than your home or office phone.

As long as we're talking cell phones, just a note of caution here: If there's somebody in your life who has access to your cell phone bill, your entire life will be laid out, chapter and verse. Ma Bell has single handedly wiped out adultery as we know it with the combination of itemized bills, star (*) 69, and caller ID.

Phone number alternatives

There are a number of ways to give out a phone number without actually giving out a phone number:

- ✓ **I'm listed:** If you want the person to get in touch, make sure you've made the listing clear as it appears in the phone book. In many cases, though, directing someone to the phone book means you've given out your home address as well. You can be a bit more suave, but if your name is hard to spell, you may have blown the deal.

- ✓ **Business card:** A business card usually has a work phone number, often a fax number, a business address, and an e-mail address.

    If you don't have a business card, for very little money, you can have one printed up that gives out whatever information you want to share. (You can usually get around 500 business cards for between $15 and $25.) If you are self-employed or work at home, having a business card can make you feel a little more professional as well.

- ✓ **Home address:** Giving out a home address is a bit risky. Of course, sooner or later, if the two of you hook up, you're very likely to exchange home addresses. The question is, sooner or later? My advice is later — when you're sure this is someone you trust to behave respectfully and appropriately after he or she knows where you live. If you have even the most minor inkling that this person may surprise you by lurking on your doorstep, trust your instinct for heaven's sake, and don't give out your address.

- ✓ **E-mail:** For many folks, giving out an e-mail address is a safer alternative than giving out a phone number. Of course, you have to balance your sense of safety and your need for intimacy. I may be old-fashioned, but I think that actually hearing a voice is a nice way to begin to connect with someone. Also, e-mails are often less private than you think, and you NEVER want to use your office e-mail for personal anything because the company can almost always monitor and store it. Many a career has been scuttled on the shoals of personal e-mails that weren't nearly as private as previously assumed.

Talking Once You're on the Phone

Talking on the phone is a nice way to begin getting to know one another. It's personal without being overly intimate: You're at arm's — or, literally, at phone's — length from one another but not as far away as an e-mail.

During the first conversations, keep things short and casual. Those let's-put-the-phone-on-the-pillow-and-listen-to-each-other-breathe-as-we-fall-asleep things come much, much later. So don't worry about the sweaty palms (as long as the phone doesn't slip), don't hang up, and don't try too hard.

Never make a date with a machine. Whether it's the first date or the fiftieth, unless it's an emergency, get in touch with the person mouth-to-ear so that you know the message has been received loud and clear.

Chapter 7

Plotting the Perfect (Sorta) First Date

. . . .

In This Chapter

▶ Using some basic rules in deciding where to go

▶ Sorting out good, so-so, and bad ideas for first dates

▶ Picking the right restaurant

▶ Figuring out who pays

. . . .

*F*irst date magic . . . flowers and chocolates, pin-striped suits and off-the-shoulder dresses, cologne, waxed legs, champagne, linen tablecloths, romantic music, candlelight, violins, laughter over lobster . . .

AAARGH!

If this is how you envision a first date, add "disappointment," "ulcers," and "financial ruin" to your list, because you're setting yourself up for disaster. The ideal first date should let you get to know the other person and let the other person get to know you, without doing irreparable damage to your nervous system — or bank account or stomach lining — in the process.

Ten Rules for Planning a First Date

A first date may never be a relaxing experience (after all, no matter how down-to-earth you are, you'll still worry about the broccoli in your teeth), but it doesn't have to be ulcer material either. This section outlines the basic rules. In fact, these rules are so basic, they may sound a tad silly, but you'd be surprised how often they're disregarded, with dire consequences. So a word to the wise: To make your first date as comfortable as possible, follow the ten rules outlined here. Doing so will increase the probability that you'll have fun — not teeth-clenching, knuckle-biting, stomach-hurting agony that may (or may not) get you to either date two or heavy sedation.

Rule 1: Pick an activity that you enjoy

A first date should be something that you like to do. *Do not* pick something you hate just because you think your partner will enjoy it. Although this may be a good strategy later on, the goal during the first date is to set the tone. If you choose something you like, at least you have that in common with your date (presuming, of course, that your date accepted the invitation because he or she likes the activity, too). If your date hates the idea, hopefully he or she will say something like "I really would like to spend time with you, but I hate jazz" or "I'm allergic to Chinese food" or "I get claustrophobic (car sick or whatever) in submarines."

Picking something you enjoy has a few advantages: First, it ensures that at least one person will be having a good time. Second, it offers an insight into who you are — you know, that *honesty* thing. Third, it means that you've set the stage for something you can afford — since only a phony or a masochist or a nincompoop would break his or her own bank on a first date. Fourth, it gives you a comfortable topic about which you can dazzle.

Rule 2: Pick an activity that you can easily afford

Don't try to snow somebody on the first date by spending gobs of money. First of all, how do you keep up that type of spending? The dangers of throwing money around are that it makes you look cheap later when you scale back your spending to accommodate your budget, and you never know whether your date likes *you* or your wallet. Also consider your date's finances before suggesting an exclusive new restaurant, any formal event, dinner and dancing, or a weekend for two in the Bahamas. Even if you are footing the bill, you don't want your date to feel like she's out of your league.

I have a friend who likes to rent a limo and take first dates to the opera and then out for a fancy dinner. All this works out to a $500 first date. Then he wonders why women are always using him. Puh-leeeze. It's much better to start small and build so that your date assumes you're more invested in both of you together instead of showing off.

Rule 3: Do something that doesn't require new clothes

New clothes are often uncomfortable and can unexpectedly bunch, rip, or gap. Besides, why add the worry about spilling red wine on your new outfit to the other stress of a first date? Why worry about clothes when there are more important things to worry about, like the broccoli between your front teeth or whether your date really likes you or is just being polite. Wear your happy, easy-to-wear, good luck, appropriate-to-wear clothes. Reassure me that there is no need to point out that you are neat, clean, well–pressed, and appropriate. Beware of too sexy or too casual. Shined shoes are always a plus.

I have an aunt who says always to overdress because you'll get taken to better places and make a better impression. But if I ran the world, I'd make sure that on first dates, everyone would wear his or her oldest, most comfy clothes; women would not shave their legs; men would not buy new after-shave; and all men and women would be who they really are, right from the get-go. Obviously, I'm not in charge. As noted above: Shoes should always be shined, cuffs unfrayed, and everything neat and clean — not rigid, new, starched, and impressive.

Rule 4: Go where you can talk without getting thrown out

I know America's favorite date is a movie, but if you talk in a movie, I will personally come and haunt you. Not only is it rude to the other customers, but it puts your date in the awkward position of either siding with the people who are trying to shush you, or talking with you and getting the usher to evict you both. See the section "Good places for a first date," later in this chapter, for a list of places that are cheap and fun and where you two can chat happily away. When in doubt, take a walk. Find a street fair, check out a museum. You may even want to Google "local freebies."

Rule 5: Go to a place that's easy to get to

Long car, bus, train, and — God forbid — plane trips may be fun once you get to know one another, but for a first date, it's really risky. Although these trips have occasionally worked as a way for two people to get to know one another (at least you can talk), you run the risk of using up your tolerance for one another before you arrive at your destination, and then, boy, are you both stuck. If you'd just gotten to know each other in smaller doses, however, you may have been okay.

Rule 6: Do something that isn't competitive

Avoid arm wrestling on the first date. Although some relationships thrive on tension, it's hard to put competitive feelings in a context when you don't know each other. Even if you're not competing with each other, how you deal with someone trying to beat you while the date you're trying to impress is watching gets pretty dicey. Beating someone on a first date means that one of you feels like a winner and one like a loser. Not a cool idea.

I walk fast. For years it was my primary form of exercise, and I still use it to keep in shape. When I say fast, I mean *fast*. Often, without realizing it, I've left my companions no choice but to carry on a conversation with the back of my head. Oops. The point is that different people are comfortable with different levels of activity. Bear this in mind before you suggest a Saturday hike, in-line skating, break dancing, or bungee jumping from a hovering helicopter.

Rule 7: Pick an activity that doesn't involve a lot of alcohol

Alcohol has been, is now, and will continue to be for the foreseeable future the major drug of abuse in this country. (More Pilgrims drowned in the canals after getting drunk and falling overboard on Saturday nights than were killed by Native Americans.) Both of you are going to feel a bit nervous anyway. Why add the temptations and problems of alcohol, especially if you have to drive home?

Rule 8: Leave time to get to know each other

A date that is chock-full of activity keeps you busy, but if the purpose is a chance to get to know one another, some quiet time is a great idea. Without a bunch of distracting noise, activity, or an audience, you can talk to and get a sense of one another.

Rule 9: Do something that doesn't involve high-ticket others

High-ticket others include friends, family, exes, kids, animals, or colleagues. Audiences are fine if you're an actor giving a performance. They are tricky if you're trying *not* to perform and just *be,* which is the point of a date. If your first date involves your parents, sibs, workmates, or people who know you and love you, the date is going to feel like an audition. You don't need other people's opinions at this point. (If you don't have enough confidence in your abilities and think you *do* need the opinions of a bunch of other people, you ought not to be dating yet.) Later on, when the two of you know each other and feel a bit more solid, showing each other off and getting feedback from your friends (always a bit dicey) may be cool, but for heaven's sake, not yet.

Videotaping your date for YouTube or your Facebook page is also not a great idea. Believe it or not, I know some people who actually did this. I talk more about keeping things private in the Chapter 1 discussion of Facebook.

Also, even if the digital camera on your smart phone is brand new and fantastic, refrain from taking photos together on the first date that can get uploaded to MySpace, Facebook, Flickr, or Photobucket. You want to retain your privacy while getting to know each other. Turn your phones on vibrate, and don't use them during your date. Or — dare I suggest — turn them off. Yeah, *off*.

Rule 10: Find an activity that doesn't last more than a couple of hours

Brevity is not only the soul of wit, but it is also the essence of a good date. In *Chapter Two,* a Neil Simon play, the male lead (played by James Caan in the movie version) tells the female lead (played by Marsha Mason), after a ten-minute introduction, that he's really enjoyed their time together and thinks it's time to plan a second date. He leaves and knocks on the door. When she answers, the two begin their second date, much more relaxed.

The key is to leave 'em wanting more. If you both had a good time, you'll both eagerly anticipate date two. If one or the other of you didn't have a good time, keep in mind that one of the ways to limit the damage is to limit the time. If the date was only mildly troublesome and not prolonged agony, you may well recover and be willing to try a second date.

Exploring First Date Ideas

Some places and events lend themselves to successful first dates, and others practically scream, "What could I be thinking?!" To help you tell one from the other — would you believe that Valentine's Day is a first date no-no? — read the following sections.

If your first date is fun and relaxed, you're home free. Worst-case scenario, you may end up friends rather than potential lovers, but a casual approach decreases the probability that the two of you will be unhappy enough with each other to end up enemies.

Good places for a first date

Following are the cream of the first-date-ideas crop: All can feel wholesome and nonthreatening during the day and only slightly sexier after dark.

- **Museums:** At a museum, you get to meander through the halls, look at exhibits, and chat about anything that inspires you. It's a great place to get to know each other and to see each other's tastes in art — or whatever. Also, most museums are usually easy to get to and offer a place to eat (which may be overpriced for what you're getting but won't break the bank). A museum is relaxed, easy, and inexpensive and doesn't bump into any of the ten rules for first dates.

- **Amusement park:** Unless it's really hard to get to, going to an amusement park is usually fun and makes everybody feel young and carefree. The only real problems? Sticky fingers from cotton candy and rides that make you so queasy you'd give up your firstborn for an antacid tablet. But all in all, a good choice.

- **Walks:** You can take walks (almost) anywhere: parks, zoos, botanical gardens, and so on. It's cheap, fun, and pressure-free. Plus, you can often hold hands.

- **Street fair:** You're outside, nothing costs very much, you're around other people, and there are a lot of things to talk about.

- **An auction:** An auction is a fun date as long as you don't get carried away and you resist the temptation to bid. I actually had a great time at both a livestock auction and a farm machinery sell-off, although I did buy a cow at the former once for a guy I was seeing — but that's another story.

- **Outdoor activities in general:** Sporting events, concerts, county fairs, zoos, and picnics are great ideas for first dates. You can talk, and because you're outside, everything feels less claustrophobic. It's easy and relaxed, and figuring out what to wear usually isn't a problem.

- **Miscellaneous indoor events:** When the weather turns ugly, consider car shows, boat shows, art shows, antiques shows, planetariums, and aquariums. You can talk to each other with no worries about being shushed!

It may seem that in a big city there are more options, but an awful lot of people who live in big cities don't know how to act like tourists. Don't assume that if you are living in a small town there is nothing to do. Even if you live in a small town, my guess is that there is an obscure museum or park that you haven't been to, a historic monument, a fun and unusual event, or a local sporting tournament. You can certainly look into special exhibits at museums or art fairs. Traveling carnivals or dances work too, because what you want a first date to be is a little unusual, a little fun, but not uncomfortable. If you know everyone in town, what you may want to do is go to the next town over so you don't feel like your first date will appear in the local gazette.

There is no such thing as an area that doesn't have special events, and what you need to do is become a little bit like a detective. Look in the Friday or Saturday paper and see if there is an art festival going on, or if you live in a college town find out if there is something going on at the school. Don't assume that you've done everything that there is to do; I guarantee that with a little bit of energy and ingenuity you'll find something remarkable.

The Internet is terrific for helping you find obscure activities that label you as creative and caring from the get-go. Search "great first dates" for your local region and do some research so you have a few options to pose and discuss with your date. Depending on what the two of you already know about each other, from friends, phone conversations, Googling, or checking out social networking sites, you can tilt your choices in your date's direction — assuming that its not something you loathe (remembering rule one).

So-so ideas

The ideas in this section, although very common, aren't necessarily your best choices for a first date. Of course, they aren't your worst choices either.

- **Movies or plays:** On the not-so-good-as-a-first-date side, going to the movies or a play doesn't give you much opportunity to talk, and if your tastes differ, you may have a hard time finding a show that pleases you both. It also denotes a certain lack of imagination. On the other hand, having seen the same movie or play gives you something to talk about afterward, and, well, it *is* kinda fun sitting together in the dark worrying about whether or not to hold hands. It can also give you time to calm down a bit before you actually have to talk to or look at each other.

  Make sure your date hasn't already seen the show and doesn't loathe the genre. If you plan to go risky — horror flick, avant garde performance piece, or nude review — check with your date or save the shock technique for date four or five.

- **Dinner:** A dinner out is a classic, but as the focus of a date, there is too much potential for an upset tummy: deciding what kind of food, the potential to spill, and that old broccoli-in-the-teeth thing, for starters. If you're not the one footing the bill, figuring out what to order that's not too expensive is also a challenge. If you're going to eat, make it a side activity rather than the date itself, or try a casual approach rather than the Ritz. Any place that has headwaiters is going to be too expensive, emotionally as well as financially.

  Despite all these possible complications, dinner is still, by far, the most common first date. See the section "Doing the Restaurant Thing the Right Way," later in this chapter, for more info on planning this type of date successfully.

- **Party:** How good a party is as a first date depends on who's hosting the party and where it is. If your date will be the only person who doesn't know everyone, and you don't know your date, it's a bit tricky. My advice is to make other plans for your first date. Of course, going to a party is a great date for later on.

Places and things to avoid

Following are occasions and places you want to avoid as a first date. As a rule, these events create unrealistic expectations and involve too many other people. If it's fireworks you want, get thee to a wienie roast in a gasoline jumpsuit.

- ✔ **Wedding:** Going to a wedding as a first date violates just about every single one of the ten basic rules listed earlier. If you want to quibble about Rule 6 (Do something that isn't competitive), are you really so naïve as to think your date isn't trying to figure out how to beat you out the door when the ceremony's over? The stakes are just too high at weddings. Avoid them at all costs as a first date. In fact, because weddings are such a bad idea for a first date, I've made it the standard by which all other bad first date ideas are judged.

- ✔ **New Year's Eve party:** Oh, puh-leeeze, New Year's Eve is the scariest night of the year for a first date. New clothes, high expectations, lots of booze, high-ticket others — consider this a mini-wedding. Just about the only thing it lacks is a weeping mother-in-law, a crazy uncle who thinks the ladies' room is the coat check, or some well-meaning relative asking when the two of you plan to set the date. On second thought, it just lacks the mother-in-law.

- ✔ **Valentine's Day:** Valentine's Day has all the anxiety-producing elements of a wedding, all the overblown expectations of New Year's, *plus* the paper-Cupid-induced hope of true Romance. Valentine's Day is so potentially explosive that even couples who've been together for years approach it warily.

- ✔ **Thanksgiving dinner:** Think of how many traumas *you've* experienced at your family's Thanksgiving get-togethers: Uncle Harry getting plastered; sister Susie crying into the crystallized yams; brother George coming out; Mom burning the turkey; and cousin Jim wanting to bring the TV to the table to watch football. Even if your family doesn't behave like this (what, you're from Pluto?), it still violates Rule 9 (Don't involve high-ticket others) big time. In short, Thanksgiving is truly a family holiday — all the more reason to avoid it as a first date.

- ✔ **Beach:** Although a great date for later on, the beach isn't first date stuff: too much skin, do you or don't you apply suntan lotion, and if you do, to what and to whom? A first date on the beach also violates Rule 5 (Go to a place that's easy to get to), Rule 10 (Find an activity that doesn't last more than a couple hours), and often Rule 3 (Do something that doesn't require new clothes).

Doing the Restaurant Thing the Right Way

Going out to eat is one of the most common first date activities. But it doesn't have to be routine. To make your date a notch above ordinary, put a spin on the restaurant theme:

- ✔ **Go to a coffeehouse.** Unless you're meeting at a Starbucks and ordering two grande skim lattes and roasted pepper and goat cheese sandwiches (which is about the same price as the national debt), compared to a traditional restaurant, this is a pretty cheap date. It's the modern version of a singles bar: relaxed, casual, and no time pressure. Tapas bars are also relatively inexpensive and allow you to sample a bit of food in small portions over time; just beware the sangria. Wine bars should probably be reserved for later dates assuming neither of you has a drinking problem; they violate Rule 7 for a first date.

- ✔ **Go to an interesting restaurant.** Food is good. Good food is even better. Good, unusual food is the best and often less pricey than the usual, boring steak or fried chicken. It doesn't have to be the culinary experience of your life, but fun and interesting food (maybe ethnic, but easy on the spices) on a first date is a cool idea. I'm partial to weekend lunch and brunch dates, myself. It's relaxed, liquor's not required, there's plenty of time to get to know each other, and it's in the daytime.

- ✔ **Stick close to home:** If a coffeehouse won't suffice and unusual food makes you nervous, checking out neighborhood joints can be fun as well. Just make sure you have a general idea of both the neighborhood and various options ahead of time so you're not wandering aimlessly.

Food can be incredibly sexy and fun, as Hollywood readily attests: Rent the videos *Like Water for Chocolate, Babette's Feast, Big Night,* or even *9 1/2 Weeks* to see what I mean. (But I don't recommend watching any of these movies on a first date!)

General considerations

There are some way cool ways to enhance the enjoyment of a restaurant date. First, for any restaurant you consider, think about the following:

You're invading my space

Reconnaissance is valuable: Scout the locale to make sure that you're closer to your date than the dude at the next table. Turf counts. Like all other cultures, Americans have well-defined territorial areas:

✔ Intimate space is about 18 inches away from our heads. According to anthropologist Edward Hall, you'll let only close companions and pets into this private area for any stretch of time.

✔ Personal space is 2 to 4 feet all around us. Friends are allowed in this space, but that's it.

✔ Social space expands to about 4 to 8 feet away. Coworkers or acquaintances at a party are invited in.

✔ Public space is all areas beyond.

✔ **Noise level:** You got together so that you can get to know each other. It makes sense to be able to hear what your date has to say and talk without seriously harming your vocal chords.

✔ **Price:** Go to a place you can afford. You can't enjoy yourself if you worry about your date ordering an appetizer *and* a dessert.

✔ **Service:** You want the service to be attentive without hovering. And who wants to be rushed out the door?

✔ **Spaciousness:** Adequate space is an animal need (see the sidebar "You're invading my space" in this chapter). That's why we all feel a little uneasy in a packed elevator or an overcrowded restaurant.

✔ **Lighting:** You don't want it too dark or too light. Too dark and he can't see the great job you did on your makeup, or she won't notice that your tie matches your eyes; too light, and no matter what you did, you'll still end up looking like a delivery to the morgue.

Specific considerations

After you narrow your list of potential restaurants down to those that meet your economic and ambiance requirements, narrow the list down even more by doing the following:

✔ **Pick a place you know.** Menu familiarity reeks of confidence. You'll sound like Cary Grant if you lean over and say, "Try the duck. It's out of this world." Also, knowing a restaurant well means that you're comfortable with the service, the all-important table spacing, the lighting, the wine list, the taste, the presentation, and payment procedures. It's the way to ensure you'll have a good time. And if you're happy, your date stands a better chance of being happy, too. If you're being considerate and trying to stay on your date's turf, check out the options on your cell, check out the menu, and make a site visit; it will make you look knowledgeable and concerned. And keep in mind that giving your date several options in the 'hood is a way cool idea.

Avoid trendy new hot spots. Number one, they are often very difficult to get into, and number two, they can be very expensive — you don't want to put your MasterCard into meltdown. Number three, these days, they tend to be noisy! It isn't the type of place you want to be on a first date. Save the trendy, expensive hot spots until the two of you know each other better. Scout out some very nice quiet restaurants that will not keep you waiting. Getting drunk at the bar while waiting for your table will not make you look suave. Another added advantage of bypassing the bar wait is that you'll find yourself with money left over for your college education or braces on your eventual children's teeth. Most importantly, make it someplace quiet where you can talk.

✔ **Pick a place that knows you.** What could be cooler than a maitre d' smiling widely when you walk in or a waiter saying, "Nice to see you again!"? Better, though, is the fact that regulars usually get the best tables and most prompt service — both of which go a long way in creating a great first date.

✔ **Pick a place where your date can eat.** There's the obvious (don't take a vegetarian to a steak house) and the more subtle (if his cholesterol count is above 300, steer clear of the Wisconsin Cheese Fest). Chances are, unless you already know each other well, you won't know the intricacies of your date's dietary preferences. Simple solution: Ask ahead of time. Less simple: Keep everyone's options open by selecting neutral territory, such as a restaurant with a large menu or a coffeehouse with a small one. When in doubt, it's perfectly okay to give your date several choices and let him or her pick or offer alternatives.

Who Pays?

In deciding who pays for the date, follow this two-part rule:

✔ **The person who asks, pays.** This practice ensures that whoever does the inviting knows what things will cost and has budgeted accordingly. As the person extending the invitation, if you can't afford the activity, scale down and figure out something else to do.

✔ **The other person offers but doesn't insist on helping.** No empty gestures please. Don't offer to pay unless you can and are willing to do so. No fights to the death. It's charming to offer, but don't push it, and be willing to treat next time.

It used to be easy to figure out who paid for a date: Men paid for everything (because they were the only ones doing the asking), and women kept their mad money tucked neatly in their little velvet purses and paid for nothing. Of course, after so many eons of men feeling that they *had* to pay and women feeling that men expected something for their money, women got a bit more aggressive about paying their share (rather than being fearful that the guy would "take it out in trade"). But it gets pretty tedious figuring out what your fair share is when you order the salad and your date orders the prime rib, and you still have to figure in the tip. My solution was to play *liar's poker,* which is a game played with the serial number on dollar bills in which bluffing is allowed until you are called. Whoever lost had to pay for dinner. I got really good at offering and *really* good at liar's poker, which seemed to cover all bases. These days, it's okay for a woman to offer to pay the tip, buy the popcorn, pay for the next date, bring the picnic, pay for the gas, and so on, not only on the first date but as an ongoing statement of equality, friendliness, and generosity — unless it drives your date nuts.

Oh, and pleeeeze never use a coupon on a first date . . . it screams cheap. I love bargains, but never on a first date, thank you very much.

Part III
The Big Day: Preparation and Action

In this part . . .

No matter how many dates you've had in your life, each new D-Day is a big day. Feeling a bit nervous, excited, giddy, hopeful, and scared is par for the course. Pretending it's just another ho-hum Saturday night can be a recipe for disaster — or at least lost potential, which can feel even worse. God is in the details, so this part will help you chill out, get ready, and plan to have a faboo time. I'm gonna hold your hand; help you get dressed; and give you a last-minute checklist, a rundown of things to talk about (and things to avoid like the plague), and a bunch of quickie relaxation techniques to tide you over until you're relaxed enough and confident enough to fly solo.

Obviously, you want to have a good time, and so does your date. But it's not always a done deal. So to make good dates even better, so-so dates okay, and awful dates endurable, this part offers pointers on all kinds of dates: the good, the bad, and the holy-nelly-was-this-a-giant-mistake ugly. I'll help you minimize awkward moments from the first hello to the last-minute kiss question so that you can maximize your chances of having a wonderful time that naturally morphs into date number two and beyond. And equally importantly, I tell you when to blab from the rooftops and when to keep your own counsel, which is psychology speak for "keep your big mouth closed and stay off the computer."

Chapter 8

Getting Your Outside Ready

● ●

● ●

*T*hink of the astronauts suiting up for launch, your first day of school, the moment just before the curtain rises — we're talking the thrill of possibility, and with it, adrenaline, anticipation, action. Even though your palms get sweaty and your tummy may hurt a bit, you feel alive and ready, especially if you've practiced your landing sequence, packed your lunch, and learned your lines. If so, anticipation is a wonderful thing. It's the perfect imaginary meal you can almost taste when your growling tummy notices it's been a while since you last ate. It's the white sands of Tahiti that inspire you to see your boss about that raise, the bacon you can see sizzling when that first whiff wakes you up in the morning.

If you handle it right, anticipation is not only a motivating factor ("I think I'll call a friend for lunch, write a memo to my boss, haul myself out of bed") but also a way to enjoy an experience twice: You can enjoy it in your imagination, and you enjoy it again when it's real. That's really good news. An emotional twofer. The not-so-good news is that anticipation can backfire if you're careless with the way you handle it.

It's up to you: You can poison a neutral or even positive situation by being negative, by building up the dreaded worst-case scenario. Or you can choose to be delighted about your upcoming date and focus on doing what you can to make things click. You can choose to label your nerves "excitement" and look forward to having a great time as opposed to anticipating the doomsday date that is every horror story you've ever read, heard about, or imagined.

Once you've decided to enjoy the tingle rather than let your nerves become hives, the adrenaline-jazzed anticipatory period before your first date is the perfect time to get yourself, your mind, your body, and your soul into the "date state."

Considering cosmetic improvements

Let's talk for a moment about a rather alarming, expensive trend: the idea that somehow a person is not going to be lovable unless completely and forever wrinkle- and cellulite-free, gorgeous, and hard-bodied with an adorable upturned nose and a full head of luxuriant hair. Okay, before you accuse me of being hopelessly old-fashioned, if you have a bump on your nose that you've always hated and you're deciding that now you have the time and the money to get it fixed, so be it. It's cool with me. But if you think changing that bump on your nose is going to help you find love, forget about it. You're likely to be disappointed in not only your nose job but also the rest of your life.

Plastic surgery is no longer only for movie stars and international socialites; today people in all socioeconomic classes are undergoing cosmetic surgery. Most people getting plastic surgery make less than $30,000 a year, which I find vaguely terrifying. If you want to have plastic surgery, it's okay with me, but please don't do it to increase your chances of finding a date. If you want to think about a chemical peel to make your skin look better, no problem, but it won't make you more lovable or a better conversationalist or less angry with your mom while looking for a date. If a cosmetic surgery procedure — or Botox injections or hair replacement treatments — makes you feel better, so be it, but if your entire sense of self is based on the smoothness of your skin or more hair, we need to talk.

Before you decide that I'm the spokesperson for ugly, I'm the first to admit that confidence is attractive and that a good haircut, a flattering outfit, or gaining or losing a couple pounds can boost your confidence. Well, terrific, and I am actually in favor of a couple of new cosmetic procedures that are relatively inexpensive, noninvasive, and easily available, including those that literally put your money where your mouth is: tooth whitening or, if the enamel is hugely discolored, veneers for your teeth, both of which are becoming more popular and affordable and available. One of the top turn-offs for both men and women is bad teeth. If you haven't had those choppers looked at and cleaned recently, start with a routine checkup and cleaning; it's the cheapest, easiest, and healthiest place to start. If you're feeling that your smile isn't as vibrant as you like, teeth whitening is a relatively inexpensive and common procedure. Inner beauty is truly something that may need work and can't be bought, but giving Ma Nature a minor shove in the smile department is quite kosher.

In this chapter, referring to "date state" focuses not on cosmetic surgery before a first date (can you say overkill?) or why your wardrobe needs an immediate major overhaul, but why your teeth, hair, and pits need to be squeaky clean. It also includes advice on what and what not to wear. Time, transportation, money, and directions require the same attention before you head out. Finally, tada, a handy checklist of smart things to do during those final ten minutes before your date arrives.

Suiting Up

Because your date evaluates your appearance from the outside in, I'm starting with the least important part of you, but the most important part of an initial impression: how you look.

What you wear — your "costume" — counts. A person dressed as a clown is seen as silly; a clown dressed as a judge is taken seriously. Think about the clichés that apply: *You are what you wear. Clothes make the man. Beauty is in the eye of the beholder.* There's a reason these clichés, hackneyed as they are, stick. Though everyone hates to admit it, we're an externally-oriented society. So expecting (hoping, praying, making a deal with the dating gods) that your date will look beyond your favorite sneakers with the toe hole or that muumuu you bought at the souvenir hut in Hawaii to see the deep, spiritual, real you hidden within is spitting into the wind. In other words, you're all wet. Get over it. Looks matter . . . no matter how much you wish they didn't.

You can do something quickly and easily without working out, consulting a plastic surgeon, or spending a fortune. The place to start is with your own sense of yourself — your personal style — your statement about yourself. Yeah, you do have one. Your handwriting, laugh, and sleep position are all uniquely you. Guess what? Creating an external, aware style can be really fun. See Chapter 2 for tips on developing and revealing your own style.

To get ideas for updating your outfits or hairstyle, go ahead and search online or check out fan magazines or beauty salon catalogs or those glossy women's mags. Just keep in mind that you want to look like an improved version of you, but still you. There are online hair sites featuring literally thousands of hairstyle ideas for all ages. Some even let you upload a photo of yourself to "try" a hairstyle on yourself before committing to it. Also, you can try on new fashion trends on digital models of your body type to see if that fashion flatters your physique or figure. Aim for stylish, not fashion slave.

When you think about what you plan to wear on your date, keep the following points in mind:

  ✔ **Comfort is key.** Even if your attire makes a fabulous first impression, avoid any outfit that pinches, binds, rides up, or threatens to burst at the seams. Believe in the Law of Murphy: All these things can and will happen at the worst possible moment.

✔ **Plan to perspire.** Even the coolest cat sweats on a date. Even in winter. It's nature's way of lowering your overheated body temperature. Choose clothes that are loose in the armpits and on the back. Let air get in there and dry you out before the fabric presses to your flesh like a wet tissue. Antiperspirant is always a good investment.

✔ **Save the skin show.** Your date doesn't need to know if you're an innie or an outie just yet — unless, of course, your date is at the beach (see Chapter 7).

✔ **A date is about getting to know you, not your outfit.** Yes, what you wear is right up there with remembering to brush your teeth, but if the first thing he sees is your ostrich feather, or she has to don sunglasses to look at your Day-Glo polyester pants, your outfit may never be asked out on a second date.

✔ **Avoid "get-ups."** If your mother would dub your date outfit a "get-up" (as in, "You're going out in that get-up?"), play it safe and get up and get something else on. Moms, after all, do occasionally know best. This is no time to test the truth of the theory.

Now is the time to control your urge to splurge. I know it's tough. (My favorite four-letter word is "sale.") But beware of the 50-percent trap (if you wouldn't buy it for full price, don't buy it at half price). Ostensibly, this is the first of many dates. You don't want to rope yourself into a lifetime of revolving debt *or* watch your date's face fall after your horsemen have turned back into mice and your carriage is one big fat pumpkin again.

Dressing for real-world dates

When it actually comes time to choose an outfit, what do you put on? Well, if it were up to me, everybody would have a first date in his or her grubbiest, most comfortable clothes (grubby in terms of well-worn, not dirty). Men wouldn't shave, women's legs would remain bristly, and new clothes wouldn't even be contemplated. This non-dress code (or dress non-code) would complement the activities planned, which, if it were up to me, would be active and fun and casual. None of this fancy restaurant stuff, worrying about prices and the right fork and not dribbling and stray bits of broccoli between your teeth and a snooty waiter and tight shoes or collars or tables. But, since I'm not in charge of the universe, I promise to help you get through getting dressed for your date in the real world.

Understand that no one, not even cute little ol' me, can or should tell you exactly what to wear on a first, second, or fifth date. You already know. Just trust yourself. Use that 3-pound blob of gray matter sitting atop your neck (no, you don't have something large caught between your teeth). In other words, if you use your head — and not your credit card or your *Vogue* or your MTV or your rose-colored glasses or your mom — you'll look and feel just fine. Don't panic. I know it's hard to keep your head on straight, let alone your wardrobe pulled together, when you're prepping for a date. But if you keep the following in mind, you'll do just fine:

- ✔ **Rule 1: Preparation before, comfort during.** Worry a lot about what you're wearing and how you're smelling and looking *before* you leave the house so that you never have to waste a moment thinking about it after you've left.

- ✔ **Rule 2: There is no one right way.** Creating a look is very different from the way you would sound out a word or learn to dance or memorize French verbs. It's not like "Put your left foot here and your right foot there." Dressing yourself up to go out is a recognition of who you are, your personal style, what you want to say about yourself, how you want others to see you, and, in a way, a reflection of your unique sense of yourself. You go, guy. You go, girl. If you're thinking this is a mini exercise in Relationships 101, you go to the head of the class. You've been paying attention. Do give serious thought about how you want to look; just don't obsess about it.

A surefire way to make sure you end up in the right outfit is to think about your outfit in terms of what looks and feels good on you, how appropriate the outfit is for the activity, how your date is dressing, and so on. The following sections lead you through this examination.

What do I look good in?

A date is a time for the tried-and-true: the outfit you already know inspires everyone to ask, "Have you lost weight?" — or the male equivalent, "Have you been working out?" If you find yourself musing, "You know, I've always wanted to try spandex," immediately do the following: Drop this book, run to the bathroom, turn the faucet on cold, and shove your face beneath the icy stream. If no water is available, a gentle but firm slap on both cheeks will do. Save your experimental urges for dark, stormy nights full of lightning when you're trying to jolt a green-faced monster with a giant flat-top back to life.

BIOLOGY

First impressions count

You can visually absorb someone's appearance in two seconds. Two seconds! Talk about your once-over. That's exactly what's going to happen in the vibrating, potential-packed few moments between the time you open the door, flash those pearly whites, and say "Hi." Ba-da bing, ba-da boom. An impression has already been burned into your date's brain, so you may as well make sure it's a great one. Even if you've seen each other before, the context has changed. Now it's official. It's a date.

That two-second stare, called the *copulatory gaze,* triggers a primal reaction in the person being gawked at: advance or pull back. It's a biologically buzzed moment. Pupils are dilated, and heart rates are up. Staring too long is threatening, so take it easy. Take a look, and then look away before your date runs away.

BIOLOGY

Just an average quiz

What would you say is the average height and weight of the average American man or woman?

The average height of a man is:

a. 6'   b. 5'10"   c. 5' 9"

The average height of a woman is:

a. 5'6"   b. 5'5"   c. 5'4"

The average weight of a man is:

a. 150 pounds   b. 160 pounds   c. 170 pounds

The average weight of a woman is:

a. 120 pounds   b. 130 pounds   c. 140 pounds

Answer: C . . . for all of them.

According to the National Center for Health Statistics, the average man, between 18 and 74, is 5'9" and weighs 170 pounds; the average woman is about 5'4" (actually 5'3.7") and weighs about 140 pounds. The point is, hardly anyone looks like Brad Pitt or Halle Berry. Striving for such an image, and/or wishing your date would, too, is not only a losing battle but not much fun for either of you.

If you're not sure what you look good in, put on a potential outfit and stand in front of your mirror. Then really look at yourself, from head to toe to the back of your heels. You'll be tempted to be judgmental. Don't. This is a time for honest appraisal, not nit-picking.

If you're not good at figuring out what looks terrific and what qualifies you for arrest by the fashion police, ask a best friend to be brutally honest. (If one isn't handy on the day of the date, do this beforehand.) Friends see stuff you've been overlooking for years.

Also keep in mind:

- **Select substance over style.** Style is great, and great style is truly fabulous. Often though, the latest, latest, latest style is a tad too trendy for anyone other than the very young and very hungry. Again, go for it only if it looks good on you.

- **Pick the right color.** Yeah, I know. You guys aren't about to hold an orange scarf up to your face to tell whether you really are an "autumn" instead of a "winter." I don't blame you. Who needs the devastation of discovering you've spent your life as the wrong season? Yet, a little color savvy goes a long way. Often, it's hard to tell if a color really does look good or the salesperson was pulling your leg when she said, "Puce is you!" Once again, a trusted friend can come in handy. One quick rule: If your skin has a yellowish cast to it, you probably look best in soft browns, golds, and reds. If your skin is more pinkish, try grays, blues, and purples. When in doubt, hey, there's always basic black.

✔ **Consider the breadth and scope of the entire date,** not just the sashay to the car or to the table in the restaurant. If there's dancing after dinner, for instance, that jacket's going to come off, so you'd better make sure it isn't the cornerstone of your look (or at least that your shirt is ironed).

✔ **Choose fabrics that wear as well as you do.** Satin? Linen? Fuhgettaboutit unless you're dating a Shar-Pei who loves wrinkles.

What do I feel good in?

Comfort is crucial. You'll have enough emotional turmoil to grapple with without fussing over a shoulder pad that keeps slipping or a silk shirt that suddenly feels like a plastic bag. Here's how to feel comfortable:

✔ **Select cozy fabrics.** Cotton or velvet or any other material that feels soft against your skin is a good choice, as long as you consider both temperature and season.

✔ **Make sure that the fit is fabulous.** Take the penny test: Drop a penny on the floor, and then pick it up. If your waistband is too tight, heels too high, skirt too narrow, slacks too snug, shirt too short, or gold chains too heavy, rethink your look until you can easily scoop that penny off the floor. If your outfit doesn't pass the penny test, put it back in the closet.

✔ **Wear what you already own.** The temptation to rush out and buy the perfect outfit will be strong. Resist it. You don't want to take chances with an outfit that hasn't already proven itself at least once. "New" doesn't necessarily mean "flawless." Hems fall, button threads unravel, perspiration shows. Again, play it safe and go with what you know. Most of us have a magic shirt or a tie that has never let us down. Now's the time to trot out the oldie, goody, trusty, never fail.

Where am I going?

This point is simple but often overlooked. Ask yourself, "Did she really mean it when she said, 'We'll grab a bite to eat'?" If so, case closed: Wear a catcher's mitt. But if you're not entirely sure, there's no harm in asking, "Is this a casual affair?" — only, leave out the word "affair" so he won't get the wrong idea.

Did I pay attention to detail?

Shine your shoes. Press your collar. Check for errant threads. Rub the lipstick off your teeth. Tuck in the tag. Clean under your fingernails. Sniff for excessive aftershave or perfume. Unstuff your purse. Freshen your breath. Match your socks. Check out the rearview in a full-length mirror (don't forget the back of your hairdo). In short, pretend you're going to Sunday school and grandma's watching, and keep the following in mind:

The light fantastic

I was once on a canoe trip with a very beautiful female friend who arrived for our wilderness vacation in full makeup: foundation, powder, shadow, eye liner, lip liner, mascara — the works. From afar, she looked as gorgeous as ever. Up close, however, in the blinding glare of sunlight, she looked a bit like a Kabuki dancer. Once we got rowing and sweating and sprayed with white water, her makeup ran faster than two-dollar pantyhose.

The moral of this story? Lighting is everything. Makeup is not just makeup. You need to know how you'll be seen before you can create the best look. Before your big date, know how the setting will be lit and apply makeup accordingly. This may require a little research, but believe me, it's worth it.

If you're . . . *ahem* . . . a certain age — and worry about it — it's to your distinct advantage to file a few softly-lit hangouts in your mind for future reference. When he asks, "Where would you like to go?" you can toss off candle-lit venues with aplomb. ***Note:*** There's nothing wrong with blowing out that votive candle in the center of the table. Who needs to set a menu on fire?

- Department store dressing rooms are notoriously overlit. If you look good in there, you'll look good anywhere.

- Bathroom mirrors are typically underlit for bright, daylight makeup. If you can, apply daylight makeup close to a window flooded with natural light. If you can't, recheck your makeup once you get outside and blend in any areas that look a little thick.

- Unless you're covering surgical scars or other major skin care challenges, you should always be able to see your skin through your makeup. Foundation is designed to improve Mother Nature, not replace her.

Have I figured my date into the equation?

Dressing for your evening out is primarily about making you feel like a million bucks, but while you're at it, throw a few cents of sense your date's way. Tom Cruise aside, most short guys feel a tad shy with an Amazon woman at their side — especially if he has a bald spot previously seen only by birds or passengers in low-flying aircraft. Date night may not be the right night to break out those 4-inch heels. Grungy rock stars aside, most women prefer a guy who at least ran his fingers through his hair — unless, of course, he's been working on the car or in the garden or out in the stables and his shower is broken. (In that case, the whole date will be a wash, so you may as well reschedule.) The point is, a date is a twosome. Some consideration on your part can help make it one heck of a great time.

Think about what your date will probably wear. If you're beaching it, lose the tie. If you're going to a barbecue, don't wear something suitable for a funeral. Dress age-, place-, and weather-appropriate so that you're not likely to be taken for her father or his baby doll. This is also not the time for gender-bending outfits. When in doubt, think about both your comfort *and* your date's. Remember that it's easier to remove a tie than wish you'd worn one. Plus, overdressing makes you look elegant, and underdressing makes you look sloppy, so if you can't hit it exactly right, try a bit over rather than under. My aunt has always maintained that overdressing will get you taken to a better restaurant.

Bearing other factors in mind

Here are a few other things to keep in mind as you prepare:

- **Allergies:** Many people are sensitive to a whole lot of allergens; it's no longer just the cat or dog. One biggie: perfumes and colognes. To some, wearing a strong scent in a public setting is tantamount to lighting a giant stogie in a doctor's waiting room. Play it safe by either going *au naturel* or, before you get dressed, spritzing your scent into the air and walking into it instead of squirting perfume or cologne directly on your skin. It also doesn't hurt to apply scent right out of the shower or bath so it has time to settle a bit.

- **Sore spots:** Although you can't avoid offending all of the people all of the time, you can avoid stepping on potential toes by considering what your date may think about fur, cleavage, big hair, smoking, drinking, drugs, and photographs of Mother pinned to your lapel. Because you don't know each other at this point, pretend that you're dressing for a job interview or a meeting with a bank to consider a loan. You can make political statements on date three.

Profile of the politically correct date: A joke

DON'T

- Drink more than two glasses of red wine . . . if you drink at all.

- Eat meat (fish and chicken are okay).

- Set your hairstyle with hair spray from an aerosol can.

- Wear fur, leather, perfume, cologne, or chemicals of any kind (including sunscreen and antiperspirant).

- Discuss politics (unless you met at a rally).

- Call her "babe" or him "sir."

DO

- Ask for bottled water in the restaurant.

- Discuss whale watching and spotted owl spotting.

- Praise family values.

- Insist on splitting the check.

Thanks, but no thanks

I was once asked out by a guy I had seen at my gym, who said, "I'll swing by after I work out." Silly me. I pictured a freshly shaved and showered stud, muscles lithe, the glow of endorphins still rosy on his cheeks. What I got was a grubby, sweaty grunt who asked whether he could use my shower. The basketball grime was still on his hands as he reached out to (unsuccessfully) give me a hug.

"My shower isn't working," I said, smiling. "Why don't we postpone?" In my nightmares, I can still see the drip of perspiration dangling from the tip of his nose — bad first date karma.

Putting together an emergency repair kit

Hey, life happens. But that doesn't mean you can't be ready for any eventuality. Keep a shoebox of the following items in your closet at home so you won't be searching for them at the last minute, and keep a mini version in your car or pocketbook for a quick trip to the restroom if necessary.

- ✔ Safety pins (small, medium, and large)
- ✔ Needle and thread (white, black, and brown)
- ✔ Styptic pencil (men and women)
- ✔ Extra pair of pantyhose (women)
- ✔ Band-Aids
- ✔ Clear nail polish to stop a run in pantyhose or repair an earring, a broken acrylic nail, or loose lens in your glasses
- ✔ Hem tape
- ✔ Tweezers for that splinter, or a pesky hair that just popped up
- ✔ Antacid tablets (optional)
- ✔ Dental floss
- ✔ Breath mints

Cleanliness Is Next to Dateliness

Good hygiene is an essential element of attraction. Most people have five functioning senses, after all, and use them liberally to evaluate a potential mate. In fact, your sense of smell is intimately involved in your choice of a mate. In essence, proper hygiene is attractive. Or, at the very least, it helps you avoid being chased by wild dogs and shows that you care not only for yourself but for others as well.

When you smell an aroma, any aroma, it stimulates the olfactory nerves that, in turn, activate the limbic, or emotional, center of the brain. Heady stuff. That's why certain smells make us feel luscious (think freshly baked chocolate chip cookies) and other odors make us grimace (think freshly minted cow patties). Scientists now believe we all have an "odor print": *pheromones* that silently lure the opposite sex. These pheromones are released through natural secretions of the body. Poor hygiene, therefore, can interfere with our natural "smell" selection.

Don't sweat it

Sweat is the Stooge Factor. You know, the thing that really separates men from women. Men love the Three Stooges; women just don't get it. A few weeks ago I was loading my sweaty 'tards into a laundry bag at the gym when a cute fella walked by and started to chat with me. I cautioned him that he was standing dangerously close to the rather ripe scent of my exercise gear. He got a dreamy look on his face and said, "Yeah, smells like sweat, baby, baby." Like I said, a difference between men and women.

Oral exam

Bad breath is most often caused by:

a. Stomach acid

b. Tongue bacteria

c. Plaque between the teeth

d. Poor oral hygiene

e. Sinus problems

f. All of the above

Answer: b.

Surprised? The latest research on halitosis has found that by-products of bacteria called *volatile* *sulfur compounds* (VSC), usually found on the back surface of your tongue, cause nearly all cases of bad breath. Everyone has these little devils in their mouths. In fact, they help with digestion. But the 25 million (yes, million) men and women with chronic halitosis have an overabundance of the critters. No one knows precisely why, and on D-Day, who cares? The best temporary solution is a good tongue scraping after you brush and floss. Then contact a specialist (breath clinics are popping up in many places, often associated with dental schools) to eradicate the problem for life.

The sweat guide

Sweating, when you're nervous or hot, is natural. Excessive sweating, called *hyperhidrosis,* can be problematic. It happens when your sympathetic nervous system is out of whack — working harder than it needs to in regulating your body temperature. Sweat appears on the palms of your hands, your face, feet, and torso, as well as your pits. Remember the Albert Brooks flop sweat scene in the movie *Broadcast News?* No one wants that to happen on a date. If you sweat profusely (or even just a little), here are things that can help:

- **Antiperspirants:** The active ingredient in most antiperspirants is aluminum zirconium trichlorohydrex (or tetra-chlorohydrex) GLY. Some people do apply antiperspirant to the soles of their feet or the palms of their hands, but most use it on their armpits. The purpose of an antiperspirant is to stop sweat from reaching the skin. A deodorant, on the other hand, is used to mask perspiration odors.

- **Powders:** Brushed on the hands and feet, talc, cornstarch, and baking soda–based powders absorb perspiration as it reaches the surface of your skin.

- **Relaxation:** Particularly before a big date, sweat may be more of an emotional response to stress than a physical problem with your armpits or hands or forehead. Take several deep breaths and try to chill out. *Square breathing* — inhaling to the count of four, holding to the count of four, exhaling to the count of four, and holding to the count of four — when practiced and repeated can do wonders at calming the mind as well as the body and soothing your sweat glands.

- **Surgery:** In severe cases of sweating, surgery is possible to remove *axillary* sweat glands, or the sweat glands under the arms — but don't try this at home.

Men think sweat is sexy; women think it's fairly disgusting. Maybe sweat reminds men of all the sexy ways they can get sweaty, and women get embarrassed by the same thoughts. We don't have to convince one another, but guys beware: Women find stale sweat smelly and quite uncool. Got it? Good.

Blotting papers, which you can buy in many cosmetic departments, are handy, inexpensive makeup aids to absorb facial oil so you don't have to re-powder or wash your face and reapply makeup. They also work on sweaty hands. If you don't happen to have them with you, not to worry. In most public bathrooms, those paper toilet seat covers work just beautifully. (Please use them *before* you put them on the toilet seat.)

Blotting papers work for you, too!

Hair apparent

At one time, our whole bodies were covered in hair. Hair, once merely a protection against the harsh elements of nature, is now symbolic of everything from virility to athletic prowess to financial status to sexuality to sensuality to youth to creativity to gang affiliation. Amazing how a mass of dead protein cells can have an emotional impact on the mating ritual we call a date. If your hair looks great, you feel great. If it resembles road kill, you'll feel just about as flat and lifeless.

Women: One way to tell that you're not ready to go all the way is if you don't shave your legs before a big date. Men: One way to tell that you're not ready to make out with a woman is if you don't shave your stubble.

Don't get a haircut on the day of the date. Men always have a harsh white scalp line on the backs of their necks, and women can't stop staring at their hair until they've lived with it a day or two. Getting your hair done is a different story. If it's a big date (wedding, formal dinner at the White House) a professional 'do will do quite nicely. If it's a bit more casual event, think clean, neat, comfy, and flattering, and leave the hairspray or elaborate updo for later.

Women lose about as much hair as men do — they just lose it all over their heads instead of in the more obvious pattern of male baldness.

Let your hair dictate the style, not the other way around. Go, literally, with its flow instead of your own. Your hair will fall into its own place by the end of the evening anyway, so why fight it?

D-day hygiene checklist

To make sure you covered all the bases, check out this D-day hygiene checklist:

- ❑ Shower.
- ❑ Wash your hair.
- ❑ Wash your ears (inside, out, and behind).
- ❑ Brush and floss.
- ❑ Clip or file your nails (don't forget your toenails — hey, you never know).
- ❑ Shave (face, legs, armpits). *Note:* "Hairless" is not a synonym for "clean." Personal preference rules.
- ❑ Pluck. (Guys: pay special attention to the bridge of your nose and earlobes; women: don't skip the chinny chin chin.)
- ❑ Apply deodorant (go for the gold; use an antiperspirant).
- ❑ Wear clean underwear (Mom was right again).
- ❑ Wear freshly laundered clothes.

Taking Care of Business: Practical Details before You Leave Home

Make sure you take care of these four essential areas in advance: time, transportation, money, and directions.

Time

Most people have a thing about time. Some people, like me, are always early and hate being kept waiting. Tardiness can feel really insulting. (I've always been prompt, but being a broadcaster makes me especially careful. If you're a minute late, you can lose your job. The "on air" light waits for no one.) Some people always keep you waiting as a sign of power. They feel important when they make people wait for them. What's really important, though, especially in the beginning of a relationship, is to show consideration for each other and be on time. It lowers the adrenaline and anxiety in an already tense situation.

For those of you who are always late, remind yourself that you're late for your mom or your little brother because you can be. You know they'll put up with it. You're probably not late for your boss, because she won't put up with it and will can you. Ask yourself whether you're using time as a way of arm-wrestling for attention. If so, figure out a better way to get attention.

Promptness is the courtesy of kings, and isn't that how we all want to be treated?

I know it's considered cool to keep your escort waiting downstairs for your descent, but think about it: Is it any more acceptable for you to keep him waiting than for him to keep you on ice? It's rude and can really throw plans and stomachs into turmoil.

Time on my side

I once had a business associate who taught me an incredibly powerful lesson. (She was 6'2", which may have had something to do with her willingness to assert herself.) I took a phone message for her one evening from someone who said he was going to be late. The next day, I asked her whether they had hooked up. She said no, he was too late. She told me that she would wait 15 minutes for anyone, but 20 minutes for no one. Her reasoning was that after 20 minutes, she was so irritated that she was unfit company. Hmm, I thought. I think she has something there. Apparently, so did everyone else. Folks were always on time for her. And once I share this story with tardy friends, it definitely lessens my waiting time. Which is exactly the way I want it.

If you want to make sure you're on time, try these techniques:

- **If you're not sure where you're going, plan a dry run the day before.** Getting lost will make you late and nervous.

- **If you always tend to be late, give yourself an extra half hour to get ready.** This is a great idea even if you're not dating!

- **Decide to be on time.** Clocks are simple to read if you actually look at them.

- **Don't overbook.** If you can't easily make it to the cleaners on your way home from work so that you have enough time to walk the dog before you shower, shampoo, shave, and blow-dry your hair, make a later date or get a cat.

For those of us who treat wasting time as a cardinal sin, grab a paperback or a Sudoku or crossword puzzle and keep it at the ready, so you can be on time or even early without feeling like you've wasted precious moments.

Transportation

No, you don't have to pick your date up in a stretch limo to be impressive. What you do need to do is gas up and clean out your car (especially if you still smoke). Empty the ashtray, wipe down the dash, and pick up the lipstick that rolls to the front every time you hit the brakes. Use all five senses. If your auto smells like a locker room, spritz air freshener after you clean up. If it looks like you pass through a fast food drive-thru each time you hit the road, vacuum and scan for shriveled French fries and errant ketchup packs in the crevices beside your seat.

Unless you want your date to think you moonlight as a cab driver, take that dangling air freshener (and anything else that dangles above your dash) off the rearview mirror.

Many city folk, some youngsters, and future billionaires who'd rather spend time in front of a computer screen than behind the wheel don't have a car. If you're in that category, you can do the following:

- Have a (clean, undented) cab waiting.

- Plan to meet at the date destination.

- Rent a car.

- Borrow a car.

- Go somewhere within walking distance.

- Hire a car service for the night.

- Okay, impress your date with a stretch limo (but not on a first date).

There's no shame to having no wheels. Where a reprimand creeps in, however, is when the "autoless" treat the "auto-ed" like chauffeurs. Don't go there. Most importantly, don't make your date go there to pick you up.

Money

The time to swing by the ATM is the day before your date. Nothing kills the illusion of a together, take-charge person faster than fumbling with your PIN while your date waits in the car.

If you ask, you pay. So be sure to do the following:

- **Stash plenty of cash.** If you can't afford where you're going, go someplace else.

- **Don't assume the place you're going takes credit cards.** If you don't know (meaning you haven't called in advance to make sure), bring enough cash to cover the most expensive item on the menu or at the venue. Or better, call in advance to both the place and your credit card customer service to make sure that your card will be accepted there (or anywhere).

- **Have a few dollar bills handy for tipping valets, and so on.** For a rough estimate on how much you'll need for tips, use Table 8-1 as a guide.

Table 8-1	Tipping Guide
Service	*Amount of Tip*
Waiters/waitresses	15 to 20 percent of total bill
Cab drivers	15 to 20 percent of fare (but never less than $1)
Valet parkers	$2
Coat check	$1 per coat
Restroom attendant	$1

Directions

Take a deep breath, guys. I'm not going to suggest that you ask for directions. But what I will say to both men and women is this: Know where you're going and the best way to get there *before* you pick up your date. In addition, know how to navigate the location once you arrive: Know where to park the car, where the front door is, and (if you really want to impress your date) where the restrooms are. Beware of an over-reliance on Google or GPS. I ended up nearly missing a wedding by following less than groovy directions I downloaded from Google, and I've been misled my share of times by the GPS lady.

I know you would never *not* know where you're going, but heaven forbid you get lost and have to look at a map. Until you know each other really well, beware these seven words: "A map is in the glove compartment." This seemingly innocent statement sends shivers of fear through otherwise normal people. *Orient the map* may mean "find China" to one of you and "get out the compass and find true north" to the other. One person reading a map while the other is driving in foreign territory is asking for trouble: One of you helplessly watches highway exits whiz by while the other frantically searches for the name of the city you're in. If (heaven forbid) you must consult a map, do you *and* your date a favor and pull over, pull the map out, and leave the radio on something soothing. Never, even when you do know one another really well, utter these nine words: "Let's find a gas station and ask for directions."

One Final Checklist

Pilots have a checklist they consult so nothing ever crashes — not a bad metaphor for dating. The best way to appear casual and relaxed is to have done your homework. The Boy Scouts are right: Be prepared. Preparation creates calm and security. There's nothing like knowing you have it all under control and the bases are covered. Conversely, what's more anxiety producing than being caught short? Besides, preparation is the realm of grown-ups. Only little kiddies frantically dash around at the last minute trying to tie up loose ends. To not only appear grown-up but to be way cool:

✔ Know where you're going.

✔ Know how to get there.

✔ Make sure you have enough gas.

✔ Know how much (more or less) things are going to cost.

✔ Make sure you have enough money.

✔ Make sure you have $20 tucked somewhere for emergencies.

✔ Make sure your watch is working.

✔ Check the following:

- Breath
- Teeth
- Wallet
- Condom (always be prepared!)
- Pits
- Wardrobe
- Babysitter (when appropriate)

- Curfew (when appropriate)

- Calendar (make sure you've got the right day, date, and time)

- Date's phone number (for emergency traffic snarls, lost directions, and so on)

- Date's address

- Tickets (for time and date)

- Credit card and/or bank balance (no embarrassing surprises needed)

Fellas, if you want to win a huge number of points, make sure you always have two clean, ironed handkerchiefs on hand. You can buy them very cheaply at street fairs or discount stores. Keep a bunch around because nothing will stun a woman more than offering her a clean, white, pressed, unscented handkerchief when she gets something in her eye or when she's crying at a movie. You instantly become the man. Tissues will not work.

Ten Minutes to Lift-Off

The final ten minutes while you wait for your date can resemble either a tornado or the calm eye of a hurricane. It's up to you. Again, advance planning is the significant factor. Table 8-2 shows you how to gracefully straddle the fine line between getting ready and being ready in ten minutes flat.

Table 8-2	Countdown to Date Time
Time Remaining	*What to Do*
10 minutes	Scan your reflection in a full-length mirror. Check for hanging threads, lint, and cat hair. ***Note:*** If you see a thread dangling from a button, don't pull the thread. It'll fall off as sure as leaves vacate trees in autumn. Instead, wrap the thread around the button and make a mental note to sew it on before date two.
	Important: Don't panic if a button, hem, seam, or anything else lets loose. See the section "Putting together an emergency repair kit," earlier in this chapter.
9 minutes	Use the restroom. If you don't have to go now, you probably will in ten minutes, so give it a shot.

Time Remaining	What to Do
8 minutes	Double-check your purse or wallet. Make sure you have your driver's license, cash, credit cards, lipstick, tissues, keys, and breath mints. Stash your purse near the door and your wallet near your heart.
7 minutes	Give your shoes a quick buff with a shoe shine brush or soft cloth (not the back of your pants — that's for emergencies only).
6 minutes	If you're going to wear an overcoat or jacket, take it out of the closet and drape it over a chair near the door. It's rarely wise to let a date see behind any closed doors until you at least know the person's middle name.
5 minutes	Grab a hand mirror and check out the back of your head. Make sure your hair looks as good going as coming.
4 minutes	Quick tooth check. Lipstick? Dried spittle in the corners of your mouth? Parsley? Chocolate? Take care of it immediately.
3 minutes	Quick breath check. Because no one can smell his or her own bad breath, play it safe and pop one of those breath mints you've stashed in your purse or pocket.
2 minutes	Deep breathing. Shut your eyes, inhale, hold, blow it out through your minty-fresh mouth. Repeat for the full minute.
1 minute	Guided imagery. Close your eyes again and picture a calm person answering the door with an easy, inviting smile. (You can find more details about controlling your stress in Chapter 9.)

Now, the only thing left between you and your successful date is the door. But before the door opens, take a few moments to open an interior door to yourself, explained in Chapter 9.

Chapter 9

Getting Your Inside Ready

*Y*ou know that delicious feeling when you're with someone who knows you, has seen all those ugly warts, and loves you, not in spite of but because of the *real* you? Like your Mom or your best bud or your Great Uncle Louie who swallows you in a giant bear hug and makes you feel special. When you're with them, the real you shines so brilliantly, it's blinding. You're insightful and charming and intuitive and unbelievably profound. Completely at ease.

That's how I want you to feel on a first date.

Yeah, right. And I might as well ask you to memorize *War and Peace* so that you have something literary to talk about! I know it sounds like a trip to fantasyland to imagine you could actually be so cool, calm, and collected that your date would see the real you from the first hello, but that's exactly what I'm going to explain how to do in this chapter. Relax, it's simple — not easy, but simple. Realistically, it's unlikely that anybody would ever feel that secure. But what to be sure *not* to do is to offer a brittle, unrealistic, misleading picture of who you are, and that's what panic is likely to do for you.

Understanding the Psychology of Stress

In previous chapters, I discuss the physiology of stress: how your body shifts into the fight-or-flight mode and pumps you up with adrenaline when you face a tense situation. Later in this chapter, I give you step-by-step instructions on how to calm those heart-racing, stomach-churning, mouth-drying, palm-sweating symptoms. Now, though, I want you to explore the other side — the psychology of stress.

Stress is your system's response to being overtaxed by anxiety due to excess fear, drink, sun, food, work, or even fun — too much of anything, even good stuff, stretches the boundaries. Stress is a spring that's wound too tightly. It's your body's equivalent of a flashing yellow light, a Caution sign, or a Slippery when Wet warning.

When you're just getting to know someone, your senses rally all their resources to help you evaluate whether this human being is a friend or foe. Intuition, past experiences, present observations, your ability to trust — they all come into play and keep cooking as new "cues" come your way. Until you've had enough positive cues to convince you that — *whew!* — this person is okay (he or she isn't going to hurt me, humiliate me, or leave me holding the check), you're going to feel a tad stressed, and the yellow light continues to flash, meaning you're not ready to let your guard down just yet.

You can reduce your anxiety by understanding that stress is a natural and useful response to an unknown and potentially scary situation. Instead of dismissing your stress, you can leave yourself on guard and then, as you feel more confident, allow less and less of a barrier between the two of you, which is the whole point of dating. It's okay to leave this wall of protection in place for a while, while you peek around to see what's on the other side.

The stress wall

A stress wall is a barrier most people build to keep strangers from getting too close too soon. It keeps others at arm's length. Like small talk, the walls we construct to protect ourselves have gotten a bum rap. When built properly (out of movable and removable building blocks rather than cement), emotional walls serve a very handy purpose. They keep dashing, yet deadly, Attila the Huns from jabbing a spear into the center of your heart, or nine-headed Hydras from swimming across your emotional moat and slithering into your life. The notion that instant vulnerability is a desirable trait is dangerous, indeed. After all, we're not in Eden anymore.

What I'm trying to get at is the sense that some feelings of stress are a normal and essential part of being alive, and — dare I say it? — of staying alive. Dating, by its very nature, is one big, fat unknown. It's okay to feel a bit of trepidation. It's good to drive cautiously with your eyes on the road and your hands at "ten and two" on the steering wheel. What's not productive, however, is to work yourself into a tizzy because you're suddenly convinced a serial killer must lurk in the soul of anyone who would date you or that a vengeful psychopath in an 18-wheeler is about to cross the median and obliterate you.

The goal of this section is to show you how to manage your stress and make it work for you, not wear you out. First, ask yourself the following questions:

Stress history

I'll tell you one of my secrets as a psychologist: I'm trained to evaluate patterns of behavior more than single incidents. You can always tell more about a person by examining what they do repeatedly than by holding a magnifying glass up to one mistake or one incredibly romantic moment. Unless this is your first date ever (in which case you can look at your behavior in other stressful situations like final exams, sports tryouts, school play auditions, and so on), think back to other first dates you've known. Did you feel the same way? Act in a similar manner? Call everyone in your address book and obsess for days? My guess is the answer is yes. And there's a very simple explanation why.

When stressed, we *regress,* which means that we revert to an earlier form of behavior that's familiar and comfy. It's why kids become unpotty-trained when they get a new sib, or why most of us become childlike when we get sick. Often, you return to the way you behaved with your family when you were growing up. This doesn't mean the circumstances were always good, just familiar. Remember that old joke about the man who wouldn't stop banging his head against the wall? When asked why, he responded, "It's the only thing I know how to do really well, and it feels really good when I stop."

We all learned really well how to respond to stress. This does not mean we all respond really well.

Think back to the morning of one of your childhood family vacations. Or just before Thanksgiving dinner at your house. Or watching your parents get ready to go out. Pick the scenario that best describes the scene:

✔ **Serenity reigns.** The bags were packed the day before and are lined up at the front door. The kids are lined up, too, ready to march single-file into the station wagon. Or, the table was set the night before. Roasted turkey smells fill the calm air. Your mom relaxes on the couch watching her kids play tiddlywinks. Or, the babysitter is early, Mom is dressed and waiting, Dad has the directions in hand and made the reservation weeks ago and is always so efficient Mom never once has to ask him, "Did ya remember to . . .?"

✔ **Chaos reigns.** You're riffling through the pile of dirty laundry in the corner of your bedroom searching for your favorite T-shirt to stuff into your suitcase. Dad keeps yelling, "If you don't get into the car now, we're leaving without you." Or, you're polishing silver as the doorbell rings, the kitchen looks like Hurricane Andrew blew through, and your mother vows, "Next year, Thanksgiving is at Grandma's!" Or, Dad is yelling at Mom, who's been in the bathroom for the past 45 minutes, "If you don't get in the car now, I'm leaving without you!" When Mom is finally ready, she asks your dad if he has the address of where they're going, and he says, "I thought you had it."

If you picked the second scenario, your family is like almost everyone's family. If you picked the first, your parents were probably hatched from an alien pod. In most families, chaos is a part of all big events, at least to some degree. Your family life was the school in which you learned how things are "supposed" to be before a big event in your life right now.

✔ Was I sober and of sound mind when the date was originally arranged?

✔ Have I spoken to this person since the date was made?

✔ Is excitement buried beneath my feelings of stress (as opposed to dread)?

✔ Is this someone I would unhesitatingly introduce to my mother?

If all or most of your answers are "yes," your stress wall will probably start lowering a bit as soon as your date laughs at your first joke.

Creating chaos

If your family life was a roller coaster ride (see the sidebar "Stress history"), you're probably feeling the same sort of thrill/terror right now as you get ready for your date to begin. You're likely running a teeny bit late, you're not totally sure what you're going to wear, and you *think* you know where you're going. What you're doing, in essence, is re-creating the same chaos you experienced as a child because that's familiar. In this time of stress, you're regressing to the comfortable days when, even though your family life was nutty, you knew your way around.

I can hear you now: "Just a minute, Dr. Joy . . . I'm running late because my boss called me into her office just as I was leaving. I haven't settled on an outfit because I wasn't sure what the weather would be. And for heaven's sake, I'm a grown-up. I don't need to pin the directions to my sleeve — I'm pretty sure I know where I'm going!"

All fine and accurate, but irrelevant. They're cool excuses, but excuses nonetheless.

You don't have to do this anymore. You don't have to replay your old family scenes in your current life. You can tell your boss you have an appointment, you can wear a jacket if the weather's cold, you can drive with confidence because you know where you're going. You can feel cool, calm, and collected before a date. It's a choice you can make a little more upfront so that you can sweat a little less later. Your choice: cool short-term or cool long-term. (Hint: Always go for the long-term — it lasts longer.) If you want to never let 'em see you sweat, sweat when they're not around. Nothing comes easily to everyone. Trust me on this.

Easing Your Mind

Stress is overtaxing the system — in this case, a physical response to an emotional state. One way to minimize the physical symptoms (discomfort, sweaty palms, rapid heartbeat, anxiety, queasy stomach) is to ease your mind, and your body will follow suit. Dealing with your emotions, fears, and worries is probably your best defense against freaking — you know, that state in which even the smallest inconvenience or most insignificant problem can send you over the edge.

COOL IDEA

Stress busters

Here are some cool gadgets and gizmos on the market that can help chill you out before a date or anytime you need to kick back a bit:

- ✔ Rain chimes (the sound of falling rain)
- ✔ Aromatherapy pendants
- ✔ Relaxease glasses (calming flickering lights)
- ✔ Herbal pillows
- ✔ Tub Tea (giant herbal tea bags for the bath)
- ✔ Meditation CDs and MP3 recordings
- ✔ Hypnosis recordings

- ✔ Electric foot massager
- ✔ Flexaball (giant ball on which you roll around)
- ✔ Indoor fountains
- ✔ Shower massagers
- ✔ Video bubble wrap, or even the real stuff (my personal fave)

All this great stuff is widely available in New Age stores, in catalogs such as Stress Less 800-555-3783 (www.stress-less.com), or at www.drjoy.com.

Mind over what's-the-matter

Stress can snowball. If you're not careful, it's easily an avalanche. If one thing goes wrong when you've let yourself become really tense, you're suddenly tossing your hands up in the air and ready to forfeit the whole game. Don't go there. Instead, it's time for a reality check. Ask yourself the following questions:

- ✔ **What do I really feel?** Have I jammed a couple of unrelated memories and fears together to make a stress sandwich? Stop and ask yourself what's the worst that could possibly happen. Believe it or not, allowing your fear to be specific rather than abstract, putting a face on your fear as it were, can really help because doing so defines, and then lessens, the fear. The bogeyman thrives in the dark.

- ✔ **Are my nerves talking, or am I?** How many times have you tripped over your tongue or your good manners and said to yourself, "I can't believe I just said that!" If it should happen to you on your date (and it happens to everyone), you always have the option to 'fess up right away. Apologize. Tell your date you were momentarily possessed. Just don't let one faux pas fester into an ugly, giant, oozing ball of stress.

- ✔ **Am I trying to make sure my date doesn't get too close?** Intimacy is a scary thing. If you find yourself running for the dugout before the seventh-inning stretch, get back in the game and see how it ends up.

✔ **Is this just old family baggage I'm keeping alive?** If you notice that you seem to be falling back on tired old patterns left over from childhood to make you feel comfortable, give yourself a good talking to. Take a deep breath and tell yourself you're safe. It's okay to feel a little afraid. Don't worry — you'll hold your hand every step of the way.

Looking at every dater's fears

Everyone who dates feels anxiety or stress sooner or later (usually sooner). After all, dating isn't meant to be boring. In earlier sections, I explain the source of stress and give you techniques for coping with it. In this section, I identify the fears experienced by anyone who has dallied in the dating world so that you'll know you're not the only one beset by insecurities and worries. Then I give some tips for dealing with these fears.

✔ **I'll say the wrong thing.** If you worry that you'll say, "I see," to someone with really bad vision or, "I'm in a really foul mood," to someone who looks like a duck, or make a Freudian slip or burp or blurt out the wrong name when addressing your date, join the club. It happens all the time. Just take a deep breath, apologize *once,* and explain that you're nervous.

✔ **I'll do the wrong thing.** You set your menu on fire by the votive candle or swallow down the wrong pipe and spend the next five minutes choking, gasping, and wiping your eyes; ask an usher for a program only to discover she's really another audience member who, for some reason, thought wearing a black-collared red vest to a play would be a good idea; or mispronounce the name of something on the menu. Everybody periodically makes mistakes — and sometimes very silly ones. So why obsess about it? Relax. You're human. If your date is cool about it, it can become part of your lore; if not, aren't you glad you found out now?

✔ **Broccoli will get stuck in my front teeth.** You could avoid smiling all evening just in case, but what's the fun in that? Run your tongue over your teeth occasionally, check the mirror in the restroom, or don't order anything green. And relax. Better to take your chances with stuck broccoli rather than fidget all evening, unless you're dating a broccoli bigot. And if you're lucky enough to have a date who does that running-a-finger-over-the–teeth thing to demonstrate your green faux pas, marry 'em. That kind of honesty and caring is hard to come by.

✔ **I'll get an erection.** Most women won't notice, and if your date does, she'll likely be flattered. Don't try spilling a glass of water on yourself as a distraction.

✔ **I'll get my period.** Only if you wear white — just kidding. The point is, nerves rev the system. It's natural and normal. Carry change or protection and don't sweat it. If you're worried, wear a panty liner just in case.

✔ **I'll hate my date.** You're going out because you hope to have a nice time and good company. But what happens if your date turns out to be a huge boor, intolerably arrogant, or — *eek!* — the spawn of Satan. You remember that it's only one night and see Chapter 12 to find out how to handle this situation.

✔ **My date will hate me.** As charming and warm and funny and wonderful as you are, you're occasionally going to stumble across a few people who just don't like you. As hard as it may be to imagine, that's life. If you want tips on extricating yourself from this situation with the minimum of pain, skip to Chapter 12 as well. All options are covered.

Regardless of what your fear is, try to put it in perspective and then put it behind you. Even the most embarrassing blunders are seldom fatal. Plus, they make great stories later.

Relaxing into your sweet self

Just before your date begins, I want you to try the following relaxation technique to make sure your body and mind are in a relaxed state. Later, as a sort of "booster shot" during your date, I want you to periodically do a relaxation "spot check." (It's okay to go to the restroom to relax.) You may want to scribble a few of these steps on a piece of paper to tuck into your pocket or purse.

If the right outfit makes you look like a million bucks, what does the wrong outfit make you look like?

I have a friend who went to a seafood restaurant wearing an outfit that, unfortunately, was nearly indistinguishable from the uniforms that the waitresses were wearing. On her way back from the restroom, she was stopped by an elderly couple who wanted more tartar sauce, another guy who wanted lemon for his tea, and so on. By the time she made it back to her table, she had handed out condiments to nearly half the people in the restaurant. Her date thought she'd taken a powder and couldn't understand why everyone tried to tip her as they left the restaurant.

---

1. **Check your breathing.**

   Look down. Is your stomach expanding with every breath? If not, stop worrying about your waistline and breathe deeply.

2. **Relax your shoulders.**

   Do they look more like earrings than shoulders? Lower those babies! While you're at it, gently swivel your neck in a figure eight.

3. **Look at your hands.**

   If you have fingernail marks in the palms of your hands, you're a little too tense. Lay your hands flat on your knees (you can do this under the table, and no one will be the wiser) and stretch your fingers and your palms.

4. **Check your face.**

   Particularly if you've been smiling nonstop, your face can freeze into an uptight mask. Open your eyes and mouth as wide as you can. Hold. Release. ***Note:*** Don't try this at the table in the restaurant or in the front row of the play. After your date is underway, excuse yourself to the privacy of the restroom stall.

5. **Check your mind.**

   After your date is in full swing, ask yourself whether you are "scoring" the evening. You know, one point for you when your date laughs at a joke, one point for your date each time his or her fingertips brush your arm. If so, cut it out! Bring your mind back to the present moment, stop overseeing the project, and, hey, enjoy yourself! Stay in the moment and experience.

Relaxing Your Body

The great thing about emotional stress is this: Because your self is unconsciously telling your body how to respond, it can consciously tell your body to cut it out. After you decide you want to connect to a quieter, calmer, more centered part of yourself, peace of mind is only a few minutes away. In the previous section, I walked you through a quick and easy relaxation technique to use just before your date begins in those crucial last moments before liftoff — or even in the midst of it. Here, I show you some more detailed relaxation techniques to use in the minutes, hours, or days leading up to your date — addressing more of the chronic than the acute phase of the jitters.

Step 1: Heavy breathing

Breath is, quite literally, the essence of life. Deep breathing is the essence of relaxation. Breathing is the cornerstone of almost all meditation. It's *chi* in

Eastern philosophy. Energy. Life force. If you watch a pitcher on the mound, a gymnast before she leaps onto the balance beam, or a professional bowler as he stands, ball in both hands, staring down the pins, they all do the same thing: take a deep breath and blow it out. Which is what I want you to do right now.

On the day of your date, before you get dressed, block out ten minutes for your peace of mind. Put your phone on vibrate or turn the little dickens off, whether cell or landline. Let your voicemail take a message. There's nothing that can't wait ten minutes — even if it turns out your date was lost and calling from a gas station — especially if it's your mom calling to tell you she wants (or doesn't want) grandchildren. They can call you back. For now, here's what to do:

1. **Pick a quiet room that isn't too dark, too light, too hot, or too cold.**

2. **Select a comfortable chair, one that supports your back, arms, and legs.**

3. **Make sure your clothes are comfortable.**

   Take off your shoes. Wiggle your toes. Remove your belt. Loosen your collar.

4. **Sit down and let your eyes fall closed.**

5. **If random thoughts enter your consciousness, allow them to gently float away like a fluffy cloud.**

6. **Tune in to your body.**

   Listen to your heart pumping, your breath inflating and deflating your lungs, and the blood pulsing in your ears.

7. **Feel very heavy in the chair.**

8. **Breathe deeply in through your nose for a count of four, hold for a count of four, and exhale for a count of four out through your mouth. Then hold for two counts of four.**

9. **Begin again. Repeat four times.**

Now, you're ready to move on to a deeper phase of relaxation.

Step 2: Progressive relaxation

You can banish stress from your system in several ways, including exercise, meditation, Tai Chi, Pilates, and Yoga. But one of the quickest and most effective ways is a technique called *progressive relaxation*. It focuses on each muscle group, from your toes to your head, and releases tension. I will walk you through the process, step by step. Still seated in your comfortable chair, with your eyes gently closed, start with the tips of your toes. Repeat each muscle group sequence twice.

The sounds of the universe

Since I originally wrote this book, both Yoga and Pilates have become even more popular. I practiced Yoga years ago and then switched to Pilates, which is really good for strengthening your core and square breathing. I now combine the two and freely integrate the mind-body connection not only in my personal life but on the air as well. I have been describing square breathing as a relaxation tool for years, as well as dabbling with Yoga at various times in my life. My switch to Pilates was partially because, while I'm not particularly flexible, I'm strong and have a lot of endurance, so Yoga is hard, and Pilates is easier for my body type. After September 11, 2001, when I was at the World Trade Center for five and a half weeks helping people, I really needed a place to go to regain my equilibrium. I found a nearby Yoga retreat and spent a week doing Yoga for eight hours a day. The Yoga not only grounded me and made me able to take a deep cleansing breath and deal with the universe in a much calmer way but also really reaffirmed my commitment to the mind-body continuum.

Deciding to try either Yoga or Pilates right before a date for the first time is unlikely to have much of a calming effect. But if you decide to incorporate either technique in your life on a long-term, regular basis, you may find that you're better able to center your self before any stressful event. You'll discover breathing techniques and ways to focus, which are helpful when you're dating, asking your boss for a raise, or trying to sleep at night. Several studies have found that women who practice Yoga are more content with their bodies regardless of their weight, so women, maybe this is one of those things to get your inside matching your outside.

You can find many varieties of Yoga, an ancient discipline that was practiced in both India and China. Its migration to the New World, specifically the United States, has resulted in a transmogrification into a regular buffet of possibilities.

Depending on your personality, strength, body type, and commitment there are myriad possibilities. You can find a number of demonstration video clips at YouTube of each type of Yoga. Watching a few minutes of a style online is like comparison shopping for which one best suits your needs now. Make sure that you opt for one that will reduce your stress level — not increase it by making you competitive or nervous. The term *Yoga* can include tapes, studios, practices, gear, mats, wardrobe, props, and Christy Turlington. In alphabetical order, here's a list of options:

✔ **Anusara Yoga:** An aerobic Yoga that stresses alignment while increasing the heart rate. It's a lot faster paced than traditional Yoga but less of a cardiovascular workout than a step or high-impact class. Purists hate it, but if you're looking to work up a bit more of a sweat, give Anusara a try.

✔ **Ashtanga Yoga:** A more fundamental Yoga that utilizes a sequence of postures involving synchronized breathing, so you basically have one breath to do any particular movement. If you've done Yoga before and you're looking for a challenge, this may be your particular cup of tea.

✔ **Bikrum Yoga:** Done in a very hot room; popular because you can lose a lot of weight due to excessive sweating and become lightheaded due to dehydration, which can be mistaken as altered consciousness. Many folks swear by it, but it seems to me overly taxing, and weight loss due to sweat is offset at the drinking fountain.

✔ **Hatha Yoga:** Considered classic or basic Yoga, this is for those who are looking for inner peace rather than panting, sweating, and weight loss. You hold postures for a long time, and the emphasis is on deep breathing. Beginners get a taste of the basics here.

✔ **Iyengar Yoga:** Emphasizes procession and purity of form. To be quite honest, this is my favorite because it really does focus on holding a posture for a long period of time and doing it absolutely correctly, although my instructor says the difference between beginning and intermediate is the ability to hold the wrong posture for longer.

✔ **Jivamukti Yoga:** Combines physical practice with foundations in spiritual teaching. *Jivamukti* means "liberation from limitation."

✔ **Kundalini Yoga:** A style of yoga that specifically focuses on energy flow and is recommended for relieving emotional stress and awakening psychic energetic power by those who swear by it. Sting has made this famous by incorporating it with tantric sex positions — tee hee.

✔ **Vinyasa Yoga:** Moves from one posture to another and tends to be a bit more vigorous. *Vinyasa* is the name for a Yoga posture.

So pick and choose, try different ones, and see what works best for you. For more about Yoga, check out *Yoga For Dummies,* by Georg Feuerstein, PhD, and Larry Payne, PhD (published by Wiley). And if you'd like to find out about Pilates, see *Pilates For Dummies,* by Ellie Herman (also published by Wiley).

1. Make a fist of your toes. Squeeze. Hold. Release slowly. Repeat.

2. Roll each foot slowly, all the way around from the ankle, clockwise. Then roll each foot slowly counterclockwise. Point your toes, then flex them. Repeat.

3. Tense and relax your thighs. Repeat.

4. Make a fist of your buns. Hold tight. Relax. Don't forget to inhale deeply through your nose, exhale through your mouth. Repeat.

5. Tighten your stomach muscles. Relax. Repeat.

6. Lift your shoulders up to your ears as high as you can. Now, a bit higher. Slowly lower both shoulders as far as you can, pushing them down gently, using only your shoulder muscles. Repeat.

7. Make a fist with your hands. Clench your biceps. Slowly extend your arms out. Relax. Repeat.

8. With arms extended at shoulder length, flex your hands, palms facing the far wall, fingers reaching straight up to the ceiling. Press out. Relax. Repeat.

9. Turn your head all the way to the left and then all the way to the right. Be sure to keep your shoulders pressed down. Repeat.

10. Scrunch your face up into a ball. Slowly relax it. Repeat.

11. With your eyes still closed, slowly rotate your eyeballs clockwise. Then counterclockwise. Repeat.

Your whole body should feel very heavy. That's good. Now, before you open your eyes, you need to do one final thing: Visualize. If you'd like a little help with this, you can order my relaxation tape at www.drjoy.com or any other tape that helps you to tune in to you and out of the chaos for a moment.

Step 3: Visualization

The mind is an incredibly powerful tool for turning stress on and off. To turn stress off, you want to create a safe place in your head where you can always retreat when the going gets tough. The best way to do that is through visualization. With your eyes still comfortably closed, take another deep breath in through your nose, out through your mouth, and then do the following:

1. **Think of a place you've been that makes you feel happy and comfortable.**

   You may think of the seashore, a forest, or your childhood bedroom — wherever you remember feeling totally content. "See" that place in your mind's eye. Smell the smells. See the colors. Hear the sounds. Be there. See yourself in that blissful environment.

2. **Think about a special person in your life: someone you love unconditionally, someone who cherishes you.**

   See the person slowly walk toward you as you stand in your joyous place. Feel suffused with comfort and well-being and happiness. Feel delighted to see this person and feel how delighted the person is to see you. Let the person's love wash over you as he or she gets closer and closer. Finally, when the person is right next to you, look in the person's eyes. Don't say anything, just look in his or her eyes. Everything you need to know and say to one another is said in your eyes.

3. **See a pinpoint of pure, bright, warm light.**

   Watch it expand until it fills the entire space. Feel its warmth. You and your special person are bathed in the glow of that special light. You have no cares, no worries. You feel comfortable and warm and loved and accepted. Experience what it feels like to be surrounded by that light.

4. **It's time for your special person to go, but you don't feel any sadness. Feel the love remain as the person leaves.**

5. **It's time for the light to recede, but you feel no loss or sadness. Instead, you still feel the warmth and well-being the light gave you.**

6. **It's time to leave your wonderful place. But you're really not leaving for good; you're taking it with you.**

   Now and forever, this spot, this feeling, will be available to you whenever you want to go there. It's you. In you. Always.

7. **With your eyes still closed, slowly become aware of your surroundings.**

   Feel the chair, hear your heart beating. Feel happy, warm, accepted, content.

8. **Slowly open your eyes. Sit for a moment.**

Know that the calm you feel now can be the calm you feel throughout your entire date . . . if you let it happen.

Pre-Date Affirmations: Sweet Talking to Yourself

An *affirmation* is a positive statement about yourself made in the present tense. A few kind words to yourself can calm you instantly, as well as quell any surges of anxiety you may feel as liftoff draws near. Feel free to play your favorite relaxation music as you repeat your affirmations. Repeat after me:

✔ "I'm a fun, interesting, worthy person."

✔ "I deserve success and happiness."

✔ "A date is only a date — it's not do-or-die time."

✔ "I'm calm and fearless."

✔ "I will enjoy myself tonight, and my date will, too."

You're now internally and (if you've read Chapter 8) externally ready to have a wonderful time.

Chapter 10

Impressions: First and Lasting

. . . .

In This Chapter

▶ Making small talk

▶ Sticking to safe subjects

▶ Steering clear of taboo topics

▶ Reading body language

▶ Learning to listen

. . . .

Irst impressions count, and you never get a second chance at them. No pressure, no panic. You're there — ta-da! — on the street where your date lives. Or you're tucked into the back booth of the restaurant where you agreed to meet. It's full steam ahead. In a few minutes, your date officially begins. So, too, begins the task of letting someone in, of being yourself, of allowing someone you don't know very well to get to know the real you. It's okay to be a little nervous. Most everyone is under the circumstances.

So what do you say when you want to make a smashing first impression? How do you look, what do you talk about, and how do you act? That's what this chapter tells you. You also find a list of topics you should avoid and a helpful primer on body language.

Before You Begin

First, try to relax. I know, name a quarterback who's relaxed on game day. But truly, the key to letting others in on who you really are is lowering the barriers you construct to keep from getting hurt. Vulnerability is irresistible. You don't want to be a puppy's belly, but the last thing you want to resemble is Fort Knox.

Second, get three questions ready — three things you want to know. Only three. You're not auditioning for Barbara Walters' job. You're breaking the ice. You're launching communication, not preparing for Interrogation 101.

Googling: Yes or no?

I know you're thinking "Should I Google or not? Or check out Facebook or mutual acquaintances?" All very tempting, but there is so much misinformation online that you may walk into a trap unwittingly. Additionally, many people feel your checking out their lives online before you've been on a few dates is an invasion of privacy. Unless they have specifically invited you to read their professional biography at their company's Web site, wait until after at least three dates before researching them online or in any way connecting with them at a social networking site. Or, my little darling, if you simply can't resist the temptation, don't

'fess up; don't lie, but don't broadcast it either. Getting to know each other really shouldn't require a cheat sheet.

How about for the first date, you more or less play it by ear and ask what you want to know rather than assuming or skirting around things you think you know. The discovery process can be fun, and short-circuiting it seems more than a little risky — and potentially takes some of the pleasure out of those early encounters. Yeah, knowledge is power, but dating isn't about power, and the knowledge may or may not be accurate or helpful.

Third, prepare three things about yourself you want to share. Be ready to talk about the work you do, movies you've seen and liked (and why), and a current event or two. Again, this isn't the time for in-depth analysis; you're not defending your life's work here. Still, you want to stimulate a dialogue instead of listen to a monologue (or dead silence!), and that takes two.

Finally, take a couple of deep breaths and tell yourself that you're safe and deserving of love and that no matter what happens, Mom will always be there with a plate of brownies and a hug. Hey, life is good!

Say What? Knowing What to Say

Opening lines, small talk, topics of conversation . . . unless you have a real gift of gab, it's not a bad idea to have an informal list of things to talk about.

Opening gambits

Because everybody's most nervous at the beginning — once you get past "hi" — an opening line can give you some confidence. There is a universal opening line that's guaranteed not to fail: Tell your date she or he looks fabulous (beautiful, handsome, delicious, ravishing, divine . . . you choose the adjective). The more specific, the better — but stay away from body parts between the neck and the ankles. Such a compliment as an opening line immediately puts both of you at ease: Your date knows the preparation wasn't in vain, and you fly past the first hurdle with several inches to spare. Plus, there's a bonus: Your date will probably return the compliment, and you'll both feel your confidence surge.

Of course, a great opening line is only the beginning of an entire date full of conversation. After all, you can't keep telling your date that he or she looks fabulous (stop after 20 or 30 reps). Eventually, you'll have to actually talk to one another. That doesn't mean you have to initiate a discussion of nuclear physics or the meaning of life as we know it. Start small with small talk, discussed in the cleverly named "Small talk" section later in this chapter.

The last thing you want to do in the first five minutes is let your date see you cower. Gobs of nerves are contagious, and so is serenity. This isn't the final round of the National Cool Talk Competition. Relax. Take deep breaths and say what's on your mind, *unless* it's one of the following:

- **How are you?** The question is trite ("Fine, thank you. How are you?") or too personal, depending on the response, especially on a date when a truthful response probably sounds like, "I'm feeling a bit nervous, slightly sweaty, a tiny bit nauseous, excited, filled with anticipation, and hoping we end up really liking one another."

  Yikes!

  Even a clever response (like "I've never been better" or "I worked out today, and I'm on an endorphin high" or "I'm looking forward to our wonderful evening tonight" or "I'm starved and raring to go") is kinda cute but a waste of time.

- **Why are you late?** If there was a ten-car pileup, it will be the first thing mentioned. If your date overslept, he or she may or may not tell you. I know you were kept waiting, worrying, and wondering if you'd written down the wrong date, and I know that's not okay, but the first five minutes of a date is a tough time to begin sounding like an angry parent.

  Make a decision. If your date's too late for you to forgive and forget, cancel the date and explain why. If the tardiness is slightly irksome but you're willing to overlook it, let it go. I mean *really* let it go. Don't bring it up. Not now, anyway. (When you make the next date, explain that you're a bit compulsive about being on time.)

- **How do I look?** When you're nervous, it's easy to fall into the trap of focusing on yourself and your insecurities. Don't go there. The quickest way to ease date-stress is to get out of your head and into the moment. Assume you look fab and try to relax yourself and your date. No fishing for compliments.

✔ **Mind if I smoke?** Believe it — most people do mind. Unless you met in a cigar bar, this question is far too risky to even attempt. I know, you smokers out there are thinking that one puny puff would sure take the edge off the first moments of a date. You may want to light up so much that your fingers are twitching. But there are two reasons to give your addiction a rest right now: First, smoking is like taking out a billboard and announcing you're nervous. Guys on their way to the guillotine were offered a final cigarette! Do you want your date to feel as though you've been sentenced to death? Second, cigarette smoking inspires passionate feelings on both sides of the issue (I know lots of folks who wouldn't go out even once with a smoker). The first five minutes of a date are time for vanilla ice cream, Wonder Bread, and sensible shoes. In short, don't even go close to controversy.

No matter what your question is, make sure you don't make the same mistake one famous interviewer often makes: You get so involved in the elaborate question that you pay no attention to the answer. Also, make sure your date can't answer your questions with a simple *yes* or *no;* otherwise, you'll feel like you're in a batting cage with an automatic pitching machine.

In times of stress, we tend to regress to childhood behaviors that may have calmed us or felt safe. Many women slip and fall into a sort of "mothering mode" when they feel anxiety tighten their chests. Questions like "Do you need a sweater?" "Do you have the directions?" and "Are you sure we have enough time to make it?" just make your date feel like an inadequate little boy. Even if he freezes his buns off or doesn't have the directions or botches the reservation, keep quiet and let him work his way out of the mess he made. *Remember:* You're not his mom; you're his date.

Okay, so you know what *not* to ask. But what are some good opening gambits? These are:

✔ What did you do today? (The focus on the other person shows interest, and presumably *everyone* did *something.*)

✔ What book (movie, TV show, and so on) is your favorite?

✔ Are you a cat person or a dog person?

Social Skills 101

It's not that some people are born charming and the rest of us are losers. Social skills are learned, and you can learn the basics by watching others. It's okay to pick someone to mimic to begin with — just like a child copies a parent. After you learn the basics, you can begin to add personal variations and style — a sense of humor, characteristic ways of speaking. Each social situation is a new opportunity to practice being you, a social creature. Don't be a hermit. You won't learn anything except how to be alone.

Are we speaking the same language?

Men and women communicate differently: Women are taught to create intimacy through talking; men view conversations as negotiations, a way to jockey for position. Neither style of communicating is better; they're just different.

If your conversation with your date begins to resemble a sparring match, take a breather and try to figure out what's really going on. Your problem may be different styles of communicating.

The point here is that you're gathering the building blocks of a conversational bridge, a way of getting from no knowledge to important stuff. You can't go from "Hi, my name is Fred" to "What do you want in life?" Talking about weather, books, friends you have in common, and so on is a way to lay the foundation across the chasm that separates strangers so that they can meet in the middle or comfortably go back and forth. You can see why Googling your date isn't the world's best idea (see the sidebar "Googling: Yes or no?"). It's okay to say, "I was tempted to Google you, but then I thought it might be more fun for you to tell me what you would like me to know." You get double credit in one fell swoop.

Small talk

Small talk has gotten a bum rap (excuse the pun) because it's mistakenly linked with air-headedness. The assumption is that those who engage in small talk only chitchat about life's piddling moments without a concern for the deeper, burning issues underneath. Poppycock.

Small talk is a necessary and important part of our social fabric. It's a way to adjust to one another, get comfortable, and find your conversational seat. Without small talk, we'd all be walking up to acquaintances and saying, "Hi. How would you create peace in the Middle East?" or "Nice to see you. My father is an alcoholic."

Getting good at small talk, or at least comfortable with it in small doses, will hold you in good stead not only on a date but in life as well. Small talk is just a means of chatting easily and comfortably about day-to-day issues without rancor or intensity. Big talk is about politics, religion, family, gun control, abortion, whether chocolate should be a controlled substance, or why none of your marriages have worked.

Safe subjects

Words can knit a warm blanket or cause an explosion. Your directive here is to create a conversational comfort zone by having a group of icebreakers ready. These tidbits are designed to put both you and your date at ease:

- ✔ **Weather:** I know, this is so trite it's almost a national joke. However, comments about the weather have more to do with presentation than subject matter. The old chestnut, "Nice weather we're having," is a waste. But confiding that the sky was so clear and beautiful you spent your lunch hour barefoot in the park is another story entirely. (Besides, that data gives you a great chance to talk about a great old Neil Simon movie, *Barefoot in the Park,* starring Jane Fonda and Robert Redford — and right there you've taken your budding relationship to another level.)

- ✔ **Location:** Where you are right now is a great subject for conversation. Commenting on the colors, smells, sounds, and tastes in a positive way (no griping allowed) allows you to share the experience. Point out the décor if you're inside, the shrubbery or architecture if you're outside . . . you get the point.

- ✔ **Friends in common:** Beware of gossip, but establishing links is a very good idea.

- ✔ **News events:** Be up-to-date; read the paper, a news magazine, *People,* whatever.

- ✔ **Popular culture:** Talk about plays, movies, concerts, rock stars, and so on.

- ✔ **Facebook pages:** It's okay to ask if your date is on Facebook rather than admitting that you've perused his or her page endlessly. It's a great conversation topic as well, love it or hate it. Beware trying to finesse if you've already peeked, so again, you're better off not checking it out before the date. Besides, some of the special features on Facebook and other social networking sites report to the person who has viewed his or her profile. It's best to refrain from viewing that profile until after a few dates and after mutual interest has been expressed and demonstrated. There's no good reason to be busted as a snoop or busybody from the get-go.

Avoiding Taboo Topics

You want to get (and keep) the conversational ball rolling without a flurry of true confessions or 20 questions. Taking a sudden vow of silence is a major faux pas. You want to be open, not transparent. Friendly, not needy. Witty, not desperate for a laugh. To ease you over dating's conversational speed bumps, here's a primer on the four deadly taboo topics to avoid like the plague.

Sex

Even if sex is the first thing on your mind, let it be the last thing on your lips. This covers past, present, and future sexual encounters (both real and virtual). Ditto your sex drive, appetite, and online liaisons.

Talking about sex before you know someone fairly well is not only threatening, but it's also confusing. "What did he mean by that?" "Is she coming on to me?" The last thing you want on a first date is ambiguity. You're trying to build trust here, not test it. Even animals know there's a ritual involved before mating. Don't try to short-circuit eons of evolution on a first date. (Which is not to say that your date has to seem like opening day at Celibates Anonymous. Flirt. See the upcoming section "Flirting Fun" for pointers.)

Exes

If you're not over your ex enough to avoid mentioning him or her on a first date, you're not ready to date (see Chapter 4). Even if you were married to Jack or Jackie the Ripper, or dated Jack or Jackie Kennedy, let past relationships come up naturally another time. Talking about a former lover dredges up a *c* word even more feared than commitment: *comparison.* Who wants to start off a relationship wondering if you measure up? Or worse, whether you'll ever be able to erase the sins of another? Besides, on a first date, three is always a crowd.

Politics

Current events are good conversational fodder. But your position on the death penalty? Abortion? Welfare reform? The president? National health insurance? The Teamsters? Gun control? Fox News? A bit risky.

The potential payoff isn't worth the risk. If your date shares your political views, is he being truthful or just agreeable? Do you really want a full-scale argument on your first date?

If you show up in a red tie, navy blue blazer, button-down white shirt, khaki pants, and brown penny loafers (or wearing suspenders, a belt, and a bow tie), she's going to assume that you're a Republican no matter *what* you say.

Political hot potatoes to avoid at all costs:

- Police brutality
- Immigration
- National health insurance

- Women in the military
- Any current war or conflict
- September 11 (Geographic location may come into play here.)
- The designated hitter rule
- Spanking
- Body piercing
- And, of course, Elvis

Religion

If the word "Christmas" or "Hanukkah" slips out while you're relaying a funny family story, so be it. If the Bible or the Torah or a Jehovah's Witness brochure slips out while you reach for your wallet, that's a bit over the top. Religion and your relationship (or non-relationship) with whomever you may or may not believe in is your own business — at least for now. You don't want to put your date on the spot. If your date puts you on the spot by asking, say, whether you believe in God, simply change the subject by asking her whether she believes O. J. was guilty.

If you two met online, you may already know each other's religious views, including denominations and frequency of attendance at services. When that information is in your online dating profile, your date may inquire about it; any topic in your dating profile is fair game for a first date conversation. However, misunderstandings are so easy here. It's best to keep the conversation brief and move on graciously to a safer topic. Again, not to beat a dead Internet horse, but if you haven't checked your date's online profile, you won't have the info and you avoid that pitfall.

Flirting Fun

Remind yourself that you're here to have fun, and your jaw unclenches, your shoulders drop down, your eyes sparkle, your breathing slows, and you're ready to flirt.

Flirting is a delicious, low-budget, irresistible, safe-sex sort of way to make you and your date feel tingly all over. The essence of flirting is interest. No one ever flirts with someone he or she doesn't want to know a little bit better. That's why flirting on a first date can be so alluring. You're showing your date you didn't make a mistake. You're interested and ready to go. What could be sexier that that? (Okay, I know, but not yet.)

Here's a quick list of what to do (and not do) when flirting with your date:

✔ **Use your whole body.** Talking the talk without walking the walk is utterly ineffective. Don't believe it? Try telling a woman she's beautiful or a guy he's hunky and then shift your eyes away, and see if you're believed. Flirty body language begins with the eyes and works its way all the way down to the tips of your footsies. Lean forward, make eye contact, smile, bend your knees a bit, and untense your hands and arms. Remember to relax a bit; this should be fun, not like defusing a bomb.

✔ **Make eye contact.** Looking someone in the eyes is very compelling. It makes a person feel like he's got your undivided attention, which he should.

✔ **Smile, don't smirk.** There's a reason why synonyms for *smirk* include *sneer, leer,* and *grimace:* Smirking is an unattractive and unpleasant expression. Avoid it. Smile openly and sincerely — it's irresistible.

✔ **Pay attention.** No looking like you're trying to remember whether you fed the cat.

✔ **Lighten up; don't bulldoze.** Telling your date he or she is incredibly hot isn't flirting; it's steering your dating experience directly into a mountain. *Attractive, smart, charming,* and *lovely* are all okay, but not *hot.* Women: Don't call a guy *cute;* they all hate it even if they let it go on the first date. Trust me on this one.

✔ **Focus on your partner, not yourself.** Without slipping into a Katie Couric–type litany of prefabricated questions — such as "Whom do you most admire?" or "If you were a farm animal, what kind would you be?" — make your date feel as though every word is a pearl of wisdom.

✔ **Don't think you can't do it.** Anyone can flirt . . . even if only a little. Flirting is a sign of confidence, and even if you're feeling a teensy bit shaky, give it a try. Practice makes perfect and flirty. You don't have to be smooth — just sincere.

✔ **Enjoy yourself.** Fun is the flirter's playground. Once you're having fun, getting others to play is easy.

Interpreting Body Language

Your body speaks louder than words. So does your date's. How many dates will tell you flat out that they're having a rotten time? Few, if any. Yet how many will catch periodic glimpses of their watch? Hopefully, not many.

In the mating game, women use their heads, and men use their chests. Literally. Women toss their hair or sweep their heads back as a sign of attraction; men simply puff out their chests. It's a throwback to our primitive pasts when big, burly Cro-Magnon men and savvy Cro-Magnon women were the kings and queens of the veldt. Now, in our modern jungle, the signs are still there. You just have to know what to look for.

GIRL STUFF

Flutter those lashes, girl

A German scientist, Irenäus Eibl-Eibesfeldt, once studied women's flirting behavior and found that nearly all women make the same facial movements when they flirt, in the exact same order. They

1. Smile.

2. Lift their eyebrows in a fast, jerky motion.

3. Open their eyes wide (a sign of sympathetic system arousal, which means that the "Hey, pay attention!" part of our nervous system has kicked into gear).

4. Lower their eyelids.

5. Tilt their heads down and to the side (a universal sign of submission in the animal kingdom).

6. Look away.

Sound like anyone you know? These flirting gestures are so universal that Eibl-Eibesfeldt believes they're innate sexual signals evolved from the beginning of human history.

If you spend all your time looking at nonverbal cues, you're not going to be focusing on what your date is saying and you're not going to be doing your part about spontaneously responding. So chill out here and don't spend more than a millisecond of your precious time together "studying" your date. If you do, you'll both be miserable.

Reading body language is far from an exact science. It's one part observation, two parts interpretation. People cross their arms when they're cold as well as closed off. Look for consistent groups of gestures or a suddenly inconsistent movement. Look for patterns, but don't get hung up here. Focus on what you're saying verbally to one another and look to nonverbal clues only when in doubt.

Positive signs

If your date is using a lot of the following signals, you can take it as a good sign that he or she is interested and having a good time. Congratulations!

- **Good eye contact:** Gazing (not staring) into someone's eyes is a good sign.

- **Leaning forward:** Making the space between you two smaller and cozier signals that interest is on the way up and walls are on the way down.

- **Relaxed posture:** Sitting or standing comfortably and breathing smoothly indicate that your date is open and non-defensive.

- **Palms up:** Open hands indicate a warm and receptive heart.

✔ **Touching:** If the touching is warm rather than suggestive, you're making contact. Careful here: arms, okay; shoulders, iffy; waist, probably not; and butt, don't even think about it.

✔ **Nodding:** If your date nods periodically as you speak, you're on the same wavelength.

✔ **Mirroring:** Unconsciously reflecting each other's behavior — leaning forward at the same time, breathing in sync, crossing the same leg over the other at the same time, speaking in the same tone — says that you're attuned to one another.

✔ **Synchronization:** Simultaneous breathing, blinking, and shifting in your seat means you're in sync.

Negative signs

Your date may not be finger-drumming the tabletop, but displaying any of the following signals can be a warning:

✔ **Frequent nodding:** The Yin and Yang of body language, a little nodding is a good sign; continuous head-bobbing means you've lost the connection.

✔ **Open mouth:** If your date always seems to be trying to break in, you may be too long-winded and have lost your partner's interest.

✔ **Hands on mouth:** This is a censoring mechanism, literally stopping the words as they come out of the mouth — *not* a good sign.

✔ **Arms crossed:** Any type of closed-up body posture indicates a barrier between the two of you (unless the room is cold — look for goose bumps).

✔ **Arms behind the head:** On a first date, this is a classic sign of dominance . . . or the attempt to gain it.

✔ **Yawning:** You guessed it — bored to tears.

We've all been learning to interpret nonverbal cues since the first time our mothers cradled us; survival depended on spotting Dad's mood or Grandma's pride or our sister's sulking. Studies have shown that kids who can easily read subtle facial cues survive the perils of grammar school far better than their more obtuse peers. If you suspect that your date is annoyed or bored or impatient, it's okay to test the waters. See whether changing the subject works or even, egad, say, "I seem to have turned you off." Then ask, "Was it something I said?" You'll score points for sensitivity. But ask only once. No nagging!

Go on YouTube and check out videos on reading body language for some quick demonstrations. Seeing examples of body language is often the best way to fully grasp them. Being yourself works better than trying to pretend via body language to be something or someone you're not. Notice the negative (arms folded across chest, bouncing foot, hand covering mouth), and let the rest go. Relax and let your hips tell the truth.

Body language quiz

Just for fun, try to match the behavior with the interpretation below to see how well you can really read your date.

Behavior	Interpretation
___ 1. Playing with hair	a. Impatience
___ 2. Rubbing eyes	b. Confidence
___ 3. Biting fingernails	c. Lying
___ 4. Stroking chin	d. Insecurity
___ 5. Drumming fingers	e. Doubt
___ 6. Hands on hips	f. Anticipation
___ 7. Tugging at ear	g. Lack of self-confidence
___ 8. Rubbing nose	h. Aggression
___ 9. Hand on cheek	i. Indecision
___ 10. Walking briskly	j. Dejection
___ 11. Rubbing hands together	k. Trying to make a decision
___ 12. Walking with hands shoved in pockets (don't even think that)	l. Evaluating all the options

Answers: 1. g.; 2. e.; 3. d.; 4. k.; 5. a.; 6. h.; 7. i.; 8. c.; 9. l.; 10. b.; 11. f.; 12. j

Mirroring

Okay, now that you know all this stuff, should you become Sherlock Holmes or just enjoy your date? Elementary, my dear: relax and enjoy. However, if you want a way to check out your own unconscious reactions, you don't need to study a videotape to see if you're mirroring.

You know that great feeling when you and another person are totally in sync? You laugh at the same jokes, love the same food, and both think the Japanese versions of horror flicks are much scarier than the American remakes. Similarity is the essence of connection, and connection is the essence of trust, and trust is the foundation for true love.

You're mirroring each other if you're

✔ **Duplicating your date's body language.**

Are you both leaning forward at the same time, each sitting with legs crossed?

✔ **Adopting the same speaking rhythm.**

Are you both talking softly, going back and forth conversationally, sharing the same pacing?

✔ **Echoing style or energy level.**

Are you both mellow or energized, calm or hyped?

Subtlety is the essence of good mirroring. You don't want to get caught mimicking your date. The trick is to have your date feel connected, not pick up on a monkey-see, monkey-do act. You'll naturally either fall into — or out of — a sort of relationship sync, which you can't fake for long. Rather than direct yourself to do it, see whether mirroring just occurs normally.

Listening Attentively and Effectively

Trust me on this — I make my living listening to others — your date will tell you everything you need to know about him or her in the first 15 minutes. Not 50. 15. Train yourself really to hear what your date's saying (and believe it). Of course, therein lies the rub: While love may be blind, dating is almost always deaf.

My friend Elaine "bought" a date with a soap star at a charity auction. She could scarcely afford her winning bid, but she had such a crush on the guy she was willing to brown bag it for the half year it would take to make up the deficit. They met at a trendy New York restaurant. He looked incredible. She was flushed with the thrill of it all. Their first minute of conversation, as she later relayed it to me, went a little something like this:

> **HE (laughing):** I can't believe you paid so much for me. I'm not worth it.
> **SHE (also laughing):** It went to a good cause — me.
> **HE:** I'm really not into the dating scene. I barely have time to learn my lines and go to bed.
> **SHE:** Thank you for squeezing me into your busy schedule.
> **HE:** I barely made it. I'm leaving for L.A. tomorrow.
> **SHE:** Business?
> **HE:** Hopefully. I'm up for a series.
> **SHE:** Good luck. I hope you get it.

Of course, she was lying, and he was telling the honest-to-goodness truth. Elaine thought their date went smashingly well and was devastated when he didn't call her again — which she could have known he wouldn't do if she'd listened with open ears instead of a too-wide-open heart. He'd told her flat-out he wasn't worth it, didn't date, and was going to move 3,000 miles away. And he'd said it all in the first 30 seconds of their evening together.

Learning how to listen is not easy, but it is simple. You have to train yourself to focus on the present moment only — not on your witty comeback, the follow-up question, the stupid thing you can't believe you just said, the parsley you can feel lodged in between your teeth. You have to be in the *now*. Period.

If you want to be a good listener, you have to

- ✔ Train yourself to stay with the talker, word for word, until he or she is finished. Simple concept, but really difficult to practice.

- ✔ Suspend judgment and open your heart and head, as well as your ears. Listen to what the person is actually saying — not what you want to hear; it's crucial not only to dating but to all human interactions.

I know I mentioned it before, but the temptation to find out everything you can about your date before the date is ill-advised. If you've Googled your date or checked out his or her Facebook page, you're going to be trying to verify, understand, or remember instead of learning, gleaning, and responding. I think it's worth repeating because I know you're tempted.

Chapter 11

Having a Way Cool Time

*P*resumably you've planned your date carefully and are fully prepared. (If not, flip to Chapters 8 through 10 for a refresher course.) At this point, I'm confident you not only know where you're going, how to get there, and about how much it'll cost, but you're also dressed appropriately and have fully factored your date into the equation. You've selected a destination you both will like and haven't decided that now would be a good time to start smoking, wearing fur, or pinning a campaign button to your lapel.

If you're the askee rather than the asker, you may be in a more passive position since you may not know all the details, but you know the *where* and you certainly can have Googled the venue to know the atmosphere. (Even if the place is not your fave, going with the flow is a better way to start off than asserting your will from the get-go.)

Now you're all set to have a good time. This chapter tells you how to make the most of your date, how to deal with the unexpected catastrophes that may creep up, and how to end the evening gracefully.

Enjoying Yourself

It doesn't have to be the Fourth of July for you to have a great time on your first date. The sky doesn't need to erupt in fireworks for you to consider your date a winner. What *does* need to happen is that you create an environment that allows both you and your date to relax a little, let your hair down (or at least loosen it a bit), get to know one another, and have fun. The basics of enjoying yourself are fairly straightforward:

- ✔ Be relaxed.
- ✔ Be yourself.
- ✔ Be prepared to talk — and listen (see Chapter 15 for conversation pointers).
- ✔ Be prepared (think Boy Scout — money, time, place, directions, and so on — and see Part I).
- ✔ Be okay about silences (if they don't go on too long).
- ✔ Be realistic about expectations.
- ✔ Resist the temptation to snoop (much more about this later).

Don't sweat it — it's pretty hard to really screw things up. Besides, it's only one date. With a bit of pre-planning on your part — which is, essentially, what all the earlier chapters have been about — this date can be a really cool one. Pace yourself. A date has a beginning, a middle, and an end. You're not on the clock. Your date doesn't have to love you in the first five minutes or it's the ejector seat. You don't have to love your date instantly either. Keep reminding yourself what a date is really all about: getting to know one another. Relax. Enjoy yourself. And take it easy.

Making the Most of the Place You Picked

In Chapter 7, I talk about great places to take a first date. My general feeling is this: Why add one more worry with an unknown location when you can boost your confidence by going someplace you already know is terrific? It just makes good sense.

Restaurants

Food is part of a time-honored traditional date activity, so figuring out how you can make eating out a delicious experience is time well-spent. (Eating "in" is for later on — after you get to know each other.)

Order food you eat with a fork

Forget about sandwiches (unless that's all there is — in that case, the fewer ingredients, the better). Food you lift with your hands can easily fall from your hands. High-rise sandwiches are notorious for collapsing on the way up to your mouth. Stringy pizza cheese dangles from your lips like you just swallowed twine, sushi is rarely served in petite bite-sized portions, and tacos spill.

Foods to fear on a first date

Stay away from these foods unless you have breath mints, dental floss, and guts:

- Caesar salad (because of the garlic in the dressing)
- Corn on the cob
- French onion soup
- Fried chicken
- Garlic

- Parsley, broccoli, or anything else green that is going to stick in your teeth
- Pasta with marinara sauce
- Popcorn
- Poppy seeds
- Ribs
- Watermelon
- Whole lobster

Don't drink

I know, I'm going to lose a lot of you here — if you're nervous you may be trying to relax yourself. But Miller Time can become mildew time before you know it. Be very careful about alcohol. If you've ever had a problem with alcohol, fuhgettaboutit — don't drink. I can already hear you muttering, "Hey, a drink or two will relax me. I can handle it," but it's you that I'm talking to here. Moderation when you're nervous is difficult to achieve, so err on the side of caution and believe that alcohol on a first date is dangerous for several reasons:

- **Nerves magnify the effects of alcohol.** You get drunk faster.

- **Alcohol has been proven to dismantle your appetite control.** While one of you is ready for the check, the drinker is ready for a second round of desserts.

- **Too much alcohol creates a sort of "tunnel vision."** You can't see or fully comprehend anything that's not right in front of your face. That's why it's so dangerous to drive, handle heavy wallets, or — heaven forbid — open up your body and soul.

- **The risk of drinking and driving is huge when you've been drinking . . .** and nonexistent when you haven't.

- **Alcohol is the solvent of the superego.** Suddenly, you're saying, doing, and feeling things you'd never say, do, or feel if you were sober.

- **All your guards are down when you're tipsy, including your sexual judgments.** The chances that you'll say "yes" when you really mean "no" or hear "yes" when you're told "no" are much greater.

Your date doesn't have to be an AA meeting, but club soda and a lime will do just fine. If your date has a drink, you can smile sweetly and say that you may have wine with dinner, you've taken a two-week pledge, or you're cutting calories. No need to make your date worry that you're going to go Carrie Nation on him or her. (Don't know who Carrie Nation is? Google her. She's the one who took an axe to the bars.) I don't drink and have never had a problem with it. If your date does, I'd wonder why, wouldn't you? Just don't make a big deal of either your behavior or your date's. You can always explain to your date that you want a clear head, the better to appreciate his or her charms.

Eat!

Okay — so I've put alcohol off-limits, but it's okay to indulge in some calories. Most men are much more comfortable with women who eat reasonably rather than the "Oh, I'll just have a small salad with the dressing on the side" syndrome. (Surveys show that women put much more pressure on themselves to have a "perfect" body than men ever put on them.)

It's okay to share a dessert. First, you'll find out if he works and plays well with others. Second, it sends a loud and clear message that you're not anorexic or obsessed with your weight. Watching your waistline is one thing; entering a convent is another. Eating is a sensual, pleasurable experience that's meant to be savored. I'm not saying you should throw calories to the wind and use date night as an excuse to imitate Miss Piggy, but enjoying yourself means letting go enough to enjoy your date, the conversation, the location, the colors, the smells, the sights, the sounds, *and* the meal — the whole enchilada or creme brulée.

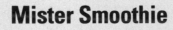

Mister Smoothie

I once dated a man who nearly knocked me over with his James Bond–type style. Smooth as silk. He took me to a nice restaurant, one that he'd obviously been to before. After we finished our cappuccinos and dabbed our lips with our pink linen napkins, he asked, "Ready to go?" Noticing the check had neither arrived nor been paid, I replied, "Shall we make a run for it?" He laughed and told me it was all taken care of. Later, I found out that he'd gone to that restaurant the day before, given them his credit card number, and instructed them to add 20 percent for the tip. A slight nod from the waiter (which I never saw) let him know the whole money thing was a done deal.

Is that cool or what? What struck me most was his effort and advance planning. He confided in me later that the check arrival and tip calculation had always felt awkward to him so he worked out a way around it. Smooth move.

I actually used the same move later on him for his birthday so there would be no awkwardness about my treating him.

GIRL STUFF
♀

Lip service

To do it, or not to do it? You know what I'm talking about — it's the ghastly decision every woman must make at the end of a restaurant meal. Does she reapply her lipstick at the table, excuse herself to the ladies room, or just sit there, a lipless wonder, hoping her date has the class not to stare at the thin beige lines that were once her luscious pout? Alas, there is no simple answer.

Etiquette pros cringe at the notion of a woman pulling out a compact and rolling up a tube of ruby red and applying it meticulously at the table. Such things are a private affair, best suited to the restroom. I have to agree . . . at least to a certain extent. On a date, three is always a crowd. You don't want to end a fabulous meal with him and you and your reflection. However, a quick swipe (sans mirror) seems to me to be a perfectly acceptable compromise. I don't believe in leaving your date languishing alone at your table, staring into space, twiddling his thumbs, just so

you can retreat to the restroom to properly apply lip liner before your lipstick. It's not nice.

That said, here's what I do: In an accessible pocket of my purse, I stash a neutral-tone lipstick just for such occasions. In two seconds flat, I whip it out, swipe it across my lips (hey, I've had these same lips for years — I know where they are), and return it to my purse, barely missing a beat. The neutral tone makes sure I'll still look okay even if I accidentally cross over a lip line or two. Use a neutral color; save the Evita red you wore on the way in, or you run the risk of looking like Baby Jane (not a soothing sight after your date just ate).

If I do have to use the facilities, I can do both simultaneously. But if we're lingering over decaf, I'd rather feel happy and with non-chapped, freshly colored lips than get up and leave.

Mind your manners

Good manners count. Make no mistake about it. Tip well

I'm talking 20 percent. At least. Generosity is attractive. Trust me, the miser never gets the girl. He may keep a few extra dollars, but a person who is tight with money is unlikely to be generous with time or self.

Nothing is a bigger turn-off than seeing food churning round and round inside your date's open mouth. Ugh. Or being rude to waiters, talking too loudly, picking up peas with a knife and sliding them down your throat. Think Jane Austen or *Masterpiece Theater* or that guy who pulls up in his Rolls and asks, "I say, have you any Grey Poupon?" You want to be prim and very proper. At the very least, do these things:

✔ Chew with your mouth closed.

✔ Be polite to the waiters.

✔ Talk softly.

✔ Use your napkin.

Movies or plays

I know, dinner and a movie is the most common date in America, but I don't love it. Talking in a movie will cause your toenails to ingrow, and a play can be a bit pricey for a first date. Show more creativity and you will likely be rewarded. However, I include the trite in this section because it's what most people do in spite of my perspective.

A date at a theater is a double-edged sword. On one side, you're creating a "shared experience." Good for bonding. One of the stepping stones of intimacy. On the other side, most of your date will be spent in the dark staring not at each other. Not the ideal way to get to know somebody. To make the most of a movie or play, be open to discussing it afterward. You can talk about the plot, the casting decisions, the money it cost to make it, other movies you've seen that you like better, childhood memories this movie evokes — anything. If it was horrible, you can talk — and laugh — about that as well.

I know I already mentioned this in Chapter 7, but it's worth checking to make sure that your date approves your choice. Surprises will be more effective once you are more certain of each other's tastes!

Concerts

A concert lets you relate to each other while the music plays, or in the midst of a break. So relate already: Bob back and forth together with the beat, scream in each other's ears to be heard over the noise, and, when your ears are ringing afterward and you can't hear anything anyway, just smile dopily at one another. This type of date shows a great deal more creativity than going to a movie, and you can talk, even if you have to scream.

Besides, if you aren't having a good time, you can leave a concert mid-stream without wondering all night if you missed the really good part. Simply buy the CD.

Sporting events

It's often much more fun attending a live sporting event than watching it on TV. Even if you're not into football, you can get into nachos and peanuts. It's outdoors (usually) and in daylight, and you can even paint your face the color of your favorite team.

A word about silence and technology

Everybody worries about not having anything to say, but if you can remind yourself that you're the "you" expert and you're curious about your date, then you'll be able to maintain the conversational flow without panicking over silences. In general, you want to reveal who you are without confessing every flaw, be sexy without being sexual, and seem funny and light without being desperate for a laugh. If you're not sure what to talk about, check out Chapter 10.

One thing you *don't* want to do is fill the silence by communicating with people other than your date. You don't necessarily want to leave your cell phone at home because it's handy to call if you get lost on the way to the restaurant, but don't even think about answering a call, answering e-mails, or texting during the date. It's just plain rude. It's the technological equivalent of flirting with someone else on a date.

Unless you're on call for a heart transplant (receiving, donating, or performing), keep your cell on vibrate. Pay attention to your date so you actually have something to call and report to your best buddy about *after* the date.

Let me emphasize: undivided attention — good; rude, distracting behavior — bad. You already know this, but it's alarming how often I see couples walking hand in hand, talking on their cells, presumably *not* to each other. It's not cool or hip, just rude and disrespectful. Granted, texting is slightly less noisy, but it's still major on the Richter Rude scale.

Of course, if you two met online, having your cell phone with you and turned on is just an added layer of personal safety. You're not being paranoid; it's just smart to do. And you're smart.

Special events

If you have two tickets to a remaining Beatles reunion tour, you've got a great first date on your hands. Once-in-a-lifetime events are your basic date shoe-in. If Paul and Ringo do decide to go on tour, I'm available. (I once turned down a cruise for two on the QE2 because I had Rolling Stones tickets.)

Fielding the Curve Balls

A curve ball (or two or twenty) is waiting for you on this first date. You can take that to the Dating Bank. No matter how well you prepare, something may go amiss — or at least, not according to your Pentagon-perfect plan. It's Murphy's Law of Dating. The trick is to prepare for the worst and then relax and field whatever may come your way.

Big date do's and don'ts

It's prom night, your sister's wedding, your 30th birthday, New Year's Eve, a retirement party at the firm . . . whatever. When it comes to a BIG date, as in not-just-any-old-Saturday-night date, these guidelines help you have a great time:

✔ DO plan ahead. Big dates are almost always dates you know are coming weeks in advance. Arrange your date as soon as possible so he or she can mark a calendar, rent a tux, buy a great present, and so on.

✔ DON'T make a first date a big date. It's too risky and too loaded. See Chapter 7.

✔ DO ask someone with whom you're really comfortable. Big dates tend to be longer than your average date and often include family members. The last thing you want is a high-maintenance date.

✔ DON'T make your big date such a big deal that your companion feels like it's a pre-marital date, too. It's okay to go out on a big date with Mr. or Ms. Kinda Right or Right Now.

✔ DO substitute a platonic date when a great date isn't in the cards. It's better to have a fun time with a friend (or alone!) than have a miserable time with a date who doesn't work out.

Surviving dating's most embarrassing moments

One of my best friends remembers her first big high school dance as bitter-sweet. It was a formal affair (as they were in those days), the guy she'd had a crush on all year had asked her to go, and her dress was to-die-for. That's the sweet part. Her bitter pill was waking up the morning of the dance to find a giant pimple perched on the tip of her nose like Mount St. Helens. The more she fussed with it all day, the worse it got. That evening, as the doorbell rang, my friend was squirreled away in the bathroom frantically powdering the tip of her nose — which by now rivaled Bozo the Clown's. A bona fide disaster. She left for the dance with one white-gloved hand hovering over the front of her face. Perhaps, she consoled herself, her date wouldn't notice. He did. After all, her uncomfortable behavior was as plain as the nose on her face.

"So you've got a pimple on the end of your nose!" her date finally exclaimed. Apparently, he was tired of gazing into a glove. "Is it the end of the world?" Of course, the answer was "no" (it only felt like it), and the lesson was learned. From that moment on, she heaved a huge sigh of relief, held her date's hand, and had a great time. Which is what you can do, too, as soon as you master the perfect remedy for the following dating disasters.

The first rule: No matter what the problem, 'fess up immediately. Your date will sense something is wrong and think the problem's her or him. And remember, no matter how bad it gets, really, is it the end of the world?

Table 11-1 offers some ways to deal with potential mishaps.

Table 11-1	**Solving Dating Dilemmas**
Disaster	*Solution*
Your pants (skirt, shirt, bra) split.	Tie your jacket or sweater around your waist; buy or borrow a jacket or sweater to tie around your waist. Borrow a safety pin from the waiter.
You forgot your wallet or billfold.	Throw yourself on the mercy of either your date or the manager (if you're a regular there). If your date likes you, at least he or she will know there will be another date — one for which you pay in full.
You get carded.	Be grateful for it. Sooner or later all of this will come to an end. But make sure you do have identification with you. Don't be trying to sneak into a movie or order a drink if you're too young. I promise you, this problem will clear itself up in the long run.
You get sick.	Hey, sick happens. Just don't deny it so long that you get sick right then and there. Tell your date you're not feeling well and need a few minutes in the restroom. If you really don't think you're going to make it, ask your date for help. Passing out in a bathroom stall will only make a bad situation worse. It's okay to ask for a rain check — or a barf check or a nasal drip check.
You pass wind.	Most importantly, avoid breaking out in a 15-minute nervous laughing jag. Apologize once and then (if possible) open a window.
You run into an angry ex.	Remind yourself that you are not responsible for anyone's behavior but your own. Stay calm and let your ex be the only person in the room who makes a fool of himself or herself.
Your car breaks down.	Presumably you belong to an auto club so you won't have to flip through the Yellow Pages app looking for a reputable tow. Best thing to do is make the best of it. Don't sink into a quicksand of self-blame. See whether the tow truck can drop you off at the restaurant on the way, take a cab home, and deal with your dead car tomorrow. *Remember:* A little reconnaissance means you won't run out of gas or get a flat without a spare.

Tarzan to the rescue

One of my all-time favorite cool/horrible date stories was told to me on a dark and stormy night in Colorado by my Girl Scout advisor when I was interviewing to be an international spokesperson. (Little did they know I'd convinced a couple of Air Force cadets to chop down a tree in a national forest for a campfire . . . I digress.) She told me a terrific tale of being asked to her senior prom by her next-door neighbor because neither had a date and they'd been friends forever. Her mother made her a strapless formal dress, and the last butterfly was alighting on the bodice when he rang the bell.

As they danced their first dance, he suddenly pulled her to him and held on for dear life. She was suitably impressed and figured, hey, me Jane, you Tarzan — until he hissed, "Waltz toward the ladies room." Her dress, it turned out, had fallen down. In a moment of true chivalry, he figured it would be less noticeable if he held her tightly all the way into the ladies room. What a cool guy. Only 18 years old and such presence of mind.

If you're old enough to date, you're old enough to understand menstrual cycles and periods and accidents. Should your date experience such an unfortunate mishap, it's up to you to help diffuse her mortification. Don't make light of it (believe me — she won't think it's funny), but don't use this opportunity to "bond" with her by confessing your horror, either. Try what's been known to work well before — tell her you're sorry it happened, and then lovingly add, "Hey, it's not the end of the world."

Lighten up

No matter what happens, the biggest thing to bear in mind is this: It's a date — just a date. Not brain surgery or the cure for cancer or the Bill of Rights or *Macbeth*. It's not serious drama with dire consequences. It's a date. So while you're in the midst of it all, why not lighten up?

The punsters weren't kidding when they said, "Laughter is the best medicine." Several studies have found that jovial belly laughs not only improve circulation and work muscles all over the body, but they relieve stress much in the same way aerobic exercise does. Even in our darkest moments, laughter can instantly make things seem, and feel, much better. Though I don't recommend tossing one-liners nonstop, looking on the bright side of a dim moment can mean the difference between a disaster date and one that's the beginning of a great relationship.

Picking Up the Check

The moment has arrived. You dab the corners of your mouth with a napkin as the waiter strategically positions the check halfway between you and your date. Now what? I provide the answer in Chapter 7, but it's worth revisiting here: If you asked, you pay.

I know I'm going to catch a little heat, but my rule for the first date, at least, is the asker (male or female) forks over the dough. After that, you can negotiate other arrangements. Or you can let the check sit there and stew.

What paying means:

- ✔ You're investing in this relationship . . . no matter how briefly.
- ✔ You're not cheap . . . on any level.
- ✔ You've got class and style and a little jingle in your pocket. Everyone loves all three.

What paying doesn't mean:

- ✔ You've just bought sex, too.
- ✔ You've bought yourself another date.
- ✔ Your date now owes you.

Ending the Date Gracefully

At first glance, it would seem easy to know when a date is over. The empty dishes have been cleared off your table, the check is paid, the theater lights are up, or the sun has risen. There are definitely markers. But a date is an emotional event. What's an empty restaurant and five glaring waiters when this could be true love? Plus, if things are going well, you're also battling your biology.

When you're in the throes of infatuation, a chemical in your brain called *phenylethylamine* (PEA) causes those tingly feelings of euphoria. Other neuro-chemicals, namely norepinephrine and dopamine, may also play a part in your "lover's high." These natural "uppers" are what cause lovers to stay awake all night gazing into each other's eyes or talking into the wee hours of the morning. Sadly, or perhaps thankfully, this chemically induced elation fades. Your brain can't stay in a revved-up state forever!

Pacing yourself may seem like a waste of time if you and your date have clicked from the start. But in the long run, it's always better to leave someone wanting more than feeling like the date was just this side of too much. Assuming your date has gone well (if it hasn't, see Chapter 12 just ahead), you want the end of your first date to be the beginning of a beautiful relationship, not the grand finale of one memorable night.

Lots of details on various dating outcomes are coming up in the next chapter. For now, though, here are some general rules on how to end the date gracefully.

Successful date

If your date is going well, mention date number two before date number one is over. You don't have to fish out your PDA or whip out a cell phone to check with your secretary or your mom or your boss, but the subject can be broached. This is important: Be honest (don't say you'll call just to be nice). When the date ends, do either — or both — of the following:

✔ **Make out:** You know, share soulful kisses and tender caresses — *but don't have sex*. (See Chapter 25 for info on the sex question.)

✔ **Follow up:** Call, e-mail, fax, text.

So-so date

Sometimes you're not sure how you feel until the excitement dies down, real life takes over, and you regain your perspective. That's perfectly fine. Just 'fess up. Tell your date you had a good time, your head is spinning, and you need a little time to sort out your feelings. It may sound a tad insensitive, but it's much better than the "Hey, baby, I'll call you" line if you're really not sure you will.

If your date says to you that he or she needs a few days to digest it all, smile sweetly, say "Great," and go home. Not go phone. Simply go home and live your life. Remember, a watched phone never rings.

So if you're not sure about the date:

✔ **Wait for follow-up — but live your life:** Don't spend all your time waiting next to the phone.

✔ **Give yourself a week or so to ponder:** Upon reflection, the scales usually tip one way or the other.

✔ **Don't have sex:** If you're not sure how you feel about the date, you are definitely not ready to have sex.

Ten signs it's a disaster date

Your date:

1. Goes to the bathroom and never returns.

2. Stiffs you with the bill after ordering the most expensive thing on the menu.

3. Sits at another table.

4. Flirts with the waiter or waitress.

5. Says, "I just forgot, my father's having surgery," "I'm having a root canal," or "I'm taking final vows," when you suggest getting together again.

6. Asks to borrow your car keys after taking a call from an ex and doesn't return.

7. Asks to practice your signature and then steals your credit card (or, having realized it's a debit card, texts you for your password).

8. Calls a parent to come pick him or her up without telling you.

9. Calls the police.

10. Buys an attack dog.

Disaster date

If you don't want to see each other again, don't say you'll call. If you're bored to tears, don't say "Yeah, that would be fun" when your date suggests a follow-up day at the beach. It's icky, it's awkward, it's painful, it makes your forehead sweat, but honesty is ultimately the best way to go.

If you have no intention of seeing what's behind date number two:

- ✔ **Don't say you'll call, fax, e-mail, or text.** It's not nice to be dishonest about what you intend to do.

- ✔ **Don't have sex.** The reason is pretty obvious, right?

- ✔ **Don't make the gruesome deets public.** Your date won't appreciate you sharing your true feelings on your Facebook page upon arriving home.

Be polite, be firm, be honest, be brave. Do the right thing. You can say, "I'll be busy for the next six months," "I feel a migraine coming on," or "I'm taking final vows on Thursday." Your date will get the message. Just don't say, "I'll call" or "Maybe we can do this again" if you have no desire to do either.

The Contact Issue: Handshakes, Hugs, or Liplocks

The all-important question looming large at the end of almost every date is as simple and as complicated as two pair of lips. Should we kiss?

Hug index

A hug is a many-splendored thing. It's intimate, motherly, fatherly, consoling, sexual, and casual. The manner in which the hugger hugs and the huggee hugs back may communicate a lot about the way they feel about each other. Take a look.

Hug Style	Description	What It Usually Says
The "tent"	Head and shoulders touch; feet are far apart	"I'm not sure how I feel about you yet."
The "quick press"	A hug that lasts one second or less	"Hi. How are ya?"
The "grind"	Major pelvic press	"Hel-lo, gorgeous. I want you."
The "bear"	All-engulfing, full-body, mind, soul hug	"You're yummy, and I dig you."
The "circle"	Relaxed, full-body press, accompanied by a kiss	"You're mine, and I adore you."

Kissing is an intimate act — at least, intimate kissing is. You're literally opening up to someone. Your eyes are (usually) closed, and your neck is exposed. Physically (and primally), it's a very vulnerable position. Emotionally, it's incredibly vulnerable. How many folks have lain awake at night, dreamily remembering their date's kiss?

A college friend of mine once confided that if she kissed a man, she'd sleep with him. I was shocked at such a confession, until she explained it further. Kissing is such an intimate act, she said, perhaps the most intimate act, that she'd never kiss someone unless she was ready to go all the way. Others feel kissing is foreplay, and lots of folks like kissing all by itself.

Keeping your lips to yourself

Before I jump into all the kissing details, I need to mention two types of less-intimate physical contact and what they may mean about the success of your date:

- **Handshake:** If your date extends his or her hand instead of lips, it means one of two things: One, he or she is trying to do the right (as in respectful) thing and not move too fast. Two, the moment is awkward, and your date isn't sure what to do. A handshake isn't necessarily a brush-off. A kiss-off is a brush-off. If you want more, try a gentle, friendly hug and see what happens.

✔ **Hug:** Since your entire body is involved, a hug can be the gateway to more intimacy. It's also what Uncle Wally and Aunt Mildred do to you just before they pinch your cheeks. The duration of the hug determines what happens next. If it's a quick body-pressing, take it as the equivalent of a quick kiss (see the next section). If your date holds you close, and you like it, a simple tilt of the head and, voilá, you're in perfect kissing position.

It's in his (or her) kiss

Okay, we've finally arrived at the Super Bowl, the World Series . . . okay, at least at that first, magical moment, the first kiss.

According to Boston College professor William Cane, author of *The Art of Kissing,* there are 25 different ways to smooch. 25! There's the eye kiss, the wet kiss, the butterfly, the friendly, and the ever-popular lip-o-suction. That's just naming a few. Unless you plan to end your date with a "see ya" peck on the cheek, it's important to know the difference between a quick kiss, a serious kiss, and seriously making out:

✔ **Quick kiss:** Quick kisses are everywhere. People who barely know one another quick kiss on the cheek when they meet. In France, the double-cheek quick kiss is part of the national identity. If your date leans forward at the end of your time together and quick kisses you on the cheek, say a quick goodbye. Though a major smooch session may be coming later, it's the last thing on your date's mind tonight.

If, on the other hand, your date quick kisses you hello, especially if it's more sweet than scary or sexy, you're picking up on some fairly serious chemistry.

✔ **Serious kiss:** This is a kiss you can see coming. Your date has been preparing the proper approach in his or her mind, and there's a thrilling tingle of anticipation in the air. A serious kiss is one of intention. It's sensual more than sexual and takes time when done properly. A serious kiss is one of the best signs that your date can't wait to see you again.

✔ **Making out:** All about lust, making out is an earnest lip-lock intended as a prelude to something more — not always sex . . . though the promise and possibility of sex are definitely part of the scene. Making out is characterized by a full-body experience. Your lips are only the initiators.

Making out uses the hands, hot breath on the neck, bodies pressed together. ***Warning:*** Don't make out with a date you don't want to see again. It sends a mixed message, as well as a mess of hormones that have nowhere to go.

In general, men view kissing as a prelude to the main event: sex. For men, a woman who kisses well promises to be a tiger in the sack, too.

Women often see kissing as a perfectly good activity in and of itself, rather than a means to an end. Women could kiss all night, and then say goodnight without feeling "cheated" out of sex. For women, a guy who's a "great kisser" is a guy who takes his time, a guy who's capable of love as well as lust.

The signs

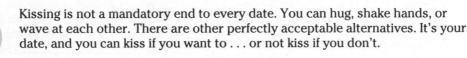

First kisses are so loaded with possibility, expectation, sexuality, sensuality, tenderness, and emotion, it's a wonder people don't explode on the spot. Before you get to the door, or to the moment of truth, I want you to make sure your date is sending all the right signals that he or she is ready to take your relationship to level two.

Kissing is not a mandatory end to every date. You can hug, shake hands, or wave at each other. There are other perfectly acceptable alternatives. It's your date, and you can kiss if you want to . . . or not kiss if you don't.

Her signs

You can tell that a woman is interested in a kiss if

- She's facing you, arms down, body relaxed.
- Her head is tilted upward.
- She doesn't appear to be ending the date with some definitive remark like, "Thanks. I'll call you."
- Her lips are parted.
- She gazes into your eyes.

If she's not interested, she'll

- Clamp her jaw shut.
- Fumble for her keys.
- Avoid eye contact.
- Turn her body away from you.
- Glue her chin to her chest.
- Hold out her hand and say, "Thanks."

His signs

A guy looking forward to a little lip action will

- Position his body between you and the door.
- Act nervous.

How to kiss

A first kiss, whether you're 15 or 50, is thrilling, sweet, nerve-wracking, intimate, awkward, and incredibly vulnerable — all in the first five seconds. Forget about what you've seen in the movies (show biz kisses are well-rehearsed — mostly so the kissers don't cover up each other's faces) or on stage (actors sometimes skip the lips and kiss between the lower lip and the chin to preserve the actress' lipstick!). You'll bump noses and knock teeth and giggle nervously as well as feel tingly all over — which is all perfectly okay.

Though there is no "right" way to kiss, here are a few pointers to help you successfully land a lip-lock:

✔ Check out your date's body language. Some signs your date is kiss-ready: head tilted up, eye contact, uncrossed arms, body facing you.

✔ As soon as you decide to go for it, do it. Hovering near some girl or guy's lips will only make both of you freak out.

✔ Maintain eye contact on the way to your date's lips. Don't shut your eyes until you arrive, or you may get lost on the way.

✔ Start gently. Press your lips sweetly against your date's. Save the tongue action for later.

✔ Pull back. Gaze into your date's eyes. If it's a go, you'll know by the way he or she looks longingly back at you. If not, smile and say goodnight, and your face will be nicely saved.

✔ The second lip-press is when you can go French. This means tongue. This doesn't mean gagging your date or thrusting home or swallowing his or her tongue as soon as it darts into your mouth. Instead, gingerly part your lips and venture forth.

A light, flickering touch with your tongue can produce major results. The tongue is a cluster of nerve-endings. Imagine "caressing" your date's tongue and lips and mouth.

✔ Don't overdo it. Variety — kissing the eyelashes, neck, nibbling on the lips — is the spice that flavors all great kissing.

✔ Show no visible signs of leaving or ending the date.

✔ Tilt his head upward.

✔ Lick his lips.

If he's not interested, he'll

✔ Walk you directly to your door or car, without hesitation.

✔ Keep his hands in his pockets.

✔ Look at his feet.

✔ Avoid eye contact at all costs.

What about sex on the first date?

On a first date, sex should be out of the question. You're just getting to know each other, emotions are running hot, your head may be swimming in infatuation hormones — not an ideal time to take such a dramatic physical and emotional step. Which is what sex really is.

There are several really compelling reasons not to have sex on a first date:

- ✔ **Health:** In addition to AIDS, there are a lot of sexually transmitted diseases, or STDs, running rampant out there: chlamydia, genital warts, syphilis, gonorrhea, and herpes (a virus you're stuck with for life). Another STD you don't hear too much about is hepatitis C, an incurable virus that causes a liver infection.

- ✔ **Translation:** Sex doesn't always mean the same thing to men and women. You may think it's no big deal, but your partner is mentally picking out china patterns. You simply need more than one date to make sure you're both headed in the same direction.

- ✔ **Exposure:** On nearly every level, sex is about exposure. You're (at least partially) naked. You're opening your body and a piece of your soul to another person. Major stuff, *not* to be entered into lightly.

- ✔ **Intimacy:** Sex is a very intimate act. Even if it feels more physical to you, it's a primal union that opens up all sorts of emotional nooks and crannies you may not even know you had. The intimacy of sexuality is a powerful, loving, amazing thing. It's to be nurtured and cherished, not taken lightly.

For more info on the timing and impact of sex on a relationship, see Chapter 17.

One final, tacky word here about sex on the first date. Even if both of you think you're both special, sex on the first date raises the doubt in the land of the insecure (which is everybody): If they'd sleep with me on the first date, they probably sleep with everybody. "I've never done this before" won't ring true even if it is, so something special and rare has been transformed into something common and suspect. Hold off, and see if it doesn't pay great dividends.

Post-Datem

You said goodnight and locked the door behind you. Her sweet kiss is still on your lips, or his whisper of affection is still warm in your ear. This was a first date that will go down in the annals of dating. It was so delicious you can still taste it. It's now time for the post-datem.

Gaining a little perspective

Every date has one — a sort of "after" date where you relive each moment that happened in the hours before. Think Sandra Dee in baby-doll pajamas writing passionately in her diary. Or Frankie Avalon singing to the stars on a moonlit beach. This is the post-datem. I must warn you, it's a very precarious time. Memory can magnify both the good and the bad. By morning, you'll believe you were out with either Adonis or The Monster from the Blue Lagoon or one of the Desperate Housewives or just somebody desperate. Or worse, you'll be convinced you single-handedly ruined what was potentially the love match of your life. None are true.

A date is a series of moments, looks, exchanges, sighs, touches, blunders, brilliance, possibilities, disappointments, and delights. It's subliminal, on the surface, conscious, and unconscious. It's the apex of your past experiences and the launching pad for the future. It's an emotional and intellectual stew. No single moment either made or broke your date. Even if your date swears it's true ("The moment you said you like pizza, I knew it was love"), it's not.

I know it's hard to do, but in your post-datem, I want you to put your date into perspective. You don't have to squash your lover's high just when you're feeling so good, but remember what I mentioned earlier: A date is just a date. If you take it too seriously, you're in for both heartaches and headaches. Instead, when you get home from your date, I want you to take a deep breath and relax. Don't decide that you blew it — or that you want your best friend to be your maid of honor at the wedding.

Chilling out

Take ten minutes to calm down. Give yourself the same gift you gave yourself before your date — a toe-to-head wave of relaxation. Clench and release your body parts in this order: toes, calves, thighs, buttocks, abs, biceps, shoulders, neck, and face. Progressively tighten each muscle, then release, and do it twice. (See Chapter 9 for details on this technique.)

If you think it's going to be hard to sleep, write down what you're feeling and, later, you can burn, flush, or preserve the record for your unborn grandkids.

Doesn't that feel good? Now you're ready to go to sleep and dream and wake up tomorrow to evaluate your date in the cold light of day and decide where you want to go from here.

You may be tempted to call a friend, e-mail your ex, text your date or anybody you figure is still awake, or write a diary's worth on your Facebook page. Resist the temptation. Instead, write down in a private diary all that you need to get off your chest. Writing in a private diary will allow you to savor without sharing and give the fairy dust a few hours to settle before you go off the deep end emotionally and publically.

Chapter 12

Not Having a Way Cool Time

*L*et's face it — everyone isn't going to like you; you're not going to like everyone. That's life. Admittedly, it doesn't feel terrific when someone would rather not see you again, but it's only one person, one person's opinion, one date on planet Earth. The ground doesn't have to tremble or swallow you up to put you out of your misery. Lighten up. Actually, a semi-awful date can be a gift from the gods of dating, an opportunity to take a look at yourself, your expectations, the signals you send, the people you pick to date, your behavior, your level of relaxation, and your ability to communicate who you really are.

Note: The possibility of a bad date is more likely with someone you've met via the Internet than someone you've already met in person. The Internet simply can't give you any hint about physical chemistry no matter how recent the picture.

Your Date Hates You

This section is a look at the stomach-churning, gut-wrenching, queasy possibility that you haven't knocked 'em dead — that the whole thing has turned deadly for them but not for you. Don't be tempted to turn the page as quickly as your little fingers will allow. It happens to EVERYONE.

The trick is not to become overly sensitive or obtuse. The last thing I want you to do is sit across from your date scanning his or her body language to determine if the date is a dud. Dating requires a leap of faith that the two of you can have a good time together for an hour or two. Think positive. Enter any dating situation with the expectation that a fun time will be had by all. Reevaluate, if necessary, when evidence to the contrary bubbles up. Life isn't a mood ring. I'm going to give you some warning signs, but context is everything when evaluating whether your date is having a good time or would rather be home with a pint of Häagen-Dazs.

A yawn can be the end of a really tough week as well as boredom. Looking at your watch doesn't always mean you can't wait to get the heck out of there — it can be an old habit or a new watch. Lack of eye contact may mean your date is shy rather than sneaky or unwilling to let you see how much fun he or she is not having. A stumbling conversation may simply be faulty social skills or nerves rather than an unwillingness to expend air or thought on you. Use all your senses — including your sixth sense, intuition — to evaluate what your date is really trying to convey. Relax a bit.

Me, paranoid?

Should you sense that your date is less than thrilled with you, undoubtedly the question will arise, "Am I right, or am I paranoid?" Good question. Dating is an emotional experience. You're vulnerable. You're letting someone you barely know see the real you. Pretty scary stuff. It's only natural that you might feel a little insecure. You may misread nuances or misinterpret a yawn or a glance at a watch as a sure sign that you're on the verge of a dating meltdown — especially if you've had any dating disasters in the past (and who hasn't?). (See my book *Dating Disasters and How to Avoid Them* [Hay House] to feel instantly better.) But this may not be the case at all. Sometimes a yawn really is just insomnia. Glancing at a watch — well, some people need to get up early the next morning, even when they've had a great time the night before. So before you write this date off, find out if you really are being paranoid by asking yourself these questions:

- Was I dreading this date?
- Did I figure it probably wouldn't work out before the date even started?
- Am I trying to decipher the "hidden meaning" in everything my date says?
- Am I obsessed with how I come off?
- Does my date keep protesting that he or she was misunderstood?
- Has anyone ever told me before that I'm oversensitive?
- Has anyone ever called me "paranoid" before?
- What's reality and what's delusional — do I need a new date or serious medication?

If you answered "yes" to most of the questions, you may need to do a reality check before you dismiss this date. Or you may be too fearful to date at all.

See whether the answers you yourself give would make sense if your best friend were telling the story. Would you be calm or dialing for the paramedics?

If you wouldn't see anything all that alarming in these answers if they were your friend's, you've probably passed your own test, and it's time to shift the focus from you to your date.

Reading the signs

It's easy to tell when someone hates your guts. They sneer, they scowl, they scoff, they storm off in a huff. They won't make eye contact, they mace you, they call their Rottweiler and the fashion police. They take phone calls during dinner and text while you're telling your life story. Unless we're talking major meltdown or atomic winter, it is really unlikely that the clues will be so obvious. What is much more likely when a date goes sour is a slow process of disconnection, a major lack of chemistry that becomes more apparent as the date ticks on, rather than dramatic magnetic repulsion. Here are the six warning signs of potential date disaster:

- ✓ **Lack of eye contact:** Eye contact is the very essence of connection, the "window to the soul." If your date won't make eye contact, nothing else will connect.

- ✓ **Sullenness:** Your date is unresponsive and says as little as possible. Make sure that you're not monopolizing the conversation or asking too many personal questions, but if your date consistently responds with "Yeah," "No," and "Don't know," you have a pretty clear sign that things are not going well. This doesn't mean there will never be a gap of silence (or two or three), but when the gaps yawn like the Grand Canyon, something isn't working.

- ✓ **The "I" focus:** If your date's conversation is focused exclusively on him- or herself, without any apparent interest in you, it's a sign of either no interest in you or a preoccupation with self. Yech.

- ✓ **Emotionally out of sync:** Have you ever been with somebody who totally "gets it"? Every nuance, every joke, every raised eyebrow? You're in tune. Conversely, if you find yourself laughing alone a lot during your date, explaining punch lines, or finding humor where your date finds horror (or worse, nothing), you and your date are likely really different and are going to have a rough time finding any common emotional ground.

- ✓ **Physically out of sync:** A body speaks volumes of feelings. Connected, interested people lean in toward each other or sit close to one another. If one body consistently says, "I'm out of here," or "Not interested" and remains aloof throughout the date, it's a fair bet the head feels the same thing.

- ✓ **Edgy or anxious or sad:** A wee bit of nerves is understandable, but if your date is in an obvious emotional turmoil that doesn't let up, it's a sign that your time together is in the dumps, too.

Getting more info

When you feel disaster in your gut, or see it in your date's response, bring it to your lips. I don't pretend this is always easy to do, but trust me on this: It's better to know than to stumble around in ignorance. If you feel like your date is not going well, here are some things you may want to say:

✔ "I'm sensing you're not having a good time. Is this true?"

✔ "I'd appreciate your honesty. Are you having fun?"

✔ "Is there something I've said or done to offend you?"

✔ "Are we not quite clicking here?"

The truth isn't always fun to hear. Sometimes it's downright painful. But, when you give people the chance to be honest with you, they usually will in a kind and gentle way. You don't want to date someone who doesn't want to date you. It's as simple as that. You don't want to have to convince someone to like you, or ask them to hang in until chemistry kicks in. This is not an endurance test or some dating karmic reincarnation where you're doomed to repeat every awful experience and where your cosmic score in each category is added up and totaled at the end before you can escape.

A date is an organic process as much as it is planning and prep work. Mother Nature is in there orchestrating the event, right alongside your careful blueprint for the perfect outing. Sometimes you just have to chalk it up to fate — this date wasn't meant to be. Find out what went awry — don't blame yourself or your date. Then move on. Don't obsess about why it didn't work out. Try not to take it too personally. Most importantly, no whining.

No whining!

If you've ever been in a long line on a hot, sweaty day with a bunch of tired little kids, you know what whining is all about. It's annoying, cloying, tiring, and, most of all, unproductive. Whining never gets you anywhere but on someone's nerves. Don't do it. If your date tells you he or she is having a rotten time, suck it up. Yeah, you're right. It hurts, but no whining. It isn't the end of the world. All of the following constitute the whine response:

✔ "Just my luck."

✔ "My last date dumped me, too."

✔ "Boy, I sure do know how to pick 'em, don't I?"

✔ "This always happens just when I start liking someone."

If you feel these words — or their ilk — bubbling to the surface, stop immediately, press your lips together and refuse to speak again until you've shed that whole sackcloth-and-ashes routine and are ready to respond like the mature person (not victim!) you are. The time to lick your wounds is later, when you're home running a hot bubble bath, or calling your mom for a hug or a best friend for support or the bakery to see if it has any double fudge brownies left.

Ending on a positive note

Your job, when your date isn't dazzled by you, is to listen gracefully and non-defensively and smile sweetly and make a swift exit as soon as the coast is clear. No need to prolong a bad date.

One of the biggest pitfalls to a date that feels like it's heading downhill is the "snowball effect" — you sense something's wrong, you panic, you clam up, you overreact, and it just makes matters worse. Suddenly, a not-great date is on its way to disasterville. If things are really awful, it makes more sense to call a polite and gentle halt rather than hurt someone's feelings for hours or waste your time or your date's time. It really is okay to say, "You don't seem to be having a good time. Shall we just chalk this up to experience?" Be honest. 'Fess up. Stop the snowball before it becomes an avalanche and buries you both. Ignoring an overwhelming feeling; trying to hide, squash, cover up, or pretend it isn't there; or wishing it weren't there isn't going to change the reality. You're not responsible for your feelings, just your behavior. If you can gently acknowledge your feelings, you can deal with them.

A lousy date isn't a reason to inflict pain on either of you. It isn't necessary to hang in there and finish what you started. It's okay to say, "I think we should call it a night." It's also okay to use that universal come-down line almost all daters have heard at least once, "I think we should just be friends." Not every couple has chemistry. That's what dates are for — to find out.

Hey, chemistry happens, or it doesn't. It can't be faked or manufactured. The feeling is out of your hands. If your date says he or she just doesn't feel any chemistry between the two of you, don't take it personally, but also don't assume a few more hours will make a whole lot of difference. While it's true that a deep love can develop slowly over time, this is a date, not an arranged marriage. Chemistry up-front is helpful on both sides for future promise; it gives you both motivation to explore further — unless it's so overwhelming that you both ignore every other part of what might be going on between the two of you. Overwhelming initial passion can move you both at the speed of light past things you ought to be assessing slowly and carefully (see Chapter 16 on taking things slow). Don't worry too much if you're not turned on as long as you're not turned off.

Don't I know you from somewhere?

A male friend of mine was fixed up on a blind date by a couple he'd known for ten years. He was excited. Divorced two years, he'd only been on sporadic dates since. So he got himself all spiffed up and showed up at the woman's front door precisely on time. As soon as she opened the door, however, the date went south.

Taking one look at him, her face fell. Even though she made a quick recovery, he saw her disappointment. Conversation was stilted, which made him feel even worse. When she excused herself to make a "quick phone call," he was convinced she was complaining about

him to their mutual friend. Dinner was agony as his insecurities mounted. Finally he blurted out, "What have I done to make you hate me?"

She admitted that it wasn't his appearance, but the fact that she had coincidentally been in group therapy with his ex-wife. My friend's date recognized him immediately from her description of the unusual color of his eyes and height and felt that she knew too many intimate details of his previous marriage to approach the relationship with an open heart. Both would have been spared some anguish if she'd blurted out, "Weren't you married to Mary Jo?"

Do be careful about being negative about your date because your feelings got hurt. The Internet is forever, so resolve that only good stuff that is appropriate for public consumption will ever appear next to your name or picture. Additionally, avoid negativity in your Tweet Stream or Facebook updates. Not only is it bad manners, but also it reflects badly on you when others, possibly future dates, see what you've said. To avoid bad Internet behavior, simply stay away from your Facebook, Twitter, and MySpace updates for the 48 hours after a date.

Tuition for Dating 101

If your date goes down the drain, give yourself a break. It happens. Life is a curve ball, an off-speed pitch, a fast ball low and inside. Even Ted Williams struck out more often than he hit a home run. It may feel lousy right now, but remind yourself, once again, it's only one date. You'll have tons more nights on which you can strut your stuff. Use the experience to learn something so it won't happen again. An autopsy is a great idea. The date died — figure out why. Answering the following questions in your dating notebook (see Chapter 1) can help you figure out what went wrong.

Answer these questions as soon as you can after the date ends, when your impressions are still fresh. By keeping these notes, you can begin to look for patterns in your behavior (see Chapter 4).

Tomorrow, after a few hours have passed between tonight's date and the rest of your life, I want you to reread your responses and see if they say anything to you. Don't pass judgment; don't look for hidden meaning. Simply read through and see what it says. If you haven't already, read Chapter 5 for tips on how to attract great dates into your life. For now, give yourself a non-chemical treat (unless it's chocolate), take a deep breath, prop your feet up, and chill out.

First, at the top of a sheet of notebook paper, write your date's name, the date (day, month, year) and time of the date, and where you went. Also note when and where you first met. Then on a scale from 1 to 10 (0 = meltdown; 10 = divine), rate the date as a whole.

From there, reflect on the date and answer the following questions. Make sure you're being *really* specific here (for example, nice smile when we met, good table manners, well-groomed).

- ✔ What positive stuff happened? In what ways did the date go well?

- ✔ What was icky poo poo? In what ways did the date stink?

- ✔ What were your expectations? (***Tip:*** See if you can make yourself aware of what disappointed you, which will instantly focus on what you expected.)

- ✔ Were your expectations based on how someone acted before?

- ✔ What patterns emerge that you have noticed on previous dates, in the other relationship? Is this déjà vu all over again?

Now reflect on your current feelings.

- ✔ How are you feeling right now?

- ✔ What do you want to do? For example, do you want to try again, talk to a friend, join a monastery, reread the whole book, take a vacation from dating?

- ✔ What can you do differently on your next date to offset this problem and change the pattern?

- ✔ Did you feel that your date saw the real you, yes or no? If no, why not?

Answering these questions after every not-so-hot date and/or journaling about your experiences can help you learn from rather than focus on less-than-successful dates. But please avoid sending a "this is why you shouldn't have treated me badly" letter or e-mail to your date, which falls into the whining category I address earlier in this chapter. Every once in a while, in an effort to save face and salvage some remnant of dignity, you may be tempted to contact your date explaining why you deserve better or how the creep hurt your feelings. Resist this urge. You should never put anything into a letter or e-mail that you are not willing to have advertised on the front page of *The New York Times*. Even something like "have a nice life" can sound sarcastic. I know you may be hurting, but don't write down your feelings anyplace, except for in a diary that no one else will see.

It's chemistry

Chemistry is mentioned a lot when two people click. "I just knew," "It was love at first sight," "We were destined to be together," "Soul mates" . . .

Beware. While some couples feel an instant and powerful pull to one another (which isn't always sustainable or prolonged), for most, the response is slower and subtler. An interest. A tingle. A thrill. A desire to get closer. In a word: chemistry.

A number of physiological changes take place in your body when you encounter a person who turns you on. Your pupils dilate (you want to see more of them), your heart races, your palms get sweaty. You feel energized, like you could stay up all night. And you probably could — that's what the expression "turned on" really means. Physically, your body is totally awake, alert, and raring to go — basic biochemistry 101. Hormones turn you on — lust in its most basic, uncomplicated, thrilling form. Your body is saying, "Let's party."

Unfortunately, as convenient as it would sometimes be to be able to bottle it, chemistry is either there, or it's not — and it's impossible to fake.

You Hate Your Date

The assumption in this section is that your date seems to be having a good time and you definitely are not. (If the situation is reversed — that is, you're having a good time and your date isn't — see the preceding section. If both of you are miserable, see the next section.) Hey, it happens. Though there's always at least some fun to be had on a date with anyone even if it doesn't seem so at the time, not every date you go on will be one for the scrapbook. That's okay. You can learn as much about yourself and your likes and dislikes from a date that fizzles as you can from one that's sizzling hot. Dating, by its very nature, is getting to know someone better. Naturally, you're not going to hit it off with everyone, nor will everyone hit it off with you. That's just human logic. Learning how to bow out gracefully, that's human kindness — and the topic of this section.

Making it to the (not) bitter end

Doing the right thing and letting your bad news date naturally run its course will score you several brownie points with the great Datemaster in the sky. If you believe in karma, an act of generosity will be returned to you someday. Don't get me wrong — I'm not saying you should grit your teeth and bear it until the clock strikes 12 and you can safely call it a date. What I am saying is that there are ways to make the best of a not-so-hot situation.

If you're not having a good time but your date is, give these strategies a try. Not only can they get you through the evening, but they give you the opportunity to discover interesting and worthwhile things about your date and yourself — and *that's* never a waste of time.

- ✔ **Identify three things you like about your date.** Everyone has at least a few interesting and unique qualities.

    When a date starts to go south, we tend to magnify the negative moments in our minds and discount the positive. Reverse this trend: Find three things you like about your date. They don't have to be big things. You don't have to suddenly realize you love this person's personality. Start small. Do you like her hair? His hands? Her laugh? His quirky sense of humor? Her small pores?

- ✔ **Become a good listener.** View this as a great opportunity to sharpen your listening skills. Stay in the moment. Don't second-guess what you could have possibly done here or worry about what you're going to tell your friends or how you're going to get a good night's sleep. Really listen to what your date has to say — without judgment. You may hear something interesting.

- ✔ **Relax and tune in to your surroundings.** Enjoy the food, the atmosphere, the popcorn, the movie, the biscotti, the sunshine, the snow, the sound of bowling pins falling each time you score a strike. Shift your focus away from a date that's not working out to all the things that are perfectly fine.

Avoiding blame

Understandably, you're going to feel disappointed when you first get the inkling that your date isn't working out. Either people click, or they don't. When they click, their communication is like a tapestry — each shared experience and similarity intertwines. Each giggle, stare, brush of a hand is a gossamer thread, one on top of the other, until a beautiful scene is depicted. When folks don't click, the date is more like a wrinkly paper bag — uninteresting, unappealing, and just plain un-wonderful. When you discover that the situation has slipped off the edge, don't be tempted to blame your date or yourself for the unpleasantness — no need to accuse your date of:

- ✔ Using you
- ✔ Being an idiot
- ✔ Being ungrateful
- ✔ Being uncivilized

Sometimes two perfectly nice people can just not mesh very well. If you take that perspective, you don't have to take offense or blame or a position — just take a deep breath.

Being polite

Your mom has explained the purpose of good manners: to avoid making another person feel bad. Well, your date may not be going as well as you wanted, but now is not the time to abandon all those skills that your parents spent a lifetime drilling into you. The basics of being polite include the following:

- **Stay put.** No leaving out the back door, faking a headache, or spending the entire date in the restroom reading phone numbers carved into the wall.

- **Have a conversation.** Sitting stone-faced is the ultimate slap in the face. Find something to talk about even if you discover you two are worlds apart. Seen any good movies lately?

- **Maintain eye contact.** You don't need to gaze into your date's eyes, certainly, but staring up at the ceiling is rude.

- **Listen.** Your date may not notice that things aren't going swimmingly. Tuning this person out will only cause him or her to try harder to reach you, and panic isn't pretty.

- **Make nice.** As Elvis said, "Don't be cruel." Your date didn't kidnap you. If things aren't going well, so be it. Without being overly encouraging (you don't want a bad date hoping for bad date number two), be civil and kind.

- **See your date home.** It's impolite to abruptly end your date the moment the check is paid, the ending credits roll, or the coffee cup is empty. You don't need to prolong it, but you do need to finish what you both started. If you drove, drive your date home. If your date drove, accept a ride home. Or share a cab, a subway, a bus ride. No bolting or escaping is necessary. The only exception to this rule is if you are genuinely fearful of this person. It happens, infrequently but occasionally. If there is even a morsel of paranoia, call a cab and skedaddle, but it's still okay to be polite.

- **Behave as you'd like to be treated.** Show common courtesy. Smile, laugh at jokes, and avoid rolling your eyes to the back of your head. The goal here is to be kind without being dishonest.

The key to being polite is to think of yourself as Lord or Lady Bountiful — much too well-bred to let on that your bunions pinch or your fine sense of smell has just discerned that something has died. The goal of being polite is not to lead your date on, but to treat your date with the same kindness and respect with which you'd treat anyone.

Proclaiming truth: Honesty is a tricky policy

There you are sitting across from a date who's eager and hopeful and trying her or his best to engage you. This person is perfectly nice. Perfectly acceptable. Perfectly wrong for you. For whatever reason, you know it's not going to work out. How, then, do you let your date down easy? Be honest . . . without harming the poor, unfortunate soul unnecessarily.

Truth-telling is a tricky bit of business. In the guise of "truth," many a hurt has been inflicted. Do you really need to tell someone he or she is fat, even if that is the case? Do you need to say, "No, your nose isn't big; it's huge"?

Using tact

The difference between hurtful truth-telling and honesty is four letters: tact. The best way to be tactful is to put yourself in your date's shoes. If you wouldn't want to hear it, your date most likely won't want to hear it, either. To help you out of any potential corner into which you might paint yourself during a date gone sour, Table 12-1 provides a list of some tactful translations.

Table 12-1	Tactful Translations
How You Really Feel	*Tactful Translation*
I want to go home now.	Gee, it sure is getting late, and I've got an early morning tomorrow.
You bore me to tears.	Please excuse my yawning; it's been a really tough week.
We have nothing in common.	You've led such a different life than I have!
You sure seemed nicer when I asked you out.	There are so many sides to your personality.
What a waste of time!	I've been in such a time crunch these days, I never have time for the fun stuff.
You look nothing like your picture.	Your photo doesn't do you justice.
Why don't you say something instead of just sitting there?	You seem quiet — are you okay?
Are you ever going to shut up?	You're so full of energy!
I never want to see you again.	Tonight has been an experience. Thank you.

Telling the whole truth and nothing but the truth, sort of . . .

The one time you really do want to tell the truth, the whole truth, and nothing but the truth is when your date asks, "Can I call you?" — or worse, "Will you call me?" The phone thing is fraught with nearly every conceivable emotion — hope, fear, anxiety, trust, excitement, rejection, and anticipation.

Now is the moment to take a deep breath and tell the truth. It's not fair to leave her waiting by a phone that refuses to ring or have him logging on to check his e-mail every few hours. If you're not going to call, now or in the millennium, don't say you will. Period. It's not cool. It's not fair. It's not what polite, respectful people do. That said, here are a few tactful ways to get the message across:

- "Though I had fun tonight, I don't think it's going to work out between us."
- "To be honest, I see you as more of a friend."
- "We're just too different, you and I."
- "I don't want to mislead you by telling you I'll call. I'm sorry, but I probably won't."
- "I'm going to be really busy at work for the next couple of months."
- "Family concerns are going to keep me tied up."

It's tough. No two ways about it. Everyone wants to believe in love and union and two souls who were meant to be together. But if this isn't that scene, don't make it even worse by lying and leading your date to believe it might one day be.

Handling hurt feelings

Rejection is just someone's opinion. You don't like everyone, and not everyone is going to like you. Don't allow your discomfort to make you mean. Stringing someone along, pretending you like him or her when you really don't, is cowardly and cruel. In the long run, you'll inflict more pain by pretending, which is really to protect yourself. Pretending is much harsher than saying upfront that this isn't working for you. If your date is smitten, the truth is going to pinch a bit but for less time or intensity than if you lie.

You've been honorable, have asked your date out, or have been asked out on the assumption of potential good stuff. You've now discovered things aren't working out. No need to push the guilt button. No one likes to hurt anyone's feelings. It's important to be humane and human: When the news is hard to break and hard to take, be aware of what you're feeling and why, and be specific about why it's not working for you without being judgmental. Unless you are incredibly adept at letting your date down gently (how did you get so much practice? We may need to talk), you're very likely going to hurt feelings. When you do:

Please, don't do me any favors!

I know a man in his 50s who's been dating a woman in her 50s for the past three years. Their relationship perplexes everyone who knows them. They seem miserable together: always snipping at each other, forever on the verge of breaking up. But they never do.

One day, when the man was telling me about his latest lover's spat, I finally asked him why he didn't just leave her. "I don't want to hurt her feelings," he said.

It stuck in my mind so clearly because, just the day before, his girlfriend had told me he was the most hurtful man she'd ever known. "He only pretends to care about me," she said.

Life seems awfully short for this kind of nonsense.

- ✔ **Acknowledge your date's rights to feelings.** Don't pretend everything is okay or get defensive if your date lashes out or is upset. Listen quietly and patiently.

- ✔ **Don't try to fix it.** These are your date's feelings, not yours. You deal with your feelings, and let your date do the same.

- ✔ **Apologize for the hurt, not the fact.** Not liking someone isn't a crime. You didn't do anything wrong. As a human being, you feel bad when another human being feels bad, but when you start down the "sorry" road, the next thing you may find yourself doing is trying to make it up to your date. Don't start down that slippery slope.

- ✔ **Let go.** Ultimately, you have to make peace with the whole situation by realizing another fact of life: Not every date is terrific any more than every meal is wonderful, every sunset grand, or every flavor chocolate.

Chalking it up to experience

You can learn something from every experience. Sometimes the tuition is high, and sometimes it's not. If you view this date as a learning experience rather than dashed hopes, a waste of time and money, or a night you could have spent watching *Grey's Anatomy* or *30 Rock*, the entire date will feel very different. After all,

- ✔ It's only one night (day, afternoon, hour).

- ✔ It never has to happen again.

- ✔ This date can help you figure out what you want or don't want next time.

The best way to avoid making another mistake is to figure out specifically what went wrong this time. After the date is over, after you're home and reliving the scenario in your mind (or trying to get it out of your mind), take out your dating notebook (see Chapter 1) and make two columns on a piece of paper: "What I was originally attracted to" and "What totally turned me off." List everything you can think of in each column. Be honest. No one is looking. You can burn or flush this list later. Even if what originally attracted you was her *Dancing with the Stars* bod and moves and what turned you off was the fact that *Dancing with the Stars* is her favorite TV show, write it down. Write it all down. When you're finished, you'll have a much clearer picture of exactly what went awry . . . and how to avoid making the same mistake next time.

You Hate Each Other

Bad dates happen. Just as a movie trailer sometimes looks so good you can't wait to see the film and then the film is a real stinker, bad dates can look great in preview and then pale in reality. It's nobody's fault. This date just wasn't in the cards. Time to shuffle on to the next date.

Really, this is the second-best dating scenario. Optimally on a date, the two of you hit it off and have a great time. Barring that, it's much better that both of you realize your date was a washout. No one gets hurt. No one has to be the rejector or the rejectee. You can shake hands and say, "Good luck," and go on your merry way, which is perfectly fine.

Facing facts

A date is a level-three experience: Level one is meeting someone, talking on the phone, chatting online, staring longingly at the back of his or her head all semester in class. On level one, there's enough of a connection and attraction to warrant venturing into level two. Level two is a little pre-date interaction (see Chapter 5), which gets pretty quickly to level three, the date.

Unless this is a totally blind date, meaning you're set up with someone you've never even spoken to before, it's safe to say there are at least some good feelings passing back and forth between the two of you before your date begins. Once the date gets going, however, the connection and attraction will be tested and tried on for size — from both sides. Liking or not liking each other is rarely an instant evaluation. Luckily, most of us are willing to give somebody a bit more time because we'd like them to give us a bit more of a chance, too. Deciding whether you want to invest a bit more time and effort in getting to know someone is a process of evaluating lots of verbal and nonverbal cues.

Speed bumps

Everything you and your date say and do from the moment you meet is recorded and processed and filed in both of your brains. Unless you turn each other off from the get-go (see the later section "Total turnoffs"), a sense of dissatisfaction, disappointment, and unease usually builds until you realize, "Uh-oh, this date isn't working out. I'm definitely not having fun, and I don't want to be here."

The tricky thing is making sure it's not just nerves or fear or shyness or arrogance that's convinced you guys you're having a rotten time. So first — a quick reality check. Ask yourself these questions:

✔ **Am I relaxed, or am I tense and fearful?**

Being vulnerable and letting another human being get close can be very scary stuff. Just like any other animal, scared humans sometimes lash out to keep other "threatening" animals at bay, or they retreat to the safety of their cave or shell. Perhaps this is what both of you are doing right now. If you're so tense that your true personality is hidden beneath a mass of knotted muscles, your date may dislike the tension, not you. You're not allowing the real you to emerge. If you feel completely stressed-out, take a few deep breaths or excuse yourself to the restroom and do three minutes of square breathing (see Chapter 2).

✔ **Is my date relaxed?**

The same standard that applies to you applies to your date. Your date may be so wracked with nerves that every response is stilted, every laugh forced, every reaction pretentious. Stress doesn't make anyone likable. Do what you can to make your date feel comfortable: Be friendly, initiate conversation, pull back a little. Try not to judge the success or failure of your date until things get a bit more relaxed.

✔ **Is it something my date said?**

Sometimes, one careless remark can send a whole date careening downhill. A friend of mine, who'd just changed the color of her hair, had a date attempt to make a joke. "Did they have a sale on red?" he asked her. Understandably, she was insulted, but she didn't say anything. Later her date told me he found her "cold and distant." She thought he had the class of a slug. Both were probably just really nervous. Human beings are complex creatures. One dumb remark does not a personality make. Make sure there's sufficient evidence to write the whole thing off. It's perfectly okay to say, "Wow, that comment seemed kind of hostile."

Make sure you're not letting other, relatively minor things like imperfect table manners, height, weight, sense of humor, style, driving habits, or dancing ability (or lack thereof) trigger a turnoff. You're both in a heightened emotional state, and your behavior may be exaggerated. Let things settle down before evaluating the whole date.

Total turnoffs

Although, theoretically, loathe at first sight should be no more or less common than love at first sight, loathing isn't always a slow-build. Here are ways to completely turn each other off in an instant:

- Neglecting to shower
- Eating like a pig
- Dressing like a hooker
- Talking only about yourself
- Abusing the waiter or clerk
- Whining
- Drinking too much
- Showing up stoned
- Talking about sex
- Insulting each other
- Insulting anybody else
- Acting superior
- Being a bigot
- Copping a feel
- Taking your shoes off in the car
- Tuning out electronically by texting, phoning, tweeting, or playing solitaire

If you discover that you really can't stand the person you're with — and you have a pretty good idea that the feeling is mutual — face the moment of truth without wasting another moment of your precious life.

Five signs you really do hate each other

- A piece of cilantro is stuck to your date's chin, and you don't bother to mention it. Your date knows it's there and doesn't bother to remove it.

- You both could describe every detail of the door but don't know what color your date's eyes are.

- If it were recorded, your conversation would make it on *America's Most Boring Videos*.

- You have to keep explaining punch lines.

- Your mouths are killing both of you from all that fake smiling.

Acknowledging the moment of truth

So there you are. Sitting across from your date, or next to him or her, or in the bathroom staring at your reflection, feeling afraid to face the truth. Don't. Face it. If you feel unhappy and sense that your date is miserable, too, denial only makes matters worse. Instead, do this:

- ✔ **Trust your instincts.** If it feels all wrong, it probably is — even if both of you are smiling and making nice.

- ✔ **Ask.** There's nothing wrong with asking your date whether what you're sensing is actually the truth. I wouldn't go so far as to blurt out, "Do you hate me as much as I hate you?" but asking if the discomfort in the air is real is really a good start.

- ✔ **'Fess up.** If your date is having as lousy a time as you are, he or she may ask you what's the matter. Tell the truth. Admit that things aren't zipping along as well as you'd hoped and ask if your date feels the same way.

- ✔ **Let it be.** Now is not the time to muse over what's going wrong. If there's no spark, this date's never going to jump-start, no matter how carefully you peer under the hood.

Exiting with style

The moment has arrived. You've finally faced up to the ugly truth: You'd both rather be anywhere but together, and a root canal is sounding better by comparison. Resist the temptation to duck out the back, make a mad dash for the door, or order a cab instead of dessert. The true measure of your soul is how you handle disaster. We can all be classy when the going is good. True style and honor come from handling bad situations well.

Don't worry. You don't have to sit there and imagine gnawing your foot off so you can escape the trap. You *can* call this one off — but do it with panache. Say:

- ✔ "Let's skip coffee and chalk this up to experience."

- ✔ "I'm ready to call it a night. You?"

- ✔ "The show (dinner, lunch, brunch, exhibit, walk) was fun. Thank you for sharing it with me. Can I give you a lift home?" (No need to be ugly.)

- ✔ "I'm sorry things didn't work out."

- ✔ "Let's toast this valiant effort and get the check."

Again, don't lie. Don't say you'll call. Don't say you had a great time when you didn't. Just end the date quickly and cleanly.

Reviewing expectations

One bad date doesn't mean much; a string of bad dates may mean a lot. If you keep thinking this one is "the one" and are wrong again and again, it may be time to stop, look, and listen.

When you get home, evaluate your expectations and examine your dating patterns. Only then can you stop making the same mistakes over and over. Answer the following questions in your dating notebook (see Chapter 1) so you have a basis on which to begin analysis, understanding, and change.

- ✔ What qualities must your ideal date absolutely, positively have?

- ✔ What must your ideal date *not* be?

- ✔ Why was this date a disaster?

- ✔ Think back to the last disaster date you had – what things went wrong then? (If this is your first bad date, skip this question.)

- ✔ Looking back over your lists, are there any similarities between what you put on the "My date must not be" list and the (one or) two "disaster date" lists? If so, nail those little suckers and write them down.

Is there a pattern? Is there a pit into which you keep falling? If your ideal date must not be rude, obese, or boring, and your disaster dates were rude, thin, and boring, perhaps you didn't look too far beyond the outer package when the date was first set up. Or if all your disaster dates turn out to be so self-involved they may as well be out with themselves, perhaps you don't know how to spot a narcissist early on. Don't worry. You don't have to keep falling in. Tables 12-2 and 12-3 can help you spot danger signs upfront (be aware that some pitfalls can be less than obvious).

Table 12-2	Spotting Date Danger Signs
If Your Date Is	*Your Date May Turn Out to Be*
Late	Inconsiderate
Talkative	Boring
Self-assured	Arrogant
Hard to get	Hard to please
A finicky eater	Obsessed with weight
Forgetful	An airhead
Glued to the vanity mirror	In love with him- or herself

Table 12-3	Less Obvious Pitfalls
If Your Date Is	*Your Date May Turn Out to Be*
Charming	Slippery
Glib	Superficial
Gorgeous	Self-centered
Quiet	Passive
Bubbly	Manic

Starting Over

The most important thing about a really bad date is making sure you don't obsess to the extent that you vow, "Never again." Becoming a hermit is not the antidote to a lousy date. Problem solving is. Figure out what you can do differently next time and get back in the race. Figure out what went awry and learn from the experience; you won't have to join a religious order with a vow of silence, solitude, and celibacy.

Don't rush into another date with just anybody, but do put this experience in perspective. Hey, it was *one crummy date* — no need to be bummed out about it endlessly. Pick yourself up, dust yourself off, and get ready to date all over again. Be thankful you both agreed on at least one thing — it didn't work.

Beware of the Groucho Marx School of Life that says, "I wouldn't want to belong to any club that would accept me as a member." In the world of dating, this if-they'll-have-me-I-don't-want-them mentality translates into two unappealing possibilities: "If they hate me, they must be really cool and have figured out the real me" or — even worse — "Nobody rejects me first. I'll charm them so they'll like me, and *then* I'll reject them." Take my advice: If it's lousy for both of you, let it go and be done with it. Amen.

A final only slightly preachy word: I've said it consistently throughout this chapter: Hurt feelings might be temporarily assuaged by blabbing, e-mailing, Facebooking about the whole lousy thing. Pleeeeze resist the temptation. Karma, especially dating karma, is a serious boomerang.

Part IV
The Day After and Beyond

The 5th Wave   By Rich Tennant

I'm just having trouble dating a guy whose name defaults to "Loony Fruitcake" on my Spell Checker.

In this part . . .

Hang on — you're now launched into that great gray area between a first date and a relationship. Whoa, boy. The day after date number one is 24 hours of fantasy, instant replays, post-mortems. It's a time of wonder . . . as in "I wonder what I should do next?" The day after date number two is similar but a bit more intense . . . as in "What's going to happen now?" No need to fret. I'll help you navigate these murky waters.

In this part, you'll find out how to open up without confessing, how to ask questions without interviewing, how to listen without nodding off, and how to let your date get to know the real you without scaring the dickens out of you both. If you think I'm convincing you about the danger of confession, you're paying attention, so I also give you a remedial lesson on when to share and with whom, when to keep things a secret (or at least off the Internet), and when to turn your back on Facebook.

I'll also give you a few tips on nipping this budding relationship in the bud if things aren't meant to be. Yeah, breaking up is hard to do, but not breaking up when you should is much harder on everyone. So buckle up. Hopefully, you're in for a long, fun ride.

Chapter 13

The Next Day

After a first date is over, there are feelings both men and women share: excitement (if the date went well), disappointment (if it went poorly), and anticipation (if it went well enough to ensure date number two). And that's about where the similarity ends.

Forgive the sexual stereotypes, but guys really do have a whole different take on the post-date period than women do. The difference is a fantasy thing, a time thing — not a biological thing. It's a part of our sociology, meaning that guys are socialized differently than girls are. Neither side is right or wrong. It's just what *is*. Therefore, the minutes, hours, days, and weeks after a first date are loaded with the potential for misunderstanding, miscommunication, and mistakes from both sides.

Clearing the air by understanding what's really going on, from both the male and female points of view, after the first date's over and before a second one occurs — *that's* what this chapter is all about.

Second Thoughts on First Impressions

A date-long first impression is different from the two-second once-over your date gives you when you initially meet. It's more than a primal, visceral thing. Throughout the time you spend together, your date's five senses are working overtime — taking it all in. Processing every nuance, every sigh, every touch. Even the stuff your date isn't aware he or she sees, hears, smells, touches, and tastes is seen, heard, touched, smelled, and tasted. Above and beyond the five senses are your date's sense of style, appropriateness, manners, space, self — you name it. Every part of your date's past and present being comes into play when evaluating you and how he or she feels about you. Yikes! No wonder we all get nervous on a first date!

What you can do if you don't want your first impression to last a lifetime is to create another one. As simple as that. It's okay to call your date and say, "I was a bit jittery last night. What do you say we try again next week?" Or you can lay your cards right on the table by saying, "I feel like I didn't show you who I really am. I'd like another chance to do so."

Honesty is appealing. Vulnerability is sexy. Unless you're a mass of quivering insecurity, few people can resist someone who's human enough to admit he or she didn't show a true picture and would like a second shot. (That is, unless you were truly the date from hell. We're assuming minor glitches here, not potential felonies.) It's also a great opportunity to find out about your date's tolerance for forgiveness, flexibility, ambiguity, and curiosity — all of which is incredibly valuable. Not valuable enough to purposely sabotage a date, but enough to give you the courage to ask for a second chance.

If your date was fantastic, no need to redo anything. If the date didn't go as well as expected, maybe a bit of remedial work is in order. If you have just experienced the Guinness Book's lousy-date record, you need to give yourself some first aid.

After an Icky Date

The day after a disastrous date can be full of blame, guilt, shame, and copious amounts of chocolate — if you let it. Or you can take a deep breath and call it like it is: one date that didn't ring your chimes. Period. What I *don't* want you to do is:

- Bad-mouth your date on Facebook or your Tweet Stream, to your bff or mom or even your diary. Keep yourself at least a little bit open and positive.
- Call and beg forgiveness.
- Berate yourself all day (week, month, year, life).
- Vow never to date again.
- Quickly arrange a date with just anybody to prove it's not you that's icky.
- Avoid feeling disappointed by overeating, over-drinking, over-drugging . . . overdoing *anything*.

Look, feeling disappointed is okay. It's a letdown when things don't work out as you hoped! But you can feel it without wallowing in it. You can experience a disappointment without draping yourself in black. Most importantly, you can forgive yourself and your date for not being a perfect match. It's nobody's fault. It's life.

Five ways to put a hideous date in perspective

1. Rent *Fatal Attraction*.

2. Thank technology for TiVo, DVRs, and Hulu — you didn't have to miss anything while you were out.

3. Count how many days you've been alive. Subtract only one.

4. Look at your watch — it just *seemed* like forever.

5. Check your pulse. You survived!

Paying life's tuition

Life is an education. At every turn, if your eyes and heart are open, you learn about yourself, about others, about love, about survival. Your not-so-great experiences are the tuition you pay for education; your so-great experiences are merit scholarships.

Hideous dates, if kept in perspective, are just another lesson in your ongoing education. A lousy date isn't the end of the world; it's the beginning of Dating 102.

Restoring your confidence

The worst side effect of a rotten date is the potential for ego devastation. How can you hop back on the horse when your date said you looked, acted, and brayed like one? What you may need the day after the date from hell is a real confidence booster. Even if you have to work the next day, set aside at least a teeny bit of time to do something you know you do well. Some possibilities are (this is also a good list to keep in mind if your date was so-so or even fabulous — or even if you've just resigned from dating forever):

- Get outside and take a walk or go golfing (even if it's miniature) or hiking or climb a mountain (even if it's a molehill).

- Get some exercise — you'll liberate endorphins, the feel-good chemicals.

- Make a gourmet meal.

- Make your mom laugh.

- Teach your old dog a new trick.

- Impress your boss.

- Eat chocolate — one piece, not a pound.

✔ Call a friend without referencing the icky date thang.

✔ Splurge on a magazine, CD, or book.

✔ Get a manicure/pedicure and change the color of your nails. Okay guys, maybe just a reflexology on your tootsies, though I have male friends who swear by sports pedicures. (No drop-off of testosterone whatsoever, promise.)

✔ Download a fun new dance tune online and dance in your living room.

Whatever you do, make sure it's life-affirming, fun, and filling — as in filling you up with pride. Then forget all about your lousy date and look forward to the next great one.

After a So-So Date

Obsessing about all the ways you could have made your so-so date so, *so* much better is a waste of time. Monday-morning quarterbacking works only in the NFL — not in the dating game. The date's over. Let it be. Unless it was a bona fide disaster (see the preceding section), you're probably going to get a second chance to spiff up that first impression.

Valium for the soul

Often, when things don't quite go as well as they could on a date, the reason is nerves. Nerves make you laugh too hard or too little, pre-judge every word you utter, or beat yourself up for every little faux pas. Your date was likely nervous, too. It's hard to be charming when your date is tense. It's also hard to put someone else at ease when you're stiff and uncomfortable.

When you get home from a so-so date:

1. **Sit down in a comfy chair.**

2. **Shut your eyes.**

3. **Take five deep breaths in through your nose, out through your mouth.**

4. **Visualize your date floating up and out of your consciousness like a soft, fluffy cloud.**

5. Repeat after me:

> I am not perfect.
>
> I don't need to be perfect to be loved.
>
> This was only one date.
>
> There will be another date.
>
> Next time I will feel safe enough to reveal more of myself.

Now, refer to the waiting-period guidelines in the section "Nine hints for limbo and surviving the wait" later in this chapter, and get some sleep.

All the right moves

The day after a so-so date can be confusing. Do you call? Do you sit tight? Apologize? Swear you'll never wear that puce pantsuit again? Knowing precisely when to be passive and when to charge is hard. My general rule is this: If your date derailed because of something you said or did, call and apologize. Everyone makes dumb mistakes. Everyone understands. It's saying *nothing* that leaves a bad taste with everyone.

If, on the other hand, your date just didn't sizzle like you hoped it would for some reason you can't pin down, let time shed a little light on the situation. Don't call the next day (or that night). In fact, don't call at all until you're sure of these three things:

Five ways to put a so-so date in perspective

1. Ask your parents if every date they ever had was stellar.

2. List how many good moments you had.

3. Remind yourself that not every word out of your date's mouth was a pearl of wisdom.

4. Count how many Saturday nights you have left if you live to be 85.

5. Rent *When Harry Met Sally* and *27 Dresses*.

✔ You want a second date because you like the person, not just because you want to make sure he or she likes you.

✔ You've identified what you may do differently next time, like relax, go to a place where you can talk, not bring your mother, and so on.

✔ You're not feeling so guilty and responsible that your second date becomes a "make-up" date instead of a second chance to get to know one another.

After the Perfect Date

After you've said goodnight and the ideal date has come to a close, both of you are high on life, awash in good feelings. You grin, sigh, kiss your dog on the top of his head, or nuzzle with your cat. If you're a girl, you want to do what girls do — talk about it; you want to lie down on your dorm bed or curl up with the phone and tell a good friend every glorious detail. If you're a guy, you feel all warm and fuzzy, too, but you probably carry those feelings more internally and quietly; you do your homework, turn on the TV, wash the car, read the paper, dribble a basketball, burp — your normal life stuff — all very satisfied that your date was a success. You don't need to fret. You feel like you've won the romance lottery, or at least a scratch-off ticket.

Inside your heads, however, a lush fantasy is brewing. Or, I should say, two lush fantasies: one female, one male. This is where things can get a little sticky if you expect your date to have the very same vision that you do. See Table 13-1 for what I mean:

Table 13-1	Post Great-Date Fantasies
Girl Fantasy	*Guy Fantasy*
The color of your bridesmaid's dresses	The color of her lingerie
Moonlit walks on the beach	Midnight sex on the beach
A great date every Saturday night	A great date for Super Bowl Sunday
Love	Lust
Adoration	Acceptance
Someone to watch over me	Someone to watch me

Along with these fantasies come the inevitable expectations that your date will act the same way you'd act. Table 13-2 shows how expectations vary:

Table 13-2	Expectations after a Great Date
Girl Expectations	*Guy Expectations*
He'll call the minute he gets home.	I'll see her again soon.
He'll call the next morning.	I'll call in a few days.
If I call him, I'll seem desperate.	If I call her, I'll seem needy.
If he really had a good time, he'll send flowers.	I only send flowers the day after we have great sex.
If he's thinking about me, he'll want to talk to me.	She's on my mind so much, I don't even need to talk to her, and I don't want to wimp out.
If he doesn't call within two days, the relationship is over.	Relationship?!

See the communication problem here?

Testosterone versus Estrogen Central

Really, the biggest potential for post-date communication glitches involves time. Guy time and girl time, that is, babycakes. They're not the same. Einstein was right: It's all relative. Here's what happens: You go out to a great dinner or a concert or the movies. You giggle, share popcorn. You both have a fabulous time. Sweetly kiss goodnight. Then he whispers, "I'll call you soon." Or she whispers the same. You both nod and head home.

Now, she assumes that *soon* means on the cell phone on the way home, from work the next morning, or at the very latest, within the next two days. *Soon* to him means "if I have a minute in my busy schedule," "when I get that new job," "when I have my fall class schedule in order," "when the football season is over." Or *soon* can mean "never," "if my mom pressures me," or "if the Knicks are out of contention." Problem city:

- Female is hovering by the phone; male is flipping channels on the remote control.

- If she calls right away (as she said she would), he thinks, "Whoa! She's really into me. Sex city!" She's really just saying, "I had a nice time and I'd like to see you again."

- If he calls when he gets around to it (as he said he would), she's an ice queen because so much time has elapsed (a week, a month, a year, a decade). How dare he leave her hanging! Suddenly, she's too busy to see him again, and the budding relationship blows sky-high.

What's wrong with this picture? In a word, the word *soon*.

Guys: Don't say "soon" when you're whispering in her ear or any other time.

Girls: Don't believe it if he should slip. (And your being vague doesn't help much, either. Take it to the bank — he'll expect a much longer passage of time than you, most likely.) If he does say, "I'll call you soon," try one of these responses:

- ✔ **"I'll be out of town for a couple of days. Could you call me after that?"** Even if you're not leaving town, this blows that whole "waiting by the phone" thing right out of the water.

- ✔ **"How 'bout I call you in a week or so?"** Then be sure to add the reason (when finals are over, after work lets up, as soon as I accept the Nobel Prize) so that it doesn't sound like a brush-off. Mark at least ten days to two weeks on your calendar and call him then.

- ✔ **"Instead of calling, let's e-mail each other from work."** This narrows the contact time to 9-to-5 and takes some of the intensity out of the exchange. E-mail is pretty public, so neither one of you can get too hot and heavy with the boss watching.

- ✔ **"What does *soon* mean to you?"** Though this question may sound a bit overeager, asking for a definition is okay as long as you don't sound like anybody's mother. Your date's response tells you a lot about the future of this relationship. Whatever you hear, be calm; don't panic or get hysterical.

If you're a guy: Don't wait quite as long as you ordinarily would. If you do intend to call her "soon," you'll score major brownie points if you make it more sooner than later. Women eventually write off the guy who never calls, but they never forget the man who calls right away.

If you're a girl: Wait at least twice as long as you ordinarily would. Give the guy a break. When he does call, warm up that cold shoulder, or he'll never call again. The appropriate response to a guy who calls a week after a great date is, "Hi. How are you?" — not "Hi. Who died?" He'll be so pleased with you he just may call later that night for more of your tender, loving acceptance. Stay cool. Don't notice. Life is long; phone calls can be short.

The best way to avoid the whole call/don't call scenario is to arrange date number two before date number one ends. Plan to get together again no sooner than a week, no later than two weeks. If your date doesn't bring it up, you can. No gender rules here.

Texting etiquette

By and large, texting has taken the place of beeping or paging and, for many, even the place of phoning or e-mailing. It has an immediacy and terseness that many people find appealing, but there are still rules and expectations that can't be addressed as they could be in an e-mail or a phone call. To use texting wisely in the dating realm, follow these guidelines:

Text when you had a great time and are pretty sure your date did, too.

Don't text when you want to know why your date never called you again.

Text when you have concert tickets for that night.

Don't text when your mom wants you to bring your date home for dinner.

Text when your date left something at your place.

Don't text when you left something at your date's place.

Nine hints for limbo and surviving the wait

There's a reason the first streamlined, easy-to-cradle-beneath-your-chin telephone was called a "princess" phone. It was designed to be talked on for hours in comfort — something little princes just don't do. Sure, guys call their buddies, but let's face it — they look like amateurs when it comes to the real phone talkers: girls. Girls grow up on the phone. So the day after a great date, the telephone in a girl's room or house or apartment or car or office takes on a sort of golden glow. Your cell may even have a weird aura. Women, if you're not vigilant, the phone will take over your life. Don't let it.

Assuming you're waiting for this great guy to call you for date number two, don't panic, don't write him off, don't obsess. Instead, follow these nine guidelines for handling the waiting period:

- ✓ **Don't stop showering.** I know, I know — the phone could ring while you're all sudsed up, and baths are quieter. But changes in lifestyle and hygiene don't need to begin quite so early. There are answering machines and voicemail. People call back. Hygiene is more important. You never know — he could drop by.

- ✓ **Don't call the phone company.** If you hear a dial tone, the phone is in perfect working order. Besides, the phone would be engaged while they checked the line anyway, and are you willing to take that risk? There is always call waiting, but what if someone else is calling when you're calling and then . . . directly to voicemail. Ouch.

- ✔ **Don't go shopping for new equipment.** You don't need a new phone, answering machine, doorbell, or e-mail server just because yours refuses to ring, beep, or announce, "You have mail!" Be patient.

- ✔ **Don't put yourself on house arrest.** This is not the time to develop a deep and lasting friendship with the pizza delivery guy. Get out. Get air. Cells were invented for this reason. Even better idea: Leave your cell at home.

- ✔ **Don't change your answering machine or voicemail message.** Your old voice sounded sexy enough. Detailing in a recording exactly where you are and where you'll be each day is an invitation to burglars, not daters.

- ✔ **Stare at something else.** A watched phone never rings or vibrates.

- ✔ **Stop watching the 24-hour news channel.** If he really was abducted by an alien or caught in a 20-car pile-up, you'll hear about it soon enough.

- ✔ **Get a life.** If you don't have one already, now's the time to live. Go to a museum, volunteer, whatever. Carry on with any version of existence other than an amoeba life form sitting by the phone or being on high cell alert.

- ✔ **Don't worry, be happy.** Even if it's your mom each time the phone rings, hey, at least it's a human voice. Remember Dr. Joy's prescription on dating: It's one date. Take it easy. Nothing, besides nuclear holocaust, is the end of the world.

Remember, women crave intensity; men crave comfort. Carry that thought throughout your life and you'll always understand why the other side behaves the way it does.

Men's ten-day morphing into two-week rule

This rule explains why guys wait so long to call, even if the date's terrific. Assuming your first date is on a Tuesday or Wednesday night:

- ✔ Guys don't call the next day; they see it as too needy.

- ✔ Now you're butting up against the weekend. You don't want to appear dateless. No one calls Thursday, Friday, Saturday, or Sunday.

- ✔ Now you're at Monday. No one calls anyone on a Monday.

- ✔ Tuesdays or Wednesdays are good days to call, but if work gets too busy, you leave the number at home, or you're out of town, then forget it — you're already to Thursday.

- ✔ Thursday. Too close to the weekend. It's too late to ask someone out for the weekend or to admit you don't have a date. Besides, a second date on a weekend rather than a weekday ups the ante too much.

- ✔ Now it's Friday. Calling on Friday is the same as Thursday.

✔ Ditto Saturday.

✔ Sunday is still the weekend and a refocus on work, not play.

✔ No one makes any important calls on a Monday.

✔ Tuesday. Ahhh. That feels about right. Work is calm, your head is calm, your heart is calm, and your conscience is still clean. Now pick up the phone . . . 'cept it's now been nearly two weeks. Yikes!

Guys: Win many more brownie points by calling before two weeks. Girls: Chill. The problem is the pattern, not you.

Believe in fate

As you can see in the French farmer case (refer to the nearby "The farmer's daughter" sidebar), fate happens and believing in fate helps you chill out a bit. It gives you perspective. If the relationship is meant to be, it'll happen. If your parents hadn't decided to have another kid and your dad hadn't been transferred to a new town and you hadn't skipped second grade, you two never would have met. If it is meant to be, if the two of you are meant to be, relax — it'll happen.

The farmer's daughter

When a friend of mine was stationed overseas in the army assigned to NATO, he met the young daughter of a French farmer. The generous farmer offered my friend, Brian, a home-cooked meal, and he accepted. That evening, and several evenings after, he dined with the family and slowly became smitten with the young girl. But she was only 14, and only Elvis Presley was allowed to indulge such fantasies.

Fast-forward 30 years. Brian was back home in the States, divorced, and the father of two girls. On a vacation to France, he decided to look up the farmer who was, by now, an elderly man, but he still remembered Brian and invited him over for dinner.

"How's your daughter?" Brian asked casually, as they were sipping port in the family vineyard after dinner.

"You can ask her yourself," the farmer said. "She's dropping her son off later this evening." Which she did, and she nearly lost her breath when she saw Brian standing in her father's doorway. She, too, was divorced and had never forgotten her first crush. The years melted away, and now as two adults, they fell in love. This summer marks their 20th wedding anniversary. "It was just meant to be," Brian often says, sighing.

So leave the phone alone. Get out of the house. Get on with your life and be pleasantly — and genuinely — surprised when he or she really does call. Sometimes you just have to believe in karma or fate or serendipity or whatever. Relax, the universe is on your case.

Nix the gossip

The temptation to blab about your great date will be intense, especially as the clock ticks while you wait for the call (or wait to call). But be very careful here, especially online. Stay away from your Twitter, MySpace, and Facebook updates. Don't say anything about your date or series of dates. Online, it is better to preserve both your privacy and an alluring air of mystery.

GUY STUFF

Bragging to your buddies about your date's bod or huge libido or exaggerating her affection for you is totally uncool, especially on your Facebook page. What if the two of you end up together? There's no way to erase an image once it's planted in someone's head, and your friends won't treat her respectfully if you don't.

GIRL STUFF

Sharing every intimacy is also uncool, especially on the pages of the Internet. Give your date a break. He's entitled to get to know you without all your friends getting to know him first. Say nothing about him at your Facebook and MySpace pages. Keep your expectations limited and your audience even smaller.

This is a fragile and vulnerable time for both of you and any potential future. An audience ups the ante, the intensity, the curiosity — and you're better off without it. You'll be glad you didn't blab too much about your date before your date began once you experience the emotionally charged post-date waiting period. Both your friends and your mom might be your Facebook friends, so don't say anything about your dating in the online world. That way they won't comment at their pages either. Who needs everyone and their mother asking you if he called yet or if she left you any messages on your e-mail? All the way around, it's best to keep info close to the vest until your relationship really gets going. Even then, discretion is the mother of true trust.

Dr. Joy's mini quiz

Q. Why should you put off having sex until you   A. All of the above.
know someone really well?

Chapter 14

The Second Date

*T*he first date jitters are out of the way, and it's on to date number two. Your emotions are still in a whirl but for entirely different reasons. No longer are you worried about knocking the shoes off your date with a dazzling first impression. That's done. You did it or you didn't. Not to worry. Even if you weren't James Bond or Angelina Jolie, you impressed your date enough to secure a second shot. Now the stakes are higher. If your first date was a rousing success, the next one better be fantastic. If date number one was so-so, date number two better score higher on the dating scale.

Understandably, you're going to feel a bit stressed as well as excited, hopeful, flattered, challenged, optimistic, and even giddy. That's okay. Everybody feels a smorgasbord of emotions when the flicker of a potential love match has been ignited. What you want to do is chill out, keep your expectations in check, and make sure this budding relationship doesn't burn out before it even begins.

Is It Really a Second Date?

The first thing I want you to do is make sure you're dealing with a bona fide second date. In Dr. Joy's Perfect World of Dating, you met your date through friends, asked him or her out to lunch, had fun, and arranged to meet again. In the imperfect world we all live in, you may have met your date in class, at a party, on the street, at work, or even online. You said, "I'm going to Starbucks for a cappuccino. Wanna come?" He went, bought his own cup of coffee, chatted with you, had a few laughs, and gave you his phone number when you offered yours. Technically, you had a date. But who deals in technicalities when dating is concerned? In reality, you had more of a date-ette than a date.

Dates versus date-ettes

A *date* lasts at least three hours, is planned ahead of time, and takes place after noon in ironed clothing. A *date-ette* is spontaneous, can last a few minutes or an hour or two, takes place day or night, and doesn't even require a shower.

This distinction is unimportant until we begin speaking about second dates, because you have to know when the first date occurred. So first get clear in your own head what your first date really was. If it was indeed a date, good for you: Your second date is an authentic second date, and you're right on track. If your first get-together was really a date-ette, however, then the next time you two go out, you're really on official date number one — or maybe one and a half. That's okay. There are no hard and fast rules here. But you may want to flip back to the chapters on first dates and take it from there if you've only had a date-ette. This chapter is for solid second-daters, not second-date wannabes.

First dates can be date-ettes, but second dates have to be dates. The progression flows naturally. If it doesn't — if you keep spontaneously grabbing a bite to eat or a cup of coffee — you're not dating. You're hanging out.

Anatomy of a true second date

A first date is takeoff — your seatback is in the upright position, your tray table is stowed, you've buckled your seatbelt and are listening intently to make sure that the engines are on full throttle. A second date is climbing to cruising altitude. You're on the way to your destination. You're up in the air. You hope the pilot didn't have a martini with her lunch, the flight attendant didn't have a fight with his girlfriend, and the skies are not cloudy all day. In other words, a second date is the beginning of a settling-in period (granted, the very beginning of the period, but a completely different experience nonetheless).

Sometimes, a second date is wishing you were there already. Mostly, it's trying to sit back, relax, and enjoy the flight. Whereas your first date is about fantasy — getting your hair done, being on your best behavior, and looking at your date through rose-colored glasses — your second date is the beginning of reality. You let your hair down a bit; you reveal the real — or realer — you; and you see your date through a magnifying glass, if not reading glasses. Table 14-1 continues the discussion about what a second date is and isn't.

When distraction is your best option

I am not a happy flier. Intellectually, I understand the aerodynamics of lift and speed and air pressure and that flying is the safest, quickest, and easiest way to travel. Emotionally, I'm not thrilled to be strapped into that small space with all those people. Once we're up there, flying flat, I feel more secure or at least more distracted — the movie is on, the peanuts have arrived, the club soda bubbles tickle my nose — until we hit turbulence or are in a holding pattern.

But because I have to fly a lot for work, I figure I have two options: I can make myself truly miserable and dig my fingernails into the armrests or my fellow passenger on takeoff, or I can bring my own distractions to keep me busy until the movie and peanuts (if I'm lucky) and seltzer bubbles take over. To every airline's major relief, I choose the latter. I never fly without an engrossing paperback, a crossword puzzle, or an unfinished book chapter my editor is waiting for me to finish. I distract myself before my mind can get carried away on all the "what ifs."

Should you find yourself on a second date fantasizing about gene pools or doodling your first name and his last name, stop immediately and distract yourself. Though I wouldn't recommend whipping out a crossword puzzle, you might want to try doing what you initially set out to do: Get to know your date. Not your future marriage partner or the potential father of your kids or even the guy you want to take home to meet Mom. Just relax and realize there's no substitute for time, no excuse for shortcuts, and no way to really know someone without listening, learning, caring, sharing, and being there.

Table 14-1	What a Second Date Is . . . and Isn't
A Second Date Is	*A Second Date Isn't*
A next step	A relationship
A continued search for compatibility	A pre-spouse interview
A chance to reveal yourself	A confessional
A time to flirt	A time to have sex
A shift of focus onto your date	Obsessing about yourself

The beauty of a second date is that real personalities can begin to emerge. Your date's nervous laughter mellows into a great sense of humor; his or her personal résumé becomes a story of a life. Of course, the potential downside is that real personalities emerge. The date you thought was a friendly over-tipper who dressed impeccably and arrived on time suddenly morphs into a flirtatious spendthrift who is narcissistic and obsessive. Oops. The important thing here is to take a second date for what it really is — namely, the next leg on your journey toward getting to know someone better. Period.

On a second date, there will be more . . .

- ✔ **Communicating:** You move from neutral conversational territory, like census data, to more personal stuff like family history, favorite movies, the school you went to, school you go to, hometown, work life — stuff you'd put in a personal ad, stuff your next-door neighbor knows but not the ultra-sensitive stuff you tell only your best friend. It's also a good time for follow-up. You asked the opening questions on your first date; now get a bit more detail.

- ✔ **Testing the compatibility waters:** You want to make sure you and your date are a good fit. Your attention shifts away from how you look, act, feel, talk, eat, and slurp to the kind of person your date is.

- ✔ **Probing for shared interests:** While you want to express yourself on a first date, a second date is for allowing, encouraging, desiring, and listening to your date express what he or she likes and dislikes.

- ✔ **Sexual innuendoes:** Nothing overt, but playful flirting is good and certainly fun.

- ✔ **Gazing into each other's eyes:** Most importantly, a second date is one step further along on the intimacy scale. It's about stripping away the outer layer of superficiality and beginning to know your date's soul. Few things are more intimate, or soulful, than prolonged eye contact. Don't stare. But don't be afraid to connect with the window to your date's soul — the eyes.

It is still a terrific idea to resist going online to Google your date's name or check out Facebook. Firsthand info is still superior to having to sort through fact and fiction, friending, and privacy walls. Ditto resisting the temptation to post ANYTHING about your date online. Too early, too risky, too permanent, too public, too rude, too tacky.

In Between Dates One and Two

Everything that happens between the first date and the second has an effect on date number two:

- ✔ If it was lust at first sight and you both have been whispering sweet nothings over the phone all week, your second date will look much different than it would if your date took ten days to call you again. Bear that in mind when you embark on date number two.

- ✔ Your second date may seem either more intense or more subdued than it actually is. There's simply no substitute for time when it comes to really knowing someone and understanding how he or she will (or won't) fit into your life. Don't short-circuit the time you really need to tap how you really feel.

✔ If more than two weeks have passed between date number one and date number two, your second date is likely to feel more like a first date. Adjust your expectations accordingly.

Date Expectations

One of the biggest differences between any first date and second date is expectation. Be very careful here. You don't want your expectations to be sky-high any more than you want them to be so low that you're grateful for the slightest crumb your date flicks across the table. I know it's hard trying to enter a date with a blank slate, but you really owe it to yourself and your date to try to enter with your eyes, heart, and mind open.

Expectation is no simple matter. The dictionary defines expectation as looking for what's "due, proper, or necessary." Interestingly, the word comes from the same root as "spectacle," the Latin *spectare,* meaning "to gaze at." What this all means is that you form your expectation of any event by instantaneously "gazing at" your past experiences, stuff that's happened to your friends or your parents or your family, what the media has convinced you is proper, and what your peers have convinced you you're due. So you walk into any situation with at least some expectation as to how it would, could, or — worse — should turn out.

Trouble is, your date doesn't have your same history. Your date isn't carrying the same baggage. He has a whole different set of luggage. That's when expectations can get a bit dicey. You expect your date to think and feel as you do. When it doesn't happen as you anticipated, feelings get hurt and tempers flare and the whole experience takes a kamikaze nosedive.

Don't fall into this trap. You can't erase expectation completely — it's okay to expect to have a good time with someone you already like — but try to identify what your expectations are before your second date begins. That way, you'll recognize immediately when (or if) your expectations are dashed, and you can put the whole thing in perspective. You may want to refer to Chapter 12 to understand your dating expectations.

Good places for a second date

Given that a second date is about delving deeper, getting to know someone better, flirting a bit more, and just plain being more intimate, pick a place or activity that lets you do those things:

- ✔ Quiet restaurant or café

- ✔ Public park

- ✔ Sporting event

- ✔ Museum

- ✔ Hiking the location you mention in your dating profile or, even better, the place your date mentioned in his or her profile

Following are some not-so-good places to do those things:

- ✔ Noisy bar

- ✔ Quiet bar

- ✔ Movie marathon

- ✔ Your parents' house

- ✔ Your date's parents' house

- ✔ Your place

Mind over what's-the-matter

Getting all stressed out is easy if your second date doesn't measure up to the notion you had of the way things should go or if you put so much pressure on yourself that nothing you do or say is going to be good enough. Don't go there. You won't have any fun. Your date won't have any fun. Everybody loses. Instead, if you start to feel tense, take a breather (literally) and do a quick reality check. Ask yourself the following:

- ✔ **What's really bothering me here?** Am I blaming my date for my expectations? Am I bringing up past history? Have I jammed a couple of unrelated memories and fears together to make a stress sandwich? If so, pull yourself back into the moment and deal with the here and now.

- ✔ **Am I trying to make sure my date doesn't get too close?** Intimacy is a scary thing, particularly in a second date where, presumably, you two are revealing more about yourselves. If you find yourself mentally running for the dugout before the seventh-inning stretch, get back in the game and see how it ends up.

- ✔ **Is this just old news?** If you notice that you seem to be falling back on tired old patterns to make yourself feel comfortable, knock it off. Tell yourself you're safe, that it's okay to feel a little afraid, and not to worry — you'll hold your hand every step of the way.

Remind yourself of one of my favorite bumper stickers: "Expectation Is the Death of Serenity" — suitable for muttering over and over to yourself as necessary.

Old patterns, new people

Behavior patterns — acting in a characteristic way — begin to take hold on the second date. If you tend to be a relationship sprinter rather than a long-distance runner, you'll continue to quickly fall in and out of love with each new person unless you do something to change it. If you typically scare the dickens out of your dates by confessing true love on the way to the car, you'll probably act it out again unless you do something to change the pattern. Or if you're so scared of intimacy that it takes you ten years to trust someone, you probably won't change unless you make a conscious effort to do so.

If you don't already know your dating patterns (everybody has patterns of behavior), I want you to pay attention on the second date so you can uncover your tendencies and know what to watch for in yourself. If you're already aware of patterns and like what you see in yourself, don't change a thing. But if you've noticed a destructive dating style in the past and want to change it, follow these steps:

1. **Identify the behavior.**

   As soon as you experience one of those there-I-go-again moments, pretend you're a school kid at a crosswalk: Stop, look, and listen to yourself.

2. **Define the behavior.**

   Mentally describe your behavior in a specific sentence like, "Whenever I'm nervous, I tend to be sarcastic" or "As soon as it seems like someone really likes me, I get turned off."

3. **Place it in the moment.**

   Try to pinpoint what set you off this time. Was it her arm brushing up against yours? Was it something he said?

4. **Put it on hold.**

   Patterns don't change overnight. They especially don't change smack in the middle of a date. What you want to do, once you've nailed down a behavior pattern, is to relax, file it away in your brain, and look at it later on when you're alone.

The First Fifteen Minutes of a Second Date

Unlike the extensive pre-planning that goes into a first date, less is needed for a second date. But there's a lot more at stake, so a bit of forethought will help you and your date relax. You want to solve any potential problems involving the first 15 minutes of your second date before you get underway. The immediate decisions to be made are these:

✔ *Question:* **Do you kiss your date on the cheek when you first meet? On the lips?**

Answer: Cheek, okay. Lips, no way.

✔ *Question:* **Do you take your date's hand? Put your arm around his or her shoulder?**

Answer: No hand, no arm, no proprietary touching just yet. Handshakes are okay if you opt for no kiss.

✔ *Question:* **Do you talk about your last date together? Or stick to the present moment?**

Answer: Continuing a previous conversation or asking about the status of something you already talked about is great. It's a real intimacy-builder and lets your date know you were listening.

✔ *Question:* **Do you go to someplace different from the first date?**

Answer: Yes. Especially if date number one was a date-ette. The location reflects a lot about you and how you feel about your companion. You don't have to spend a bundle, but if your goal is getting to know what makes your date tick emotionally and spiritually, a loud concert may not be the best way to go.

✔ *Question:* **Does money matter?**

Answer: Money always matters to some degree. But don't let a lack of the green stuff freak you out or keep you from asking someone out. A walk in the park can be a better second date than dinner at the Ritz. What's most important is picking a place that lets you feel free to be you and lets your date feel free to get to know you. Just don't look cheap — make sure you have enough to cover any expected expenses, plus $20 tucked in a secret compartment.

Getting to Know You

The info-exchange process on a second date is fun and exciting and interesting and a bit tricky. Unlike a first date, which is pretty superficial, a second date delves a little deeper. You already know you like each other enough to find out more. How much more remains to be seen. For now, you want to be vulnerable enough to let your date see who you really are without showing all your warts at once. (A wart or two is okay.) You want your date to feel comfy enough to share a wart or two with you.

If the two of you met online, you likely have both already cited a number of interests in your dating profiles. A second date is a great time to delve into discussing those interests in more detail. The added benefit of having expressed your interests in your dating profile is you two have safe topics to discuss without getting too, too personal too soon. Go ahead and discuss anything you each cited in your profiles.

To get the good stuff, you've got to give it. Trust me — your date won't open up if you just sit there with your arms crossed. Though a second date usually shifts the conversational focus away from you and onto your date, striking a balance between being a good listener and an interesting and sincere talker is crucial — and not always easy or comfortable right away.

First, know your personality type before the second date even starts. Are you the strong, silent type? A Chatty Cathy? Knowing who you are can help you tone down your natural tendency to clam up or blab on and on.

Second, periodically gauge how things are going. Here are some basic rules:

- If you feel you know everything about your date and your date knows nothing about you, it's time to open up.

- If your date has been nodding for the past hour, it's time to hush up.

- If your time together seems more like a stand-up routine than a conversation, take a deep breath and focus on getting more insight, less laughs.

- If your date sounds more like a job interview than a chat, it's time to get a bit more personal.

- If your date blushes each time you ask him or her a question, it's time to get less personal.

- If the conversation on your second date keeps grinding to a screeching halt, ask yourself if it's you or your date. One of you is uncomfortable. It's okay to flat-out say, "We had such fun the last time we went out. Is something making you uncomfortable?" If the answer is no and the conversation still limps along, you may be looking at a second, and final, date.

- Don't use the digital camera feature in your cell phone to commemorate the occasion thinking you'll share your Facebook or Flickr photo albums. Too soon, too much, too intense, too too. Only after the two of you have agreed is it okay to even think about sharing with others. The second date is also still too soon to friend each other at Facebook, LinkedIn, Twitter, MySpace, Google, or Yahoo!. Better to wait until you two have agreed you are a couple to share all that information with each other.

Trust or Consequences

Trusting someone instantaneously can be just as devastating as suspecting an ulterior motive behind everything he or she says. True trust takes time. No shortcuts allowed. **Remember:** Your date is just your date; he or she isn't your friend. If you've already known each other primarily as friends, you've got a head start, but dating (and the sexual subtext) changes everything. So remind yourself that you don't know this person in this context. Even if you've been chatting for months online, trust still takes a lot of together time. If your date wants you to give more than you're willing to give at this early stage, don't be afraid to say so . . . and stick to your guns.

If, on the other hand, you don't want to "slip" and divulge any clues as to where you live or work, what you do for a living, or what color your hair really is, you may be a touch paranoid. Yeah, the world can be a dangerous place. But if you trust someone enough to agree to a second date, it's only fair to let him or her get to know you. This isn't a CIA investigation. It's a date. Chill out.

Particularly if you're over 30, avoid what I call the Blitz School of Dating. That's when you've been there, done that, and you don't want to waste any time. You want to book a table in a quiet restaurant where the wait staff won't bother you for the two hours you take to chronologically pour out your life story, hear your date's, and determine if this union has legs. While the Blitz approach has been known to work on occasion, I don't recommend it. Part of the mystery and magic of getting to know someone is getting to know someone, not hearing how well that person knows himself or herself.

Finally, resist the temptation to ask yourself the $1,000,000 Deal or No Deal question: Is this the one? Is this second date with the person with whom you'll spend the rest of your life? Have babies with? Rock on the porch with? Watch go gray? While the urge may be there to weigh every second date on the "forever scale," don't give in to it. Distract yourself. It's too soon. A relationship hasn't even taken flight yet.

If your worst enemy knew what you're telling your second date, could he or she use it against you? If the answer is yes, keep it under wraps for now. If not, go for it.

The Last Fifteen Minutes of a Second Date

Two words: *No sex.*

Two more words: *Too soon.*

Even though you feel like you've known each other all your lives, it's really only been two nights, or an afternoon and an evening, or ten minutes and lunch. You get the picture. You don't know each other — don't get to know each other under the sheets.

Physical intimacy blurs the emotional intimacy of a relationship. It's hard to see things clearly when hormones are involved. A second date isn't even a relationship yet, so sex confuses the whole deal. Making out is okay. Making out passionately is cool. Just don't go any further than that until you know each other better. Ask yourself if you'd be embarrassed the next day if the previous night of lovemaking turned out to be a disaster. If the answer is "well, yeah," then the answer to sex has to be "well, no."

Never have sex with anyone whose middle name you don't know.

Chapter 15

To Blab or Not to Blab: Sharing Personal Info

I once had a guy appear at my house for a first date with a bouquet of daisies and a résumé. He thrust both at me and said, "Read this. I'll be back in 20 minutes to answer any questions." I pointed out to him that I was going on a date with him, not looking to hire him, and that anything I wanted to know, I could ask. Although I prefer the *I'll-talk-to-you-and-you-talk-to-me* approach to getting to know someone, he seemed to prefer the *here's-my-curriculum-vitae* approach. (If he asked me out now, he probably wouldn't even come to the door but would send me an e-mail telling me to check out his LinkedIn page or just Google him.) So I ended up knowing a bunch of stuff that I didn't necessarily want to know, like his work history — and the fact that he wanted to duck out on any messy, emotional stuff, which of course, like most of us, is what I wanted to know. Talk about a guy who has a hard time talking from the get-go. As you can imagine, things went downhill from there.

Not all dates begin with such a gap between what you want to know (or share) and what the other person wants to tell you (or hear), but they do all begin with the desire to share some information. After all, without an exchange of something, the two of you remain strangers; if you weren't interested in learning about each other, you wouldn't be on a date in the first place. If that's not your motivation, if you're just tired of your own company or want a free dinner or a warm body, we need to talk! The job here is to figure out what to ask, what to tell, and what to finesse. The list changes as the two of you get to know each other, but the basic guidelines remain in place.

Volunteering Information

What information you share — and when — depends on who you are and your level of comfort with openness and who your date is. If your date is open and friendly and accepting, you most likely feel comfortable sharing more. If you're dating someone reserved, you're likely a bit less forthcoming. This is called mirroring (see Chapter 10) and survival and common sense.

Some people are quite comfortable sharing some parts of their lives and less comfortable sharing other parts. What you're trying to accomplish early on is compatibility — a good fit. So volunteer what you're comfortable having most people know about you. The rest you can slowly divulge as the relationship progresses; in other words, you don't have to produce an autobiography, complete with a slew of your opinions — or your most awful secret or family scandal — all in the first couple of dates. So make your Yahoo and Google profiles invisible to everyone to maintain your privacy until you two have gone on a few dates and revealed what you wanted to in a conversation, not in your social networking profiles. Or better yet, just stay away from your 'puter for a bit . . . no hyperventilating, you're involved in the beginning of something that might be big. Enjoy and experience it in life rather than online.

Most people who date have a mini-scenario worked out in their heads of what they want someone to know about them. You, too, can create a mini-script — what you'd tell someone on a long airplane trip, for example, or someone at a party is a place to start:

- ✔ **Include a little bit about your factual life:** You know — things like where you're from, where you went to school, how many brothers and sisters you have, what hobbies you like, what kind of work you do, and how you spend your free time. In other words, this script can more or less include the stuff you'd put in a personal ad if you had unlimited space and money. (In a way, the early days of dating are a personal ad — you share who you are and what you want — with the advantage being that your date gets to respond face to face.) Age and weight are optional. I know that much of this info is included in your online profile, but we're digging a little deeper here; isn't that what intimacy is all about?

- ✔ **Share feelings:** Worries, music groups that you like, whether you're a baseball, opera, or chocolate fan, and how the weather is affecting you.

- ✔ **Keep the script positive and realistic:** Your comments shouldn't be too negative *or* make you sound like the best thing since sliced bread. Self-effacement works only for Woody Allen, and a braggart isn't much fun to be around.

When you share information, keep the following in mind:

- ✔ **As the two of you get to know each other, remember that *you really don't know each other*.** If the date doesn't turn out well, this person is going to have all the information you're now blabbing.

- ✔ **Make sure that you're not using information as a way to bind someone to you too soon and too tightly.** This tactic usually doesn't work anyway, and you'll hate yourself in the morning for telling someone you don't plan to see again that your family's completely dysfunctional and you've been in therapy since third grade.

- ✔ **Exchanging information is like dancing — you have to move together, or it doesn't work very well at all.** Some people are comfortable volunteering some things; others are comfortable volunteering other information. Just because you describe the house you grew up in doesn't mean that your date has to blueprint his family homestead. The key is to make sure that you're not doing all the talking or all the listening.

Once the two of you really get to know each other and have moved from first date to first month to first year, the ratio of what you don't talk about to what you do does — and should — shift dramatically. After all, you don't want *not* to tell anything that, after being found out, will shake the pillars of your relationship. But too much too soon is without a context for understanding.

In the old days, before the Internet, the spigot on information flow could be adjusted according to the situation, the amount of alcohol consumed, and your comfort level. Google and Facebook have thrown discretion out the window. Google can at least be dismissed as "lies and half truths" that others have planted to sabotage your reputation, but your Facebook page is on your head, darlin'. Assuming that your date will never check it is wishful thinking. Those pix of your exes, your belly ring, and your rants that grace your wall are all public, and even if you opt for privacy, it's not hard to breach. So before you date, you may want to edit or at least peruse what your page says about you. Also, do not accept your date as a social networking friend or connection until after at least the fourth date, when you two have established a mutual interest in a relationship together. By keeping this person at social networking arm's length, he or she can find out a bit about you but not your full life history. The following sections give you guidelines on what type of information is important to tell and when you should share this information either in person or in print.

Things to tell immediately

If there's something about you that you think can affect any long-term prospects and that more than two people know, you may as well 'fess up on the first few dates — especially if you feel that it may blow things. You can try to create an environment that makes sense, but keeping that big of a secret from the get-go adds pressure and nervousness at a pressurized time. If you'd tell a same-sex potential friend, tell your date. If your date is cool about it, you're relaxed. If not, at least you haven't invested much already.

Information that more than two people have isn't a secret. If your date is likely to find out sooner to later, you may as well tell sooner rather than jeopardize the relationship once it progresses and the additional factor of trust is introduced (as in, "If you'd lie about this, what else haven't you told me?"). Any long-term relationship is based on trust. If you can't trust someone, you can't love that someone, so don't start off hiding important facts.

The list of things you definitely must share includes most of the biggies in life. You should share this information by the third or fourth date. Any earlier is unnecessarily brutal; after all, if you really don't fancy one another, why parade the skeletons from your closet? Any later is viewed as a breach of trust (plus, not having shared can get you in more trouble than any upset that telling may now create).

- **Previous marriages:** How many times you've been married, how long you were married, and how long you've been apart. But don't go into too much detail. See the later section "Keeping Mum."

  Notice that you should confess *previous marriages,* not whether you're married or separated or in the process of divorce. The reason? If you are married or separated or in the process of a divorce, *you have no business dating at all* — not until one full year after the divorce is final. I'm not kidding here. If you fit into one of these three categories, you can hang out with friends, work out, paint your house, become a temporary workaholic, take courses, volunteer — but you can't date. If you want to find out why, return to Chapter 4 or hop ahead to Chapter 19.

- **Previous convictions and parole violations:** What crime you were convicted of and how long you were in prison. (I'm sorta kidding here, but stuff happens.)

- **Previous bankruptcies:** How long ago you filed for bankruptcy and why.

- **Previous kids:** How many, how old, whether they live with you, and if they don't, how often you see them.

- **Previous sex change operations:** What can I say?

When should you share this information? You don't necessarily have to share it when you first lay eyes on one another, but before the end of the third date at latest. If the information is readily available elsewhere (the Internet, the *National Enquirer,* the local paper, or the police blotter), start talking sooner. Confessions of any kind — even "I think you're swell" — need to be seen and heard in context. The best rule for when to tell is when *you'd* want to know if you were the one about to hear what you have to say. Making your date the last to know won't endear you to him or her, so if it's under your control, make sure that your Facebook page says only what you want everyone to know.

Things to tell eventually

Sooner or later, the I'll-do-anything-you-like-to-do phase has to stop; not only is it boring, but it's also not entirely honest. After all, you must have some likes and dislikes. They're what make you the person you are, and jettisoning them all in the interest of harmony is a short-sighted perspective. At this point (I'm talking date three or four, max), you want to be honest about who you are and what you enjoy doing. This information is not first tier — it doesn't need to be understood as the bedrock facts of the relationship on date one — but it is important enough to be risked even if the result is mild turbulence; otherwise, you run the risk of being trapped by your pretenses.

If you can't keep up the ruse forever (and you can't), it's best not to keep it up at all. But realistically, at the beginning of a dating experience, we all resonate a bit; we want to be liked and likable and agreeable, and so we soften our own preferences because we want the relationship to endure. But sooner or later, the real you has to come out, and the sooner the better. After all, you want as few unpleasant surprises as possible.

Almost everyone has strong feelings about something. See if I push any of your love or loathe buttons with the following:

- Aerobics
- Ballet
- Boxing
- Bullfighting
- Football
- Sky diving
- Types of food (Chinese, Mexican, French, and so on)
- White-water rafting
- Your date's
  - Perfume or aftershave
  - Temper
  - Drinking
  - Sense of humor
  - Socks

Note: As you get seemingly closer to the loathe side of the list, it becomes even more important to temper your firm opinions with gentleness.

As you share your likes and dislikes in the name of honesty, be gentle. Telling someone you're not crazy about football may be jarring to a die-hard fan, but you need to be especially careful about mouthing off about your date's:

- Best friend
- Parents

- Dog
- Hair color
- Haircut
- Height
- Weight
- Religion

Things to tell before sex

I can't say this often or strongly enough: *You must have a frank and honest discussion with your clothes on and no alcohol or other mood-altering substances coursing through your bloodstream before you hit the sheets.* If you're not sure what this frank and honest discussion should include, take a look at the following list and keep in mind that if you're not ready to talk about these things, you're not ready for sex:

- **Condoms:** Who's supplying them? Don't even *think* about not using one, even if you use something else for a contraceptive. Nowadays, a condom is as much a safety issue as it is a contraceptive issue.

- **Contraception:** What type and who's providing it?

- **Medical sexual history:** Be sure to mention AIDS test results, herpes, and any other sexually transmitted disease that you currently have or are being treated for.

Unless you're on medication whose primary side effect is impotence (for example, blood pressure medicine and some antidepressants), the fact that you've occasionally had problems with impotence need not be discussed here unless the problem has been going on for quite some time and happens more often than not. If so, get professional medical treatment; otherwise, keep in mind that impotence happens to all guys sooner or later. If you explain to your partner that you really want to impress her and that's a lot of pressure for the little guy (okay, big guy), you can turn what seems to be a problem into a compliment.

- **History of sexual abuse, if you think it's relevant:** For example, if you can't tolerate certain positions or words, say so. Also, you need to work these issues out in therapy with a professional — not on a date.

- **Past relationships:** This is not a time to get into long, drawn-out discussions of the misery of your past relationships (see the later section "Keeping Mum"), but if these relationships are going to affect how you behave with one another, you may as well get it out in the open now. The *it's-not-you-it's-me-dear* defense is much more credible if you've brought up the subject before the problem occurs.

✔ **Fears:** Claustrophobia and fear of pillows, dogs, heights, oral sex, pink lights.

✔ **Excitement:** What turns you on.

✔ **Positions and fantasies:** Eventually, it really is okay to talk about favorite positions and fantasies, but see if you can lay some groundwork of trust before you go technical on one another.

✔ **That you're just not ready yet to be sexual either in the relationship or at the moment:** Just because you've been sexual together before doesn't mean either of you can't say no now.

✔ **That you want to wait till you're married, engaged, or surer:** See Chapter 16 to find out how to say no gracefully.

Given this list of topics, you can understand why putting off having sex until a relationship can really take hold makes sense. Knowing and trusting and liking one another makes these issues loom a lot less large.

Things to tell if asked or pushed

The preceding sections outline the types of information you should share at some point in the relationship. But what about the information that you're not obligated to share but have been asked for? You know the type of questions: the ones — like "How many relationships have you been in?" — that come out when you least expect it and leave you sputtering in your dessert. Do you avoid answering? Subtly change the subject? Look at your date like it's none of his or her business (which it isn't, really)? Or just 'fess up?

Although historical accuracy isn't required in answering a question like this — in other words, you can avoid giving too much detail (think of Andie MacDowell's character in *Four Weddings and a Funeral*) — if you stonewall completely, you're likely to make your date think you have something to hide. So the best answer is to give a brief history — more or less what you'd put on an entry in who's who in American dating circles — and then move on without editorial comment that includes who, how long, how many, or preferred positions.

One way to answer such a question is "Why do you ask?" Lamentably, that question is usually answered with "I just want to know," which leads you nowhere. A cooler, smoother way of avoiding the whole messy, *it's-none-of-your-business* issue is to say, "You're so dazzling that I've forgotten everyone but you."

Some questions are so hard to answer that you really should feel compelled to answer only if you're pushed — that is, if your date won't let the subject drop and not answering is likely to hurt the relationship more than a tactful but honest answer would. Some questions that fall into this category are:

- Why didn't you have an orgasm?
- What is wrong with me?
- Why don't you like my friend?

Sharing Feelings

Setting guidelines on when to share feelings is a bit trickier. Admittedly, the coin of the realm for dating is feelings and intimacy, but in the early stages of dating, everything is a bit fragile. What you're trying to do at this point is to set a firm foundation for everything to follow — but what this *everything* entails is almost impossible to predict.

A new dating situation is an investment between the two of you. You need to establish the ground rules together and get a feel for who both of you are and what you want all the while watching the interest mount, getting a return on your investment, and trusting the stability and reliability of the institution (that is, the idea that neither of you is going to rip the other off or create grievous harm or pain). Building this kind of trust takes a bit of time. Just as if you were to borrow money from a bank and be late on your first payment, the bank very well may see you as a bad credit risk and recall the loan. But if you've had the loan for years and have never been late or missed a payment, being late or missing a payment in year three will feel very different to both you and the bank.

When you share feelings, follow these basic rules:

- **Be a tad cautious.** Over exuberance (for example, taking a pledge of undying love) can feel pretty scary if it's in the first 15 minutes of a date. No, you don't have to be Gary Cooper, strong and silent, or Mata Hari, the keeper of mysterious secrets, but blurting out unformed and unexamined feelings à la Pee-wee Herman can scare the daylights out of both of you.

- **Live with a feeling a bit before you express it.** Make sure that what you're saying is true for more than the moment. If you've just tripped over your date's tennis shoe and you're feeling angry, saying "I hate you, you slob" probably reflects emotions stronger than you'll be feeling in ten minutes. If the sentiment isn't going to be true for more than ten minutes, stifle it.

- **Get some perspective on your own emotions and some control over your mouth before you speak.** Otherwise, you can mislead yourself and your date. Saying "I love you" when you mean "Thank you" or "I'd like to have sex," for example, isn't fair or kosher, and it misleads both of you. As the two of you get to know each other better and feel safer and more comfortable with one another and develop some history, your words will have a context and can be evaluated that way. You'll have a track record together and will have enough experience to know what is characteristic and what isn't.

✔ **In deciding what feelings to share and when, think about what would be reasonable to expect at any given time.** A promise of undying love and devotion on the first date might feel kinda cool until you think it through. All of us long to be loved and appreciated, but on the first date? Nice — sorta — but completely unbelievable except in movies or romance novels or from folks who are a bit unbalanced, really needy, or really manipulative. So although "I really had a great time with you and I'd like to do it again. How about you?" isn't quite as flamboyant as "Will you marry me? I knew from the first moment (five minutes ago) that you were the one," it *is* a lot more believable. If you want to tell your grandchildren "We knew from the very first moment" 50 years from now, okay, but when in doubt, go slowly.

Guys' proposing marriage on the first date is sorta cute and makes a girl feel really special. It also offsets the notion that all men are commitment-phobes who love 'em and leave 'em. But it is pure fantasy at best and blatant manipulation at worst. Dating should be fun, not a mind game or delusion.

When to say "I love you" (and when to keep quiet)

Few things are more memorable than the magical, angst-ridden, fingers-crossed, breath-held, passion-filled moment when either you or your date says, "I love you." The phrase is much more than three little words. It's also a silent question. As in, "Do you love me, too?" Properly managing this moment can spell the difference between euphoria and humiliation. Tips:

✔ Wait at least several months, a minimum of three but preferably longer, before confessing your true love — even if you feel it on the first night. It takes a while to gain and build trust. Zooming ahead too fast can easily backfire, and it's really embarrassing to find out you changed your mind and you don't really love 'em.

✔ If your date says, "I love you" and you don't love your date back, don't say "Love you, too" just to be nice. You'll open a can of worms that'll only make a gigantic mess.

✔ If you've been together a while and you're just waiting for your date to spill the beans first, take a chance and tell him or her how you feel. Your date may be waiting for you to take the plunge.

✔ Realize that "love" doesn't always mean the same thing to everyone. For some, the word "love" is followed by the word "marriage." For others, "love" is always followed by "ya." Make sure you're clear on how you feel before putting your feelings into words, and give a thought to the way your date might receive what you're about to say.

✔ Understand that true love implies commitment. If you're not ready to be monogamous, connected, open, and loving, don't say "I love you" just yet.

✔ If the only time you're tempted to confess love is during sex or when you're apart, close your mouth, open your eyes, and see what's really going on.

So do share your feelings, but beware of temper and elation. Make sure they're feelings you've been feeling for more than one second and can live with in an hour or two or a day or two. If you really must say it, finesse a bit — for example, "I know it's too soon to be feeling this, but it sure feels good to me right now" — and then laugh sweetly. Trust is a fragile thing. You need to trust not only each other, but yourself.

Keeping Mum

Between honesty and duplicity is silence.

None of us is completely honest. If you told everything, you wouldn't have time to do anything but confess, and your conversations would be riddled with lines like "Who in God's name told you that puce is your color?" or "The bunion on my toe is driving me insane" when you're asked "How are you?" On the other hand (and other than the kindly social prevarication), lying isn't an acceptable alternative either. The solution? Keep quiet.

People do things for reasons. Before you confess something, write it down on a piece of paper, even if you have to make a quick trip to the bathroom to see whether it makes any sense. Also evaluate why you're about to spill these particular beans. Are you looking for absolution? Trying to put the worst foot forward? Trying to get the person to go away because you're not really interested? Setting up a test to make your date prove intentions? (Don't even think about it — manipulation isn't a pretty sight.) Ask yourself why you want this person to know what you're about to tell. If the only reason you can come up with is "I'm just being honest," look harder or keep your mouth firmly closed.

Following is a list of topics you should keep to yourself unless you have a compelling reason to do otherwise:

- Details of past loves
- If you've cheated
- Sexual stories
- Your own inexperience
- Your own incredible experience
- Your bank account
- Your poverty
- Gossip
- Your innate superiority or inferiority
- Your friends' feelings about your date
- Previous hospitalizations (until month four, at least)

✔ Your parents' bigotry

✔ Your bigotry

Past sexual experiences

When in doubt, keep your mouth shut. If there was ever an area about which to draw a blank, it has to do with past sexual experiences. Over, done with, irrelevant. Don't ask, and don't tell, even if tempted. You'll both regret any departure from this policy.

And if there are racy pictures of you with or without a partner on your Facebook page, we need to talk — unless you live in Nevada and work at the Mustang Ranch. Discretion even in the age of information is much to be cherished. This is not only for the sake of your romantic life but also to preserve your career. Employers frown on seeing such items on your social networking profiles. *Caution* is the watchword for the day. Remind yourself that the Internet is forever and your run for higher office may not be boosted by youthful (or not so youthful) hook-ups.

All of us want to be loved not in spite of our warts but because of them; you want to feel that someone knows and loves the real you. But confessing sexual issues feels good for you for the moment and bad for the person who has to listen; it will come back and haunt you both.

See any pattern in the following list? You should. All these topics relate to past sexual experiences to keep a lid on:

✔ Previous love affairs

✔ Previous one-night stands

✔ Previous indiscretions

✔ Flings with the boss

✔ Flings with your best friend's significant other

✔ Sexual preferences

✔ Ménage à trois or more

If you have fantasies of being with someone else, remember that you're not the only person who has occasionally thought about an old love or a movie star when you're with your current date. The question is not "Is it okay?" but "How often does it occur, and how necessary does it feel?" If this type of fantasy happens most of the time, you're not ready to be with this person. If it happens only occasionally and, in general, you're pleased with your date, keep your mouth shut and enjoy the once-in-a-while forbidden pleasure of letting your mind wander.

You're an adult, and human beings aren't perfect. Learn from your mistakes and move on. Like everybody else, you're a compendium of everything that's come before: the people you've known (teachers, parents, sibs, the kindergarten bully, Sunday school teachers), the things you've done (your first kiss, dance lessons, strike-outs), and the things you've experienced (getting bad haircuts, developing crushes, receiving a favorite Valentine, getting a bloody nose, adoring favorite rock stars, losing report cards), and so on. Your sexual history is part of you, but the more you talk about it, the larger it's likely to loom. And a looming sexual history does nothing but taint your current dating situation. If you need to confess about past sexual experiences, find a priest or a therapist, but with everyone else, adopt the Clinton plan: Don't ask, don't tell. You'll *both* be happier and wiser.

Past relationships

In general, talking about past relationships is a really bad idea. They're over and done with. When you talk about them, the tendency is to paint either your ex or yourself as a bad person. If you paint yourself as bad, you may plant the question in your date's mind, "Why waste time with this loser?" If you paint your ex as bad, you can end up looking paranoid and unintentionally bringing up the uncomfortable question "How would this dude talk about me behind my back?" Talking about exes is just too much negativity.

If you can't find something better to talk about than your exes, you need a therapist, not a date.

Showing Interest

The earlier sections deal with information you must or must not share. But presumably, at some point, you're going to be curious. What questions are okay to ask? Which ones need to be avoided?

Good questions to ask

It's important not only to be interested but to *seem* interested in your date by asking cool questions like the following:

- ✔ What do you do?
- ✔ What sports do you like?
- ✔ What's your favorite free-time activity?

- ✔ What movies have you seen?
- ✔ What restaurants do you like?
- ✔ What do you think is the most important invention of the last 100 years?

Avoid questions like the following:

- ✔ **Do you come here often?** Trite, silly, and demeaning, leading nowhere.

- ✔ **How's your food?** The most common response is "Fine." Complaining is tacky, and what are you going to do about it? If you want to focus on the food (I wouldn't suggest it), you can offer to share. You can find out gobs about your date very quickly by his or her willingness — or unwillingness — to share.

- ✔ **Can you believe the weather?** Pleeeze try harder than this. It's a dead-end question that runs the risk of making you sound desperate.

Good questions are those that draw your date out without putting him or her on the spot. The goal here is to learn about one another, not scare the daylights out of your date with your investigative prowess. You're trying to show interest, not terrorize. Talk, explain, find out what makes your date tick a bit. It's fun, so lighten up and follow these easy guidelines:

- ✔ **Be prepared to talk about a lot of things.** You can see why keeping up with current events, the latest movie, a local political scandal, or (in a pinch) your horoscope is a cool idea. If all you can talk about is work or your exes, it's going to be hard to begin building those conversational bridges that give you the feeling that you're getting to know someone and letting him or her get to know you.

- ✔ **Don't worry about your next question.** Listen to your date's response. It's even okay to be quiet for a minute or two.

- ✔ **Don't fall into the Spanish Inquisition phenomenon.** See the next section for all the gory details.

The Spanish Inquisition phenomenon

The Spanish Inquisition was established by the Catholic Church to root out heretics in 1480. The inquisitors' methods were brutal, employing, among other horrible torture devices, the rack, thumb screws, and boiling oil. You do not want your date to be reminded of this historical era as you tastefully peel away the protective layers and find out who this person is.

Any question can feel like an intrusion, so make yourself and your date comfortable:

- ✔ **Share some things about yourself without dominating the conversation or showing off.** The best way to elicit information is to offer some. I'll show you me if you'll show me you.

- ✔ **Ask thoughtful, nonaggressive questions.** Doing so shows that you are genuinely interested and paying attention.

- ✔ **Avoid the enough-about-me-what-do-you-think-about-me? approach.**

Remember, the trick is seeming interested enough to ask gentle questions that show interest rather than reportorial zeal.

Avoiding Pitfalls

"Tell me a little about yourself" can always be countered by "What would you like to know?" which can be sidestepped by "Whatever you'd like to tell me."

Don't be tempted to lie, even for effect. If you don't plan to see this person again, stay on neutral subjects, talk about the weather, or — okay, okay — go to the movie where, at least, you won't have to talk. (*Note:* If the date has gone this far wrong, you both may want to pull the plug; the only reason to maintain the polite fiction is if you're truly chicken, your date seems impossibly needy, or a reallllly good friend or your mom has set you up. Life is short; this much resistance this early is the universe writing large.)

Another pitfall to avoid is the tendency, when you hear a problem, to move in to fix it, becoming parent, therapist, or confessor. It's awfully early to become a fixer.

If you do plan to see each other again, don't worry that everything has to be said now or forever hold your peace. You have time, so relax and be as much like yourself as you can. Pretend that you're talking to a friend who doesn't know you very well but likes you and isn't going anyplace.

Chapter 16

Speed Bumps on Life's Highway

*T*he time span between the end of date number two and the beginning of the rest of your love life is a sort of "like/lust/love" limbo. It's all about potential. You're in the *what's-going-to-happen-next?* mode. It's not a relationship yet. It's not a full-fledged friendship, either. It's an exciting, sexy, mysterious, scary, thrilling sort of thing — which is just what this stage is supposed to be. It's a time to take it slowly, take stock, keep it all in perspective, and accept your topsy-turvy emotions for what they really are: a natural reaction to what potentially, plausibly, conceivably, hopefully, fingers-crossed, if everything works out, may one day (possibly) be.

This is an especially important time to stay in the moment. Enjoy and don't get too far ahead of yourself. Don't be tempted to peruse your date's Facebook page and study his or her photo albums and interest Pages or get too far ahead of yourself in daydreaming about sharing all those interests just yet. Take time to smell the roses, the coffee, the perfume, the cigars, and the wind. Slowing down: That's the focus of this chapter.

GIRL STUFF

♀

Women are particularly prone to begin planning the color of the bridesmaids' dresses, practicing writing his name as theirs, getting into the prince-on-a-white-stallion mode. It's too early to think about riding off into the sunset. Chill, girl!

GUY STUFF

♂

Just as you're getting comfortable, understand that your date may begin planning ahead. Stay in the moment and resist memorizing her social networking pages. Don't dominate her Tweet Stream, and avoid direct messaging her at Twitter or e-mailing her at Facebook. Playing dumb and/or oblivious will cost you more than it's worth in the long run.

Scoping Out the Four Stages of Attachment: The Gospel According to Dr. Joy

Although each dating situation is unique, each progresses in a fairly predictable way. This progression from first date to budding relationship is what I call the four stages of attachment:

- **Stage One: Ignition (from first date to first month):** Your interest is just starting up. Hopefully, there's enough fuel on both sides to ignite a spark. You're on your best behavior, wear your best clothes, shine your shoes, wear clean socks, pluck your eyebrows, thin your sideburns, and stash breath mints in your pocket.

- **Stage Two: First Gear (from 1 month to 3 months):** If all's well, you didn't pop the clutch and kill the engine or flood the carburetor. You're getting to know each other and checking the rearview mirror a bit, but mostly you're keeping your eyes on the road ahead, trying really hard to mesh those gears without going too fast. You're relaxed enough to be real, to fumble with the check, to wear a shirt straight from the dryer without ironing it, perhaps even to wear something comfy rather than spiffy. You offer your date a breath mint, too, instead of just sneaking one for yourself.

  Depending on how things are going, though there are no hard and fast rules, somewhere around here, after the two of you have discussed it, low-key connecting on a social networking site may feel great. If either of you is reluctant or feeling a bit claustrophobic, hold off. Curiosity is dangerous to budding relationships as well as cats.

- **Stage Three: Acceleration (from 3 months to 6 months):** Foot on the gas pedal, you're raring to go. Physical and emotional attraction are steaming up the windshield. You like each other a lot. You feel so comfy you invite your date over to your place even when you haven't picked the newspaper off the floor. You order extra garlic on the pizza. You feel a sense of give and take. Some of the nervousness about whether you're on the same page, map, or galaxy or in the same car has lessened a bit — okay, mostly a lot.

  You're probably taking lots of candid photos together with your smart phones, which are starting to show up in your Facebook, Flickr, Photobucket, or Picasa photo albums. Have fun and still play it cool, though a little honest excitement and an occasional giggle is okay too.

- **Stage Four: Cruise Control (from 6 months to 9 months):** Sit back, relax; you're on the freeway. It's a bona fide relationship-to-be. You love each other, though you may not have said it yet. You've seen each other's flaws and find them adorable. You ate cold garlic pizza for breakfast, and your mate asked you to, please, brush your teeth. Happily, you complied. Not only are you in the car together, you can take turns driving (right . . .), choose destinations together, and really enjoy the trip.

It's okay to change your Facebook status from Single to In a Relationship with each other and share it just a little with the whole world, assuming you both agree to change both of your statuses.

Applying the Brakes

Remember when you were a kid, and your parents were driving the whole family to Disneyland or Magic Mountain or Lion Country Safari? As soon as you saw the signs on the highway telling you there were only a few miles left to go, you hopped up and down on your seat and squealed, "Faster! Faster!" You couldn't wait to get there. Remember what your parents said in response? "Calm down. It'll still be there when we get there."

The same holds true for this thing you're on the verge of experiencing. Calm down. It'll still be there when you get there. You're still in the ignition stage. As you read through this chapter, I want you to envision a flashing yellow light. Proceed cautiously. Don't come to a complete stop, but slow down and look both ways. Enjoy the scenery. I know it's hard chilling out when you can't wait to arrive. (I have a daughter. We've been to Disney World.) But there are lots of really good reasons why it's a good idea to take a deep breath and gently apply the brakes, or at least be a little less lead-footed with the gas.

Ten ways to ruin your life with technology

- ✔ Pose nude on Facebook
- ✔ Twitter from the bathroom on your first date
- ✔ Use your home address online
- ✔ Share sexual fantasies on Facebook
- ✔ Bad-mouth your exes
- ✔ Text your date several times an hour
- ✔ Leave sexy messages hourly on your date's cell
- ✔ E-mail your date's parents and exes detailing your love
- ✔ Make sure there is a video record of your sex life together and apart
- ✔ Make sure to e-mail your date at work

Love at first sight

Phil Donahue once asked me about love at first sight in the presence of three couples who had fallen madly, passionately in love with one another upon the initial locking of eyes. Not wishing to rain on their parades and be seen as the Wicked Witch of the West, I declared love at first sight to be "lust with potential" — nothing wrong with it unless you confuse it with anything else, such as love, like, knowledge, reality, or reason. (FYI: Within a year, a follow-up of the program reported that all three couples were either separated or divorced.)

On the other hand, 32 percent of couples married more than 25 years report that they felt love at first sight, which may be attributable to impaired memory, luck, or willingness to do the work of getting to know someone. Love at first sight isn't bad if you remember what it really is: Lust with potential, not a reuniting of soul mates.

In previous chapters, I talk about the chemistry of love. What you're dealing with in this early stage of dating is the chemistry of lust, which can be much more compelling and much more confusing. When your dates go well, your brain becomes flooded with natural amphetamines, or uppers, that make you feel — literally — high on life. You're full of happiness, energy, optimism. If you were on an old *Mary Tyler Moore Show* episode, you'd toss your hat up in the air. It feels like this excitement will last forever, which is lust's practical joke on us all. It doesn't last. Eventually, the chemicals fade, and if deeper feelings haven't developed, your fledgling "relationship" fades as well.

When you race into a relationship instead of meandering along the scenic route, not only do you miss out on all the good stuff you'd never see otherwise, but you also set yourself up to drive straight off a cliff if things don't work out. It's hard to see all those Dead End or Detour or Slippery When Wet signs when you're speeding, so the ultimate crash and burn take you completely by surprise.

Moving slowly is as much about self-preservation as it is about laying a proper foundation. Like I emphasize in Chapter 15, trust takes time. As in months. As in lots of face-to-face, nose-to-nose (not lip-to-lip or hip-to-hip) communication. Put in enough trust time and ask yourself some major soul-searching questions:

- ✔ **Focus:** Why do I really want this person in my life? Is it about liking him or her or how good it feels to have this person like me?

- ✔ **Motive:** Is this a romance or a rescue mission? Do I need or want this person?

- ✔ **Rationale:** Do I think I'll lose him or her if I don't give all I've got right away?

- ✔ **Function:** Is this more about getting into bed rather than getting to know someone?

Be honest. It's important to know what's truly lurking in your head and your heart. Misleading a date is uncool. Misleading yourself is unwise.

Putting Off Sex

Chapter 17 explains everything you ever needed or wanted to know about sex and dating in this modern, complicated, out-there, in-your-face, boob tube, wonderful, memorable, technologically advanced, Internet, no secrets, full disclosure, transparent, virtual day and age. For now, I want you to understand the emotional reasons why waiting is a good idea. Not forever. Just until you know each other pretty well.

Sex changes everything. Trust me on this — it just does — which is reasonable, if you think about it. Sex is, after all, how human beings are created. If sex meant nothing, what would that say about all of us? Still, no matter what you believe about premarital, post-marital, extramarital, or even marital sex, there is always an emotional metamorphosis after two people make love. Always. The relationship is never the same again. It can be better or worse, but it's never the same. Just look at the vocabulary. For instance, here are some synonyms for the word naked:

- Bare
- Defenseless
- Exposed
- Helpless
- Raw
- Revealed
- Stripped
- Unprotected
- Vulnerable

Now, take a look at some synonyms for the word dressed:

- Adorned
- Bedecked
- Covered
- Decorated
- Embellished
- Guised
- Spruced up

Five ways to say no gracefully

- It's too soon. I'd rather wait.

- I'm not that kind of guy/girl.

- I have a ten-date rule. If you want to know what it is, ask me out again . . . and again.

- I'll know when the timing's right. It's not right, right now.

- I'd rather have something to look forward to than back on.

The point is, sex is ultimately about exposure: physical, mental, spiritual, and emotional exposure. There's no more covering up. You're letting it all hang out, exposing a very intimate part of yourself (your head may be even more vulnerable and tender than your genitals) to another human being, not to mention the potential health exposure as well. All of this is why sex at this point is so dicey. If you're not ready to be that vulnerable, that open and unprotected, you're all the more vulnerable to getting hurt the next day or a bit farther down the road.

Baring your soul

The early stages of relationships — getting to know one another, tingling in each other's presence, daring to think this might be the one while steadfastly trying to stay in the moment — should be savored and enjoyed, not rushed. This is the time when you want to start baring your soul, not your body. It's a time to tiptoe into vulnerability, not leap into bed. The potential emotional cost is simply too high. Why risk it? Your mom was right. If he or she is worth waiting for, he or she will wait.

For now, I want you to relax and focus on letting your date begin to see who you are inside. Most people wish they'd waited just a bit longer to get sexual — not because of the sex but because sex moves you at the speed of light past things you ought not to be moving past at all. Don't ever go to bed with someone if you have the slightest notion that it's too soon, that you're feeling pressured, that you don't really know each other well enough, that you'd be devastated if this person didn't call or you'd feel used — *please* wait. It's not that I'm against old-fashioned lust, but it is a surprisingly unstable basis for love.

Trusting your emotions

I once met an artist who sculpted these incredible horses out of marble. Some were ebony, some a sort of salmon color. Others were a pearly white. Each one, horse after horse, had a distinct look, a personality that literally leapt off the pedestal where he'd mounted them. It was stunning. I asked him how he did it.

"Did what?" he asked back.

"How do you create such unique beauties?"

He grinned and told me it was simple, really. "I don't create anything," he said. "I just free the horses."

When he began chipping away at a block of marble, he explained, he focused on getting out of the horse's way. "It's all in there," he said. "You just have to figure out how to open the stone and let the horses out."

At this early stage of dating (I'm talking about the first several weeks or months), I want you to forget about sex for now and "free your horses." Be yourself. Let your date see the real you. Get out of your own way and reveal your unique beauty. Instead of making love, make another date to do something that will bring you closer emotionally, such as:

Will the real Barbie please stand up?

The entire American culture conspires against our getting real with who we are. Look at the images all around us. On TV. In the movies. Mannequins at the mall. If Hollywood were an accurate reflection of who we are, most women would look like giant Barbie dolls, and most men would have full, lush heads of hair and washboard abs. Everyone would sit around at work in $1,000 suits tossing barbs at one another, and kids would solve all their problems in 22 minutes or less.

The media's portrayal of even the dark side of life is distorted. Ask people if our country is more violent than ever, and most will say yes. The fact is, that's not true. According to the FBI, violent crime has consistently decreased every year since 1993 and shows no indication of leaping up any time in the near future. Yet the number of murder stories broadcast on the network news rose 721 percent from 1993 to 1996, according to a study done by the Center for Media and Public Affairs. Get the picture? What we may think is real, right, just, or the way everyone else is simply isn't true.

Ch-ch-ch-ch-changes

Remember the song from *Guys and Dolls* about marrying the man today and changing his ways tomorrow? I'm convinced women view men as clay. They fall in love with them and then decide to dress 'em differently, teach 'em to talk, to like ballet, and to be nice to their moms. Men, on the other hand, want women never to change — to remain the same size, weight, IQ, and sophistication as when they met.

Wow, how do relationships ever work out?

Miraculously, they work out when both people decide to accept the basics and understand that change happens but that the most successful change is self-generated.

- Taking a walk along the beach
- Going bird-watching in the woods
- Taking a drive
- Strolling the mall
- Having a picnic
- Sipping high tea together
- Snuggling up in front of the fire
- Baby-sitting
- Baking
- Visiting a museum
- Helping deliver food to shut-ins
- Visiting a nursing home or hospital
- Gardening
- Skating together, roller or ice
- Rediscovering your inner kid at an amusement park

Not Getting Ahead of Yourself

Nailing your heart, head, and toes to the present moment is what you want to do here. The temptation is strong — to fantasize about your glorious future, to dump your desires onto your date, to project that your date feels the same way about you, or to imagine that this is the person who will solve your past relationship problems. Resist it. Bite the inside of your lip, if necessary, to remind yourself, "Hey, I'm dealing with one person now, one moment in time, one original situation." It's hard to do, I know, but you owe it to yourself and your date.

Getting real about the person you're dating — and leaving your own Fantasy Island — is important if you want to build a relationship that lasts. The way you do that is to keep your attention on the here and now, on the date before you, not on other people you've dated before. Here's how to identify some warning signs that you're at risk of judging your date based on a past, future, or fantasy life. Ask yourself these questions:

- ✔ Does my date remind me of anyone? Old girlfriend? The guy who got away? My mom?
- ✔ Do I spend a lot of time thinking about my date's potential (like, he or she would be great if only . . .)?
- ✔ Do I obsess about what my date meant by something he or she said or did?
- ✔ Do I ever feel uneasy when my date says or does something my old girlfriend or boyfriend used to say or do?
- ✔ Do I assume my date feels the same way about me as I feel about him or her?

Feeling these things is okay. Judging new folks based on the old folks you know is understandable. But I want you to be aware of what you're doing so you don't make the mistake of misjudging a date based on something that has nothing to do with that person. Take it one date at a time, one moment at a time. Evaluate what's there, not what could, would, or should be.

Smokey says . . .

In the 1989 movie *Always,* John Goodman, Richard Dreyfus, and Holly Hunter played forest rangers. (It's based on the remake of *A Man Named Joe,* but that movie was before my time.) At one point, John Goodman is explaining love to Holly Hunter, using the metaphor of the two kinds of forest fires — one that is explosive and burns hot and bright and then burns itself out, and the other kind that is quieter and less noticeable and dramatic, but if you put your hand to the ground, you can feel its heat. It's the kind of fire that will burn forever.

We're all enthralled with the idea of love being the first kind of fire because it's so dramatic and beautiful and scary. But if you think about it, it's wiser to be drawn to the second kind because it'll keep us warm forever.

Reality versus unrealistic expectations

Picture one of my favorite TV commercials: A gorgeously dressed man strolls into a lovely room with white gossamer curtains gently blowing in the wind and a candelabra with flickering candles; he moves sinuously toward a beautiful woman in a lovely white gown as she expectantly waits for him to come to her. The whole scene is beautiful and blurred in soft focus.

Suddenly, he trips on a tablecloth and spills wine and knocks over a flower arrangement and breaks the china. The ad is for a carpet stain remover, but it could just as easily be an ad for understanding the blurring reality and unrealistic expectations in dating and the unquenchable need for romance to the detriment of reason, sanity, and reality — and your fine china.

Don't talk about your date with other people until you're in the Acceleration Stage (you've dated 3 to 6 months and are pretty comfortable with each other). The fewer people who know you've passed the second-date threshold, the better — and that means (especially) your mom and casual friends. It's okay to tell your best friend, but the last thing you want is an audience that can't wait to hear every juicy detail. Yeah, right, keep it off the Internet as well. Same rule applies to asking your friends about their post-second dates. Give the thing a chance to get going before asking *how* it's going. With an audience, everything — the good stuff and especially the bumps — will be exaggerated. I know this is really hard, and it's tempting to want to blab in the early first stages, but keeping the whole thing secret is tantalizing and a lot safer.

Being Patient: You Can't Hurry Love

Diana Ross was right: You can't hurry love. You just have to wait. No two ways about it. True love is a slow-burn. Lust is spontaneous combustion that soon burns itself out. Here's how to tell the difference:

✔ **Like:** When you like someone, you're still in checklist mode. You're keeping a mental scoreboard — plus one for showing up on time, minus one for taking a call on the cell phone, plus one for laughing at your dumb joke, minus one for biting fingernails. "Like" is an evaluation of compatibility — literally, seeing if you two are enough alike to get along. Think about how you describe a friend. You go through a list of attributes; it's all in sharp focus.

- **Lust:** More physical than mental, lust is tingling fingertips, sweaty palms, pounding hearts, and breathless kisses. Lust is wanting to engulf someone with a bear hug and make out (or more) till the sun comes up. Lust is powerful and fickle. It's a sexual faucet that can seem to turn off almost as quickly as it turns on — pure energy.

- **Lust with direction:** After date two, before date twenty-two, the LWD phase is sexy with street smarts. You've lost your head over this person but not your mind. Not only do you desire to whisk him or her off to bed in a cascade of kisses, but you want to read the morning paper together, too. And not just the funny pages, either.

- **Love:** Soft-focus in the best sense of the word. You can see clearly, but it's pretty and mellow and pleasing. Most of all, love is about trust and time — and the time it takes to really trust someone fully. Love isn't a mad dash; it's a slow stroll. It's compatibility, acceptance, giving as well as getting, warmth, fun, and shared interests and goals. It's caring for someone, not in spite of their flaws but because of them.

Dr. Joy's love tip

If your date says "I love you" on the first date, it's lunacy.

If your date says "I love you" on the second date, it's lust.

If your date says "I love you" on the third date, it's still lust.

If your date says "I love you" in the fourth month, it's lust with direction.

If your date knows your soul and your weight and your childhood scars and your adulthood scars and your parents and your most embarrassing moments and your dreams and your failures and says, "I love you, not anyway but because," congratulations, it's love.

Chapter 17

Getting to Serious

• •

In This Chapter

▶ Understanding the differences among casual, serious, and heavy dating

▶ Knowing what sex is and isn't

▶ Determining when to say yes and when to say no to sex

▶ Evaluating your relationship

• •

*W*hen does dating move from the casual phase to the serious phase? Obviously, the answer is different for every couple and often for both participants. One of you may view the dating as serious from day one; the other may never view the dating as serious (which obviously creates problems for you both). In this chapter, I give you guidelines from which you can begin to evolve your own personal perspectives and discuss them together.

Casual versus Serious versus Heavy Dating

Any relationship can survive if you're both on the same wavelength, and any relationship is going to run into problems if you're not. Like anything else, heavy dating may best be defined by what it is and what it isn't: It's not casual dating, and it's a step beyond serious dating.

Casual dating

Casual dating means that neither of you is taking the relationship terribly seriously because one or the other of you is

▻ **Dating others:** You like each other but see other people as well.

▻ **Living far away:** You live so far away from each other that you can see each other only occasionally.

- ✔ **Only in town temporarily:** This is similar to a holiday romance; you know that the relationship will last only as long as the business trip, vacation, or whatever does.

- ✔ **Not interested in a commitment:** You want the relationship to be without long-term expectations.

- ✔ **Not being sexual:** You're abstaining.

- ✔ **Not being seriously sexual:** You're not being monogamous (not a terrific idea).

- ✔ **Available less than twice a week:** You get together less than twice a week, either because you're not interested in seeing each other more frequently or because proximity keeps you apart.

- ✔ **Still listed on an Internet dating site:** You're keeping your options open.

- ✔ **Still listed as single on your Facebook account:** You aren't defining this relationship as a relationship. You tell yourself it's about privacy, but you know it's not.

Even though no one is crazy about auditioning for the role of significant other, casual dating isn't all bad: It allows both parties to get to know one another without the pressure of exclusivity, and it allows for comparisons that are natural and not necessarily odious.

Serious dating

Serious dating is a transition between casual dating and heavy dating. With serious dating,

- ✔ Your relationship is exclusive.

- ✔ You see each other once or twice a week.

- ✔ You live in the same city.

- ✔ You are possibly sexual, possibly not.

- ✔ You've cancelled your online dating membership or let it lapse.

- ✔ You've both listed yourselves as involved in a relationship on your Facebook pages.

Heavy dating

The idea of dating is to see who's out there and to keep *do-si-do*ing and switching off until you find someone who seems a cut above the rest, someone worthy of additional time and effort and consideration. Once you decide that you have someone who is worth abandoning all others for (someone for whom you're willing to change your Facebook status — at least temporarily), you've moved into exclusivity, which is a precursor to heavy dating. Heavy dating involves:

- **Being mutually exclusive by design:** You discuss and consciously agree to see only one another.

- **Having three or more dates a week:** You take time and effort to be together often.

- **Dating on weekends:** You spend weekends together rather than with the guys or girls, and when you do have to be with others, you often go as a couple.

- **Living in the same area code:** Living relatively close to one another makes it possible to see each other often.

- **Often being sexual and, certainly, practicing sexual exclusivity:** In other words, if your relationship includes sex, you are monogamous.

- **Abandoning online dating sites:** Neither of you even thinks about trolling through your old online dating profiles or checking out anyone else's.

- **Committing to your relationship on Facebook:** Neither of you lists yourself as single, in an open relationship, or "It's complicated" online.

Sexual intimacy, although not necessary to a committed relationship, is often one of its hallmarks. Whereas some people think the key is the "sex" part, the real key is the "intimacy" part: a connection deep enough to involve body *and* soul. But intimacy depends on a number of factors, not just (and not necessarily) on the sex act. If you think that you can achieve intimacy solely through sex, you're mistaken.

What do men and women really want?

"What on earth does the other sex want?" a lot of people ask me on my radio program. The answer is simple. While men and women aren't the same, they're not from different planets, either. What they all want is this:

- To be accepted for who we are . . . not for who you think we should be.

- To be known . . . warts and all.

- To be heard . . . even when we say something you don't want to hear.

- To be appreciated . . . for small things as well as big.

- To be cherished.

- To be needed.

- To be wanted.

- To be liked.

- To be loved.

The Role of Sex in a Relationship

In our society, sex is a big deal. It's commercialized and romanticized; it's used to sell everything from toothpaste to chewing gum, cars to condos, jeans to Jacuzzis; and it's wrapped in ribbons and adorned with hearts and flowers. No wonder there are so many mixed messages. For example:

✔ Everybody seems to be doing it on sitcoms, afternoon talk shows, the news, the movies, the soaps, and in "reality" hot tubs . . . *but it's sacred and special* (according to your pastor and papa).

✔ To be a great lover, you've got to have many partners . . . *but save yourself for the right person.*

✔ Sex is wholesome and natural . . . *but venereal disease is a punishment.*

Wow, if we used the same criteria for words, we'd all stutter all the time, and sexually we are a stuttering society.

What sex isn't

I can't tell you what sex should or shouldn't mean to you, but I *can* tell you what it's not. Sex is *not* AIDS, commitment, necessary, wicked, beautiful, or ugly. In its most basic form, it's scratching an itch. Everything else is something we project on a very simple act. It's the psychology, not the biology, that's complicated.

What sex is

But sex can be all of those things listed in the preceding section and much more. It's you and your body and a way of feeling close to another person. Whether sex is wicked or beautiful, intimate or ugly, depends on you and your partner and all the perceptions and feelings and intentions and expectations you both bring to the party. Whether sex makes you feel close to another soul depends on you and your partner and timing and position and the ability to laugh or cry.

Sex occurs everywhere. After all, it's how little birds and buffaloes and Bobbies happen. Of course, for most animals and plants, there is a season; in other words, their sex drives are controlled purely by biology. But although we humans still have the monthly reproductive cycle, we let our heads and our hearts and our genitals completely overtake it. Add to that the fact that sex has various social and economic connotations, based on the societies in which we live, that affect the meaning and variety and acceptance and rules of sex. Yeah, the equipment is all the same, but the meaning and variety and acceptance and rules are all governed by heads and hearts, not genitals. The point is that we all live in a society that has rules about sex; what's important here is what sex means to you and your partner.

Virtual sex

What virtual sex and virtual dating often mean these days is logging on to the Internet and clicking into an online image gallery, cyber chatroom, sex link, virtual sex club, Facebook page (especially one with privacy settings), or video conference call. Most of this stuff is little more than an online peep show. You have to be (or pretend to be) at least 18 to enter, and the costs can really rack up — many sites charge by the minute. Facebook has taken the opportunity for raunch to an unprecedented level (though maybe not intentionally), and it's free. The notion of privacy is seeming more and more old fashioned and anachronistic. Please remember that the Internet is eternal.

Be very careful here. Porn sites can be expensive and no substitute for the real thing — dating someone you can actually see, touch, and talk to in person. I would argue that many of the social networking sites can be described in the same way. They don't have to be that way, but without some care your time on a social networking site can morph into something significantly less than wholesome, and the seduction of a blank screen cannot be overstated.

If you're getting the feeling that sex is tricky stuff, you're right. So what does this mean to you and your partner?

It means that first and foremost, you have to decide what you want and what sex means to you. Are you ready to be that open and vulnerable to another person? Are you ready to be gentle enough with someone who trusts you not to intentionally harm him or her? Are you prepared for the responsibility of sexuality with another person? I guarantee you, your body will urge you well before the rest of you is ready, and *that's* the rub, so to speak.

The Thing about Sex

The thing about sex is not that you're naked physically, but if you do it right, that you're naked emotionally. The whole point of dating is to feel connected and less alone. Sex can certainly accomplish that if both of you are careful. If you're only horny, you're going to either hurt someone or get hurt, and then you'll feel lonelier and less connected than before.

In some ways, it's quite convenient that the urge to merge should be both sexual and emotional, physical and mental, but we all know that it isn't always this way, that sex isn't necessarily intimacy. Think of the friend you love but with whom you have no "chemistry"; conversely, think about the sexy thing you know who is unprincipled, self-centered, and mean and who has the attention span of a gnat. I know I sound like your cranky Aunt

Mathilde, but if you have to give up one for the other, it's a better bet to give up the sex and go for the intimacy. (I hear you — you're saying "girl thing," but guys get tired of meaningless, impersonal sex, too.)

Identifying the right time

The right time to have sex is when you aren't asking anything more than sex from your partner. You know this person, like and trust him or her, and aren't using sex to get power, presents, or a date or as a sign of anything other than mutual interest. If you're looking for signs, read tea leaves or traffic lights. It's never the right time until

- ✔ **You've talked about it.** By talking about sex, you find out what each of you thinks (that's why before you can talk, you have to know your own mind). If you can't talk about sex, it's too soon to have sex; if you don't trust each other enough to talk, why would you take your clothes off in front of the other person?

  Have this conversation about sex when you're both dressed and sober.

- ✔ **You know each other's middle name.** If you don't know each other's middle name, you probably don't know enough about each other for this kind of trust and intimacy. (Of course, swapping middle names on your first date doesn't mean that you're ready for sex.)

- ✔ **You feel passionate about this person.** Sex is urgent. If it weren't, who'd go to the trouble? (It is a physically vulnerable position if you think about it.) If the point of sex were merely species survival, for example, why do we humans spend so much time talking and reading and writing about it?

  But is urgency passion? It can be, but not necessarily. To understand the difference, think about a full bladder or an excruciatingly tight pair of shoes. Both situations are urgent, but neither is passion. Now think about your favorite meal. Yeah, hunger is an urgent need, but *passion* is when you care about what slakes your thirst or fills you up. You're going for passion here, not urgency.

- ✔ **You've had more than three or four dates.** No, this doesn't mean everybody has to have sex by the sixth date, but certainly, have it no sooner than the fourth date. How can you trust your judgment, let alone know your heart, before that?

- ✔ **You love touching each other and being touched.** You've played kissy face, and there's a lot of hand-holding going on here. You talk a lot in person and on the phone.

- ✔ **You see each other more than once a week.** This moves you into serious and heavy datingland.

✔ **You're not having sex with anybody else, and your date isn't either.** You know because you have talked about it together.

DR. JOY SAYS

If either of you is having sex with someone else, you don't necessarily have to stop seeing each other. But good sex feels preemptive, and if either or both of you are involved sexually with others, that situation sets up conflict. It increases the probability of lying, which isn't a great idea when you're trying to develop some intimacy and trust, and you'll probably have to deal with jealousy and possessiveness before you've established a basis of knowing and liking and respecting one another.

✔ **You're ready to practice safe sex.** You are prepared to make sure that nobody gets pregnant, hurt, diseased, or misunderstood. You have to be prepared for the responsibility of safe sex — safe medically, emotionally, and prophylactically. Men and women must both be prepared, so carry a condom, everybody.

✔ **You're both ready and having fun.** Nobody feels put upon or martyred or co-opted.

✔ **You're both willing to deal with the reality that the sex may not be great for either of you.** Men often experience impotence or premature ejaculation with a new partner, and women often don't feel comfortable enough to have an orgasm. If either of these common occurrences would blow your relationship out of the water, wait until the relationship has more stability outside the bedroom.

Anticipation

I once did an on-the-air poll about whether people wished they'd had sex earlier or later in their lives. Most 93 percent, in fact — said that they wished they had waited longer both in terms of age of first sexual experience and time in the relationship.

Waiting isn't so terrible and can even be fun. Anticipation is a powerful aphrodisiac. The longer you wait to have sex, the better the foundation, the more you know about each other, and the easier it is to talk about sexual things when the time comes.

And even if the sex isn't great initially, you both have something to fall back on, so to speak. You know and like each other, so one mediocre time in bed doesn't make either of you bolt. Friends talk; strangers don't. When it comes to sex, friends give you a much safer place to feel vulnerable. On the other hand, I know a woman who dated a guy exclusively for five years, slept with him in the same bed, and never had sex with him. Chastity is one thing; manipulation and mixed messages are quite another. If you're not intending to have sex with each other, don't go to bed with each other.

When sex is right, you're physically and emotionally naked. If your goal is sexual release and not an emotional connection, seriously consider masturbation. If you still decide to have sex, at least promise yourself to be honest upfront so that you don't mislead your partner. Remember, one of the assumptions of this book is that you are not a predator — that is, you're not someone who uses or exploits another person just for your own pleasure. The bottom line is that you have to wake up with yourself every day of your life, so don't do something in a fit of sexual heat that is going to make you dislike yourself. Lecture is temporarily over.

Saying yes

Saying yes to sex is easy and should be fun once you've had the discussion; if you're not sure what discussion I'm referring to, see the previous section. There is one and only one reason to say yes to sex: because you honestly and sincerely want to have sex with this person. The following are *not* reasons to say yes:

✔ You want to lose your virginity.

✔ You want to tell your friends you've done it.

✔ You want to prove you're not gay.

✔ You want to prove you're over your ex.

✔ You're afraid that if you don't say yes to this person, someone else will.

✔ Dinner was good.

✔ You're high.

✔ You're low.

✔ You're tired of saying no.

✔ You're afraid.

✔ You want him or her to call you again.

✔ You never want him or her to call you again.

✔ You feel sorry for him or her.

If the sex is good, I don't need to give you hints. Enjoy. If the sex isn't so good, keep in mind that some things take getting used to. Remember the first time you danced (probably no one mistook you for Fred or Ginger) or played mixed doubles (maybe you both ran to the net when one should have stayed behind). Getting in sync physically with another person takes time, patience, and a little practice, unless you're really lucky.

Keep a couple of things in mind about saying no:

✔ When you want to say no, just say no. It's okay to explain why it's not *no forever* but *no for now* because "I want to wait until . . ."

- "We're married."

- "We're engaged."

- "I'm sure."

- "I know you better."

- "You know me better."

- "My infection clears up."

- "I'm sure I'm straight."

Remember: Saying no has always been okay. See the next section for tips on how to say no.

✔ Just because you said yes once doesn't mean you have to say yes again, this time or ever, to that person.

Saying no

Saying no is everybody's right and privilege. Lots of folks say no all the time. Just make sure that you *never* say no when you mean "convince me" or "maybe." Regardless of the circumstances, *no means no,* no ifs, ands, buts, or I-thought-you-wanted-it, or I-know-you-want-it, or I-promise-I'll-stop-when-you-want-me-to, or any of the other responses to no. No means "Stop! Go no further." Period. Just so there is no misunderstanding on what part of no you understand:

✔ **No means no.** If you want to be convinced, say so.

✔ **Women own their own sexuality as much as men.** Guys, you can say no for any reason. Gals, you can say no for any reason.

✔ **If you know you're going to say no eventually, make that point upfront so you don't mislead anyone.**

✔ **If you change your mind either way, say so.**

Soul Mates: Fact or Fiction?

Everybody's looking for a soul mate, a carbon copy of feelings, thoughts, and values. We have been brainwashed into thinking that somewhere there is a mirror image of who we are, who is as much like us as a pea in a pod, which means we never have to change a thing or adapt or compromise. You can see why this is such a seductive thought but also completely silly.

Be careful of assuming the two of you are destined to be together. Doing so can make you overlook important distinctions, like that one of you is a morning person and the other is grumpy; one of you loves rare steak, and the other is a vegetarian; one is in the National Rifle Association, and the other is for gun control. Believing in soul mates can also make you much more vulnerable to the all-or-nothing school of relationships, where someone must be exactly like you in all things or completely unworthy of your time. It's hard enough to know our own soul; figuring that you know someone else's soul and it's a complete match is a recipe for disappointment and disaster.

Relationships aren't made in heaven or previous lives. They are living, breathing entities that require the same care and nurturing that any other living thing requires. If you buy into the soul mate nonsense, you're much less likely to do the work and have a reality-based relationship.

Fish or Cut Bait: Relationship Evaluation

There comes a time in any dating situation when you have to decide whether to go to the next stage or the next relationship. Going to the next relationship is exciting and can re-create the fun early days of getting to know someone. But if you're not careful, you may find yourself doing only dessert and never the meal, because in dating the dessert part comes first. If you're looking exclusively for excitement, it always makes sense to move on. If you're looking for intimacy and even semipermanence, sooner or later, you have to trade off novelty for depth. How can you tell if you're settling or steering?

The following questions help you evaluate your relationship. The list of questions is divided into particular areas. Answering these questions can help you decide whether it's time to move on or move up. Keep track of your answers in your dating notebook (see Chapter 1).

✔ **Compatibility**

- How much time do you spend together?
- How much do you enjoy your time together?
- Is your time together increasing or decreasing?
- How much do you have in common?
- Do you fight a lot or a little?

✔ **Common interests**

- Do you like to do the same things?
- Do you have friends in common?
- Do you like each other's friends, family?
- Are you each willing to try something new together?

- Are your religious convictions and behaviors compatible?

- Do you like the same kinds of music, sports, and so on?

✔ **Goals**

- Do you have the sense that you want the same things in life?

- Are you at the same stage of life?

- Are you both headed in the same direction?

- Do you want the same thing from a relationship?

- Do you have similar ideas about money and time?

✔ **Background**

Note: While opposites can attract and then aggravate the daylights out of one another, common backgrounds allow the two of you to respond in similar ways.

- Are you equally comfortable talking about feelings, friends, work, external events, and so on? Okay, realistically most women are going to be better at the feelings part than men, but still, a Chatty Cathy with stoic Stan is going to create problems eventually.

- Do you both come from screamer families or sulker families?

- Do you share religious, educational, and economic backgrounds?

- Do you both spend about the same amount of time and energy with your families?

- What part do family traditions play in your interactions, and are they compatible?

- Do you both feel essentially the same about alcohol, smoking, drugs, sex, and rock and roll?

- Do you have similar philosophies about money, spending, and saving?

- Do you both want/abhor children?

✔ **Fun**

- Do you share a sense of what's fun?

- How high do each of you rate leisure time?

- Do you do fun things together?

- Do you share a sense of humor, adventure?

✔ **Energy**

- Are both of you morning people? Night people?

- Are you both couch potatoes or exercise freaks?

- Are you both hyper or laid-back?

- Are you both healthy?

✔ **Problem-solving**

- Are either of you control freaks?

- Do you listen to one another?

- Are you able to negotiate?

- Do you ever disagree?

- Are you afraid to be angry or make the other person angry?

- Are you possessive?

- Is jealousy clouding your discussions of other things?

- Are you able to solve problems and move on?

- When you argue, do you insult each other?

The purpose of these questions is not to tally up points so that you can fit your relationship into one of three categories, like the two of you are okay, need a couples' counselor, or are toxic for one another. The purpose of these questions is to help you understand what you should be asking when you think about your relationship. When you evaluate your answers, try for the middle ground:

✔ **Don't settle for a lousy dating situation because you're afraid to be alone.** Being lonely because you're not seeing someone is one thing; being alone in a bad relationship is a lot worse and even lonelier.

✔ **Don't jettison a perfectly good relationship because it's not perfect.** There aren't perfect people, so it stands to reason that there aren't perfect relationships. If you took a job and never learned new skills and kept doing the same old thing, you'd get either bored or fired or both. Why should relationships be any different? You need to grow and change and work to make love rich and powerful and rewarding.

Chapter 18

Breaking Up

. . . .

. . . .

*D*ating is usually about wanting to make sure that the time and effort being invested pay off, so the hope is that the relationship will last forever (assuming it's wonderful and positive). The reality is that relationships don't always last. You may be comforted to remind yourself that people are put into our lives for one of three purposes: a reason, a season, or a lifetime:

✔ A reason may be a specific need to be met, a lesson learned, assistance, guidance, or support — something that we haven't been paying attention to. It's the universe's way of saying, wake up! We may have decided that we're too old or too unlovable or that we're fine by ourselves. Someone is then put in your path to remind you of the fun of having somebody with whom to share your life and by definition, once that support has been tendered, lesson learned, guidance given, it's time to move on, however painfully.

✔ A season offers us the chance to share, to grow, to learn a lesson that hasn't yet been learned. The lesson may be to be patient, more outgoing, or a bit more generous. Once we've learned or taught that lesson, the person who teaches or was taught is no longer necessary or relevant, so he or she moves on.

✔ Then there's the wonderful category in which most of us invest heavily, which is a lifetime and beyond, a person with whom we build a foundation.

Because a relationship didn't or doesn't last doesn't mean that it's not valuable, productive, or positive, or even that it's anybody's fault.

Like the song says, breaking up is hard to do. You've invested time and effort and emotion, but the relationship is just not working. Most people know well in advance when things aren't working out, but the world is divided into two sets of people: those who hang on too long and those who don't hang on long enough.

Aha, you're asking yourself, what about people who get out at the exact right time? Theoretically they exist, but knowing the exact time to split is generally something understood in retrospect.

Painful as it may be to contemplate, it's likely that all of us will face a breakup or two in our lifetime, so we may as well be prepared. In this chapter, I detail the warning signs of a breakup, tell you the how and when of discussing an impending breakup with a partner, and include a list of the most common reasons causing splitsville. Before you are completely bummed out, there is a first-aid kit of things to do that may save a relationship and advice on how to say it's over and what to do after you've called it quits.

Decoding Warning Signs

People often stay in relationships that aren't working so that they don't have to be alone — especially for the holidays, a wedding, a vacation, a birthday, Mom's anniversary. They may think, "This relationship isn't terrific, but it's better than the last one — or better than none at all."

But how do you know it's time to call it quits? You can count on a few warning signs:

- ✔ You fight over nothing.
- ✔ You're not as affectionate.
- ✔ You don't see what you ever saw in this person.
- ✔ You decided all your friends were right and have been all along.
- ✔ Your parents absolutely *adore* your date and that really frosts you.
- ✔ If there was ever sex, it has stopped.
- ✔ More time passes between dates.
- ✔ There are longer and longer silences.
- ✔ You start mentally (and maybe verbally, but I hope not) comparing your date unfavorably to others.
- ✔ You are more tempted by others.
- ✔ You're looking for excuses to be alone but not together.

✔ You're looking for excuses to hang out with other couples.

✔ You've renewed your online dating membership.

✔ You list your Facebook status as "It's complicated," "Single," in an "Open relationship," or "Widowed" (and nobody died).

✔ The two of you have no long-term plans.

✔ You take separate vacations.

✔ You buy a car, house, or pet without consulting or informing the other person.

✔ You're never there when he/she calls.

✔ You don't return your date's phone calls.

✔ You get a post office box.

✔ Your date moved, neglected to inform you, and didn't leave a forwarding address.

✔ You have your number changed and don't tell.

✔ A love child has been left on your front porch.

Hey, look, hopefully it hasn't gotten as bad as all that, but some people have a hard time letting go. You might convince yourself that just a little more effort or time or a good therapist would do the trick. The first thing you need to do, though, is figure out whether you're the only one who has noticed that things aren't going well or whether both of you seem to be miserable. If you feel that most of the preceding warning signs apply to you, it's time to call a halt. If your partner seems to be the unhappy one, it's perfectly reasonable to sit down in a public place (without alcohol) and say, "I've noticed that we're fighting a lot or not spending much time together. Do you want to see whether we can fix things, or do we have a dead fish here?"

Look, if your relationship gives you more misery than pleasure and more pain than fun, sit down with a pencil and paper and figure out what you want and what you're willing to offer to get it. If you discover that there is nothing the other person can give (or anything you're willing to relinquish), that should tell you something. Similarly, if you're in a relationship that used to work but has now turned rancid because one of you has moved or changed or cheated, you can't go back, but you can evaluate whether there is anything your partner can offer that has value to you and anything that you're willing to offer to get it. If so, get busy and figure it out and offer it. If not, it's time to do that grown-up thing and break up without bloodshed or nastiness.

Breaking up is as important a skill as any other part of dating. It's not fair to just disappear without a word. The world's too small a place, and you're too big a person, so don't even think about it.

Dealing with Evidence of Problems

While it usually takes six to nine months for a couple to decide whether or not a dating situation has the potential to become a relationship with a capital R, the bad news can become much more evident much sooner:

✔ If you've been out on only a couple of dates, there can be any number of reasons why things aren't working, including things beyond either of your control — work, family, finances, health problems — and it's sometimes hard to admit your confusion or unhappiness to someone you like but don't know very well.

✔ If the problem is just that the two of you have gone about as far as you can go, it's probably pretty apparent to you both. If you're really brave, you can talk about the specifics, which are listed in the next section. A cowardly no-no is to weasel out by not asking the person out and seeming to be really busy. The problem with this approach is twofold: First, it isn't very good communication (or very honest). Second, if the other person is really nice, he or she may be very understanding about how busy you are, and that makes you feel even worse. It's better to explain that the dating scenario just isn't working out and why.

✔ If both of you seem to be mutually uncomfortable, the problem is a lot easier to handle, and if you're honest without being brutal, you may even become long-term friends and go on to introduce each other to future dates.

The problem occurs when one person is seemingly content and the other is miserable. (But don't be fooled by a difference in styles. If one of you is really miserable, chances are the other person isn't having all that much fun either but may have a less confrontational style, be a better actor, be clingier, or have a worse track record, which tends to make people hang on for a longer time.)

✔ If you're the one having the problems, I encourage you to be honest and ask for help or a time-out rather than act aloof or uninterested. If the relationship has some potential, it's a lot easier to resume if the other person doesn't feel trashed.

✔ If you're the one who wants out, you have an obligation to be kind but honest. If you're the one who's being dumped (pardon the expression), you have a right to ask why, if you can do it without whining.

✔ If your partner seems to be having the problem, it's all right to say, "Seems to me you're a bit distracted these days. If you feel comfortable talking to me about it, maybe I can help, or if you'd rather not, I understand if you need to take a break right now." These days, most people feel they're better jugglers than they really are, and just having someone acknowledge that you don't have to be perfect can feel really good and be quite a relief.

Resist the temptation to send messages via your friends or bad-mouth your partner either online or in real life. It makes you look tacky and vindictive, and if you ever get back together it'll make you look unstable and mean.

Okay, it's obvious nothing is working: You've talked and tried, but it's just not much fun anymore and seems more trouble than it's worth. Get out your dating notebook (see Chapter 1). No, you're not going to write a Dear John or Jane letter; you're going to do some soul and relationship searching. Do an inventory of what's working and what's not by being very, very specific. For example, maybe you can talk (good) but the sex stinks (not so good). Weekends are okay, but you snarl at each other on Wednesdays; his mother is great, yours is driving you both nuts. The more specific your list, the cleaner the path. And don't ever be tempted to say, "We can't communicate." Communicate about what?!

Understanding the Break Up

People do things for reasons, and dating works or doesn't work for a surprisingly limited number of reasons: timing, incompatibility, money, geography, and so on. The following sections look at how each reason can and does impact the intimacy and time involvement necessary to move a dating situation forward.

Timing

This factor tops the list because if you both have time, everything else can be sorted out. If you don't have time, even the most compatible of couples is going to hit the wall.

Trading up

I once interviewed a man who said each of us should get in touch with exes who had dumped us. His position was that we should thank them because we could not go on and date more wonderful people until we had gotten out of a non-workable relationship, and some people are just better at noting the handwriting on the wall, even if it is graffiti. He contended that we never go backward: The next person is always better than the last because we know that someone at least that cool and good and kind and smart and cute exists, so we'll never settle for less.

An interesting, optimistic, and comforting notion.

The six- to nine-month itch

Perfectly viable relationships hit the watershed area around the sixth through ninth month. At this point, it's no longer just a brand-new thing, and nobody can keep up the pretenses for that long. You're both seeing who you really are. It's about this time that you either fish or cut bait, either move on to becoming a full-fledged relationship (my next book) or remain in dating purgatory, having neither the fun and excitement and awkwardness of getting to know one another nor the richness and serenity of moving to a deeper level of involvement and commitment.

You and I both know couples who seem to stay in six-month relationships forever and ever. Not a cool idea. If somehow you've gotten yourself in a relationship that has become long distance, unless you've known each other for a year or more and have been apart for a short period of time with intent to resume the relationship within a month or so, follow the rules for long-distance relationships. Long-distance relationships are primarily based on fantasy (you're apart a lot more than you're together) and have to be managed in completely different ways than traditional dating, which moves into serious and then heavy dating patterns.

Your timing can be off because one of you isn't out of a relationship, isn't finished with school, or isn't old enough or young enough, or you should have met earlier or later in your lives. This is the stuff of which heartaches and country songs are written. If not now, maybe later, and if not later, maybe your next life or last life.

Timing is a huge stumbling block, but it is not very negotiable, at least for the time being. If one of you is at one stage of commitment and the other isn't there yet, a classic way of dealing with the timing issue is to let some time elapse and see whether anything changes. I recommend six months apart with a ten-minute phone call on a designated day once a month so that no panic sets in. If you've been together less than six months, dispense with the phone call and agree to meet for lunch in six months, provided both are interested.

Incompatibility

Sometimes perfectly nice people just want completely different things in life, have different rhythms, different energies, different belief systems. These incompatibilities aren't necessarily instantly obvious, so it can take time to unearth them, but once they're out in the open, they're really hard to negotiate. Following are examples of significant incompatibilities:

- ✔ One of you wants to travel; the other one wants to settle down.

- ✔ One of you wants kids now; the other wants to finish a four-year college degree and then apply to medical school.

- ✔ One wants a Porsche; the other wants a poodle.

Some things are negotiable, but if the basics aren't in place (those things that are hugely important to the two of you — shared goals, attitudes, values), you'll spend all your time negotiating, leaving very little time or energy for true crises because everything seems like a crisis.

Obviously the two of you connected on some level, or you wouldn't have gotten this far. Being incompatible doesn't mean that one of you is right and the other wrong; it just means that you're wrong for each other. The more specific and honoring of the differences you can be, the easier the split is — making it bitter-sweet rather than just bitter.

Hauntings by ghosts

Old loves leave impressions. A song, a smell, a look, a place can conjure up a love that was. This is why the time rules exist, so the ghosts can find a resting place that's not actively in your head or heart.

But sometimes someone from the past pops up and completely disrupts a perfectly good relationship. It's not that anything's wrong; it's just that the prior situation seems more right, no matter how careful you are about waiting until someone is completely out of a relationship (the one-year-past-divorce rule, for example). These things happen. If it happens to you (whether the resurfacing former love is yours or your partner's), believe in kismet and don't take it personally — and don't be sneaky or vindictive, either. Sometimes we just have to bow to Fate. Fortunately, it doesn't happen all that often. As you're reading this, I'm sure visions of reunions and Facebook pages dance in your head. It's one of the primary reasons I urge married couples to attend high school and college reunions together and to be extraordinarily careful about friending an old love on Facebook. Nostalgia and ghosts can be realllly seductive.

Kismet kiss-off

One of the nicest brush-offs I ever got was from a guy I'd been seeing for a week or two who explained to me a ghost had reappeared in his life, someone he hadn't seen or heard from in years, and he felt he needed to pursue the ghost so that he could either put the whole thing to rest or marry her. He ended up marrying her and inviting me to the wedding. I remember it as being a classy way to tell me not to wait by the phone.

Geography

Long-distance relationships stink. They have too much of a fantasy component with too little reality. If you are dating someone you see less than a couple times a month because of distance, you need to adopt the Clinton plan: Don't ask, don't tell — what the other person is doing, whom they're with, where they were when you called — and don't consider it a "real" relationship until the two of you live within the same area code and can see each other at least a couple times a week. (Browne doctrine also dictates you don't live together, and both of you get jobs and date each other "normally" and see what develops.)

This is another case of not no, just not now.

Sex

Initial attraction can wear thin even if you're not hitting the sheets, and because we're talking dating and not friendship here, a complete waning of sexual interest or attraction doesn't bode well for the dating part. You may turn out to be great friends, but dating assumes some sexual interest.

Obviously, some minor change in the initial excitement is not unusual, but what you hope for here is a deepening of the interest and immersion in the other person's soul — as well as body — rather than ennui or boredom.

If you've become a sexual predator who is just interested in conquest, it's time to get some help, not a date. Not only will you be hurting other people who are silly enough to love you, but you'll view yourself, with some accuracy, as a creep, and I guarantee that the only person you'll always end up in bed with is yourself. Hating yourself isn't a good basis for dating or anything else.

Money

A huge discrepancy in financial resources can cause problems, especially if you didn't know about the discrepancy up front or if someone's situation has changed. Even winning the lottery is surprisingly hard on relationships. Losing a job or having a car stolen or major medical problems all create emotional problems, but then having to deal with the money factor is also very difficult. Do you borrow money, loan money, talk about money, ignore it?

When you get down to it, money isn't just inert, wrinkly, green stuff; it's power and lifestyle and freedom and self-definition. One person getting or losing a lot of it undoubtedly changes things.

Friends and family

The approval or disapproval of important people in your life about your date matters very little at the beginning but more and more as time goes by. It matters not only because the juggling that is necessary becomes more characteristic of longer-term relationships but also because a longer-term relationship gets taken more seriously by all parties. Friends who may have been amused or stunned are now actively and vocally worried, and parents who didn't know one way or the other or thought it was a passing phase are now weighing in with their two cents' worth. Tricky stuff.

If you're old enough to be reading this book by yourself, you're old enough to make your own decisions, but support from friends and family is a lot easier than active opposition. If nothing else, it's important to listen to their concerns. After all, they do love you. That doesn't mean that they know what's best, but they do have a different perspective. It is never okay to say, "I'm breaking up because my friends hate you," but it is okay to listen to your friends' concern and see whether it squares with that quiet little voice in your own head that you've been ignoring.

If you're dating someone just to make people you love miserable, you're a mean, self-involved child, and you should go to your room and repent now. There are better ways to show your independence — like moving out, getting a job, and making a success of yourself and your life — than finding someone to serve as a symbol of your rebelliousness. Grow up.

Kids

One of you wanting them and the other not is not very negotiable, and hopefully you sorted this out before the two of you got involved. (If not, make sure you do the next time.) If you're sure you don't want kids and have absolutely no doubt, get yourself sterilized, get a T-shirt that says as much, and never take it off: You'll save yourself a serious amount of heartache. If you've changed your mind, be honest about it; people do change. Still, it's a hard issue to compromise.

A major cause of breakups of otherwise promising relationships is someone else's kids. If you or your date has kids from previous relationships, it's a good idea to make sure your relationship has legs before you get the kids involved. Once the kids are involved, they become attached, and the relationship between the adults becomes that much trickier. If the two of you are really cooking, but the kids hate the idea, you may want to seek out some good couples' counseling before you call it a day. Kids can be incredibly disruptive, but adults owe kids even when it's hard on a social life.

Work

The *M.A.S.H.* philosophy of life is the assumption that you can find all of your goodies in one place: your father figure, your social and sex lives, your work, your neighbors, your meals, and anything else your little heart desires. Both men and women are spending more time at work these days — an average of 45 hours (out of 168) per week plus commute time — resulting in a serious proportion of awake time devoted to work. Most of us see more of our colleagues and bosses than we do our families. So there is a tendency to make colleagues our surrogate family — always a bad idea because work is about competence. Anything that gets in the way of competence is the enemy at work.

Believe that there is nothing that gets in the way of competence more than an office romance. Even though you may think that no one knows, people always do. (Think about it. You always know when somebody is getting it on.) These days the law forbids not only sexual harassment but also sexual acting out at the office. I have a friend who got sued because she was having an affair with the boss. Her coworkers sued because they felt the affair was creating an overly sexualized environment and suspected that she got special privileges. In the bad old days, when office affairs occurred, the woman traditionally was fired because the man was usually in the position of more power; however, these days, men are getting fired as well.

Whether the law gets involved or not, having all your eggs in one basket is a lousy idea. And should the two of you break up, you've got a real disaster on your hands because throwing ourselves into work to get over an unhappy love affair is a standard response to heartache, and if it is all happening in the same place, you're very likely to lose your love, your job, and your marbles. So although having your work life and your love life in the same place may seem efficient initially, it can be incredibly dangerous. Don't even think about it.

In addition to the pitfalls that work can present to both sexes in terms of temptation and distraction, guys have an added burden. Most men between the ages of 25 and 55 are defined by their work. Is this reasonable or right? Probably not, but it's true. If you try to get between a man and his job, you'll lose, even if you win. When a man feels his work is getting away from him, he feels he is dying, and he will jettison everything else to save this part of himself. Unfortunately, as more and more women enter the work force, they are taking on some of the same characteristics.

Traditionally, women have defined themselves in terms of their love, and men have defined themselves in terms of their work. It's changing, but not all that quickly. Hopefully we can learn from each other, but a man whose work is in trouble is a man who is going to have a hard time balancing a relationship.

Freud said it all when he said, "We all need work and love."

Health

A major illness can scare the daylights out of anyone. It's not only the scare, but also how the partner responds, that impacts a relationship. Health problems sap energy and humor and time and money, and a serious illness can either cement a relationship or give both people pause when thinking how the other would respond in the future.

No one likes to think of himself or herself as a fair weather friend, but before "I do," not everybody is in it for richer or poorer, in sickness and in health.

Substance abuse

If you're in a relationship with someone who has a drug problem, whether the drug is alcohol or cocaine or marijuana or prescriptions or crack or any of the other ways people have invented to make themselves temporarily happy and truly miserable for the long term, you need to think about bailing. Getting clean and sober is hard work and doesn't leave any time for anything other than that task.

If you're the person with the problem, do yourself a favor and get yourself straight before you inflict yourself on someone else. Your partner can't love you if you're high, and you won't even know who the real person is.

If you love someone with a drug problem, you don't really know the person and you can't trust him or her. You don't have to hate the person, but you *do* have to leave until he or she straightens out. I just completed an audio book for St. Jude's that they and I believe can be very helpful in helping someone to confront and overcome his or her demons without referencing the "sick" model. You can find out more at either the St. Jude's Web site (www.stjude.org) or mine (www.drjoy.com).

If someone's drowning and you don't know how to swim, don't go in after the person. You'll both perish, and if someone comes along to help, the rescuer will have to choose which of you to save. Save yourself, and let your partner do the same.

Lack of trust

You can't love someone you can't trust. Once trust has been breached, it takes time and effort to repair the tear, and it's never like it was before. When trust has been broken, the wounded party has the right to ask why, how the transgressor can promise both of you it won't happen again, and what the penance is for the next time. Without that kind of three-part understanding, being together is hard.

Both of you need to be aware of what the understanding was and why the breach happened. Taking time off can allow some of the pain to diminish, but it still takes a lot of work to put things back on some kind of even keel.

Violence

If you are in a violent relationship, ***get out now.***

- ✔ If you're the violent one, get away from your target and get some help.
- ✔ If you're the target, get away now. You're not doing anybody any good by allowing yourself to be used as a punching bag.

Making Last-Ditch Efforts

When you know the relationship is in trouble, for whatever reason, you may not be ready to give up on it yet. This section gives you some ideas of things to try that may make a difference.

Apologizing

Unless you're completely sure that your relationship is toast, the end bitter or not, you may want to try the greatest cure for couple misery ever invented: the apology. An apology is only really useful if it's sincere, specific, and timely. If you did something wretched and thoughtless and selfish — look, you're human, not perfect — be specific and grovel. The bigger the boo-boo, the larger the apology. If the mistake hurt your partner, the apology should pinch your soul, your pocketbook, and your conscience. This isn't about buying your way out but rather reminding yourself and your partner that you are truly sorry. If repentance is expensive enough, it may give you pause the next time you're tempted to blunder in that direction again.

It does no good to say "I'm sorry" if you're not: It means you're lying, and you'll only make the situation worse. If you don't feel you did anything wrong, try problem-solving, not apologizing. Also, saying, "I'm sorry you feel that way" *is not* an apology. It's sniveling and self-serving and mean, so don't even think about it.

Taking responsibility

Sometimes you get caught, and try as you may to wiggle out of it, you find out it's just too late. Too late is when your partner's anger and tears and passion have all been replaced by bland uncaring. You may think this indifference is easier to deal with, but it signals that you are closer to the end than you want to be.

If your latest boo-boo meets with resignation rather than rage, you're in trouble and maybe out of chances. When what you've done in the past simply doesn't work anymore, your apology may be too little, too late. What this means is that, when in doubt, don't try and get away with something important. Face up, apologize, and take responsibility, because once your partner doesn't care anymore about your mistakes or your apologies, your partner doesn't care anymore about you.

Keeping your fantasies to yourself

Look, there are always temptations in this life: a dollar to pocket that's not yours, a tax form to cheat on, a cute face at work, a stolen kiss or drink, a broken promise, a sense of who will ever know. There is a part of all of us that finds temptation sexy (otherwise, it wouldn't be called temptation), but if you're tempted to stray, at least be smart enough not to be tempted to confess. If your partner has received no pleasure from your behavior, your partner shouldn't have to suffer any pain.

If you find yourself constantly tempted by another person, maybe it's time to sort out whether you are looking for an excuse to bail from your current relationship, and if so, you need to take a good look at your relationship and either fix it or leave it. Whatever you do, don't complicate it by cheating. In the long run, cheaters cheat themselves first and foremost. There are better ways to get out of a relationship than being thrown out for being a liar and a cheat.

There is nothing wrong about feeling tempted as long as you don't act out the temptation. Remember, fantasies can be useful pressure valves if you keep your mouth shut. Part of the reason it makes sense to toe the line is to have a clear conscience and not have to confess or apologize or hurt someone you love.

Avoiding ship-sinking mistakes

Never move against your own best interest. If you want the relationship to last, work on it. If you feel it's beyond redemption, leave because you feel it's over, not because you think the other person will leave if you don't. If you want the relationship, work on it; don't leave something you think is still viable.

No one likes to feel foolish, but doing something absolutely stupid to save yourself from the imagined pain of being left by someone is not a terrific idea. First of all, the person who leaves always feels guilty, at least for a while, and it's hard to feel guilty when you feel justified. So don't problem-solve by doing the following:

✔ Having an affair

✔ Pretending not to care

✔ Getting violent

✔ Getting the kids/friends/relatives involved in a who-do-you-love-better contest

✔ Playing the martyr

✔ Doing the online flirtation thang

None of it will work and is guaranteed to make everything even messier.

Taking time out

It's okay to take mini-breaks if you think you can gain something by doing so. Sometimes both partners can use the perspective of missing one another, and decreasing the day-to-day aggravation and unhappiness. Maybe one or the other of you is going through a tough time and needs some space. Maybe outside factors make it impossible to give the relationship the time and effort required for it to thrive. As long as both of you can agree on what the purpose of the time apart is, what the rules are, and why you both think it's a good idea, time can really be used to your advantage.

✔ If the two of you are crazy about each other, and one wants a break and the other doesn't, take a break.

✔ If the two of you are crazy about each other and can't get along, take a break and think about doing some couples' work together.

✔ If one of you is ready for the next step and the other isn't, take a break. When you reconnect, you may have moved closer together in your thinking.

✔ If both of you are bored or violent or uninterested, take a permanent break. See the next section.

Time apart is the hole in the donut: It is defined by what goes on around it. Because you can't make someone love you more, you can give both of you a breather to figure out what's going on in your head and heart and other organs. A breakup can be mini or maxi, temporary or permanent, but if you work it right, it can be a really important learning experience.

As is true of most things in life, timing is crucial. Be willing to see whether your relationship can stand time apart as well as time together.

Making a Clean Break

Okay, okay, the relationship isn't working for you. It really is the end. Now the goal is to end it with minimum blood loss, nastiness, and pain. When you finally decide to make the break, how do you actually go about doing it? This section gives you some ideas.

Avoiding blame

The first temptation to be avoided is the need to blame somebody or something. Because there are only the two of you, it's logical that you will decide, heroically of course, to make it all your fault, even though you know it's not true: "You're too good for someone like me," "I don't deserve you," — both of which mean you want out now. Or you could blame your partner: "You never loved me enough," "You cared more about your work than you did me," "You've never really gotten over your first love," "You've put on weight, lost hair, gotten moody. . . ." Yada, yada, yada.

It's not necessary to fall into either trap. All you have to do to be dignified about this whole unpleasant thing — breaking up is *never* easy — is to be specific about your feelings without laying blame. It really doesn't matter in the long run whose fault it is, and avoiding blame spares you both a lot of bloodshed.

To avoid the blame game, try saying, "I feel . . ." rather than "You are . . ." and no, it isn't kosher to say, "I feel you're a rat." The "I feel" rather than "You are" scenario is only okay if you follow up with something about yourself, like, "I feel neglected when you work weekend after weekend." (Of course, if you had been able to say this when you were feeling it, the relationship might not be beyond redemption at this point.) If you're specific now, at least both of you can look at the data as dispassionately as possible rather than feel that either of you failed.

Don't ask why

Once a relationship is over, the "why" is less relevant than the "how" — how are we both going to walk away and be able to live our lives without scars or regrets? Let me reiterate that trying to read someone else's mind and motivation is a waste of time — understanding your own is crucial! Sometimes a perfectly good relationship is only a perfectly good relationship for a while. That doesn't mean it was bad, only that it wasn't long-term.

If the two of you are specific, you'll know what went wrong and what, perhaps, either of you could do differently next time. The *why* may be lost in the mists of time or be a proper subject for therapy, but when you're going your separate ways, getting stuck in the past feels incredibly painful. The *why* is in the past, often clouded and sometimes unknowable. Once you're reduced to asking *why,* you're both sunk, and there are no comforting reasons to be had.

Beyond the Breakup

You probably thought that the hardest part of breaking up was getting up the nerve to tell your partner why and actually doing it. Yes and no. Because you're not a robot and you cared about this person, it's very likely that you have at least one or two teeny, tiny reservations. Maybe a part of you even wanted your partner to argue with you and explain why you were all wrong and everything was going to be fine and you'd both be happy again. This may be especially true if your partner agreed that it was time to pull the plug and call it quits, thereby depriving you of the opportunity to prove your case. All of us believe much more strongly if we can convince ourselves by stating our case against opposition.

Now you're broken up. You've gone through the first hard part, the misery has ended, but another kind of misery is about to begin: the unhappiness of doubt, the "did I do the right thing?" second-guessing. You'll do this whether or not you've got someone waiting in the wings. (If you do, it's important that you not only read but also memorize Chapter 19 to save yourself shame, grief, and gobs of misery.)

This section gives you tips on how to make the aftermath of a breakup a productive time.

Looking for patterns

If this isn't your first breakup — and if you're old enough to read, chances are it isn't — take this opportunity to privately examine whether your relationships are following a pattern, beginning with your first love in second grade who hit you with the teeter-totter.

Do you pick unavailable people and then feel neglected when they're unavailable? Do you need to be in control all the time or else you feel anxious? Do you take care of people and then get angry when they don't take care of you, even though you've set yourself up as the caretaker (which is really just a variation on being a control freak)?

Looking for patterns is a really good thing to do for yourself because most people get involved again eventually (and, usually, much too soon, before they've sorted out the last disaster). You'll most likely want to get involved again, too, and knowing your patterns may help you avoid making the same mistakes.

Parental influence and self-fulfilling prophecies

One of the most important places to look for the genesis of any dating breakup is with your parents. This doesn't necessarily mean your parents didn't approve, although that may offer some insight, but the real question is, were you being rebellious or trying to get attention or punish old Mom and Dad for not loving you enough? I'm talking about something a bit more psychological and buried, not only how your parents treated each other — after all, watching Mom and Dad is the place we first learn how men and women behave to one another — but also your relationship with both of your parents.

If you felt Dad was never there for you, are you picking a date who is aloof like your dad and hoping if you can just make this aloof person love you then your relationship with Dad will be okay? This tendency may or may not be conscious, but if you look for it, you may find it. And of course, you're dooming yourself because you've picked a person who has a hard time showing affection again, and those folks *always* seem aloof. Talk about your self-fulfilling prophecy.

It isn't always about Dad either. If you felt Mom always loved your brother best, have you picked a nurturing person who will be a good parent to your children in the future but who will then make you feel that you are second best to your own offspring?

No matter who our parents are or how they raised us, the rules get changed every ten or fifteen years, so parents, by definition, are always wrong. You don't have to get caught here, but the breakup of a relationship is a good opportunity to go back and do some psychological archeology and dig up those buried skeletons that Mom and Pop helped create. This isn't about changing your parents or even your attitude toward them, but freeing yourself from the need to repeat unproductive and negative past patterns.

For more information on how your parents influence your dating behavior, see Chapter 4.

Talking to your partner about the patterns you see in yourself isn't very productive. And *puh-leeeze* don't, under any circumstance, point out the patterns you see in your partner's behavior. You're not the parent or the therapist, and no matter how keen your insight, your remarks will be viewed as self-serving. So keep those deathless pearls for a hundred years from now when you're the best of friends, and even then, best swallow them.

Accepting that things don't last forever

Just because something doesn't last forever doesn't mean it's not good. A smile on the street as you pass is a good relationship. A cheerful person who bags your groceries is a relationship. Unfortunately, many people have the sense that if something doesn't last as long as they wanted or expected it to, somebody must be blamed, someone has to pay, and it wasn't a good relationship at all. (If you haven't gotten the idea here that it takes a while to get to know someone and even perfectly nice people can find that there just isn't that much cooking between the two of them after some time passes, then you haven't been paying much attention.)

A wise woman's words

At one point in my life, I was involved in one of those situations that was fraught — and I do mean fraught — with lots and lots of misery. I can remember confiding to my grandmother, whom I loved dearly and with whom I shared secrets, that the relationship really wasn't going very well at all and that when he wasn't around, I felt a part of me was missing.

She said, "Oh honey, that's wonderful."

"Wonderful?" I said. "Gram, whose side are you on?"

She said, "Darlin', people live their whole lives without feeling that passion. Be glad that you've had it."

Even after all these years, my head understands exactly what she meant, even though my heart still has a bruise with his initials on it.

If a relationship that doesn't go on forever doesn't have to be bad or a failure, then neither party has to be the bad guy or at fault. The only perspective by which you can evaluate whether the relationship made any sense or was a good or not-so-good investment of your time is with time. And time takes time.

If you think of every experience as being tuition in the school of life and love, then you can understand that some tuition is higher than others, and some classes are more fun or stick with you longer or teach you more than others. But it's only after time passes that you gain the perspective to see which things you really benefited from.

Always looking forward

It is humanly impossible to go backward in a relationship. Once you know that someone can be both kind and smart, you'll never settle for one without the other again. Therefore, every breakup is an opportunity to go forward, and after a while, you may even be able to say thank you to the one who gave you your walking papers, even though it felt awful at the time.

If you feel someone has done you wrong, it's pretty hard to have the perspective that someday you'll thank them for this, even though that line comes up in movies a lot. One of the reasons it comes up so often is that it's basically true. You are the product of all of your experiences, good and not-so-good, and sometimes it's hard to tell the one from the other without a scorecard, 20/20 hindsight, and some time.

Scrutinizing the details

I've said it a gazillion times before, and I'm sure I'll say it at least that many more: God, genius, and salvation are in the details. If you can pare things down to basics, you can problem-solve, and if you can problem-solve, you can free yourself from the need to blame and hurt yourself or someone else.

If you can give up the need to be right or be martyred and just think things through, you'll know exactly what to do next. You may not like it, but you'll know, and in that knowledge is salvation and serenity.

Spending time alone

Time is a great healer. The nerve endings get anesthetized, and the pain becomes a memory. (Fortunately, human beings have very little capacity to remember pain, which isn't to say that vengeance isn't a real human emotion.) So take the time you need.

Don't immediately begin another relationship, whether on or offline. Rebounding feels logical, but it's really not (see Chapter 19 for details). It's only a way to postpone dealing with the issues you have to deal with if you want to be a happy, healthy person.

Be careful when you update your Facebook status from "In a Relationship" back to "Single." You will get both lots of sympathy comments and new singles starting to send your Facebook e-mails of interest. While flattering, it's really too soon to jump back in the water. Chilling out may make the most sense. Don't change your status until you're ready to publically deal with your status change.

Sidestepping emotional pitfalls

It's certainly okay and appropriate to ask yourself whether you can live with your decision over time. But be aware of the emotional seductions that are part and parcel of this experience; they go directly for the gut or the jugular and completely ignore that grown-up, smart part of you.

Rats and relationships

At one point in my career as a psychologist, I actually had to run rats through a maze. The reason to run rats (yech) is to study learning theory. You place a piece of cheese in the maze and wait until the rat consistently goes to the cheese. Learning theory begins when you move the cheese and figure out how long it takes the rat to relearn the maze. For a while, the rat will continue to go to the place it went before, looking for the reward. After a while, depending on how smart the rat is, it will begin to look elsewhere, finally discover the cheese, and then go there consistently.

Human beings, on the other hand, won't try to relearn the maze because they are convinced they are right, even though there is no cheese. In relationships, you can either be right or you can go for the cheese. I would heartily recommend going for the cheese.

Our song

Music is as old as human history and is part of each of our personal histories. Lullabies your mom sang you; the first time you heard the "Star Spangled Banner" or "Yesterday" or "Heaven Help Us" or "Feelings"; singing "The Itsy-Bitsy Spider" in kindergarten, hymns in Sunday school, and fight songs at football games; the first musical you saw; and so on. If the two of you were together more than ten minutes, you probably have a song that is linked to your first date, kiss, fight, and make up. It is wise to avoid this song when you're alone for at least a year. You will not believe how quickly you can be reduced to quivering jelly upon the opening chords. If you want to get back together, fine, but do it for reasons other than musical ones. Think about why you broke up and whether anything has changed or is likely to, but don't put yourself back in a dicey situation based on a ditty.

Our place

Memories can certainly be evoked by going to that special restaurant or beach or woods or park bench. Hopefully, the masochistic part of you is under enough control not to be seduced by revisiting your past before it is really past, and you're certainly smart enough not to try and take anybody new there. If you find yourself back in an old haunt, at least try a different table, order something outrageous, or fake an attack of poison ivy. You'll know that the relationship is truly in the past when you can revisit without nostalgia or nausea, but don't try the test too soon.

Being friends

Inevitably the person who was the dumper says, "I love you — I'm just not in love with you. Let's be friends." The dumpee, grasping at straws, is tempted to accept the morsel, hoping it will morph back into love. Note to dumpee: Don't be tempted. The only way to go from dumping to friendship is with time, a lot of time, so that kindness won't be misinterpreted as interest, sexual feelings can be neutralized, and longing can dissipate. Time (I'm talking at least six months, more likely a year or more) allows for a perspective on whether you even like each other. In many ways, liking is much harder than loving since we do one primarily with our head, the other with our heart, and hearts are more easily fooled!

Pity parties

This little experience is mentioned throughout this book because it is one of the most common social (or antisocial) experiences on human calendars. We, as a species, have an enormous capacity to feel sorry for ourselves and indulge in lavish celebration of our misery. I am all in favor of 24 to 36 hours' worth of misery after a breakup. If you wallow in self-pity for a day or two, pulling out all the stops, visiting the old haunts, listening to your song, looking at the pictures, stubbornly reviewing all the good times and great things, and assuring yourself there will never ever be another love like this for you, you will likely get bored and then you can begin healing.

But don't invite other people to your party because they will get bored sooner, and you might still have some residual pity left that can ooze out for months and months. Other invitees might also divert attention to their own misery, and misery *doesn't* love company or competition. Worst-case scenario, your friend may want to talk you out of your pity, which simply won't do at all.

Have a personal, solitary pity party and get it out of your system so that you can escape the gooey quagmire of self-indulgence and get a perspective and get on with your life. If you find your party going on for more than two days, or you can't stop crying or obsessing, it's time to get some help.

Stalking

You may have a tendency to see how your partner is doing without you, especially if you believe that your ex is seeing someone. There is a wish to spy and keep an eye on what you may have viewed as yours (which is a problem that needs to be addressed before you try and move on to another relationship). But these actions can be characterized as stalking, and stalking is both dangerous and illegal (see Chapter 21 for more on stalking behavior).

Possessiveness and jealousy are poisons that must be lanced and exorcised if you are ever to have a sane, happy, serene relationship. If it's over, it's over, and spying on someone is demeaning and dangerous and destructive. If the relationship couldn't work, it didn't work between the two of you; anything else is outside the two of you and therefore can't be affected by you. Making someone feel afraid is a statement of your need to be in control, to punish, or to hurt. It's not nice, and it's not legal. So don't sit outside their house, follow them, call them at work, ask friends about them, or call and hang up.

All kinds of phones offer a caller ID feature, which tells you who's calling and documents who and when and how often someone calls. Harassment is illegal as well as irritating, and who wants to end up in jail where you aren't allowed to call anyone without permission? Letting go is almost as hard as breaking up, but it's necessary, and police involvement isn't going to make your life easier or more pleasant.

Violence

I hesitate to even mention this because it is so distasteful. Understand that it is not unusual to feel angry and want to lash out when you're hurt. You just can't do it. Being violent is both dangerous and illegal. If you're feeling particularly nasty, write a poison pen letter *but don't send it.* Write a story of death and dismemberment and send it to a magazine to publish (lots of best-selling authors have gotten revenge and rich simultaneously with this technique), draw a picture, dream of destruction, dump on your diary. But stay away from your ex and guns, baseball bats, arrows, pills, and razors.

Violence toward your ex or toward yourself isn't a way to solve your heartache. It will compound your misery and keep pain alive for much longer than necessary. If you feel you can't control the impulse to damage yourself or someone else, get yourself to a therapist or, if need be, a hospital, and take yourself out of harm's way.

Trust me, everyone has had these feelings. It's just a matter of controlling them or controlling yourself, and if you can't, put yourself in a position (like a hospital) where you don't have to control them because someone else is in charge. The anger and hurt do pass, and most people learn to control their negative impulses so that they don't have to be afraid or make others afraid of them. They learn to love and feel close and trust. In the final analysis, that's what *Dating For Dummies* and life as we know it are all about. Take a deep breath and relax and understand that coming together and coming apart is the dance people do until they find the right partner.

I suspect you're tired of hearing how dangerous it is to take your frustrations out online, but when you're feeling hurt, lonely, vengeful, and angry, it's hard to resist the temptation to unload. If your computer screen is beckoning, at least go offline and put your musings in a folder that you can revisit when some of the bile has ebbed. You will save yourself grief, embarrassment, and a possible lawsuit.

Chapter 19

Rebound

When I say *rebound,* I'm not talking about basketball and the skill it takes to dunk someone else's shot amid fierce opposition. I'm talking about a much more dangerous sport that involves catching yourself or someone else on the bounce from another relationship whose momentum hasn't stopped enough for the person in question to come to rest after the tumult of a breakup.

Rebound is easiest to understand when looking at someone else's behavior and hardest to apply to oneself because the end of a dating situation, especially if it's gone on for more than a month or two, hurts; it's natural to want to get some relief from that pain. Unfortunately, time is crucial, especially if that time is spent in active recovery, trying to figure out what happened, why it happened, how it happened, and what you can do about it next time. (***Note:*** Asking someone else or the universe "why" is a waste of time, but asking yourself why you behaved a certain way is *always* time well spent.)

In this chapter, I discuss several aspects of rebounding, including how to recover from a breakup and what to do while you're healing from the end of a relationship. I also warn you about the dangers of dating newly divorced or married people.

I absolutely guarantee you're going to hate this chapter, but I also absolutely guarantee that if you understand it and can discipline yourself enough to heed the dire warnings and stay clear of big league emotional involvement that I detail here, you can save yourself some serious wear and tear on your head, your heart, your soul, and your psyche. (If nothing else, think of all the cool ways you can spend the money you would have otherwise spent on therapy or a good lawyer to get yourself out of the results of not paying attention to the rebound rules.)

Loosening the Ties That Bind

People get involved and enmeshed with one another. No news flash. We smile at someone we see every day on the way to work. We say "Hi" to a neighbor who lives down the block. We chat with someone in our aerobics class. But once we've dated a person, we're into the foothills and heading toward the Mt. Everest of human interaction; the involvement and entanglement are that much greater.

We're humans, not robots. The feelings we invest can't be unplugged or turned off like a faucet. When you see someone you like, you put out a fragile, wispy tendril. If the person shows interest, he or she too puts out a thread, and so it goes. The longer the involvement, the deeper the commitment, the more levels on which there is communication and caring and interaction, and the greater the number and the stronger the ties.

When a relationship starts to break down, the result is often *more* tendrils rather than less. The reason is that you up the energy because fear and anxiety increase the strength and intensity of the threads in an attempt to bring the other person closer, pretend that everything's okay in order to try and return to the good old days, or continue the illusion that you are cared for and adored even with evidence to the contrary.

When enough is enough and one or the other of you calls the whole thing off, those tendrils aren't like retractable cords on a vacuum cleaner that quickly whip back into the socket. There is no instant shut-off valve. Even when the two of you don't see each other, the heart, the brain, and the mind remember. You can be haunted in your dreams, your memories, your fantasies. And each of those remembrances has tendrils. Because these tendrils are not based in reality, often they are particularly stubborn and hard to get rid of.

If you've been going out only a couple of weeks, there aren't going to be gobs of connections between the two of you. If you've been going out for months, it's going to be harder to pull away because of the increased number and strength of those ties; even the thought of severing them may seem really painful. Sometimes rather than begin the painful procedure of pulling away, couples just let things drag on in the futile hope that things will either improve and there will be no need to break off, or things will get worse and it will be easier to walk away. But anybody who's attempted this Cleopatra technique (Queen of Denial . . . get it?) can tell you how ineffective it is. The idea that it's easier to leave something if it gets worse overlooks the fact that staying in a lousy relationship takes time and energy and that even diseased tendrils are tendrils and can be amazingly tenacious. (People can convince themselves to stay and nurse a nasty relationship rather than admit the problems and either make things better or get out because sometimes it feels easier to ignore problems than to solve them.)

Connection is connection. If the tendril thing doesn't work for you, try another analogy or metaphor. Two people in a relationship become intertwined, like two saplings that are planted in the same pot, which is one of the reasons why it's hard to leave a situation that was once good: Uncoupling is truly the pits. As each tree grows, its limbs and roots become tangled around the other. Even if one of the trees dies or is cut down, the other tree's shape has been changed forever, and unless the tree wants to die as well (don't even think about it), it will take time and soil and sunshine for the remaining tree to regain its strength, to be straight, and to find the sunshine on its own. The ending of the best relationships leaves us a bit shaken but able to function on our own eventually, to find the light and the soil we need to grow, and to not have to worry about sharing nutrients or water or shade or space or sun with another until we're sure we can survive.

People are resilient and crave intimacy and involvement, but any dating situation works best when two little saplings *choose* to be together rather than *have* to be together to survive. When a dating situation works, the strength of both contributes to a greater strength as a couple, but uncoupling is truly the pits.

Defining Rebound

The kind of rebound that we're talking about here doesn't actually involve a basketball. It is feeling like you've been slam-dunked or even that you've slam-dunked someone else and aren't real proud of yourself about it. Either way, you're going to feel wounded or guilty, and asking another person to tell you that you're okay is too much of a burden for another soul and too needy on your part.

Rebound is one of those useful words that says exactly what it is: It is a recoiling — yeah, like a gun — a springing back from a disappointment. Those of you who are physicists know that for every action, there is an equal and opposite reaction. The greater the pain, the bigger the bounce. You don't want to catch somebody when they're still bouncing around because who knows where they will land. For the same reason, it's important to resist the temptation to use someone to slow your own flight. People get hurt and bruised and feel used when used as a backstop.

How then do you regain equilibrium after a disappointment? You allow yourself to bounce around a bit without getting other people involved in the motion. You're dangerous to yourself and to them. Just allow the motion to continue until it's stopped, and then wait a little longer until you're absolutely, positively certain there haven't been even teensy, tiny bounces for a couple of months. Rebound is one of those situations where talking about it, on or offline, works against recovery unless your audience is a therapist; talking about the relationship to a friend or online keeps the whole thing alive and kicking at a time when quiet reflection and even deflection is much more appropriate. Sympathy is much to be desired but of very little real help and can help you to feel good about feeling bad.

Bounces are really tricky and deceptive. Your head stops bouncing well before your heart does. Even if you're convinced the breakup was for the best and both of you will be better off, the sense of being a bit woozy, a tad shell shocked, and less than your most stable self takes a bit of time to get over.

Everybody wonders deep down if the breakup is really their fault, if they are completely unlovable or capable of loving. The simplest short-term solution is to go find an emotional Band-Aid quickly so that you can put those panicky feelings aside. Don't do it. Having somebody waiting in the wings is a short-term solution to a long-term problem. If you've catapulted yourself into a brand-new relationship, where is the time or energy to figure out what went wrong in the old relationship going to come from? If you take the time from the new relationship to figure out the old relationship, your new love will be understandably miffed; if you don't take time, you increase the probability that you'll do the same thing again. If it happens over and over, you're going to be one unhappy or unfeeling cookie.

Beware the bounce. Take the time to let the motion stop before the emotions start again.

Using the Time Productively

What now? I won't let you date, so are you supposed to become a hermit? Nah, that just makes you vulnerable, and you lose all that hard-won poise. Time is really the only cure for healing emotional bruises, and the healing can't go on if you're busily diverting yourself with growing new tendrils and sending them out. If you don't take time to heal, those tendrils will be super sensitive, not very healthy, and very, very needy — not an auspicious beginning, and beginnings are hard enough as it is.

The first rule is to stay away from romance. How can you convince your heart and your bruised ego to avoid flirting back or using the soft or strong shoulder of that person you sorta had your eye on to cry on? Stop it — and divert yourself. Here are some suggestions on how to use the rebound in a productive rather than destructive way:

  ✔ **Work on same-sex friendships.** Friends are those people who sustain us through breakups and traumas and share our good times. I'm sure you're sensible enough not to ignore or neglect your friends when you're in a love relationship, but now is a terrific time to really work on and polish the part of you that is a wonderful friend.

✔ **Sift through the ashes of the old relationship.** This is the time to become an emotional archeologist. No one is completely to blame when a relationship tanks, so get out that trusty paper and pencil and see what you can learn. This exercise isn't much fun, but it's truly time well spent. If nothing else, it should absorb enough time and energy temporarily to put you off dating until you've figured out what to do next time to avoid the bruises.

✔ **Stay away from one-on-one.** That well-meaning buddy can easily turn into a wrongheaded fling if you're not careful, and what an icky thing to do to a friend. There is strength and safety in numbers. Hang out with friends, large groups, small countries.

✔ **Work out.** This is a good time to join a gym or a softball team or play some b-ball at the local high school. Take tennis lessons (avoid the cute pro), practice yoga, or learn to swim. Keeping physically active helps cure the blues and the blahs naturally with endorphins, and once you're ready to get back in the swing, you'll look faboo.

✔ **Paint your house, clean out your closets, trim the hedges.** Taking care of those chores you never have time to do when you're involved will make your living environment that much more pleasant and give you a real sense of accomplishment. Planting a community garden, cleaning up a park, or helping construct a home for Habitat for Humanity also gets you being physical and social with a specific goal in mind without pairing off or staying alone.

✔ **Become a workaholic, temporarily.** In the flush of a new dating situation or one that is going poorly, work often suffers. Now is a great time to spend that available time at work, which allows you that much more time and money to lavish on yourself once you begin dating again.

✔ **Become a volunteer.** Doing good makes you feel better about yourself. You can also meet like-minded souls, and it gives you an invaluable perspective on others' problems.

✔ **Take a course.** Learning a new skill or just learning is also a perspective giver and offers an opportunity to interact on an intellectual basis. Joining a great books discussion group will also do the trick as long as the reading list doesn't focus on romance novels.

✔ **Stay away from alcohol.** A lovely bottle of wine might feel like it helps you relax, but alcohol is actually a central nervous system depressant. So drinking right now will neither help your mood nor heal your heartache while you are on the mend.

✔ **Hide your plastic:** They don't call it "Retail Therapy" for nothing. When you want to get on with your life, shopping 'til you drop and running up your credit card debt won't help. Better to fill your life with friends, exercise, and even the occasional pity party. If you must, window shop but beware expensive panaceas.

Projects under construction

I was walking down the street beside a building that was being rehabbed. As I stopped at the light, the foreman came over, took my arm, and said, "Projects under construction are dangerous. Things can fly off and hit you. Why do you think we're wearing hard hats? Anytime you see a project under construction or rehab, cross the street. It's dangerous."

I think his advice works for situations that aren't new buildings in the literal sense. Any dating situation is an attempt to build something on a firm foundation. If it feels dangerous, you'll end up wearing a hard hat for your heart. If one of the pillars of the relationship (you or your date) is on the rebound — the person is unstable and trying to rebuild his or her own life — walk away until the rehab is done, and there's time and energy to work on your new project together.

Remember, lives under construction are unstable and therefore dangerous foundations on which to build a new structure.

Taking the rebound time to work on yourself and your world pays gobs of dividends: You'll sleep better, look better, and act better (and the alternative is really awful to contemplate). If you don't give yourself time to get out from under the shadow of your bruises, you're going to *go postal* (overreact and blow everyone away) or *batmobile* (put up impenetrable shields that will deflect any potential incoming hazard). For example, if your old date was always late, the first time your new date is three minutes late, you're going to be convinced that you're the last polite person left on the planet and start ranting and raving. Very nice, right? Wrong! — and so much fun to be around. Not exactly the frame of mind conducive to getting to know someone and letting them get to know you, which is the only purpose of dating.

The person on the rebound either clings for dear life or begins to run through dates like Kleenex tissues on the assumption that there is either something wrong with everyone else or something desperately wrong with them. Disposable or cement — not a nice choice.

A breakup is a tempting catalyst to retire to your room; fire up your computer; and complain, troll, and whine. Your life will be significantly improved if you can resist this temptation. Take yourself off house arrest, resist the misery loves Internet company phenomenon, and work on improving the product . . . YOU, not because you're lacking but because we can all use a bit of progress. Growth is the only alternative to stagnation, and a breakup is a great catalyst to do a personal inventory and clean out your emotional closet.

Waiting It Out

Please, please, *please* do yourself a favor and give yourself enough time to recover. Stay away from your Facebook page. No moping online. How long does the process take, you ask? Some who are stricter than I am think you need to wait one month for every two you've been involved. I think formulas are a bit rigid here.

A good rule of thumb is to double or triple the time you think it will take, and no fair cheating. The basic idea is to wait until you can think about the ex without pain or embarrassment or sadness, and you can avoid talking about him or her. There is nothing more tedious than having to listen to your date's recitation about why his or her ex was terrific or terrible. If you still need to talk, find a therapist, not a date.

The longer you dated, the longer the recovery period. If you talked about the L word (*love,* not *lust*) or even the M word (*marriage* — don't you dare break out in hives), or you dated for more than six months, the ratio gets closer to one-to-one — it will take as long to get over it as it did to get into it. Sad, but true (it's the tendril thing). If you were talking about the M or the L word and the relationship had been less than six months, you were rushing things and that may be part of your problem. It takes six to nine months to get to know anybody.

If you dated for over a year, the waiting period is at least a year. One whole calendar sequence so that you know you can make it through your birthday, Christmas, New Year's, Thanksgiving, the Fourth of July, Easter, Passover, the ex's birthday, the anniversary of your first date, the anniversary of your first kiss, and so on. Once you know you can do it by yourself, any future relationship will be based on choice, not need, and *that's* a much healthier beginning.

Don't think of my dreaded one-year rule as deprivation but rather a gift to yourself . . . to be able to indulge your every whim without relationship repercussion or consequence. Eat crackers in bed, stay up late, don't bathe on a weekend, and burp whenever you feel like it. I'm not talking degeneracy here, just the best kind of selfish; the kind that refreshes and restores a sense of balance and self reliance.

Dependency offers a really useful short-term basis for a relationship, but it simply doesn't work for the long run. Any good relationship nurtures, and in a nurturing relationship, the dependent one becomes less needy. This change leaves the powerful person in the position of feeling useless or trying to make the other person still need him or her, and the best way to make someone needy is to belittle that person. In psychology, the tendency to use power to make someone dependent is called the *Bad Mother Syndrome:* You're a bad, ugly, nasty child, and no one will love you but me, so you had better never leave me. It's bad mothering, and it's lousy relating.

The need to go back to the good old needy days is destructive and dangerous, like ouch.

If the person you're thinking of dating has been married or you've been married, the rules get even stricter. The waiting period is one whole year *after the divorce has become final.* This is such a crucial and important point, I'm going to say it again: *WAIT ONE FULL YEAR AFTER THE DIVORCE HAS BECOME FINAL!* No exceptions.

Everybody universally hates my one-year rule, but instead of viewing it as a prohibition issued by the Wicked Witch of the East (cute lil ol' me), what if you view it as a gift to yourself: a gift where for a whole year you don't have to be altruistic, thoughtful, generous, or compromising. You can do exactly what you want to do, when you want to do it, how you want to do it, without explaining it to anybody. What a gift! That way, you can get it all out of your system, and you understand a lot more of who you are when it's time to start dating. Then when that year is over and you start dating again, the idea of compromise or doing it someone else's way is going to feel like a novelty and a pleasure as opposed to a burden. So *please* give yourself the gift of the one-year rule.

Advice for the friend of a friend

One day on the street, I ran into a friend who introduced me to his friend who was just divorced. My friend explained who I was, and I explained that I was writing this book. The guy, without taking a breath, launched into a feverish account of his date last night. He had mentioned that he wouldn't buy an apartment until he found the right woman, and he'd want her to help him pick it out to make sure that it was big enough to have kids (this was a first date). Fifteen minutes later she said, "I really don't want to have kids." He was offended, couldn't understand why she was making such a big deal of it, and then he immediately said, "My ex-wife always. . . ."

I said, "How long have you been divorced?"

"Three months," he said.

I said, "You ought not to be dating at all right now."

He said, "You don't know my situation; there was no emotional. . . ."

I interrupted, "I know everyone's situation."

"I'm different," he said.

Yeah right. This guy could be the rebound poster boy. He's an accident actively seeking a place to happen. He thinks a woman being honest when she hears something that doesn't suit her is overreacting. I told him to buy the book. He didn't ask to join my fan club . . . yet.

Avoiding the Still Married, Separated, and Newly Divorced

Assume that you've taken all my warnings to heart and you've waited the appropriate period of time. One of your friends at the office tells you his ex-sister-in-law has just moved to town, and he thinks the two of you will be terrific together. Your first question is not "How old is she?" or "Can I see a picture?" or "Does she have kids?" It's *"How long has she been divorced?"*

The only people who are eligible for sane dating situations are people whose divorce has been final for at least one year. You know how crucial that waiting time was for you, and you can do the world, your potential date, and yourself an enormous favor by immediately asking the question, "How long has the divorce been final?"

The following words and phrases are all fancy or not-so-fancy ways of saying, "Still married":

- Separated
- Staying together for the sake of the kids
- Living like brother and sister
- Waiting for her mother, brother, aunt, or dog to die
- Can't afford to live separately right now
- In the hands of the lawyers
- Have almost everything worked out
- Working on an annulment
- Only until I find another job, apartment, or reason to live
- Not sure if I'm straight

Don't date married people, and if you're married, don't date. Married people who date are unhappy, dishonest, and confused, or they're people who use other people. Who needs to be in that kind of situation? And even if you're tempted, maybe I can convince you not to if you realize that

- You will be alone *every* Christmas, New Year's, weekend, and holiday.
- Married people who date lie. If this person really does get divorced, he or she either needs recovery time or is the kind who will cheat on you since the pattern has already been established.
- You'll be viewed either as someone who cheats (if you're the married one) or as someone who has so few scruples that you'd date someone else's spouse.

Who needs to date someone who is already proven to be capable of adultery, bad judgment, or both? Who needs the heartache? Walking into a propeller is just plain dumb, and dating someone who's still married is walking into a propeller. Even if that someone hasn't been living with his or her not-really ex, what makes you think the person doesn't use his or her legal purgatory as a way to keep potential dates or mates at arms' length? You truly can't win. You can only lose.

The proper response to finding out that your prospective date has not been divorced the required one year is, "I've read (or I know) how crazy that first year is. I think you're special enough to wait for because I think we might really have something here. I'll call you in (fill in the blank) months, and we can celebrate the anniversary of your divorce together."

Anniversaries of separations are not to be celebrated. If you're feeling like you really want to be the emotional Red Cross, go take a cold shower. Once you've dried off, donate some time to a worthy cause, but *not* to a walking disaster area that is a person freshly out of a relationship. I promise you will be an emotional Band-Aid, and we all know what happens to used Band-Aids. You deserve better.

You don't have to walk away forever, but you do have to walk away. Everybody needs to regain his or her equilibrium after being on storm-tossed seas. Whether the boat sank or floundered on the rocks or was commandeered by pirates, your prospective date needs to get his or her breath and sea legs back. Give that person some time. It will be time well spent even though it's hard to do.

Part V

Playing It Safe and Keeping It Fresh

The 5th Wave   By Rich Tennant

Suddenly Linda found herself mysteriously drawn to the stranger on the train.

In this part . . .

Remember when your mom and dad taught you to look both ways before crossing the street? It's not that they wanted you to fearfully cling to the crossing guard, but they wanted you to land safely on the other side. That's what I want for you, too. I want you to be adventurous, open to meeting new people, trusting — but careful. I want you to keep your eyes wide open so you can see what's coming down the road.

In this part, you'll learn how to date smart. Without scaring yourself silly or putting yourself under house arrest, you'll find out how to have fun without being foolish and how to take risks without engaging in risky behavior. Reminding yourself that information is power and the Internet is forever may be a crucial part of your strategy for your own well being. It also gives you an opportunity to think about infinity and beyond.

Speaking of infinity . . . dating, in theory, is the early part of a potentially long-term, committed relationship. But some of the same techniques that work on making someone interested in you can also keep that person interested and appreciative, helping your investment stay fresh, alive, and healthy, not to mention sexy, exciting, and rewarding.

Chapter 20

Safety First

ating can be scary and fun and exciting and challenging, but you want it to be all of the above for all the right reasons — not because you haven't taken reasonable precautions about your own safety. Crossing a street is perfectly valid and the only way to get to the other side; it's safe, too, if you're wise enough to look both ways before you venture forth. This chapter is about looking both ways, not under the pavement or being so terrified of traffic that you need to hold someone's hand as you cross. Just looking both ways.

If you've been frightened by the unprecedented number of stalking and date rape victims, don't become a hermit or assume that dating is a high-risk behavior. Just take the issue of safety seriously at the beginning. Never give out your home phone number. Don't tell strangers where you live or work. Use your cell phone. If somebody is calling you a lot or you're getting a lot of hang-ups, or if somebody is trying to cut you off from your family and friends and tells you that he or she has never loved anybody like you and can't live without you, *do not be flattered by this; be terrified by this.* This is stalking behavior.

News stories always focus on Jack the Ripper — or a modern-day monster — who preys primarily on women. But guys, it makes sense for you to be a bit cautious, too. (Please tell me you look both ways before crossing . . . macho doesn't keep you safe from Mack trucks, fella.) Don't feel you can skip this chapter or skim through it. You'll feel better and safer if you've been sensible, too. Besides, it's good to know what your date may have on her mind other than batting her baby blues at you.

It was a dark and stormy night . . .

I was once on my way to a speaking engagement and missed my connecting flight due to bad weather. Having no other choice, I hired a car to take me the 200 miles I needed to go. The driver did nothing to make me feel comfortable by asking me if I wanted to sit up front and telling me about his 12-step recovery. After we had gone 300 miles or so, I realized he was hopelessly lost. There were no lights and no cars and no signs. It also occurred to me that he knew I had the cash to pay him because we'd discussed it ahead of time. In my most tactful voice, I soothingly asked if I could find a phone and reconfirm to my hosts, whom I had told about his car.

This was, of course, untrue. But to this day, I'm convinced that the knowledge that someone knew where I was and with whom saved me from getting dismembered by the roadside. I only wish I'd had enough sense to make the phone call I fantasized. Be smarter than I was — but have since learned to be.

Telling Somebody Where You're Going

Always let someone you trust know where you're going — and with whom — when you go out and about what time to expect you back. Unless you went to kindergarten with your date and every grade since, it makes sense to let someone know where you are, especially these days when people meet through the personals and blind dates and online chat rooms. Even if you're both safe from each other, what if the car breaks down or there's a storm at the beach or your in-line skates are hijacked? Not only is it smart to be safe rather than sorry, you'll feel more relaxed as well.

If your mom or your big brother is likely to grill you about your date for weeks afterward, pick someone else to tell — a friend who gives you the same kind of info. If you don't know a soul, the next best thing is to leave a detailed note of where you are and who you're with posted in an obvious spot in your home or apartment, such as on the refrigerator door. It just makes common sense. If you should stumble into trouble, speed and accuracy are essential.

Particularly if you're a single woman living alone, tell a friend what you're up to. While it may feel like a pinch on your freedom, it's a gift you and your single girlfriends can give to each other.

Getting Your Date's Name, Rank, and Serial Number

While researching this book, I asked several single friends, both male and female, to tell me how often they knew the home address of a first date who was picking them up or meeting them somewhere. The answer I most often heard was "rarely," which stunned me at first. Then, the more I thought about it, the more I realized it was logical — and probably pretty sensible. Most first-date arrangements these days sound something like this:

"You want to get together sometime?"

"Yeah. Sounds great."

"Great! Can I call you?"

"Sure. Here's my office number, my e-mail address, and my cell phone number."

"I'll give you a buzz."

When he or she does call, a specific home address simply doesn't come up in conversation unless it's needed for directions.

Frankly, I don't think you and your date need to exchange home addresses before a first date. After all, if things go horribly wrong, do you really want your date driving past your house the next day?

When you date someone you've met online, either at an Internet dating site or a social networking site like Facebook, you two are really total strangers. It may take several dates where you each drive and meet each other before you reveal the same level of personal contact information (such as a home address) that you would with someone you're already acquainted with in the offline world. Erring on the side of caution in the Internet age is respected between modern single adults. Be both careful and smart here.

With that said, here's what you definitely *do* need to know about the other person before your date begins:

- ✔ His or her full name (first and last)
- ✔ Where he or she works or goes to school
- ✔ The general area (such as a neighborhood) where he or she lives

If he or she is hesitant to freely offer any of this information or is confrontational or cranky about giving you any data, consider it a red flag because there are precious few reasons for not making these kinds of disclosures:

- ✔ The person is married.
- ✔ The person lives with his or her mother.
- ✔ The person is embarrassed by his or her neighborhood.
- ✔ The person lives in a car.
- ✔ The person is not who he or she says at all.

Let me take a moment here and chat about chat rooms and Facebook. Just because information is on the Internet doesn't mean it's true. Beware of assuming you know *anything* about someone you have met online. Folks have been known to lie not just about their age but also their gender, nationality, and more. Not everyone lies online, but it's hard to tell truth from fabrication by typeface, and please don't tell me you saw the person's picture . . . whose picture was it, *really?*

Finding a Safe Haven

Depending on the part of the country in which you live and your age and economic situation, your date may offer to pick you up in a cab, a limo, a scooter, a wagon, a bus, or not at all. Although a car, especially if it's yours or your dad's or your older sib's or your granny's, may sound fun, and there's something lovely and prom-like about the ritual of leaving your home on a first date and walking together to the car (will he hold the door open? will she unlock the inside?), I want you to consider other safer and potentially saner alternatives.

Meeting there

Meeting at the date location is a good option for several reasons:

- ✔ **You are in control of your arrival and departure times.** There's no nail-biting if your date's late, or frantic rushing around if he or she is early. And, if the date turns out to be a dud, you're outta there in seconds flat.

- ✔ **Realistically, you may not be so comfortable giving a near-stranger your address just yet.** That's okay. If he or she insists on coming to your house, that's another red flag right there. It's perfectly okay to say, "Let's save home visits 'til a little later so the neighbors won't gossip." Being cute and flip is okay rather than saying, "Look, I don't know you from Jack or Jackie the Ripper so chill on the address stuff." The trick is to get enough information while meeting in a public place so you feel comfortable. Trust your gut, but stay out of strangers' cars and homes.

- ✔ **You don't have to count on your date staying sober when you drive your own car.** You do, however, have to make sure you don't drink (unless you've been dropped off by a friend, parent, cab, bus, or so on).

- ✔ **Unless you invite your date to follow you home at the end of the evening, the sex question is definitely out of the question.**

- ✔ **Meeting at the location lends a slightly businesslike air to the date.** This perception can be ideal for a first meeting where you're still checking each other out.

Meeting at your workplace or school

Meeting your date at your workplace or school has some advantages, as well as a couple of pitfalls. Here are the pros:

- ✔ **Unless you work in a one-man operation, you're meeting in a public place and can keep your home address to yourself for now.**

- ✔ **Presumably your coworkers will still be around.** It's a great opportunity to see how well your date relates to others.

- ✔ **You can still exercise the option to provide your own transportation from work.** You can leave your car there and call a cab or take a bus or have a friend take you to the restaurant or theater.

Here are some cons:

- ✔ **Meeting at work or school ups the pressure for your date to offer to escort you home if you haven't left a car at your meeting place.** If you generally ride the bus to work, for example, your date may not want to make you ride the bus home at night after your date. Though it's a bit of a splurge, tuck cab fare in your pocket so you can be cool and safe at the same time.

- ✔ **Now your date knows where to find you eight hours a day.** At home, at least you can leave the machine on or change your phone number if the situation gets too dicey (for instance, your date won't take no for an answer). In some working environments — a store, restaurant, driving a city bus — it can be much harder to avoid a too-ardent admirer.

Mom versus my favorite restaurant

I took my mom to one of my favorite restaurants when she came to visit. She asked me if I ever took dates there. I said, as a matter of fact, I often did because it was close to home, all the guys there knew me, and I felt safe. Mom said, "Bad idea. They treat you like a princess here. It'll scare the poor guy to death." I told a friend this story, and she said, "Mom's wrong. It's the perfect place. They might as well start treating you like a princess from the get-go."

The moral of this story is, it's good to feel comfy as long as you don't make your date feel too uncomfy. If there are either emotional or verbal references to dates past, I might forgo the experience for a while.

The major disadvantage of meeting at work — blowing your cover — can be offset by meeting somewhere near work.

Meeting in your 'hood

Your neighborhood is your territory. It's where you feel comfy and known. Meeting at some nearby landmark — the fountain in town, the gas station, the Piggly Wiggly (I could have said grocery store, but my childhood resonates when I mention the Piggly Wiggly — a real grocery in the South and West) — has several advantages. It's public and close to home, and chances are that you'll be seen by neighbors who care about you.

Taking Cash

Always make sure you have what my mom calls "mad money." It's enough cash to get yourself home should you decide to walk away in a huff. Tuck 20 bucks inside your shoe. Just remember to take it out at the end of the evening or you'll have a shoe rack full of somewhat smelly cash.

Achieving Safety in Numbers

My number-one criterion for a safe date is to go to a public place. When you do, you're creating your own safety zone — essential for not only feeling relaxed emotionally but also for releasing your body from guard duty. Your shoulders drop, your eyes stop darting left and right, your breathing deepens and slows. Isolated, dark, quiet places may be great for romance, but on a first date, the goal is to get comfortable with each other. And comfort comes with safety. And safety comes in well-trafficked public places where you can let your guard down.

Here's a list of safe things to do on a first date (go to Chapter 7 for more information on great date locations):

Safest	Less safe	Unsafe
Going to an outdoor concert	Meeting at a bar	Going for a drive
In-line skating (unless you're a complete klutz) in the park on Saturday	Attending a private party (unless you know the party-givers)	Walking on the beach at midnight
Going for ice cream	Seeing a drive-in movie	Spending a weekend in the country

Safest	Less safe	Unsafe
Doing lunch	Going to a sporting event (testosterone levels can go sky-high if it's a violent sport)	Going to his or her home alone
Doing brunch		Hiking in the woods
Meeting for coffee		Standing in Times Square on New Year's Eve after midnight
Going dancing		
Running a 5K in the park		
Visiting a museum		

Again, this list is not intended to scare you into joining a monastic order. Certainly, a midnight stroll on the beach can blossom into one of the most memorable dates of your life, but a midnight stroll doesn't have to be a first date. Mom was right: It is better to be safe than sorry. In the dating world, avoiding iffy situations in the first place is better than trying to figure out how to get out alive and intact. This is dating, not undercover work.

Paying Attention to Your Intuition

You know that old chestnut, "If it seems too good to be true, it probably is"? Well, I want you to memorize a slightly different version: "If it feels all wrong to you, it probably is."

In fact, if you ever feel the niggling of intuition telling you that something's not quite right, do this:

1. **Listen to your gut.**

2. **Do a reality check.**

3. **Get out and sort through your intuition later.**

Intuition is . . .

The word intuition comes from the Latin *tuitionem,* which means "guarding or protecting." Your natural intuition is a sort of sixth sense that allows you to "feel" something you can't see or touch or define. It's a way of processing information emotionally as well as intellectually that makes you feel everything is okay — or not.

Intuition is also what bonds you wordlessly to a person you don't know well. "I just have a good feeling about them," you say. You're probably right. It doesn't take a rocket scientist to realize that the tingly feeling you have as you walk through a deserted parking garage or the urge to walk on a well-lit street is sensible and will keep you safer than ignoring your body's warning signs.

Women's intuition, a common notion in the American vernacular, is actually true. Women do have a more finely tuned sixth sense than men. Perhaps it's a throwback from the Stone Age when women had to be hyper-alert not only for their own safety but for their little cave babies, too.

Intuition versus paranoia

The trick is to distinguish between true intuition and the paranoia our society so easily fuels with all the in-your-face crime images on TV and in the papers. How do you do it? The best way is to start with trust. Trust your own instincts first. Tap in to how you really feel, in your gut. If those gut feelings turn out to be wrong again and again, you'll know your intuition needs a little adjustment.

When I lived in Boston, I often took the shortcut through the Commons (a large, manicured park in which the earlier citizens of Boston were — and still are — allowed to graze two head of sheep or cattle) on my way home. If I ever felt the least bit spooked, I went around rather than through. I never questioned my feelings or berated myself for being a baby. I also noticed that when I carried my umbrella over my shoulder like a rifle, I was less likely to be spooked. Body language says a lot.

It's okay to get the heck out

Before your first date begins, I want you to make a conscious decision. If, at any point, your date feels not quite right to you — if there's a look that gives you the willies or a remark that sends the hairs on the back of your neck standing on end — immediately do the following:

1. **Do a reality check. Flat-out ask, "What did you mean by that?"**

   If your date shuffles his feet or she blushes scarlet, you'll know it was probably just a faux pas and not a sign of something more sinister.

2. **Look at body language, and if your date's body language makes you uncomfortable, move yourself away.**

   Is your date standing in an aggressive manner (hands on hips, feet planted, staring) or sitting too close? You're entitled to feel absolutely comfortable, and if you don't, ask your date to back off.

3. **Survey your surroundings.**

   Are people around? Is the lighting sufficient? Does the location put you on alert?

4. **Listen to your own body.**

   Sometimes your body knows what your head may be denying. Listen to your heartbeat. Is it a smooth, steady rhythm or a deep, resonant pounding? Do you feel yourself running out of breath even though you're sitting still? Decide whether you're excited because you're turned on or terrified. There is a difference even though the clues are quite similar.

5. **Evaluate all the cues, listen to your gut, and, if you still feel uneasy, get yourself out of there.**

   Plead illness, a headache — it's okay to be a fraidy-cat. Dating is supposed to be fun and exciting, not scary!

Nobody goes on a date expecting trouble, but as your mom pointed out, an ounce of prevention will save you some serious heartache. While predatory behavior is relatively uncommon, you don't want it to happen to you. So arm yourself with information.

Dating is supposed to be fun and exciting. By being aware of potential dangers, you can be alert and informed and confident rather than naively obtuse or frighteningly paranoid. The Boy Scouts said a mouthful — be prepared. I add, be careful and be aware.

You can prepare yourself by knowing what date rape and stalking are and how to protect yourself from these behaviors, so as uncomfortable as they are to contemplate, those are the topics I cover next. Be a bit discomfited now so you can relax on your date.

Date Rape

No dating book would be complete without a discussion of the darkest side of dating: date rape, also called *acquaintance rape*. Both terms are misleading and contribute to the misunderstanding of this very serious crime. Rape is rape — a violent felonious assault that is about power, not sex, and that traumatizes and injures the victim, perhaps even more so when the victim knows his or her attacker.

The definition of date rape is confounded by the pervasive sexual stereotype in our society that men should be the aggressive sexual initiators and women should "play hard to get." Both are dangerous assumptions. When mixed with alcohol and other controlled substances (often a factor in date rapes), they can be seriously destructive to both parties.

- ✔ Rape isn't about sex; it's about power.
- ✔ Rape is anything after the word "no." Anything.

College campuses are particularly vulnerable. According to a controversial 1985 study funded by the National Center for the Prevention and Control of Rape, 25 percent of women in college were victims of rape, and almost 90 percent of them knew their assailants. Of those rapes, 47 percent were by first or casual dates or by romantic acquaintances.

Myths and facts about date rape

There are a lot of inaccurate perceptions of what date rape is. Some people (unfortunately, too many) think that date rape is a boys-will-be-boys scenario, or a case of her saying no when she really means yes, or a lover's disagreement, or a sample of overreaction, or a meaningless offense. It's not.

Those and other myths and misperceptions end up clouding the real issue: that date rape is rape. No exceptions.

MYTH: Lots of date rape accusations turn out to be false reports.

FACT: Most incidences of rape are never reported, particularly in cases of acquaintance rape where the victim feels guilty or somehow responsible. According to a survey of reported rapes in Los Angeles County, for example, fewer than 1 percent were found to be unsubstantiated — less than the false report rate for either robbery or homicide.

MYTH: Acquaintance rape occurs only between two people who don't know each other very well.

FACT: Rape is a violent crime that has nothing to do with how long the attacker has known the victim. It's not uncommon to be raped by a longtime acquaintance, former lover, or spouse.

MYTH: Rape is a crime against women.

FACT: Men are sexually assaulted as well — and not just by gay men. Rape is an act of violence and brutality, not sexuality. One survey of convicted rapists found that about half didn't care what sex their victim was; they raped both men and women.

How to protect yourself if you're a man

It can be confusing to be a guy out there navigating the treacherous waters of the dating scene. Some women do send mixed signals. No doubt about it. Some guys are a bit blinded by their desires. Still, to protect yourself, as well as the women you're dating, I want you to consider the following points before your relationships progress to the sexual stage:

- ✔ **If your date is sending a mixed message, assume "maybe" means no.** You don't want to make love to someone who is unsure about making love to you. Talk about it. Clarify how she feels. Proceed only when both of you are ready. Alcohol is the solvent of the super ego and makes it easy not to communicate or hear communication clearly. Make sure this discussion occurs with both of you dressed and stone cold sober.

- ✔ **Assuming you both want the same amount of intimacy at exactly the same moment is a mistake.** Your date may be interested in sexual contact other than intercourse. I know it's hard to do, but it's important to continuously check on each other's desires rather than just making convenient or self-serving assumptions that may be *very* dangerous.

- ✔ **A woman who says "no" to sex is not necessarily saying "no" to you as a person.** She may just want to pursue being physical more slowly.

- ✔ **Just because she's in your room doesn't mean she wants to be in your bed.**

- ✔ **Your size and physical presence can be intimidating to a woman.** If she doesn't struggle, it may be because she feels too afraid.

- ✔ **Intoxication (either yours or hers) is not a legal or moral defense for rape.**

- ✔ **No matter what has transpired, "no" means "stop now — go no further."** That's not only the moral definition but the legal definition as well. I don't care what's happened up to this point.

How to protect yourself if you're a woman

It's true that anybody can say no at any time: at hand holding, kissing, petting, right up to penetration. If you say no, that means that your partner must stop, but you have to be smart, too. You have to avoid sending mixed signals, like protesting one moment and then coyly relenting, purposefully trying to turn him on and off like a faucet, or agreeing to an intimate dinner at his place when you have no intention of becoming intimate, or making suggestive comments in public and turning cool once you're alone. That's game playing, and it's dangerous. You abusing your power is no more attractive than him abusing his. After all, if *you're* not clear on what you mean, how can you expect him to be? Be smart and follow these guidelines:

- ✔ **Avoid situations that put you at risk.** Don't go up to his room if you really don't want to be there.

- ✔ **When you say no, say it with a period instead of a question mark.** No means no, not "maybe" and not "convince me." Don't be stupid.

- ✔ **Never cry rape as a way of getting even or getting attention.** This is serious, serious stuff and can ruin both of your lives if it's not true. A false allegation of rape is illegal.

Other things to keep in mind:

- ✔ Don't invite trouble by inviting yourself into a compromising situation and then playing dumb. "What kind of girl do you think I am?"

- ✔ Understand, men have been taught that if they don't make a pass, you'll think they're gay, so no fair baiting them.

- ✔ Rubbing against a man's penis is going to get him excited, and he'll feel you should finish what you started, so don't get started.

- ✔ Using alcohol as a way of excusing yourself from responsible behavior is misleading to him and dangerous for you. Nobody ever does anything drunk they don't wish they could do sober.

How to protect yourself from the date rape drug

In the late '90s, an alarming rise in the use of a drug called Rohypnol or "roofie" was reported across the country. Known on the street as a "love drug," a roofie is a potent tranquilizer — several times stronger than Valium. As originally formulated, it was tasteless and odorless. When sprinkled in someone's drink, sedation occurs in about 20 minutes to half an hour and lasts for several hours. The effects are similar to alcohol: muscle relaxation, slurred speech, slowing of motor skills. But there is one notable exception: The drug produces amnesia as well. There were numerous reports of young women waking up in frat houses or other unfamiliar surroundings, without clothes on, having been sexually assaulted but not remembering a thing. (As of the writing of this book, the manufacturers of Rohypnol have added a substance that makes the drug give off a blue tinge when dissolved in liquid.)

Roofies, also called ruffies, roche, R-2, rib, and rope, are known on the street as the date rape drug of choice even though statistically they're present in the bloodstream in less than 3 percent of all reported rape victims. (Alcohol is still the major drug of abuse in this country — especially in date rape.) The dangers don't stop there. When mixed with alcohol and other drugs, roofies can kill. Your breathing slows to such an extent that you may stop breathing at all. To protect yourself:

✔ Don't take any type of drug handed to you at a party.

✔ Refuse a drink offered by a stranger.

If you should "wake up" and not remember where you've been, report it to the police immediately.

Even at the height of the "roofie" scare, alcohol was the number-one date rape drug — and it still is. More people have found themselves in dangerous situations due to alcohol than all other substances combined.

The current hot drug is methamphetamine, which is passed around as an aphrodisiac and also is not dropped unknowingly but used consensually to heighten sexual pleasure. It is known as crystal meth, ice, crank, speed, glass, and chalk. Methamphetamine comes in many forms and can be smoked, snorted, orally ingested, or injected. Meth is a stimulant on the central nervous system and has a high potential for abuse and addiction. Users can stay awake for long periods of time and then eventually crash, feeling tired and depressed, leaving them worse off than before they used the drug. Even small amounts of meth can produce serious negative effects, including hyperthermia and convulsions, which can result in the death of the user. The use of methamphetamines also increases the user's risk of heart failure, stroke, and brain damage.

Stalking

We've all heard about celebrity stalkers, but stalking affects an estimated 1.5 million ordinary men, women, and children in the United States each year. More and more states are passing anti-stalking laws. Many statutes define stalking as the "willful, malicious, and repeated following and harassing of another person" and add that an imminent threat of violence must be made for law enforcement to take action.

The Internet and social interaction sites such as Facebook have made stalking much easier because so much information is so readily available about people's friends, interests, schedules, looks, and wardrobes. Privacy seems to have been a casualty of the information age. We've all adopted the worst of celebrity culture, with the result being that strangers can know our every move. For celebrities, the loss of privacy is by and large the cost of fame. For civilians, it seems to be a choice to voluntarily surrender privacy — maybe in the hopes of becoming a celebrity.

Rarely will someone march up to you and verbally threaten to do bodily harm, but stalking always has an implied threat of violence. Stalking is often much more sinister and insidious than a stated threat. So that you can take steps to protect yourself, you need to understand what goes on inside the stalker's head.

Looking for signs of obsession

Remember the movie *Fatal Attraction,* in which Glenn Close plays a gorgeous, sexy, smart, available woman who was willing to be the Michael Douglas character's love slave for a weekend? You can just see him thinking, "This is too good to be true." As it turns out, he was right. She was not only a stalker but a resourceful woman who tracked him down, threatened his family, and killed his daughter's bunny rabbit.

Someone who is overly attentive, overwhelmingly thoughtful, and wants to be with you all the time — especially in these days when people seem to fear commitment — may seem terrific, but there may be a dark side. If someone is too good to be true, believe me: It's not true.

A person who is too attentive can be rationalized as a product of a match made in heaven, someone who finally appreciates the real you, but what you really have is the breeding ground for a stalker. A stalker is someone who craves that closeness in an addictive sense and whose own sense of self is so fragile that instant bonding with another is the only way he or she can quell the loneliness. A stalker will try to cut you off from your friends and wants to have all of your time because this is somebody who craves control rather than somebody who craves you. With most stalkers, the seeds of the trouble are there from the beginning, but since we all want to be loved, we write this initial clinginess off to infatuation that is engendered by our wonderfulness. You may have been in relationships with people who didn't have time for you (and who hasn't?), so you may be seduced by the notion that somebody really wants to be with you all the time, but beware: If there's any question in your mind, back off.

Understand that the unbelievable instant closeness is just that — unbelievable. Obsession is not love. It is need, and the object of the obsession is nearly irrelevant. You make yourself safer from a stalker by not letting things get started, because once a stalker gets started, he or she is really hard to stop.

Profile of a stalker

A stalker is incredibly needy and unable to carry on the give-and-take necessary in longer-term dating. The Internet has really fostered this behavior because it allows — and may even encourage — a false intimacy without ever leaving the comfort and safety of one's own bedroom for a very long time. For a stalker, this is exhilarating. He or she can be quite charming initially but turn ugly when everything isn't going exactly as planned. Stalkers are:

  ✔ **Obsessed with the objects of their desire:** Stalkers are looking for attention. If they can't get this attention in a positive way, negative attention will do.

✔ **Out of touch with reality and able to hear only what they want to hear:** For instance, "I'm sorry, I'm not ready for a relationship" translates as "Wait for me." "I have a boyfriend or girlfriend" means someone is in the way of the two of you getting together.

✔ **Persistent:** If you let the phone ring 30 times before picking up, the stalker assumes it takes 31 rings to get through to you.

✔ **Self-involved:** Stalkers are unable to see things from any perspective other than their own.

How to protect yourself from a stalker

First and foremost, the moment you sense someone is overly persistent in pursuing you, take it seriously. Denying the problem only makes the stalker try harder to get your attention. Instead, do the following:

✔ **Sever all communication.** Don't try to let him or her down easy. Be firm and be specific. "I am not interested in having any type of relationship with you, now or in the future." I know it sounds harsh, but it's important to extinguish even the faintest glimmer of hope.

✔ **Change your regular routine.** If you usually leave for work at 8:15 to catch the 8:30 bus, carpool it some days or get to the office early.

✔ **Don't react.** If the person who's been following you suddenly shows up in the cafeteria at school, try not to look scared or shocked. That's exactly the reaction he or she wants. Instead, ignore the person entirely and sit with a group of friends.

✔ **Let people know what's happening.** Tell your coworkers, teachers, friends, parents, doormen — anyone you trust who sees you on a regular basis. When you're being stalked, everyone needs to be on the lookout for your safety.

✔ **Carry a cell phone.** You want help to be three numbers away: 9-1-1.

✔ **Plan ahead.** Know where police stations are. Park only in well-lit areas. Hang with friends more than alone. Don't give a stalker any opportunity to have some private time with you.

✔ **Keep your old phone number but get a second number.** Experts suggest getting a second phone number and letting voicemail handle the first. That way, you can document threatening phone calls, and you never have to answer no matter how many times the stalker calls. Rely on caller ID; if you don't know the identification, don't pick up. I suspect that in the not-too-distant future it will be possible to block a number on a cell in the same way that you can do so with a land line. You can already block solicitors; stalkers are next.

✔ **Never meet the person for one last time.** It could be your last date ever with anyone if the person feels there is no hope and therefore nothing to lose by harming you.

✔ **Finally, if the stalking seems to escalate rather than dissipate, call the police.** Ask to speak with one of their stalking specialists who is trained to evaluate cues to determine if the threatened violence is indeed real. There is some controversy about whether restraining orders or personal orders of protection are valuable or dangerous. Talk to your local authorities about their feelings on this matter and at least establish a code word with friends and love ones to alert them to call 911 if you give the code word or phrase that says you're in trouble. I know this sounds a bit melodramatic, but it just might save your life.

Stalkers don't necessarily look like something out of a horror flick or wear T-shirts saying "I'M CREEPY," so you need to be aware of the warning signs:

✔ Someone who wants to spend every waking hour with you

✔ Someone who calls or e-mails you dozens of times a day

✔ Someone who demands to know where you are and who you're with every moment

✔ Someone who waits outside your job or home for you all the time

✔ Someone who monitors your cell phone bill

✔ Someone who wants to know your passwords

Most ardent suitors are not stalkers, but believe that if someone seems too good to be true, he or she is. You are lovable and valuable, and no one has the right to make you feel frightened in the name of love.

Online power plays: Bullying and stalking

Especially among middle and high schoolers, online bullying through Facebook has become a problem. You don't have to have a Facebook account to be popular, and you can have real-life as opposed to just online friends.

PLEEEEEZE be mindful and careful of what you are willing to share with the world at large. If you feel someone is bullying or stalking you, turn off your computer and ignore the whole thing. A bully or a stalker lives on your fear and sadness; if you cut off the source of that fuel, he or she will move on or just be starved by your equanimity and nonchalance. Care less, and this person will stop caring too much.

Chapter 21
Dating Sight Unseen

*T*here are a lot of ways to meet people (in fact, I list about a zillion in Chapter 5). You meet someone at a friend's house; you catch someone's eye in class; you both volunteer at the same homeless shelter. You meet, you talk, you make plans to get together.

When you get together online or through personal ads or through a blind date, you're really not meeting at all until the actual day of the date. While you may have chatted, if you've never laid eyes on each other, you are complete strangers. Believe it.

This chapter can allow you the freedom to indulge in this high-risk behavior with a safety net when your first date is the first time you really meet face to face. But please be really, extra, especially careful, and if you're feeling the least bit chancy, pass for a safer method of meeting someone.

Online Connections

Every week on my daily program, I receive at least one call from someone who met someone online. I'm going to tell you what I always tell him or her: This person you meet online, however familiar he or she may seem to you, is a stranger. Repeat after me: *a stranger*. My callers always protest this, as I'm sure you will, too, if you've met someone in the vast world of cyberspace. Think about the circumstances realistically for a moment:

- Each of you is sitting in front of a computer screen, alone, in your home or office.

- No one is speaking. You're writing to each other. Although you feel like you're talking, online is an entirely different form of communication. Many tongue-tied people are elegant, soulful writers.

✔ You have no way to verify that what he or she is telling you is true. You may well be communicating with a fiction writer.

✔ Your intimacy appears more intense because all of your senses, sensors, and censors are not engaged. Your online companion can (and will) tell you things he or she would never tell you to your face — for better and worse.

Numerous studies have conclusively demonstrated that our inhibitions are lowered when faced with a blank computer screen. Our normal, cautious self is deleted, and our pacing is sped up by the Send button. Beware. It's happening on both sides of the e-mail or texting exchange.

This type of false intimacy is misleading. You feel as though you know this person better than you do. Even if he or she is completely honest, you have only a partial picture. If you do decide to meet someone you've "met" online, be very careful and follow these guidelines:

✔ **Exchange recent photographs first.** Not touched-up, Hollywood versions of yourself, but the real McCoy. The fewer surprises, the better.

✔ **Meet in a public place.** No exceptions . . . no matter how well you "know" the person.

✔ **Schedule a short date that has a built-in end to it.** Go to lunch on a workday or meet for a quick cup of coffee. Daylight hours are safer and less sexy; it's also easier to make a graceful exit due to prior engagements, thus limiting lengthy, hard-to-limit time involvements.

If the initial meeting goes well, it's still critical to proceed with extreme caution. After all, you're partaking in a sort of "backward" relationship — one that begins with intense revelations and pulls back from there. The potential for heartbreak is magnified. If things don't work out, you may feel as though you've revealed your soul online and were rejected on the basis of how you look. Devastating, indeed. Take it very, very slowly.

To profile or not

You're curious and think about checking out this person's Facebook page. Yeah, I know that HALF A BILLION folks are on Facebook, but if you can resist 'til after the first or second date, you'll go in with a fresh perspective, no inherent expectations or concerns, and much less of a tendency to blurt out inappropriate questions.

When you're putting info on your own Facebook page, keep this in mind: You understand that strangers will be checking you out, so consider whether this information is what you want them to know about you before you even meet.

Phantom dating

Let me just add a word or two here about timing. As you can read, I am absolutely a fan of meeting online. It deepens the pool and widens the circle of potential dates. I am also a fan of chatting a bit before you actually meet face to face. All of which underlines the reason to make sure you're not doing the GU thang: dating outside of a 25-mile radius, making your date *geographically undesirable.* What I am NOT in favor of is prolonging the arm's length phase. We're talking dating, not typing or pen-palling. I know several couples who waited months — and in one case, a *year* — before actually setting eyeballs upon one another. Don't do it. There is an assumed intimacy, a distortion of fantasy, and a bunch of other anti-reality factors that will come into play. Sooner or later, preferably sooner, step up to the plate, take a deep breath, and see each other face to face, nose to nose — or else how are you ever going to get lip to lip, for heaven's sake?

Personal Ads

As I discuss in Chapter 3, personal ads have become an acceptable way of, at the very least, jazzing up your social life, providing that you are specific, honest, and careful. Different from an ongoing online exchange, a personal ad is literally an advertisement for yourself. It's usually well thought-out in advance — few people just dash out a personal ad. At the very least, a personal ad tells the reader what the "advertiser" wants in a date. At most, it offers a real insight into the way the person who wrote it feels about himself or herself and about others.

There's not only nothing wrong with either placing or answering a personal ad, but it also happens to be a good way to get very specific about who you are and what you want in a date. And it can be a great way to get that all-important introduction to someone. Once that happens, a natural unveiling of your fleshed out personality can take place. I know tons of happy couples who met in the personals and later married. Of course, I know many other couples who did not. That said, there are very specific ways to protect yourself when writing and responding to a personal ad:

- **Never include your full name, phone number, or address in the ad.**
- **Be honest.** Why waste time, effort, and money misleading someone with whom you want to develop a lasting relationship?
- **Arrange to meet only in a public place, for a specified amount of time.**
- **Keep your expectations in check.** Yours may be one of several ads your date responded to.

✔ **Exchange recent photographs ahead of time.**

Maybe you're feeling shy or insecure and have declined to include a picture in your personal ad. (Please don't even think about using an old picture or, heaven forfend, someone else's picture . . . we're not trying to con anybody here.) Let me convince you here and now, you're only delaying and giving the wrong impression. Including a picture increases the chance of a response eight-fold — yeah, eight times more responses — REGARDLESS OF HOW YOU LOOK. Bite the bullet: Sooner or later you're going to want to meet face to face, so give each other a chance to adjust and admire.

If you're technologically astute, a short Skype video call before meeting may be reassuring to you both. This lets you two see each other in real time without touchups. However, this advantage may be offset because your Skype ID can reveal your last name and place of employment, so you may not be comfortable using it. Skype and video calls before you meet will become more prevalent in the near future. Still, keep this phone call brief. It's just to verify how you two look and to work out logistics for your first date when you meet.

✔ **Have fun.** Remember . . . it's only a date.

Eight ways to tell if your date's married

Not every married man will be wearing a wedding ring and a sneaky look. You don't ever want to be the reason somebody uses to get out of their marriage. If you see or experience any of the following red flags, run the other way:

✔ He gives you only an office number or cell number.

✔ She's never home when you call.

✔ Your dates tend to occur outside city limits.

✔ He often excuses himself to call the "office" well after office hours.

✔ Spur-of-the-moment dates are out of the question.

✔ She picks only darkly lit, out-of-the-way places.

✔ He's never available on weekends or holidays.

✔ She has a mysterious rash (or white mark) on the ring finger of her left hand.

Blind Dates

One step up from a personal ad, a blind date can be either a godsend or the last time you ever speak to the "friend" who set you up. Married people are notorious for trying to fix up their single friends, with all the best of intentions. If nothing else, a blind date is a crash course on what your friends think you'd be interested in. Keep these rules in mind:

- ✔ **Rule 1: Know the intent of the person who's fixing you up.** If your mom wants you to meet her friend's son who "doesn't get out much," ask Mom whether she's met the dude and whether going out with him is likely to help or hurt her friendship if the two of you don't hit it off. If your best friend wants you to meet this great woman who just moved into his building, ask yourself what your friend's taste in women is like. Are you willing to give it a try? Before you do, be sure to follow Rule 2.

- ✔ **Rule 2: Get to know your blind date (at least a little) on the phone first.** You can save both of you some time and money by getting to know each other a little first (see Rule 3 for the type of info you want to get).

  Or you can drag the fixer-upper along on the first date. Having the fixer-upper come along works really well because it takes both the anxiety and the danger out of the situation. Worst-case scenario: You had fun with at least one person with whom you are already familiar, and if the date is a complete bust, you won't have to give lengthy explanations as to why. They came, they saw, they cringed.

  If you're the fixer, one of the coolest and least painful fix-up scenarios occurs when you ask both of your candidates to go out with you. Not a double date, just the three of you. If they seem to be getting along, you can scram and get the good skinny later. If it seems like a disaster, hang in there until one of them decides to leave.

- ✔ **Rule 3: Conduct a pre-date "interview."** At minimum, this interview covers the basics: *Who? What? Where?* and *Are you married?* It's also one way to feel more secure about somebody who someone else knows but you don't. In a friendly, breezy, conversational way, ask the basics:

  - Do you work? Go to school?

  - What are you studying? What do you do for a living?

- Where do you live? (Don't necessarily press for an address, but a neighborhood or area can be helpful.)

- Are you married? (Unless you already know . . . for sure never assume that because they're dating, they're single. That assumption has caused many a heartache down the road.)

- Are you recently out of a relationship?

- What are your interests?

- How do you know the person who fixed us up?

- Don't you hate the term "fixed up," as if we're broken?

It's a lot easier to get this stuff out of the way on the phone before you're face to face.

✔ **Rule 4: Once you've agreed you like each other enough to actually meet, meet in a public place for a specified amount of time.** For more guidelines on protecting yourself when you're dating someone you don't know, see the earlier sections, "Online Connections" and "Personal Ads."

Dating with an audience

A blind date is a great chance to anticipate before you participate. Beware sharing your hopes, dreams, desires, or fantasies with anyone, even your best friend or a family member. And UNDER NO CIRCUMSTANCES should you share your hopes and dreams on Facebook or any other online site. Trolling for info from mutual friends is a no-no, as is sharing any expectations, fears, and so on. Keep your secret love secret until you've at least seen each other, and then see if you can't keep your delicious secret to yourself for awhile. New relationships are like soufflés: Keep 'em in the oven, undisturbed and unseen, until they're ready to be admired. Otherwise, they can pancake out and be messy and unpalatable.

Chapter 22

Keeping It Fresh, Alive, and Healthy

....

....

I don't want to end our discussion of dating on a sour note by talking about the dangers and the difficulties of staying too long online, even though I would be remiss if I didn't include Chapters 20 and 21. But whether you love dating or view it as a necessary process, I want you to have the option to retire yourself from the search by concentrating on and enriching your — dare I say — relationship, so that if you choose, you can date each other after the wedding, the kids, the cocker spaniel, retirement, senior housing, and beyond.

Being romantic in the early days of dating is a no-brainer, but how can you keep the fun, energy, interest, and, yeah, romance alive on an ongoing basis?

In this book, you've learned how to figure out who you are, what you want, and how to set up a date. You've gone on your first date, had an incredible time, and survived the early stages of a relationship. What you want to do is not start this whole process all over again.

I've spoken about casual, serious, and heavy dating, and here is the step-by-step how-to to turn heavy dating into a potential (drum roll . . .) relationship. Think of your relationship as a budding plant complete with aluminum foil and a big bow. You can't put that faboo plant in a window and ignore it — it needs pruning, watering, and nurturing as well as the proper environment so the wonderful plant can continue to grow and thrive and make you happy. Your cool new relationship needs the same care, consideration, and knowledge. The following sections suggest ways to keep that relationship alive, wonderful, and terrific!

Send Flowers for No Reason

St. Valentine's Day conjures images of candies in foil hearts, boxed roses, and a romantic dinner. But the real romance of Valentine's Day isn't the food or the flowers: It's the feeling of being important enough to someone else to be remembered and fussed over and loved and cherished. It's sharing a loving (not necessarily sexual) experience — picking out a scent together or choosing warm, woolen mittens or a perfect scented candle or a fuzzy warm blanket or a CD you both like. It's a shared ice cream cone.

Well, I've got news for you: You don't have to wait for February 14 to get or give that feeling. Just as you can have Christmas in July, you can make any day Valentine's Day. Just try a few of the ideas in this chapter — any day of the year — and I'll bet you can melt your date's heart faster than chocolate in August, with a lot less mess.

Flowers remind us of Mother Nature at her most lovely, which is always helpful when dealing with romance. Plants are lovely, but not nearly as romantic.

If sending your date flowers worked initially, then flowers will also work eventually (and basically flowers always work). Sending flowers to your soon-to-be or is-already incredibly significant other for no reason is a great idea.

Women, this idea works for you, too, except if you are sending flowers, make sure that they vaguely look like something a guy would enjoy receiving, which means no long-stem roses (especially if it's for no reason), but maybe an amaryllis, (the so-called boy flower) chrysanthemums, or anything exotic, even a plant. Be sure that you choose something vaguely "manly," which means forget the teddy bears, kissy faces, or cherubs, especially if you are sending it to his office. Getting teased unmercifully may not make him all that pleased, amorous, or grateful.

Guys, all this advice can be completely ignored when it comes to sending women flowers. We all get completely gushy about almost anything, and if guys knew the real impact of flowers, they'd keep a florist on retainer. Just be careful not to send the same flowers for birthdays, fights, or special events. Roses are romantic, but don't get in a rut.

Even though we all know that flowers come from seeds and take work and care — they need to be watered, weeded, fertilized with just the right amount of manure, dead-headed, and so on — a beautiful flower reminds us of the bounty of life and the possibility of artistry. What better symbol than a flower to represent the birds and the bees? (Even Belle in Disney's *Beauty and the Beast* is transfixed by the glow of a frozen flower that can be melted and brought back to life by love.)

A rose by any other name . . .

Flowers symbolize new life. It's no wonder suitors give their loved ones flowers to show the blossoming of their love. Interestingly, flowers also symbolize purity and virginity. Hence the notion of "deflowering" a young bride. Specific flowers have specific meanings, as well. Though it's open to interpretation, here's a consensus of what certain flowers mean.

Flower	*Meaning*
Red rose	Passion
Yellow rose	Jealousy (though I'm from Texas, so I like yellow roses!). Some people are willing to bend the stems a bit and figure it probably means less than true love, so maybe friendship rather than passion. Who would send flowers to signify that they're jealous for heaven's sake?
White rosebud	Purity
Daisy	Innocence
Mum	Hope
Tulip	Luck
Gladioli	Strength
Violet	Modesty
Lily	Devotion
Carnation	Joy (Watch it — I'm sensitive and also from Colorado, the home of the carnation!)
Daffodil	Desire
Sweet pea	Gratitude
Chrysanthemum	Optimism

Trust me, anything that works on the designated holiday works even better on a random day and is scads cheaper. The bouquet can be hand-delivered by you or sent if you're feeling flush or shy; you can send a dozen roses or a single stem, orchids or violets, seasonal or hothouse. The point isn't the lavishness, but the thoughtfulness.

Write a Love Note

Just as flowers speak volumes, putting pen to paper bespeaks extra effort, something from the heart. Those little love notes that you wrote when you were first getting involved or maybe after you first hooked up, the sort of "what I like about you" romantic thoughts, are always a good idea. In some ways, a like note may be even better than a love note; it's more specific and bespeaks emotions that are thoughtful, literally from the head, as well as loving and heartfelt.

You don't have to rhyme, be Bill Shakespeare, or be flowery. Cards are fine, but struggling through on your own is even better. Don't try to be cute or funny. Your words don't have to be poetry (although poetry's cool), and if you're really talented at drawing, terrific, add a sketch or two. But the point here isn't so much about artistry as sincerity. Just write a sweet sentiment from your heart, something gentle and touching — and try not to make it a mash note (body parts shouldn't be too graphically mentioned).

Buying a nice sheet of paper is much better than ripping something out of your notebook, and post 'ems are to be avoided just this once. Don't even think about typing the note, and while texting has its place, this isn't it. If your handwriting is lousy, print — and no pencil, please. Also, try not to mis-spell a whole lot. Just make sure your note's legible, and don't worry about points off for punctuation (after all, your love isn't your English teacher — I hope). Understand that the real value in writing a love note is that it's hard to do. We've all been talking a lot longer than we've been writing, so sometimes you can really get to the heart of the matter (get it??) a bit more quickly by putting pen to paper rather than word to mouth.

A love note is hand written, never typed, and don't even think about e-mailing — old-fashioned is romantic, thoughtful, and special.

One last word about love notes: Make sure it doesn't fall into the wrong hands. No passing it out in class. Leave it someplace private rather than someplace public. In a perfect world, a *billet-doux* or love note would be left on a pillow; don't get ahead of yourself, and no breaking and entering to leave a note, but you understand the underlying meaning, right? Also, x-rated notes may come back to haunt you; we're talking love notes, not smut notes here. If you send a note to work with someone, make sure that somebody else won't discover it. So having it fall out of a briefcase at a business meeting is not a good idea.

Reminisce about Your First Mutual Date

Even if it was a disaster, thinking back to how you two got started is fun. Sharing your history with each other can give you both a perspective that allows you to weather temporary glitches on the radar better because of the sense of shared past. *Nothing* is more romantic than the sense that you've come through troubled times together. It's the metaphorical equivalent of being cozied up in front of a roaring fire together with a cold wind blowing outside.

Reminiscing in a note or conversation can help you remind each other of some of the landmarks in your relationship — your first date, your first kiss, or the first time you both just knew it was serious — any of the things that make you feel closer to one another.

Share Baby Pictures and Stories

Your mom trots out your baby pictures for a reason: You were really cute and cuddly and sweet and innocent, and there's something elemental and basic and charming and nostalgic about seeing who you were then. I know you're feeling a little silly about this, but if you're willing to show your love a little about who you were then, your love will know a bit more about who you've become. Just don't make this sharing time a chapter meeting for the dysfunctional and abused victims of the world. No harsh episodes or horror stories.

You don't actually have to wait to visit your family to trot out old pix of the former you (as if visiting parents wasn't traumatic enough).

If you can't conjure up any pleasant memories from your childhood, you probably need to think therapy, not dating. It's really true that it's hard to love anyone else until you can love yourself. And if you can't love your baby self, get some help so that you can.

Do make sure that neither you nor the family has a hidden agenda here by conjuring up the recently dumped miscellaneous love. No manipulation allowed — just mushy sharing and no reminiscing about first loves, wild vacations, or youthful indiscretions. What seems like intimacy when it comes to sexual history can come back to haunt you. If you do happen to accidentally (and I really do mean *accidentally*) come across an old love while perusing the pix, it's time to trot out the refrain, "I've forgotten everyone but you darlin'." It's a much better idea to have done a little reconnaissance and discreet editing ahead of time if at all possible.

Give a Massage

There are ways of being physical that don't require sex. Certainly dancing, holding hands, and massages are sensual and sexy.

What you're going for here is a way to celebrate sensual intimacy independent of sexuality. A massage isn't necessarily seduction; we're not talking "complete release" here, but pleasure. It's sensual — good feelings that aren't genitally centered, feeling warm, happy, contented — not sexual. Also, the idea isn't "You do me and I'll do you." Treat the massage like a gift; you can get your own massage at a later time.

For a massage, you can either splurge on some good massage oil, use baby oil, or put a drop of almond extract in mineral oil for a lovely scent. Find a flat surface in a comfortably warm room (okay, yeah, a bed *will* work, but we're going for sensuous, not sexual here — just keep telling yourself that), and make sure that you're not messing up your best sheets or towels. Find some soothing music and soft lighting. Too bright isn't relaxing, and too dark makes it hard to find each other.

If you're giving a full body massage, remember to include the hands and feet. Because you're going for intimacy and closeness, not sex here, it's a good idea to exclude genitalia, and always offer the option of underwear kept on. (If the two of you aren't at that stage of your relationship, offer a hand and foot massage as an alternative to a full body massage or scout up a professional masseuse or masseur. The gift of massage is always lovely but even more special if it's you personally laying on hands.)

Take your time — at least an hour — and warm up the oil in your hands first. If you're still not sure about how to give a massage, look for a good book about massage; maybe consult *Massage For Dummies* by Steve Capellini and Michel Van Welden (Wiley). Also, practice on a friend first (who will undoubtedly love you forever).

Shampoo and Bathe Your Love

From earliest times, from the Romans to the Japanese, baths have had ritual status as a way of not only purifying, but also of preparing and relaxing and celebrating.

Geishas have it right. There is something very loving about washing someone: warm water, soap, bubbles. The sensations take us back to being cared for and pampered and loved. A long, careful, gentle shampoo is lovely enough to have a very sexy movie named after it, starring Warren Beatty and Goldie Hawn. If you can find some scented candles and soft music, so much the better, but resist the notion of a quicky shower; vertical just doesn't quite do it.

Bathing together (especially when there is a hygiene problem) and shampooing one another as part of lovemaking can be fun and a nifty way of bypassing those less-than-romantic odor discussions. You can also make it independent of lovemaking. In fact, all these things are probably most romantic when they are independent of sex. Playing geisha girl or boy to your loved one is a loving basic thing to do; primates groom one another. It is relaxed; it slows the pace down of a hectic existence. To set the mood, you can use rose petals or bubble bath, light candles, or play music. Giving each other the time, the space, and the energy to tune in to one another is the ultimate gift.

If your relationship hasn't moved to a sexual level, it's okay to wear bathing suits. The idea is fun and pampering and sensuality, not seduction. Reality television has given hot tubs a salacious bad rep, but you can redeem it by not making suggestive comments but being romantic and looking each other in the eyes and holding no more than hands.

Clean Your Love's Place

If baths are sexy and sensual, shampooing a rug (no, not his toupee, silly) and cleaning her sink (don't even think about it) can certainly drive some of us into a frenzy of appreciation and love. The idea of someone we love doing something we loathe just for us is really cool. Besides, cleaning someone else's place isn't nearly as icky as digging out your own. There was a recent article that suggested that men who do housework have a lot more sex than men who don't (we're talking heterosexual here, smarty pants).

If you are going to clean someone's apartment, make sure that this isn't interpreted as "you are a slob, and I can't stand the clutter around here anymore." Don't even think about throwing away things that your friend loves and will kill you for throwing out. It's not about changing someone else's behavior by manipulating, but about showing how much you care about the person. Polishing the chrome in the bathroom or waxing the floor is okay, but throwing things out is not okay.

Remember, no fair peeking into drawers, and giving a gift certificate good for doing the laundry, cleaning the oven, moving the lawn, or waxing the car or floor is probably better than risking being arrested for breaking and entering by trying to do it as a surprise.

Give a "Generous Soul" Gift Certificate

In an ongoing relationship, after the initial months of proving how much you love love love anything your date wants to do, sooner or later, it will occur to you that you're not identical and actually enjoy some activities the other one loathes.

Even though the best relationships are based on commonality of interest, into every relationship a certain amount of difference falls. She loves professional wrestling, he loves ballet; he loves horses, she gets starry-eyed over drag racing. But going someplace you loathe because you love someone who wants to be there is a sign of not only being in love, but also of being a generous, considerate, empathetic, and sensitive adult as well. So no whining! Being a good sport is way cool — especially if you keep reminding yourself that karma is a boomerang.

Recently a friend of mine shared that an old boyfriend had asked her if anyone had ever told her she was a good sport. After a suitable culling through her memory banks, she admitted that no, no one ever had. He replied, "No wonder." Not very romantic, though she gleefully told the story. Moral of the story: He was an EX.

Rather than being dragged kicking and screaming, offer an *ollie, ollie home free* good for one date, to any event you usually loathe, without complaint, and with no strings attached. Not only is it good karma, but it's also an opportunity to stop being a pain in the neck and experience something voluntarily that you may actually learn to like or at least tolerate because it was *your* idea in the first place.

The willingness to do something you hate because someone you love loves it is one of the true signs of love.

Or give a gift certificate saying "Here is a night out with the girls or boys" without recrimination, without recompense, and without whining. This is saying "I really care about you and I really want to make you happy, and even though we do lots of things together, we don't have to do everything together." It is also a good practice to remember that, if you are talking about a long-term relationship, the two of you do not have to be joined at the hip. Obviously, I'm not suggesting you spend all your time apart from each other, but there is some indication that couples who have time away from one another actually do very well.

This is a gift, not a contract.

Plan a Mystery Date

Instead of falling back on the old standbys or the "So what do you want to do?" ploy, take the time and care to plan and prepare a special date. Don't make your date responsible for anything other than showing up. You pick the place, choose the activity, buy the tickets, arrange the dinner — you get the picture.

It's important to settle on the time ahead of time so that you're not trying to whisk your love off to Paris for the weekend just before a major presentation is due on Monday or to a romantic picnic on the day the corporate boss is scheduled to come in for a review. Your feelings will be hurt at the likely response, and this is Romance 101, not Guilt for Fun and Profit. But once you've agreed on the day or the hour or the weekend or the month, let yourself get really creative. Pretend you are planning the world's most spectacular experience to delight the head and heart of the one you love.

You can pick something lavish or low-key, romantic or rustic, close or far away. Just make sure that you are planning something your love will enjoy, not *your* fantasy date and place. Focus on making a date, with all the trimmings, to delight your love. The date doesn't need to be expensive, just imaginative: A picnic can work as well as a cruise, a home-cooked meal as well as a catered affair. We're talking heart, not wallet. Just taking responsibility in doing something that you know will please the other person can be very romantic and very lovely.

Take a Hike to Someplace New

The beginning of a relationship is always about new and different. But if the two of you have been together enough to consider each other exclusive — you're in the heavy dating stage and six months into a relationship — you may find that you are repeating activities. For example, you frequently drop into your favorite neighborhood restaurant, you have a Saturday night movie date, or you hang with your posse. Spice up your relationship and show your special someone that you care about him or her by doing something new that you haven't done before, such as taking a walk to a new place. Can we please get beyond the *slice and a movie on Saturday night* scenario?

By putting some effort into the new and different activities, you are demonstrating that your honey is worth putting yourself out for. The local weekend section of your newspaper is a great source of ideas.

Yeah, I know this sounds like a metaphor, and it probably is, but we are influenced by our own behavior. A walk makes a slower pace, together in a larger world, exploring a place neither of you has ever been before. Look, don't be silly. I'm not talking about walking through a dark park at midnight and worrying about whether you're going to get mugged, and getting lost isn't necessarily romantic. Use caution and sense and your head. Go for a walk on a new beach or in a national park in daylight, a hike through the woods, or even a stroll around the block. The idea is experiencing both something new and part of the greater world together. A picnic lunch is optional. Playing tourist is fun and romantic even if it is your own backyard or hometown.

Other cool places to experience together:

- **Aquariums:** Water is always romantic; just don't go out for seafood afterwards.

- **Zoos:** Don't go on a Sunday unless absolutely necessary or you're very fond of small kids.

- ✔ **Amusement parks:** Beware of rides that make you nauseous.

- ✔ **Water parks:** Fun and water are seductive.

- ✔ **Beaches:** I love the water; I'm prejudiced. Win points by bringing sunblock for two.

- ✔ **Museums and sculpture gardens:** You can walk, hold hands, and talk.

- ✔ **Botanical gardens:** Make sure it's not hay fever season.

- ✔ **Churches:** The air is special, and candlelight is always flattering.

- ✔ **Rowboats:** Being on the water is lovely if you can row.

- ✔ **Mountains:** Don't get caught unprepared. No unnecessary risks, and bring water and decent shoes.

- ✔ **The desert:** Being outside is almost always lovely, and a desert is austere and basic. Bring water.

- ✔ **Paris:** Okay, so I love spitting cherry pits and walking on the Champs Elysee.

- ✔ **Redwood forest:** Being around something that's been around that long puts things in perspective.

- ✔ **New York at Christmas:** What can I say?

- ✔ **Carriage rides:** Lots of cities have them.

- ✔ **Fireplaces:** They get us right back to the caves and our ancestors.

- ✔ **Country lanes:** Beware of traffic.

Gazillions of dollars are spent every year on Valentine's Day when lovers conspicuously demonstrate their affection and commitment to one another. It's ironic that the original Valentine was an imprisoned, soon-to-be martyred early Christian saint who sent messages to his followers or performed a marriage ceremony for his jailers (depending on whose story you believe). You can make any date Valentine's Day by showing the same concern and love without being either imprisoned or martyred. In fact, it should make you both giggle!

The point of St. Valentine's messages was thinking about the concerns of his friends even though he was imprisoned. You're not imprisoned or a martyr, and we're talking more than friendship here, but you get the point. Working at a relationship should be fun and inspiring, but the best relationships do take work — don't you ever think otherwise.

Part VI
The Part of Tens

The 5th Wave

By Rich Tennant

"So, you come here often?"

In this part . . .

By now, you've digested the material and are a dating expert in the making. This part is your emotional cheat sheet — dating CliffsNotes. You've done the work. Good job. Time for a few reminders such as "Ten+ Do's and Don'ts of Internet Dating" and "Ten Ways to Know You're in Love." I also list the "Ten Sexual Commandments of Dating," as well as offering ten suggestions for ways to make certain that you and your date are truly miserable, if that's your goal. These chapters offer solid info in quick, snappy bursts so that, even if you're not quite there, you can fake it with style.

Chapter 23

Ten+ Do's and Don'ts of Internet Dating

The Internet has broadened and widened the playing field and deepened the pool for dating. Literally thousands of folks are out there just waiting to click or be clicked on — so how do you enjoy and profit from this brave new world? Listen up and read on.

The To-Do List of Online Dating

Many of us just love lists as a way of being organized, encouraging a sense of accomplishment, and just generally feeling we are in control of our own destiny — so here is a way of condensing a complicated, multifaceted process into succinct, comprehensive, forward-moving steps.

Be precise

When writing an Internet personal ad or filling out an online dating questionnaire, it's useful to pretend that you have to pay by the word, whether you actually have to pay for it or not. In the bad old days, personal ads were charged by the word. These days most profiles are unlimited in terms of words once you've paid your membership fee. Don't allow this freedom to encourage you to blather. Be as specific as possible.

Think about who you are and what makes you unusual, and list both your successes and your failures. Don't allow yourself to wander into abstractions or use trite phrases. No moonlight strolls, walks in the park, or "I'm a true romantic"; these descriptions of yourself are meaningless, overused, and silly. Remind yourself that a very focused intent is time saving, practical, and useful, so be thoughtful and specific. For example, you might say, "I'm a homebody who really loves cooking, but also likes camping." That description gives somebody a clear idea of your snow-flakicity, your unique self. Saying, "I'm looking for someone who is not afraid of snakes, but also is not a carnivore" sets you apart as a vegetarian camper with a big vocabulary.

The trick here is to be focused enough to winnow the field and be honest and compelling without being so narrow that nobody on the face of the earth could ever meet your criteria. You want your ad to be honest, compelling, eye catching, sane, reflective of who you are, and different from everybody else's efforts.

Even if you don't post your personal ad, figuring out who you are and what you want is a wonderful exercise.

Make your English teacher proud

Check and then double-check your grammar, spelling, and punctuation. Nothing will make you look more like a doofus than misspelled words or incorrect grammar in your ad. Have somebody proofread your ad even if you're doing this on the QT and you're trying to be very clever and have nobody know. Ask a discreet friend to read your listing to make sure it makes sense and has no major lapses of logic, taste, or grammar. Always do a spell check and run it by a supportive friend with good English skills. Another set of eyes will often catch something you've missed.

Keep the fibs to a minimum

Okay, I could say be completely truthful, but no one ever is. For those of you who know me, I think people are allowed to lie about three things in life: their age, their weight, and their sexual history. Unfortunately, on an Internet dating site, those things tend to be the minefield.

- ✔ Your age should certainly be within several years of your actual age. Everybody is allowed to shave a year or two, but no decade reductions. Beware of saying things like "salt and pepper hair" if you haven't had any hair on your head since dirt was invented.

- ✔ Make sure any physical description roughly correlates with what your mirror reflects, not what your heart desires.

✓ Beware of women who use "code" and say they're "voluptuous," which translates into "35 pounds overweight." Be honest about who you are. If you're a little heavy, then say, "I'm a little heavy. I can live with it, can you?" This is a much better approach than lying about your weight. Remember: Sooner or later the intent is to meet face to face, and neither of you should be unpleasantly surprised.

✓ As for sexual history, don't go there! Your indiscretions are best forgotten or dealt with in the confessional or therapy, but certainly not on the Web site with strangers.

Use an appropriate photo

You don't necessarily have to post a picture with your description, but the number of responses increases dramatically — like by a factor of eight — if you do. Here are some tips on using a picture:

✓ Use a fairly recent picture.

✓ Don't be tempted to use your cute friend's picture or your brother's bar mitzvah picture.

✓ Avoid flattering glam shots because you want very little discrepancy between the picture and what you really look like. (You don't want your date to receive any nasty shocks!) It's much smarter to elicit a comment such as "My goodness, you're much better looking in person" instead of "Oh my God, is this what you really look like?"

✓ Don't even think about using a picture of yourself with your arm around somebody of the opposite sex (duh), and if you're thinking about cutting the person out or pasting someone else's face on the body, fuhgetaboutit. A picture with a friend is also a mixed message.

✓ Be careful about using props like dogs, boats, or a fancy car. This is about you, so it should be a good headshot of you alone.

✓ Women, don't be tempted to be too sexy in your picture because unless you're looking for a one-night stand, you're going to send the wrong message. The same type of info applies to guys: Keep your shirt on.

Provide only a cell phone number

There's a joke about the guy who gives his baby doll wife a cell phone for her birthday with instructions to keep it turned on whenever she leaves the house. To test her, he calls her, and she is thrilled: "Honey this is wonderful. I just love my new cell phone, but how did you know I was at the mall?"

Joking aside, you need to remind yourself that a person who found you on the Web is a stranger. So don't give your home phone number, which someone could track to your address. Practice safety first by giving out only your cell phone number, which also offers the protection of caller ID, an off switch, and mobility. A cell phone allows you to be anywhere without anyone knowing where you are. In the worst-case scenario of a lunatic or a stalker, you can get rid of the phone if you need to.

Date within a 25-mile radius

You may be one of those people who looks for potential dates on vacations or planes, or with someone who is traveling through town. Be careful, however. Long-distance relationships are initially thrilling but soon become poisonous because they're often more fantasy than reality. Have people met other people on bike trips through Provence? Yes, but leave that happenstance to happenstance. When you're investing in the specific intent to find somebody, be reasonable and sensible and play the odds. Find somebody who is in your zip code if possible, your area code preferably, and your time zone certainly, so that you can actually get to know each other without the constraints that a long-distance relationship places on things. Make it as easy on yourself and your date to be as geographically close as possible, to allow for emotional and physical intimacy as an organic, unfolding project. Dealing with someone who is GU (geographically undesirable) is an avoidable hassle.

Meet publicly and make sure someone knows where you are

Remember that the person you meet online is a stranger. Let me say this again: *This person is a stranger!* If you wouldn't meet a blind date at your house, if you wouldn't get into a car with a stranger, if you wouldn't give someone you've never met before your home phone number, don't do any of these things with someone you meet online. Please reassure me that in fact you wouldn't do any of the above. Meet in a public place, and make sure that somebody you know and trust is aware of your whereabouts. Practice a modicum of sensible behavior. In real life, you wouldn't go off with strangers, and this is indeed still real life — with the computer as intermediary.

The Never-Do List of Online Dating

If common sense were common, I'd be out of business. I'm just reminding you what you already know when you're thinking with your head — consider me your favorite Aunt Mathilda who's looking out for you.

Don't stay online too long before a meeting

Studies show that looking at a computer screen gives a false sense of intimacy with a resulting loss of inhibitions. When you're dealing with strangers, as you are in online dating, inhibitions serve a valuable and healthy function. So if you lose your inhibitions without knowing to whom you're making yourself vulnerable, you put yourself in a careless and dangerous situation.

I know that receiving those first e-mails from an online dating prospect is a thrill. But a week or two of fantasy fun is sufficient, and then it's time to bite the bullet and actually meet face to face, with a brief pit stop at phone calls so you can at least be assured of gender and voice recognition. If you spend any more time in fantasyland, you're creating an artificial sense of intimacy, which is very difficult to overcome. Remember that you want dating, not danger, as the eventual outcome.

Never online date on an office computer

I know you have a computer at your office. If you don't have one at home, invest in a cheap laptop, a used computer, or a smart phone, but don't date online at the office. Keep your personal life and your office life separate. You may think that you've covered your tracks or that online dating after hours doesn't count, but the headlines and dockets are full of folks who believed that e-mail and computers are secure. Not only will most companies object strenuously to you doing personal stuff (strangely enough they expect you to do their work if you're being paid), but they also have access to anything done on their equipment. Your activity leaves electronic records and might be against corporate policy. Best not to risk your job while searching for love online. Work is about competence, anything that interferes or implies anything else is a no-no. If I need to explain this any further, you need either a therapist or a parole officer.

As long as I'm on the subject, allow me to vigorously caution you to avoid dating people at your office or even going into elaborate detail on your online dating life. Work is always about competence, and everyone will know if something is going on. Sexual harassment is a legal issue. Flirting is a potential, if somewhat risky, way of waiting until one of you has a going-away party and then you can pounce, but not before and *never* at the company Christmas party. And even flirting is not without pitfalls. You want to be gossip-free and above reproach and viewed as a team player, not a player; competent, not seductive.

Don't get seduced in online "shopping"

One of the most dramatic good news/bad news scenarios of Internet dating is that there are just so many options. Certainly that's the major reason to indulge, but beware the seduction of the "Gee, I wonder who's around the next e-mail corner" phenomenon. If you find somebody you like and you've had half a dozen dates, you may want to consider going offline for a while.

Beware of juggling too many people at the same time. While it's perfectly okay to go slowly and initially see more than one candidate, especially if your dates are continuing also online, the giddiness of "so many profiles, so little time" can be self-defeating. If you do find somebody who you think may be a keeper, both of you can agree to take your profiles off the Internet, allowing for a more normalized dating environment. Both of you always know that you can resurrect your profiles if things don't work out.

Don't rely on humor or sexual innuendo

I can hear you saying that this heading must be a misprint: "My sense of humor is the best thing I have, and dating is all about sexy!" Take a deep breath here. You don't know how strangers will interpret something as individual and personal as humor. Senses of humor can differ greatly depending on a person's gender, age, culture, mood, or ethnicity or the context in which the humor is used. Given the fact that you're not going to be privy to any of this up front, err on the side of safety by being as straightforward as possible. You can be charming and witty, but be careful of innuendo or humor until you have eyeball-to-eyeball contact. That way, you can look each other in the eye and make sure that what you're saying is going over. Humor and innuendo are intended to soften, lighten, and divert — you're trying initially for clarity with very little possibility of misinterpretation. The bottom line in all this is to stay focused: Remember what you're doing — this should be fun, but you do need to stay focused. Make sure what you're doing makes some sense.

Chapter 24

Ten Ways to Know You're in Love

*L*ove. Amour. Amore. In popular fiction, the signs of true love tend toward the melodramatic: heart palpitations, loss of sleep, loss of appetite, blowing curtains, fireworks. But let me tell you: If you feel these things, you're not so much in love as lust — or you've gotten ahold of new cheese or old meat and need a good internist or a stomach pump.

Here is a list of the *undeniable signs* of true love — and good (emotional) health. And, romantic that I am, I will concede at least *one* heart flutter.

You Actually Want to Meet the Parents

Even if you're a thousand years old, the idea of explaining yourself to your love's parents is terrifying: After all, they've known and loved the cherub longer than you have, *and* they'll question your motives, your intentions, your behavior, your lineage, your table manners, your bank account, your morals, your intelligence, and your commitment. If you're willing to put yourself through this kind of scrutiny to move into further intimacy, it has to be love — or masochism. I'm definitely willing to give you the benefit of the doubt.

You're Willing to Explain Why You Don't Want to Date Others

With all the nasty little diseases around, the idea of sleeping around is a lot less attractive than it used to be — and I'm not sure that sleeping around was ever all that attractive — so the issue here isn't a willingness to be exclusive. It's a *willingness to talk about and explain being exclusive.*

A surprisingly large number of men and women are surreptitiously monogamous, feeling that their willingness to forgo all others gives power to the partner. But when you're willing to admit that you're willing to share the power and admit your vulnerability (I really like you and hope you like me as much), not only are you in love, but you sound like a rational, fairly adult soul in the bargain. Especially if you're super grown up enough to be the *first* to bring it up rather than doing the "me too" number.

You'll Ditch Your Little Black Book

This is a statement of not only exclusivity but also *future plans* for exclusivity, essentially saying that no one of your acquaintances holds a candle to your beloved. Your willingness to get rid of the book gives tangible proof of that reality. Getting rid of the black book also says that you're unwilling to revisit past loves and that, in this relationship, there is no going back; you can only go forward. (For the record, both men and women have little black books. Or at least little black berries — get it? BlackBerries?) Throwing away the book is also a realistic acknowledgment that once you discover someone as wonderful as your beloved, you can only go on from that person anyway; there is never a reason to go back. People we love have an effect on us. We grow because of the intimacy of the relationship, and we become entwined so that even if the relationship ends, we're different from how we were before.

No fair throwing the book into the fire but keeping the database on your trusty laptop. A commitment is a commitment, and this is as much about self as other. If you pretend to throw away your black book, then you're also pretending that you're committed. Grow up; if you're old enough to be taken seriously by someone you like, you're old enough to take yourself seriously. Committed adult relationships don't have room for manipulative games. You may "unfriend" a few people at your Facebook profile and remove others from your online photo albums. You're also willing to take your profile offline and maybe even change your status on Facebook.

You Breathe Easier When He or She Is Around

Please don't misinterpret here. I'm not saying you can't breathe when your beloved isn't around. I'm saying that the world seems a bit brighter, and you feel a bit better about yourself. When you feel this way, you're also past the infatuation stage, which is the stage where you actually *do* have a hard time breathing when the other person is around (those hormones are murder on lungs) and you've gotten past the *limerence,* the phase where you're addicted to love or you love the idea of being in love. You've settled into a wonderful but manageable phase where you work hard to please but not at the expense of yourself or your beliefs. You're content and happy and energized and sleeping well and eating okay — hey, it must be love.

If you *can't* breathe when your beloved isn't around and feel like you're going to die, you're talking serious dependency. If you feel that way, check yourself into the respiratory therapy unit of your local hospital or a twelve-step program with a local therapist.

You Hum Love Songs under Your Breath

Your sense of well-being and happiness is so deep and so easy and so comfortable that even when you're not thinking about your beloved, your sense of fulfillment permeates your being. You actually concentrate better, work more efficiently, and are more resilient, but your unconscious is aware that something very cool is happening, and those love songs just go directly from your unconscious mind to your lips without ever having to disturb your intellect. This love stuff is working for you on all cylinders.

When you *do* realize you're humming a love song, you smile, think of the words for a moment, remember to mention it to your beloved, and then get right back to work. Freud was right: All we need is work and love. Good on ya.

You're Full of Energy

I'm not talking about the kind of energy you feel in the early stages of dating, when you're sure your date is "it" and you're sure you can float on air. I'm talking about the kind of energy that comes when you know you've just hit a home run or your recipe for turnip soup is actually edible or those jeans that were a struggle actually fit or when someone smiles at you on the street on a sunny day and you feel connected to the universe. This is the energy you feel when you accomplish something, and in many ways, allowing yourself to *be* in love (not fall in love) is a terrific accomplishment. You've trusted yourself and another person, and you're taking the time and care and risks to build and maintain an intimate relationship.

When an intimate relationship works — and has been working for a while — it can truly light up your life. It may not be forest fire, fireworks, explosive, dramatic stuff — which is really fun but really short lived — but it is the long-term, this-is-going-to-last-and-I-want-to-nurture-it kind of glow. It may be less dramatic, but it can burn forever.

You're Willing to Go Somewhere You Hate

I think of this as the ballet/boxing phenomenon. The willingness to go some-place you actually hate with someone you actually love — and not be a pain in the neck about it — is one of the hallmarks of love.

When you first start to date, you're tempted to do whatever it takes to get the date off the ground because you're blinded by the possibilities. During the next phase of dating, you stand up for yourself and *don't* do the activity you hate. This is a necessary evolution because if there is to be true love, it has to be based on who you are, not who you think your beginning-to-be-significant other will like. But once you actually get to love, your need to constantly assert yourself is softened by your beloved's influence and the sense that you can give because your love will reciprocate your generosity.

You don't need to keep track on a day-to-day basis to make sure everything is 50-50. (I went to her ballet; now she has to come to the Three Stooges Fifty-Hour Marathon — how tiresome would *that* get?) But the sense that there is fairness and equality and appreciation and respect means that your reluc-tance to do something you're not crazy about gets overwhelmed by your desire to do something with the person you love. In other words, the person becomes more important than the event.

Yep, looks like love to me.

You're Willing to Save If You're a Spendthrift and Spend If You're Chintzy

The point of this section isn't really about money at all, but a willingness to examine fundamental beliefs as a direct result of valuing another person and his or her perspective and opinion. (Yeah, the same phenomenon can happen with friends, but because friends generally tolerate and celebrate dif-ferences, there's less motive or incentive for change. Not to mention unless you're planning on being roomies or going on vacation together, agreeing to disagree works just fine.) If the two of you are planning a future as a couple romantically, legally, financially, and with a 401(k), it makes sense to get these babies resolved.

Any good relationship changes you. If being around your beloved makes you examine or change some fundamental part of yourself, it may not be love in and of itself, but it does indicate respect, a willingness to learn from another, and a relationship in which you feel safe enough to try something foreign and scary.

I'm not talking flattery or hypocrisy here; I'm talking about having the courage and strength and energy to examine and experiment with a fundamental belief system, be it your view on religion, politics, gun control, abortion, Chinese food, travel, having children, gardening, money, or any other position you used to consider inviolate. *(Money?* you say. Yep. It's hard to think of any one commodity that is more basic than money. If you think money is just green stuff that just sits there, you're wrong; it's power and lifestyle and control and options and freedom and interaction and upbringing and impulse control and a whole lot more.)

The Idea of Doing Nothing Together Sounds Terrific

In the early stages of dating, you're hungry to discover who the other person is, but this time also feels scary because he or she may not be what you thought or — even worse — you may not be what your date is looking for. Even though the stakes aren't very high at the beginning, you feel they are, so you play at dating, and one of the easiest ways to play is to *do something* at all times — either publicly or privately. The dating ritual is about finding places to go and things to do. Once a couple is sexual, the thing to do is sexual, and everything else seems just a holding action until the couple can hit the sheets. Then when the initial flurry of sexual activity is over, there is a tendency to want to show each other off because you're feeling connected and proud and flushed (this can occur before sex and even when a couple is sexual . . . although hopefully not at *exactly* that moment), which means spending a lot of time around other people.

When the idea of doing *nothing* together is the coolest thing either of you can come up with, you're very likely in love, because you've gone through the other stages of terror, sex, and showing off. Now, the relationship is just about the two of you. Your "normal" life has expanded to include each other, but the idea of simply being together is the most wonderful thing either of you can figure out to do — even out of bed.

You're Willing to Risk Being Yourself

Being yourself is really the big enchilada. Everything else on the how-you-know-you're-in-love list hints at being yourself, but when you truly love someone, you want him or her to know *who you are* and love you for all that you are, not just for who you pretend to be. When you're in a truly loving relationship, you can be honest and direct and take chances.

The tricky part of being in love is that it can encourage you to be yourself but ups the risk that if you show the real you, someone whom you really want to stay will change his or her mind and leave. You want your beloved to be happy now and forever, and the only way to do that is to be who you really are. Sustaining an illusion over time is almost impossible, and because you are now truly in love, you wouldn't want to hurt your beloved by living a lie. But you also need to be a bit careful of what you confess (see Chapter 15 for advice on what you should share and what you should keep under your hat). Remember that between honesty and duplicity is silence. If you're old enough to be in love, you're old enough to understand the occasional use of silence.

Chapter 25

Ten Sexual Commandments of Dating

In This Chapter

▶ Setting a slow, steady pace

▶ Taking responsibility

▶ Being honest and sensitive

*I*n the old days — when dating meant hanging out with a chaperone and the person your parents had arranged for you to marry when you were still in diapers — people could pine away for each other, and there was no risk of sex too soon. If you had sex before you were married, you were road kill, literally and figuratively. Now we've done away with chaperones, arranged marriages, and parental influence (who was the last date your parents liked?), and sex is *still* hanging there, tempting and dangerous.

Which is just fine! After all, sex is powerful stuff: basic, primordial, fun, messy, seductive — and therefore dangerous. The risk doesn't mean you have to avoid sex; it simply means you should treat sex carefully and with respect, kinda like fire. You want it to warm you, not harm you. (The burning up part I leave to your own personality structure.)

Don't Get Naked Too Soon

The problem with sex is not being physically naked but — if you're doing it right — being emotionally naked. Being emotionally naked with a stranger is really tricky. Sex moves you at the speed of light past things you ought not to be moving past at all, the getting-to-know-you stage.

There are several ways to know when it's too soon for sex: when you don't know each other's middle name, when you haven't talked about protection, when you're doing it 'cause you think it's expected, when you're just trying to show your parents they can't boss you, when you're afraid the guy won't call unless you do, or when you do it to prove that you're not gay.

If you could do it over again . . . ?

I used to do a program in San Francisco in which people could vote on various questions — yes or no, pro or con. One day, I asked the question, "If you knew then what you know now, would you have waited longer to have sex?"

Fully 93 percent of *both* men and women resoundingly responded yes, they would wait!

The reasons varied from "It was too distracting" to "I hurt too many people" to "I had to sneak around" to "It committed me too soon to someone I really didn't like" to "I never learned how to do it right."

Sobering thought, yes?

There is only one real reason to have sex: because you really want to and you can accept the consequences (and then, for heaven's sake, be responsible and make sure nobody gets hurt, sick, or pregnant). You can see why it's often wise to wait.

No House Calls until Sex

Being in somebody's house unchaperoned for any length of time is, at best, a mixed message. Home is an intimate place, and coming up to use the bathroom, have a nightcap, check your e-mail, or watch a video is ambiguous. A home-cooked meal is nice, but you had better be willing to be dessert unless the entire family is gathering for the occasion.

If you're ready to have sex, a house with a bed is a real comfort. If you're not ready to have sex, a house with a bed is either a temptation or a tease. Careful here. Likewise, don't Skype video call each other from your bed or text each other while in bed. You're sending the wrong message too soon. Don't even admit to chatting while in bed on your cell; that kind of intimacy should follow sex, not precede it since it's giving the dreaded mixed message.

Slow Down

Know the song about wanting a man with a slow hand (and we're not talking poker here)? Well, almost everything about sex and intimacy can be improved if it's slowed down and savored. Anticipation is heady stuff, and your most erogenous zone is the gray matter between your ears. If you're not convinced that going slow has much to recommend it, think about the difference between gobbling a hamburger at a fast food restaurant and dining out. You get the point.

Make sure you know what you're doing and what you want. I know sex wasn't designed to be thoughtful: It's an urgent, fast response. But you're not an animal at the mercy of your hormones. You've got that big, fancy cortex on top of all your other organs for a reason.

Not only is it a good idea to go slowly in launching the initial sexual encounter, but once you're sexual, going slowly is a great turn-on. (Think of the good old days, when waiting until you were married made the wedding, the wedding night, and sex very special.) Even if you decide to be sexual, the longer you wait and the longer you take, the happier, in general, both of you will be.

No Sleeping Together Until You're Ready for Sex

Think about it this way: You wouldn't go to a restaurant and then not order anything. Restaurants are primarily for eating.

You may be rereading this rule to make sure you read it right. After all, why else would two people who are dating climb into bed together if it isn't for sex? Well, I can give you lots of reasons: They're tired, cold, scared, or too cheap to get two rooms; they want a cuddle — the list goes on. The problem with all these reasons to get into bed together (and the words "I promise not to do anything until you're ready") is that they sound perfectly reasonable at the time. But being in bed together is not fair to either of you. If he makes a pass, he's an untrustworthy brute, and if he doesn't make a pass, you're convinced he's gay. Once you've launched the relationship and you know each other very well, being in the same bed without either of you wanting sex may be possible, but the situation is still complicated and needs to be discussed, which is a lot of hassle if you're just starting out.

Don't Have Unprotected Sex

Oh, puh-leeeze. If I have to explain this to you, you need to put this book away for a couple of years. You must protect yourself and your partner not only from sexually transmitted diseases that can ruin or end your life but from unwanted pregnancy as well.

The only way to be completely protected is to abstain; but if you decide to have sex, understand that although a condom and a degree of caution mean safer sex (is there really anything even remotely safe about sex? — truly a contradiction in terms), the parts of your body that really need protection are your heart and soul and mind. Make sure you're aware enough of your emotional needs and your partner's emotional needs to be responsible. Otherwise, fantasize, masturbate, and wait.

Women have been worried about getting pregnant since the caves, but men should worry, too. The idea of having to support and care for a child for the rest of your life because you were feeling amorous one night and had too much to drink is a terrifying one. You get a woman pregnant, you're a father, ready or not. Can you say DNA? If you're not ready, then make sure you use a condom every time, period (and make sure you put it on and take it off right). Then when you and your beloved decide to have kids (and legalize your union for the kids' sake), you won't have to worry about any surprises knocking on your door someday and asking you to take a paternity test and attach your paycheck. Do you understand me? Good!

Don't Assume Your Date Is Responsible Sexually

Assumptions about sexual responsibility can be literally fatal and, at best, embarrassing. So talk about what you're about to do and what it means to both of you. If this conversation seems to get in the way of spontaneity, talk about it when both of you are dressed, sober, and maybe even in public.

Basically, don't assume anything at any time if you don't absolutely have to. As my used car salesmen taught me when I was writing my dissertation, "Never assume. It makes an *ass* of *u* and *me*" (Get it? *a-s-s-u-m-e*). You wouldn't assume a gun wasn't loaded before you pulled the trigger (enough Freudian imagery there for us all?).

Beware of Back Rubs

I am a sucker for a great back rub, but in a dating situation, if you haven't launched yourselves sexually, a tempting back rub has to be viewed as part of a package with a front rub. In other words, lying down, taking off your shirt, and letting somebody touch you is pretty darn sexy, wouldn't you say? Don't tease.

If you want sex, a back rub may be a great prelude, but both of you need to understand that that's what's happening. If you want a back rub without sex, go to one of the storefront, great American backrub places or find a same-sex masseuse or masseur.

Don't Confess

Possibly the only behavior more fraught with potential disaster than sex is talking about previous sexual experiences. At least sex usually feels good and is fun for both; confession feels good only for the confessor. Blabbing about your sexual past is a good example of trading off short-term comfort for long-term pain — not such a terrific idea.

Beware the electronic confessional. Twitter is recorded by the Library of Congress, and Facebook is forever. Unless you're absolutely 100 percent sure the relationship is forever too, keep your mouth shut and your fingers off the keyboard. And no sexy pix downloaded anyplace to anyone! Got it?

If you want to confess past indiscretions, find a priest or a therapist, not a date. Thinking "I'm just being honest" is a terrible reason to inflict past experiences on a date. Confession is good only for the soul of the sinner, and it can wreck a perfectly good relationship. If what you want to confide is a problem, solve it yourself; if it's guilt, get over it; if it's bragging, tell your friends or your diary. Anything else will come back and haunt you. (See Chapter 15 for advice on what and what not to share.)

If you're about to do something that would be hard to confess, you may want to consider not doing it. This isn't to say you have to pretend that you've just sprung fully armored from the brain of Zeus or that you're the last vestal virgin or that you have to lie. It's time to adopt the Clinton plan pre-Monica: Don't ask, don't tell. Anything you are or aren't sexually is about here and now. If there is baggage, find a therapist, find a priest. Not only will confessing add absolutely nothing positive to your relationship, but it'll come back to haunt you. Comfort yourself with the thought that between honesty and duplicity is silence.

Don't Fake It

Faking interest or orgasms is a short-term solution to a long-term problem (and simultaneous orgasm is a myth of romance novels and Hollywood). If you're faking it, you're giving out misleading information. Nothing will ever change or get better, and sooner or later you'll be found out. Then the *if-you'll-lie-about-something-as-fundamental-as-this-what-else-will-you-lie-about?* question rears its ugly head. Sex is about intimacy, and intimacy is about trust, and trust is about integrity, and integrity is about honesty. And most of us aren't all that great at acting. (Remember how your mom always knew when you were lying? Probably hasn't changed all that much.)

If you're enjoying the sex, enjoy it honestly; if it's not working for you, figure out what you can do differently or what you can instruct your partner (gently and tactfully) to do differently.

Don't Compare

I'm absolutely sure that no one who has the good sense to read this book would ever be tacky enough to compare sex partners out loud, not to a friend, not to a locker room acquaintance, and certainly not to a current date. (If you *are* tacky enough to do this, please don't tell me about it — I definitely don't want to think of you like that — and clean up your act.)

Equally importantly, don't compare partners in your own mind. Then was then; now is now. Some folks have a great backhand, some dance well, and some tell a great joke. All of us want to be loved and appreciated for more than the sum of our parts. We want to be loved for the unique creature that each one of us is. If you don't want to be compared, don't compare. Love isn't a race to be won; it's not a competition: It's an experience to be savored and nurtured and enjoyed. So no checklists, please. You'll cheat yourself big-time.

Male and female sexuality

Sex in humans is much more of a learned response than in other species. In fact, there's a great monograph that describes two primates raised in captivity who had to be shown stag films to be able to mate. The conclusion was that their hearts were in the right place, but that was about all. But I digress. Female genitalia is hidden, and the message that society gives women is to basically ignore any sexual impulses that women may have but to use sex to entrap men. Balderdash. Everybody is sexual from the seventh month of gestation onward. It's how society teaches us to feel about our bodies that affects us. The best way for a woman to enjoy sex is to trust her partner, know her body, feel comfortable in her own skin, and be an active participant in her own life, pleasure, and sexuality.

Most guys will admit that there are different kinds of orgasms and that ejaculating and having an orgasm aren't always the same thing. Feeling emotionally involved makes things a lot more intense. Feeling close to your partner makes men (and women) much more willing to please and feel vulnerable. While it's harder for men to "fake" it, it's just as big a mistake. All God's children have the right to feel good.

Chapter 26

Ten Ways to Make You and Your Date Miserable

In This Chapter

▶ Behaving like a child

▶ Acting out or holding it in

*E*xplaining how to make yourself or someone else happy depends on personality, age, temperament, history, experience, time of the month, phase of the moon, job security, personal insecurity, commitment, versatility, imagination, and a gazillion things too numerous to mention but fun to imagine. This whole book is about understanding yourself and what you want, taking control and taking chances, getting out into the world and having fun with another person, and growing. In other words, this book is about nice stuff, happy stuff — emotionally healthy stuff — *except this chapter.*

In this chapter, I'm going to show you how to make yourself and somebody else really, really miserable. "Why?" you ask. "Can't I do that by myself?" Well, maybe, but I'm going to make things so obvious that I cheerfully assume you'll avoid these pointless and destructive behaviors like the plague and thereby move a step closer to the really neat things you can do to make yourself and everyone around you much happier.

You're undoubtedly smart enough to read between the lines, but just in case: Happy dating is realistic, active, and focused on the present. Both partners are willing to be specific in their needs and wants, take responsibility for their mistakes, be creative, and willingly stare down their own fears rather than merely respond. Both partners are willing to evaluate, change, and even write down feelings as a way of being aware and working on being the best people they can be and working at making a relationship the best it can be.

Whine

While happiness may or may not be contagious, misery certainly is. If you are miserable and negative and nasty and can always find something negative to say about anyone, you'll find that even the most energetically happy person gives up on you, gets angry, walks away, or converts to misery — and the mess doesn't take very long at all to occur.

If you want misery to ruin your relationship, think to yourself, "Why be miserable alone when I can make others miserable, too?" and then show your misery — don't keep it bottled up. The hallmark of misery is the whine — you know, that high-pitched, grating noise you make when your shoes are too tight, you're cranky and tired and coming down with a cold, and you want everyone to know? So whine, whimper, whatever it takes, and for heaven's sake, don't ever be constructive or specific, because somebody might actually be able to help then.

If you want to be miserable, be as abstract and unpleasant as possible, using phrases like, "No matter what I do, it's not enough," "Why was I born?" (or its ever-popular cousin, "I wish I were dead"), "That's okay, even my mother doesn't like me," "Go ahead and leave me; everyone I've ever loved has." Before you know it, you'll be alone again with no one to blame but everyone.

Whining doesn't accomplish anything except to aggravate and annoy the people you're around. So instead of whining, figure out what's making you unhappy and then try to really talk about it. You may be surprised how far real communication can take you.

Blame

Instead of problem solving and figuring out what went wrong so that you can ensure it doesn't happen again, assign blame; doing so assures that your date will fight you, run, or meekly admit that, yes, it is all his or her fault. The handmaiden of blame is, of course, the ever popular temper tantrum: Anger is so preemptive and scary.

Dating will be maximally miserable if you get one whiner and one blamer together. They can make each other miserable for long periods of time. We all know at least one married couple like that, don't we? We know what keeps them together: mutual misery. We know they had to have gotten their start somewhere: dating.

When things don't go well or as you expected, instead of assigning blame, try to figure out what went wrong so that it doesn't happen again.

Keep Victimology 101 out of your Facebook updates and Tweet Stream. Any potential date will read it and figure it's only a matter of time until the blame game is played on his or her head.

Compare

Whatever you do, don't live in the present; living in the present is a good prescription for happiness and therefore contrary to your plans if your goal is being miserable or spreading misery. Instead, compare your date or yourself to others. By doing that, you move out of the moment and the intimacy the two of you are sharing and widen the circle in an unpleasant, judgmental way.

Comparisons are by definition a statement of expectation, and expectations are the death of serenity. If you're just beginning to date, you can always compare your date to other people's dates or your parents or your sibs or your classmates. Even if your current date compares favorably, it will probably occur to him or her that sooner or later, he or she is going to suffer by the comparison, and your date just may get the idea to compare you to someone.

There is a great story told by a world famous journalist who was interviewing a world famous playboy who was handsome, smart, wealthy, accomplished, and unmarried. She said, rather rudely actually, "Why is it you've never married?" He replied, "I was looking for the perfect woman." "Never found her?" "Au contraire, I did, but unfortunately she was looking for the perfect man." Few of us are perfect. The need to compare self or other is an exercise in futility and misery that is a glorious waste of time.

A related note: I'm sure you're not so shallow as to preclude all but the most gorgeous of your friends on your Facebook page, and if you are, we need to talk, seriously.

Pout

Disagreements inevitably occur between two people who are trying to function, no matter how temporarily, as a unit. Each has different experiences, backgrounds, expectations, skills, strengths, weaknesses — even different sexes. The question is, what happens when there's a problem? One option is to say nothing and let the problem fester and build and mold. In other words, pout.

Why engage in constructive, helpful conversation when you can demonstrate your unhappiness without taking responsibility by acting sullen, sulking, and being unwilling to discuss the matter? Why engage when you can so easily and negatively disengage?

Pouting is akin to emotional terrorism: It's a way to walk away emotionally while staying in the same room. By not saying what's wrong and not working toward a solution, you hold your partner hostage.

Holler

Pouters always find hollerers to hang out with. Opposites attract and then aggravate the daylights out of one another. When it comes to undermining a relationship, hollering is almost as effective as pouting. The only real advantage is that there is *some* verbal communication occurring; of course, it occurs at a decibel level that can be frightening, especially to a pouter.

Hollering is usually saying very loudly, "What about me?!" In the face of hollering, most people shut down (if for no other reason than to save their hearing), holler back, get sullen and pout themselves, or walk away.

So to aggravate the situation, avoid constructive conversation, and to scare the daylights out of anyone who startles easily, shout. Keep in mind that shouting as an intimidation tool usually works a little better if you can also make the veins in your neck pop out and your face turn beet red.

Getting angry is normal, okay, and even part of good communication, but take a deep breath, pretend you're angry at your boss or the pope, and quietly explain what's vexing you.

Swear

People who holler almost always end up swearing because their noise feeds on itself and becomes angrier and angrier and more and more incoherent. Incoherence means the cool words won't come, so the cuss words emerge. Cuss words are meant to wound and shock. So forget about trying to solve a problem or develop an atmosphere of trust in which intimacy can occur, and cuss up a blue streak. String together one incoherent, objectionable word or phrase after another until you either end up alone or sputtering for the next word.

One way to curtail the temptation to swear is for the two of you to draw up a list of forbidden words and then decide that the first one who uses one of the words on the list has to pay the other $50 for every swear word, every time. I guarantee the swearing will either stop very quickly, or somebody is going to get very rich very quickly — which at least makes the verbal nonsense a little easier to take.

Cuss words have no place on something that lasts forever, like anything on the Internet. Our words reflect our thoughts, and we are our thoughts, so clean up your act; it's better to be thought of as a prig than a potty mouth.

Say "You Always . . ." or "You Never . . ."

If you want the real problem to remain unsolved so that it will come up again in another fight, say "you always . . ." or "you never . . . ." What makes either of these phrases so effective at circumventing constructive interaction is that the other person instantly thinks of a counterexample, and then the two of you are off on a tangent, and the whole point of the disagreement is lost. Using "you always . . ." or "you never . . ." is the quickest way to escalate a disagreement into a war.

Arguments are inevitable, but be specific, stay in the present, and look for solutions, not blame.

Complain

Complaining is such fun to listen to, don't cha think? It's especially pleasant if you complain about your date to people who know him or her — you know, parents, friends, coworkers. Then you can start gossip and rumors, which inevitably get back to your date. Of course, you'll discover that you lose not only your date but your friends as well. Congratulations. You've moved from misery to abject misery.

Females, you have all cut your eye teeth on chewing on problems and talking them over, but guys hate the thought that you might be sharing really intimate things about them with your best friend or sister or mom or — the ultimate humiliation — *their* best friend or sister or mom. The problem is that you gripe when things aren't going well, but you feel better when you hang up the phone, so you give him a call and make up. Then when things are going well, you don't have the time or inclination to talk about him as much, so your mom and sister and friend are left with only the bad stuff and are convinced you're dating a nasty combination of Hitler, Jack the Ripper, Saddam Hussein, and the Antichrist. No wonder they can't be civil to him. So if you want to make him truly uncomfortable, talk about him with people who know him. To push him over the edge, *tell* him you're blabbing and don't hold back any information from those (like your mother or sister or very best friend) who you want to like him in the long run. If you follow this advice, you'll stress out the people you're close to and embarrass your date. In the misery charts, that's a win–win situation.

It's best to complain to the person who's making you unhappy; then there's actually some chance something will change. If you find yourself overwhelmed by cowardice, at least complain to someone who doesn't know and will never meet your date — *ever*.

Be Passive

Passivity is a very controlling behavior. You control by withholding — words, love, sex, information, and so on — and it can inspire a frenzy in the more active partner.

Forget that this is your life, your date, your chance to do something. Don't think, don't talk, don't act, don't make mistakes. Keep letting your partner do everything until he or she gets tired of your doing nothing and moves on to someone else. After all, the best way to feel like a victim is to do nothing.

During part of my career, I spent a lot of time with people who were dying. The most striking thing that they all had in common, when they were reviewing their lives with very little time remaining, was what they regretted: It wasn't the mistakes they made but the chances they didn't take. Mistakes are life's tuition. Not doing, not risking, is a waste. It makes me think of Helen Keller, whose philosophy was that either life is daring risk, or it is nothing at all. Don't be tortured by what might have been.

Find Fault

Finding fault is sort of the crème de la crème of all the ways to make yourself and your date miserable: It incorporates blame, whining, being judgmental, complaining, and if you're really good at it, you can really be infuriating by seeming holier-than-thou at the same time.

Ignore the fact that people blossom in the face of praise. Overlook all the things your date does right and focus on the thing he or she does wrong. Be on the lookout for mistakes, faux pas, and any other missteps; then make your date feel downright lousy by keeping the negative feedback coming. It works only if you're sincere, but it really does work beautifully.

Catching your date doing something right and well will lighten up the relationship, your posture, and your life. It makes everything — including you — more fun.

Appendix

Catch Phrases

● ●

*A*t one time or another in your dating life, you're gonna hear a line. It may not be, "Come here often?" or "Where have you been all my life?" but it's going to be some sort of catch phrase that, upon translation, means more (or less) than meets the ear. Following are phrases that should set off warning bells and whistles. I'm not saying you need to immediately dump the date who dares toss you a line, but it is helpful to know what he or she may be really trying to tell you. These (sort of) tongue-in-cheek translations do just that so that you can keep your perspective, as well as your sense of humor, while you're out on a date. Make sure you never succumb to saying any such trite phrase yourself. They only blanket a number of complicated meanings.

When in doubt — go for accuracy, not smoothness.

Phrase	*Translation*
I love you; I'm just not *in* love with you.	I've called the lawyer.
	I have a lover.
	You're toast.
	Color me gone.
Can't we just be friends?	There's no chemistry.
	I'd rather die than kiss you.
	You disgust me.
	I feel really guilty about doing you wrong, so I'd like to pretend you don't hate me to ease my conscience.
	I'm seeing someone else.
	I don't want to have to find my own place.
	I'd like to borrow money.
	Will you take care of my dog?

(continued)

Phrase	Translation
You're too good for me (basically the same as "I love you; I'm just not *in* love with you").	You're funny looking.
	I'm outta here.
	Crying, begging, pleading, and threatening won't do you any good.
	I'm going to treat you badly.
Can we cuddle and not have sex?	*If a woman says it:*
	I haven't made up my mind about you.
	If you make a pass, you're scum.
	If you don't make a pass, you're gay.
	If a man says it:
	I think I'm too drunk to perform.
	I'm going to seduce you.
Can I just come up and use your bathroom?	I plan to seduce you nearly immediately.
	I want to spend the night.
	I have a bathroom fetish.
My mom would love you.	I hate you.
	I really want to get married.
	My dad would hate you.
	My mom is dead.
	I want to have sex with you.
	Will you cook for me?
You're just like my ex.	You're history.
	I hate you.
	We've just had a humongous fight.
You deserve someone better than me (a more urgent, virulent form of "You're too good").	I'm already seeing someone else.
	I've done something awful, and you're going to find out.
Believe in fate.	I'm seeing someone else.
	I've decided to go back to my ex.
	I'm leaving for a three-year trip, and I'd like you to be faithful even though I'm not going to be.
We're soul mates.	*If a man says it:* I want sex.
	If a woman says it: I want to get married.

Phrase	Translation
You'd love my friend.	I'm passing you on.
	We have nothing in common.
	I'm furious with my friend and hate you.
	We have no chemistry.
Do what you think is best.	You're about to do something I hate, and I'll never forget it and punish you forever.
	I have a graduate degree in guilt.
	Do what I want . . . *now or you'll live to regret it.*
	Don't you dare.
I've never felt this way before.	Here we go again.
	Let's have sex.
	You're standing on my bunion.
I thought I'd just stay in tonight.	I have a date.
	You have a herpes sore I don't want.
	I got a better offer.
	There's a party I don't want to invite you to.
We should get together sometime.	I'm seeing someone, but it's not going well.
	I'm passive. Ask me out and pay for the date, and I'll go.
Check me out on Facebook.	I'm too chicken to tell you I'm not interested.
	I wouldn't go out with you if you were the last person on the planet.
	If you want to do me, okay, but don't expect me to expend any effort.
	I'm gay, but don't tell my folks.

Index

Apple & Macs

iPad For Dummies
978-0-470-58027-1

iPhone For Dummies,
4th Edition
978-0-470-87870-5

MacBook For Dummies, 3rd
Edition
978-0-470-76918-8

Mac OS X Snow Leopard For
Dummies
978-0-470-43543-4

Business

Bookkeeping For Dummies
978-0-7645-9848-7

Job Interviews
For Dummies,
3rd Edition
978-0-470-17748-8

Resumes For Dummies,
5th Edition
978-0-470-08037-5

Starting an
Online Business
For Dummies,
6th Edition
978-0-470-60210-2

Stock Investing
For Dummies,
3rd Edition
978-0-470-40114-9

Successful
Time Management
For Dummies
978-0-470-29034-7

Computer Hardware

BlackBerry
For Dummies,
4th Edition
978-0-470-60700-8

Computers For Seniors
For Dummies,
2nd Edition
978-0-470-53483-0

PCs For Dummies,
Windows
7 Edition
978-0-470-46542-4

Laptops For Dummies,
4th Edition
978-0-470-57829-2

Cooking & Entertaining

Cooking Basics
For Dummies,
3rd Edition
978-0-7645-7206-7

Wine For Dummies,
4th Edition
978-0-470-04579-4

Diet & Nutrition

Dieting For Dummies,
2nd Edition
978-0-7645-4149-0

Nutrition For Dummies,
4th Edition
978-0-471-79868-2

Weight Training
For Dummies,
3rd Edition
978-0-471-76845-6

Digital Photography

Digital SLR Cameras &
Photography For Dummies,
3rd Edition
978-0-470-46606-3

Photoshop Elements 8
For Dummies
978-0-470-52967-6

Gardening

Gardening Basics
For Dummies
978-0-470-03749-2

Organic Gardening
For Dummies,
2nd Edition
978-0-470-43067-5

Green/Sustainable

Raising Chickens
For Dummies
978-0-470-46544-8

Green Cleaning
For Dummies
978-0-470-39106-8

Health

Diabetes For Dummies,
3rd Edition
978-0-470-27086-8

Food Allergies
For Dummies
978-0-470-09584-3

Living Gluten-Free
For Dummies,
2nd Edition
978-0-470-58589-4

Hobbies/General

Chess For Dummies,
2nd Edition
978-0-7645-8404-6

Drawing
Cartoons & Comics
For Dummies
978-0-470-42683-8

Knitting For Dummies,
2nd Edition
978-0-470-28747-7

Organizing
For Dummies
978-0-7645-5300-4

Su Doku For Dummies
978-0-470-01892-7

Home Improvement

Home Maintenance
For Dummies,
2nd Edition
978-0-470-43063-7

Home Theater
For Dummies,
3rd Edition
978-0-470-41189-6

Living the
Country Lifestyle
All-in-One
For Dummies
978-0-470-43061-3

Solar Power Your Home
For Dummies,
2nd Edition
978-0-470-59678-4

Internet

Blogging For Dummies,
3rd Edition
978-0-470-61996-4

eBay For Dummies,
6th Edition
978-0-470-49741-8

Facebook For Dummies,
3rd Edition
978-0-470-87804-0

Web Marketing
For Dummies,
2nd Edition
978-0-470-37181-7

WordPress
For Dummies,
3rd Edition
978-0-470-59274-8

Language & Foreign Language

French For Dummies
978-0-7645-5193-2

Italian Phrases
For Dummies
978-0-7645-7203-6

Spanish For Dummies,
2nd Edition
978-0-470-87855-2

Spanish
For Dummies,
Audio Set
978-0-470-09585-0

Math & Science

Algebra I
For Dummies,
2nd Edition
978-0-470-55964-2

Biology For Dummies,
2nd Edition
978-0-470-59875-7

Calculus For Dummies
978-0-7645-2498-1

Chemistry For Dummies
978-0-7645-5430-8

Microsoft Office

Excel 2010 For Dummies
978-0-470-48953-6

Office 2010 All-in-One
For Dummies
978-0-470-49748-7

Office 2010 For Dummies,
Book + DVD Bundle
978-0-470-62698-6

Word 2010 For Dummies
978-0-470-48772-3

Music

Guitar For Dummies,
2nd Edition
978-0-7645-9904-0

iPod & iTunes For
Dummies, 8th Edition
978-0-470-87871-2

Piano Exercises
For Dummies
978-0-470-38765-8

Parenting & Education

Parenting For Dummies,
2nd Edition
978-0-7645-5418-6

Type 1 Diabetes
For Dummies
978-0-470-17811-9

Pets

Cats For Dummies,
2nd Edition
978-0-7645-5275-5

Dog Training For Dummies,
3rd Edition
978-0-470-60029-0

Puppies For Dummies,
2nd Edition
978-0-470-03717-1

Religion & Inspiration

The Bible For Dummies
978-0-7645-5296-0

Catholicism For Dummies
978-0-7645-5391-2

Women in the Bible
For Dummies
978-0-7645-8475-6

Self-Help & Relationship

Anger Management
For Dummies
978-0-470-03715-7

Overcoming Anxiety
For Dummies,
2nd Edition
978-0-470-57441-6

Sports

Baseball
For Dummies,
3rd Edition
978-0-7645-7537-2

Basketball
For Dummies,
2nd Edition
978-0-7645-5248-9

Golf For Dummies,
3rd Edition
978-0-471-76871-5

Web Development

Web Design
All-in-One
For Dummies
978-0-470-41796-6

Web Sites
Do-It-Yourself
For Dummies,
2nd Edition
978-0-470-56520-9

Windows 7

Windows 7
For Dummies
978-0-470-49743-2

Windows 7
For Dummies,
Book + DVD Bundle
978-0-470-52398-8

Windows 7 All-in-One
For Dummies
978-0-470-48763-1

DUMMIES.COM ®

Wherever you are in life, Dummies makes it easier.

From fashion to Facebook®,
wine to Windows®, and everything in between,
Dummies makes it easier.

Visit us at Dummies.com

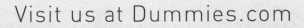